Glenn Ford

WISCONSIN FILM STUDIES

Patrick McGilligan
SERIES EDITOR

Glenn Ford

A Life

Peter Ford

The University of Wisconsin Press

The University of Wisconsin Press
1930 Monroe Street, 3rd Floor
Madison, Wisconsin 53711-2059
uwpress.wisc.edu

3 Henrietta Street
London WC2E 8LU, England
eurospanbookstore.com

Printed in the United States of America

Library of Congress Cataloging-in-Publication Data
Ford, Peter, 1945–
Glenn Ford: a life / Peter Ford.
p.   cm. — (Wisconsin film studies)
ISBN 978-0-299-28154-0 (pbk.:   )
ISBN 978-0-299-28153-3 (e-book)
1. Ford, Glenn, 1916–2006.
2. Actors—United States—Biography.
I. Title.   II. Series: Wisconsin film studies.
PN2287.F589F67   2011
791.430′28092—dc22
[B]
2010038907

To

Lynda,

my best friend and life's mate,
for her devotion and unwavering support through these many years.
To her I owe everything.

nisi canis es princeps,
semper visus est idem

Contents

Foreword

Books by the children of movie stars digging into the lives of their celebrity parents occupy a small but valuable niche in the field of film literature. As a biographer myself I prize the books I collect on my shelves that go behind closed doors to offer an alternative glimpse of Hollywood legends. Such books are rarely dull, and the best of the genre are revelatory, peeling away layers and crevices behind the mask.

A few of these books shake our basic idea of the star we thought we had known. Christina Crawford's memoir of growing up with a she-monster and Maria Riva's description of her similarly driven mother permanently altered our knowledge and understanding of Joan Crawford and Marlene Dietrich, respectively.

Peter Ford's book about his father is bound to reshape the standard impression of Glenn Ford. Until now, Ford, whose heyday was the 1940s and 1950s, has escaped the scrutiny of any substantial book, and his son's biography of him makes clear why. Ford was a tireless promoter of himself, a master at crafting an appealing persona. Off-screen, however, he was a self-absorbed personality who thrived on the perks of stardom, a difficult father, and rarely the hero he played on-screen.

Glenn Ford: A Life is three books in one. His son's memoir is modestly woven into the life story of his celebrity parents—the actor born Gwyllyn Samuel Newton Ford and the "Queen of Tap Dancing," actress Eleanor Powell.

Peter Ford also takes readers behind the scenes of Ford's 100-plus screen appearances—a daunting list to cover. The author adds private interviews and information to the background of the best Glenn Ford films, including classic comedies, film noir, westerns, and "message" pictures. The worst are also covered, and the book helps explain Ford's work ethic and indiscriminate career choices.

The star himself takes center stage throughout. To say that Glenn Ford was one of a kind doesn't begin to state the case. His persona was powerful. He usually played warm, decent, idealistic fellows with backbones of steel. His acting was never less than professional and often superlative. Yet without a script he could be a cold and steely person. He was in constant pursuit of his own self-interest. This can't have been an easy book to write. *Glenn Ford: A Life* gives the famous performer and the complicated man his honest, sometimes painfully honest, due.

PATRICK McGILLIGAN

Glenn Ford

1

"California, Here I Come"

You could say that I first got to know Glenn Ford at about the same time the rest of the world did. To moviegoers in the years just after World War II—and that really meant everybody in the world in those days before television and portable entertainment—he was the new star sensation, the good-looking young actor who had burned up the screen with Rita Hayworth in *Gilda* and romanced not one but two (identical twin) Bette Davises in *A Stolen Life*. To me, a little boy in those years, he was just Dad, the man who lived in the house and told me bedtime stories.

When you're a child, you accept the world around you as you experience it. I may have thought my father and my mother, Eleanor Powell, were special, but it would take a while to understand that millions of other people thought so too. The stately mansion where we lived on Cove Way in Beverly Hills was just home to me. Dad went to work each morning as men went to their jobs everywhere, and the people I might see sitting at the dining table or swimming in our pool, among them "Aunt" Rita Hayworth, director Billy Wilder, James Stewart, James Mason (my occasional babysitter), Harold Lloyd, and Charlie Chaplin (who very unfortunately and accidentally killed my beloved German shepherd with his car), were our family friends and neighbors. I can look back now and see that my parents and I lived in a kind of mythic kingdom, that the place where my father went to work each morning was a factory of dreams, and that those friends and neighbors were some of the most talented and colorful individuals in the world. I was regarded as a prince in this surreal world of make-believe, but in many ways I was destined to be a pauper.

My mother had been a star for many more years than my father when I was born. She was perhaps the most famous female dancer of her era. With a series of blockbuster movie musicals to her credit, she had been a star at MGM in the late 1930s and early 1940s (and you couldn't do better than be an "MGM star" in that period). But Mother had decided to put her career on hold when she married in 1943, and by the time I was born only a year and a half later she had largely faded from the spotlight and had come to identify herself almost entirely as a wife and mother. Now it was my father's time to shine, and she stepped aside.

My mother was not much more than a child when she became famous. Dad was still a young man—twenty-nine years old—when he hit it big in 1946, but he had experienced many nervous years of small breaks and middling success before then and more than one person telling him he didn't have the right stuff for stardom. At the time he returned from service near the end of World War II, he had been seriously wondering if he would ever work in movies again. For my father it had been a slow, unsteady climb to success.

The man fated to become an all-American archetype was actually born at the Jeffrey Hale Hospital in Quebec City, Canada. He came into the world, howling and healthy, on May 1, 1916, and was named Gwyllyn Samuel Newton Ford: Newton for his father, Samuel for his mother's beloved step-dad, and the exotic-sounding first name (a variant of William) as a tribute to the clan's Welsh heritage.

It should have been a day of great happiness and celebration, but the good news of Dad's birth was overwhelmed by shock and uncertainty. Just a day earlier a horrific disaster had nearly consumed the family and ended the unborn baby's life before it began. The first call came at 1:45 a.m. while the family slept. A fierce fire had broken out in the small grocery store on the ground floor beneath their third-story apartment at 58 Palace Hill in Quebec City. It was a narrow, older building, and in minutes the whole place was ablaze, thick black smoke filling the upstairs rooms and flames shooting up through the floorboards. Choking through the darkness, my grandfather had scrambled to save his pregnant wife, Hannah, and her adoptive mother, Caroline Mitchell. Burned and blistered, they hung across the window ledge until arriving firemen could reach them with a ladder. As they descended, the ladder collapsed, and the three of them, along with Fireman W. Floyd, who was carrying pregnant Hannah, fell twenty feet to the ground. Caroline was the most seriously injured in the fall. Hannah was terrified that her unborn child had been hurt. The women were rushed to the hospital, where Hannah immediately went into labor and gave birth to my dad. Caroline remained for 105 more days, undergoing a painful recovery.

That fire would never be forgotten by my grandmother. She had life-long recurring nightmares of being trapped by a fire or losing her baby to the flames and smoke. The incident left her with intensely protective feelings toward her son, which affected their relationship throughout their entire lives. While it is normal for most mothers to take pride and joy in their children, I don't think Hannah—who would never have another child—ever took another breath without thoughts of her son foremost in her mind. She never wanted Gwyllyn to separate from her, and he promised her he never would.

My father's ancestors were of British stock, English and Welsh. His parents were both Canadian-born, Hannah the daughter of English immigrants, while my grandfather Newton's people had been in the Quebec region for more than a hundred years. Newton's family had been paper manufacturers since the sixteenth century in Derbyshire, England. My great-great-grandfather Joseph came to Canada in 1850 as an eighteen-year-old stowaway, settling in the heavily wooded area of Portneuf, Quebec, along the St. Lawrence River.

With some partners—and eventually joined by his father and nine brothers—Joseph established a series of paper mills in the region and introduced hydraulic power to the industry. Small towns came into existence around the company mills. One of these was set in a glen along the banks of the St. Anne River four miles from Portneuf and was named in honor of the family—Glenford. This was where my grandfather Newton Ford was born on January 3, 1890. Newton might have stayed on with the family business in the forest, and that would likely have been the end of this story, but my grandfather had little interest in paper. He was swept up in the romance of train travel, and when he was old enough he left the mills to work on the rails, eventually becoming an engineer on the Canadian Pacific Railroad, principally traveling the route between Quebec and Montreal. Pictures of Grandpa show a tall, handsome, determined-looking young man who favored fitted suits and sported a handlebar moustache.

My grandmother Hannah's family background remains something of a mystery. "I was never sure about my mother's first years," Dad told me.

"She seldom wanted to talk about that part of her life." We know she was the daughter of James and Jessie (née Barlow) Wood and believe she was born in Hamilton, Ontario, Canada, on March 31, 1893. The Woods were forced by circumstances to return to their native England around 1897, and Hannah was left in the care of family friends Samuel Mitchell and his much younger wife, Caroline (née Pincombe) Mitchell. Hannah grew up loved and well taken care of by Sam and Caroline. At age nineteen, when she met Newton on the steps of the Methodist Church in Montreal, she was a poised-looking young woman with a slim figure, bright gray eyes, and a shy smile, attractive rather than beautiful, sensitive, and with fine manners. They were married on June 3, 1914, and had their honeymoon at Niagara Falls.

A month after my father was born, the family—Newton, Hannah, Caroline, and young Gwyllyn—relocated to Montreal. My grandfather, the railroad man, was gone more days than not, so Hannah had even more time to devote to her child. He was the center of her universe. Any spare money was spent on something to amuse her little boy. She photographed his every development and mood change either with her little box camera or at the portrait studio downtown. When he was old enough, instead of letting the boy go to the local school, Hannah decided to educate him herself. They lived in the heart of French Canada, but English was their native tongue, and no one in the family spoke fluent French; this was a factor in her decision, but it's also likely that Hannah simply couldn't bear the idea of sending her boy away for so many hours each day. She took the job seriously in any case and made sure Gwyllyn studied hard.

Hannah had Gwyllyn reading at a very early age. One of her methods of improving his mind and vocabulary was to have him read to her from the daily newspapers while she tended to her household chores. This became the first portent of the future, perhaps, as Dad, responding to his devoted audience, turned the readings into performances. "I would stand between the window and the drapes," he would tell me, "then throw the curtains open with a flourish and begin reading the paper out loud and making the most dramatic gestures. Mother, bless her, encouraged her little ham with lots of applause."

Though Newton had turned his back on the prosperous Ford paper-mill business, he remained close to his father and brothers and during summer vacations and holidays would take his family to the Ford compound at Portneuf. This was jokingly called the "ancestral family seat," a series of clapboard two-story houses built on grassy acreage in the shade of the towering pines. "Life there was rugged," my father remembered. "They were very simple, down-to-earth people. Everyone did everything—fed stock, lugged water, fished and hunted, chopped wood, and soled their shoes. We toasted bread over the open fire. All the sausages and meats were raised and cured on the family farm, and the fish we ate came fresh-caught from the river. My dad was one of thirteen, and when the whole family sat down to dinner there were twenty at the table. Each time a son was born the Fords planted a pine tree. The whole place breathed pine."

It is Grandmother Caroline who can take responsibility for bringing Glenn Ford out of Canada and landing him in Hollywood for the first time. Hannah's mother suffered from terrible arthritis, made worse by the bitter Canadian winter. She was therefore happy to accept an invitation to visit her sister Emma, who had settled far away in warm Los Angeles. Grandmother Caroline fell in love with the place—the therapeutic climate, the sunny skies, the fragrance of citrus trees in blossom—and did all in her power to convince her daughter and son-in-law that California was the promised land. Newton and Hannah made a couple of exploratory visits and soon agreed to immigrate to the American West Coast.

It took several years of planning, but on February 21, 1922, the family said good-bye to family and friends in Portneuf and Montreal and embarked on the three-thousand-mile journey to a new life. After many days of arduous train travel—crossing the border to Detroit, on to Chicago and then Albuquerque, through the desert to California—they finally pulled into Union Station in downtown Los Angeles, making one more transfer to the Red Car line that would bring them to their final destination on the Pacific shore: the little beach town of Venice, California. Eighty-some years later Dad would remember his wide-eyed arrival: "I had never seen such a blue sky and so many seagulls."

The family moved into a small two-bedroom house at 34 Park Avenue, signing a lease and purchasing the home's furnishings and appliances from the previous resident. Two years later they rented another bungalow at 15 Breeze Avenue. In 1926 the family resettled up the coast in Santa Monica on 15th Street, and finally in 1930 they moved to 1423 Arizona Avenue. This would become my father's principal home as a youth. The family lived there for thirteen years. Southern California proved a welcoming environment for the new arrivals from Canada. (Those were the earliest boom years for migration to the area, mostly from the Midwest, and the saying was that everyone in Southern California was from "somewhere else.")

With their savings spent and far from the support of family, the Fords lived a simple life with no frills but few complaints. Newton took a job with the Venice Electric Tram Company, carting folks up and down from Venice beach to nearby Ocean Park, a considerable loss of responsibility after guiding the mighty locomotives of the Canadian Pacific. (Glenn would learn to drive the tram as well and as a teenager would fill in for his father or work when an extra driver was needed.) For extra money Newton also hired himself out for carpentry jobs and every summer helped build the structures for the state fairs in Pomona and Sacramento. The experiences at Portneuf made all the Fords fairly resourceful and self-sufficient. Newton did any repairs that were needed around the house or to the black Willys-Knight two-door sedan he bought on time. Hannah was a skilled seamstress and reduced expenses by making clothes for herself and the family. Even little Gwyllyn—inheriting the Ford family knack for building things—took to making his own toys out of scrap wood and found items: a scooter, a desk, and a kite.

Many dinners for the family were provided by Newton straight from the nearby Pacific. "Dad would get up several hours before work," my father recalled. "I went with him whenever I could. We'd go out to the pier and catch mackerel and halibut. And we would eat it all week." Eating beef was a rarity for the family, as they lived thriftily. As an adult Dad recalled wistfully, "When I was a child the only things I got or found in my Christmas stocking hung by the fireplace was *fruit*—oranges and apples—and in a good year there might be a little candy."

In Venice, Hannah had begun educating Gwyllyn at home again, but the California laws were less accommodating toward such things, and soon she enrolled her son (at age seven) in the second grade at Martha Washington Grammar School. He adapted quite easily to the new regimen, Hannah less so, holding tightly to his hand as she walked him to school each morning, reluctantly letting it go, and waiting for him at the end of the day to walk him home. "I wish sometimes I had had a brother or sister," my father would say about this. "It would have made things easier. My mother was so protective of me—she was afraid of anything that might harm me. I had to fight sometimes to keep her fear from rubbing off on me." Regardless, Dad got on well at school—aside from some ribbing his classmates gave him about his name and Canadian accent.

Dad was a hungry reader and also came to love classical music. He would lie on the floor of the living room for hours at night listening to the antique family radio. He could remember sitting in a darkened room as

Chopin, Tchaikovsky, and Beethoven streamed through the airwaves, the music transporting him and igniting his imagination. He would conjure up heroic, romantic adventures for himself as a knight in armor or a vagabond on the high seas as the seeds of wanderlust took root.

Hannah encouraged him to study music. She bought Dad a second-hand violin and paid $4 a week to Mr. J. Anson Clapperton for music lessons. Dad's first public appearance was at age seven in 1923 in *Tom Thumb's Wedding* as a wedding guest in a church pageant, but his first "billing" was as a musician on June 4, 1926, when at the age of ten he played Beethoven's *Minuet in G*. However, later in life, Dad referred to his mother's musical aspirations for him as "wasted money."

The Newton Ford household was a loving but austere home, unembellished by flamboyance or emotional outbursts. This family trait, what I'd refer to as a Canadian reserve, would later be a boon to my father in his skills as an actor but became a detriment to his personal relationships. When he was an adult, at times he could be sullen and uncommunicative and take the Ford family position "if you don't have something to say, don't say anything." However, when he was a youth, young Gwyllyn's need to express himself demonstrably drove him to the one arena where this was possible—the theater.

Gwyllyn began to create little plays to be performed in the backyard, each with a bold heroic leading role to be played by him, of course. Sets were hammered together out of orange crates, a volunteer cast was found, and a school chum was persuaded to provide musical accompaniment on his clarinet. A neighbor had moved away and couldn't take his little dog. He offered the black-and-tan mutt to Gwyllyn, and after much pleading with his parents, Chappy joined the family and began his career as an "actor" onstage—very much like Petie in the Little Rascal films. Hannah encouraged her son, making colorful costumes for Gwyllyn and his co-stars. All neighborhood kids not already in the play were invited to see the show at a nickel a head. The first of the Colossal Ford Productions, a twenty-minute swashbuckler titled *The Pirates of Tortugas*, was written by and starred Gwyllyn. The handwriting, you could say, was on the wall.

As the years went by, Dad's performing skills did not go unnoticed in local circles. Members of an amateur glee club picked Gwyllyn to join the cast of the one-act operetta they were producing called *Johnny Appleseed*; he played an Indian. Another group recruited him in the spring of 1929 when he was thirteen years old; he played the best friend to the hero in a production of *The Sunbonnet Girl* at the Santa Monica Educational Little

Theatre, a role that demanded he sing onstage. Then one week before his graduation from Lincoln Junior High he was featured in the school's colorful pageant, *Italian Carnival*.

That year Gwyllyn also would join the Boy Scouts—Troop 13 in the Black Cat patrol. He would eventually earn the rank of Life Scout. In his diary he noted with much enthusiasm the trips he made to Catalina Island and the things he got to do for the first time in his life away from home—camping, hiking, and sharing "boy" experiences.

Gwyllyn's spirit of adventure combined with his thriftiness of saving his little allowance drew him to treat himself for his thirteenth birthday by joining seven others in his first airplane ride. Unbeknownst to his parents, he walked down to a small airport called Clover Field (later Santa Monica Airport) for the thrill of a flight over the bean fields of western Los Angeles.

On September 7, 1931, Gwyllyn began attending Santa Monica High School, the ivy-covered brick building on Pico and Fourth about a mile from the Ford home on Arizona Avenue. At age fifteen he had a teenager's bursting energy and yearning for experience. At Santa Monica High, when not in class, he was busy with the track and lacrosse teams, acting in school plays, and drawing cartoons and writing columns for the school paper. At home he pursued another group of interests, writing poetry and keeping a daily diary. The latter was something he would do his entire life, providing a wealth of information for family, friends, and fans about his thoughts, hopes, and dreams. Perhaps writing was going to be his career. Or maybe it would be broadcasting.

Like a lot of kids in the 1920s and 1930s Gwyllyn was excited by the new medium of radio. He would listen faithfully to his favorite programs on the old Philco set in the living room and was captivated by the deep, dramatic voices of the news readers and announcers. "I just loved those guys," he would tell me, "and I copied the way they spoke. I decided I would become a radio announcer." Too eager to wait until he was old enough to be taken seriously for such a job, Gwyllyn and a school pal named Robert Koschnick decided to start their own radio station. Using ham radio equipment, they launched station KFRG (a combination of their initials) from Gwyllyn's bedroom with an antenna strung up in the alley behind the house. For the next year or so they made regular broadcasts of local news and school gossip.

In spite of his many competing interests and distractions, Gwyllyn continued to act. Acting seemed almost to pursue *him*—he couldn't avoid the opportunities that kept knocking at his door. In addition to his inherent talent, Gwyllyn had now become a distinctive, striking-looking young man on or off a stage. By seventeen he had grown to his father's height of six feet and had a lean athletic figure. People who knew him then—like Grace Godino, who would later work with him in Hollywood—remembered the young, sometime actor as very handsome, with "wavy dark hair, soulful gray eyes, and a mischievous smile." Most memorable of all, Grace would recall, "was that marvelous voice he had. He didn't sound like any other boys his age. It was rich and low and mature."

"I get a big kick out of being in plays," he wrote in his diary. "Ever since 'The Sunbonnet Girl' I have realized what a lot of fun it is to be in plays. It would be a lot more fun if I could really act."

He hadn't yet taken acting, or his talent, seriously. But that was about to change.

In the winter of 1933 Gwyllyn got a part-time job at the local public library on Santa Monica Boulevard:

> I stacked and reshelved books for three hours a day from six to nine in the evening, and it paid thirty-two dollars a month. One evening I had gotten to the library and was starting to work when I happened to notice a stream of people heading downstairs to the basement. I was curious and went to have a look at what was going on. I learned that they were having a meeting of a group called the Santa Monica Community Players. The group put on plays in the area, and it was a semiprofessional theater company. They didn't have their own offices or rehearsal space at the time, so they arranged with the library to use the basement hall. That night they were having auditions for their new production, a play called *Death Takes a Holiday*. I thought I might give it a try—I guess I forgot I was supposed to be working that night—and I read for a small part, Corrado, the French mayor.
>
> In charge of everything was a man named Harold Clifton, who had created the Players in 1930. Clifton was born in Norman, Oklahoma, but had studied drama at the University of Oklahoma and at the George Pierce Baker workshop at Yale. Years later, I asked Hal Clifton why he gave me the part. He said he didn't know why, only that he believed me in the reading.

My father's understated recollection of that evening at the library belied its momentousness in his life. Joining the Santa Monica Community Players was the first real step down a career path, the road that would lead to Hollywood stardom.

Dad's first part in a Santa Monica Community Players production (at the Miles Memorial Playhouse) was a success. Hal Clifton immediately urged him to take a role in the next play on their schedule, *Green Grow the Lilacs,* casting him as a square-dancing cowboy, and then the next, *Rebound.* Gwyllyn was soon a valued, integral part of the Players, which was a semiamateur enterprise with a volunteer, unpaid company. But Hal ran it with the same serious purpose of any Broadway producer. My father often said, "A person who wanted to be an actor or in the theater could do much worse than to learn the ropes with Harold Clifton and his Santa Monica group." Moreover, Hal took a particular interest in Gwyllyn.

Hal would be the first person to make my father see the real possibilities, artistic and professional, in pursuing a career in the theater. Hal coached him in his performances, worked with him on voice and movement, taught him stagecraft, and lectured to him on the history of the theater. "Everything about the theater began to appeal to me then. I came to know it backwards and forwards. I read every book in the library about it and got on-the-job training at the Players. I enjoyed acting, but I also wanted to know about everything else. When I wasn't rehearsing, I would work at the other crafts, the lighting, the prop handling, set design and construction, stage managing, or whatever else that had to be done."

Gwyllyn quickly became a stalwart member of the Community Players. Over the next few years Gwyllyn appeared in every production, established standards like *Death Takes a Holiday, The Guardsman*, and *Accent on Youth* as well as more unusual works, some previously unproduced, including *No More Americans* and *Where the Cross Is Made*. As time went on he increasingly played the lead or a prominently featured part.

Since the Community Players shut down at times between presentations, Gwyllyn sought other places to pursue his new calling. He performed with amateur troupes like the Mummers and the Epworth League and appeared in stage shows at various women's clubs, in church-sponsored productions, in school auditoriums, in churches, even, one time, in a barn behind a gas station. "Looking back over that time until I got into movies," he would tell me, "I can't remember a single day when I wasn't rehearsing or acting in a play." Over a period of five years he appeared in more than sixty local productions and at one time was a member of no fewer than seven different theater groups.

The Santa Monica Community Players, however, was Dad's artistic home. And though he valued Hal Clifton highly as his director, mentor, and friend, it gradually became clear that Hal's interest in Gwyllyn Ford was also highly personal. It was an open secret among the Players that Hal Clifton was a homosexual, and rumors went around of his occasional affairs with this or that good-looking young actor. As Gwyllyn became the boss's "new favorite" and was often seen in close contact with him in the theater and around town, there was inevitable gossip surrounding their relationship. Clifton could be temperamental as a director, but he was always gentle and soft-spoken with Gwyllyn, further fueling speculation among those who had suffered his wrath.

It is a delicate subject to bring up to one's father, but Dad addressed my question with candor: "Hal at some point told me he was in love with me. I told him I could not reciprocate, and he accepted it, but it did make me nervous. Fortunately, he was always professional, so we were able to work together over and over without incident. I had deep respect for Hal's talents."

Dad never forgot Hal's help at the start of his career, and after he achieved success as an actor and was able to request certain personnel to work with him on his films, he rewarded Hal. Hal joined Glenn on *Gilda* and worked on nearly every one of Dad's films as a dialogue director and coach until I succeeded him in 1968.

Dad did develop a romantic connection at the Community Players with a winsome strawberry blonde named Donna Damon, whom he had first met at Santa Monica High. She was pretty, sweet-natured, interested in a career in acting, and devoted to Gwyllyn. They became boyfriend and girlfriend and went everywhere together. They were seen as a cute and attractive couple, two good-looking young people from the same background and with the same enthusiasms. Even Hannah, who generally looked askance at any girl who showed an interest in her son, thought Donna a "very nice girl" and accepted her.

It was an apparently chaste romance, as was not unusual in those more innocent days, though that may be one reason why they had many breakups through the long course of their relationship. During some of those periods Dad had a secret romance with another young woman at the Players. This actress—we'll call her Cheryl—evidently offered what Donna didn't. "She was a wonderful girl," Glenn would later recall. "And she was willing to go a lot further sexually than some others. I guess I took advantage of that. It was my first adult affair. We were not very smart about it, and at one point we both feared she was pregnant. I went around a nervous wreck for a couple of days until she discovered she was okay. I was very careful from then on."

These were years of the Great Depression, and times were occasionally tough, even in sun-kissed Santa Monica. My grandfather Newton was laid off from his job on the tram for months at a time, and Gwyllyn was expected to work and contribute to the family coffers. He gave up his hope of going to junior college after graduating high school because it was "too expensive." He taught a Sunday school class at the First Methodist Church in Santa Monica for a while. He and Newton both got occasional construction jobs, and at various times Gwyllyn worked as a paper boy for the *Santa Monica Outlook*, and as a roofer, weather-stripper, process server, and glass cutter. Newton had never discouraged Dad's acting ambitions, but he always insisted that he first learn something sensible, like how to work with his hands. Dad considered it wise advice and would later insist I do the same.

During his later high school days my father got a job working as a groomer for Will Rogers at his ranch on Sunset Boulevard in Pacific Palisades. It was here that he learned to ride horses while he tended to the polo ponies of the many movie stars and celebrities who would play polo on the weekends, Spencer Tracy, Clark Gable, and Walt Disney among them. Darryl F. Zanuck was also one of the participants, back in the days before he ran Twentieth Century Fox. The young groomer attending Zanuck's horse would one day make his first motion picture at Zanuck's studio.

On one occasion Gwyllyn took a job as a male model on a commercial assignment for a local photographer. This was more daunting than it sounds, as it involved parachuting from a small airplane at two thousand feet and landing in the vicinity of the photographer's camera. A pilot took Dad up in an old open-cockpit Jenny biplane, handed him a bottle of Myers's Rum to swig for courage, and then wagged a thumb at the ground below. "It wasn't so bad once I got back to earth," Dad recalled. "And it paid fifty dollars. But I didn't dare tell my mother I had done it." The shoot appeared in a Texaco ad—Gwyllyn's first appearance in print advertising.

In early 1935 Gwyllyn landed a steady job that he jokingly referred to as his first work in the professional theater:

> It was the Wilshire Theatre on 14th and Wilshire Boulevard in Santa Monica, a movie theater that had vaudeville on the weekends. I started out as what they called a "twister," in charge of the searchlight on the roof of the theater. On some nights there were previews or special events, and my job was to twist the searchlight around in the sky so that the public would know something special was going on. For twenty-five cents an hour I stood for hours on that darn roof, sometimes in pouring rain,

twisting the light across the sky. There were always things going wrong inside the theater, and I would get called down to help fix them. The curtain would come off the trolley—I'd fix it. The spotlights would have to be rewired. Film had to be spliced when it broke, and if the projectionist on duty didn't know what he was doing or didn't have time, I repaired it. One night Mr. Wells, the boss, said, "Kid, you're through standing up on the roof. You're now the stage manager."

It was quite a job. There was never a dull moment. The curtain was always sticking. Spotlights had to be rewired fast. The vaudeville actors, who appeared before the film presentation in those days, would shout instructions to me about lights and props in what seemed like a foreign language. Sometimes I'd overload the electric current and blow the whole building out. Mr. Wells was patient and paid me eight dollars a show.

In his free time Gwyllyn continued to pursue acting. He knew he had gone as far as he could working in volunteer productions and shows in church basements, and by the summer of 1935, at age nineteen, he began to make a more determined assault on the professional theater community headquartered in downtown Los Angeles. Important new plays and regional versions of the new London and New York hits were performed downtown, and local casting was headquartered there.

The single most important person in Los Angeles theater then was Homer Curran, whose name was attached to most of the big and successful West Coast stage productions. My father repeatedly and nervously tried to make himself known at Curran's office at the Belasco Theater. "He was a big, bald, jovial man," Dad remembered, "with a good sense of humor and a jovial laugh. I went to see him every Saturday, which was a two-hour trip for me each way on the trolley, bus, and foot. He would come into his office around eleven every Saturday, and I would be there. He'd laugh and say, 'Look, it's the great Welsh actor from Santa Monica!' I bugged Homer Curran so much that he finally hired me to sweep the lobby of the Belasco for a few weeks. I guess he felt sorry not having any other job for me."

Then one day Curran told Dad what he had been longing to hear. He said, "Herman Shumlin"—a famous director then—"Herman Shumlin is in town. He's having readings for *The Children's Hour*. I'll get him to see you."

Dad recalled: "I got a copy of the play by Lillian Hellman. All the parts were for women. Mr. Curran said, 'The grocery boy in the third act.' It was three lines. I hadn't even noticed. There were a dozen or more of us at the theater to try out for the part. Shumlin looked us over. He asked some questions about our experience in the theater. When I said I had worked as an actor and as a stage manager, it was settled. Shumlin said, 'Okay, you can be stage manager and on the side you'll be the grocery boy.'"

The production rehearsed in Los Angeles for three weeks, then went up the coast for a series of preview performances in Santa Barbara, then on to a lengthy run in San Francisco, finally returning to Los Angeles for three weeks at the famed Biltmore Theatre. Gwyllyn was to be paid $30 a week for his dual employment as stage manager and player. Part of his salary was immediately rerouted to the actor's union. He was now officially a professional—it said so right on his Actors' Equity card.

Three salaried lines, a bit part, seemed like a breakthrough to my father at the time. At the closing night party, Gwyllyn sat at a table with veteran actor James Dunn. "Jimmy downed his third or fourth whiskey and looked me straight in the eye. He said to me, very ominously, 'You know, kid, your chances of making good in this business are one in a million.' I told him I had to take that chance."

But Dunn's words must have echoed in my father's head in the months ahead when he was unable to find another professional stage job. He returned to Santa Monica, back to handyman jobs, shingling roofs, working in a paint store, and back to the Community Players. Then, in September 1936, after a performance of *Accent on Youth* in which he played the lead role opposite his girlfriend, Donna Damon, Dad was approached by a well-dressed older man named Oliver Himsdale, who turned out to be a talent scout for MGM Studios. Himsdale liked both Gwyllyn and Donna and invited them to come out to see him at his office.

MGM was only three miles from Santa Monica and was often the topic of animated conversation among the young hopefuls at the Players. But they might as well have been in another country for all that anyone knew about how to get inside the studios' hallowed gates. And now here was an official invitation to enter the biggest, most famous studio of them all.

It took a while to set up the appointment, but the two young actors, in Hal Clifton's borrowed powder blue Chevrolet coupe, made the drive east to Culver City. "It was Friday, November the thirteenth, I remember. We arrived wide-eyed and nervous. We parked on a side street off Washington Boulevard and presented ourselves to the guard at the front gate, who told us where to find Mr. Himsdale. He had us perform a scene for him. He seemed impressed. He told Donna she reminded him of Virginia Bruce, who was an MGM star at the time. He thought Donna was talented, but he said to me, 'You're certainly no pretty boy, are you? We're looking for leading men, not characters.' But he did promise to see if he could find something for us."

Looking back, it's interesting to note that on November 4, just nine days before, my mother and Jimmy Stewart completed the film *Born to Dance* at MGM. My mother had top billing. When Mom left the studio in those days, through MGM's vaunted gates, she was chauffeured by her driver, Eddie, in her new pale yellow 1936 Packard Roadster. The car had been an early twenty-third birthday gift to her from the film's director, Roy Del Ruth, and a young suitor who had been pursuing her, Clark Gable. Mom in her fancy car might have crossed paths with Dad and Donna on their one-day pass.

Himsdale recommended Gwyllyn and Donna to an agent named Marty Martyn, who worked out of a tiny office above a drugstore on Sunset Boulevard. Taking Himsdale's recommendations seriously, Martyn immediately signed Gwyllyn and Donna to representation contracts.

It seemed too good to be true, and it was. Himsdale left MGM almost at once in search of newer opportunities. Separately and sometimes together, Gwyllyn and Donna went off to meetings and auditions with various producers and casting personnel. One meeting at Universal Studios was with a young director named S. Sylvan Simon. Simon told Dad he was a good actor, but he did not photograph well enough to work in movies. (A decade later, Mr. Simon would direct this same modest-appearing young man as the star of one of his vehicles at Columbia Pictures.)

And so it went, until one day in February 1937. In the midst of rehearsals of the next Players production, *Petticoat Fever*, Gwyllyn got a call from Marty Martyn. Oliver Himsdale had resurfaced at Paramount Pictures, remembered the Santa Monica actor, and recommended him for something to a production executive named Ted Lesser. There were meetings, readings, then a test on Stage 12. Dad was led to a small set where a camera crew filmed him from a variety of angles as he read a few lines. He tested with Mary Lou Lender (who would later marry director Delmer Daves).

A few days later Dad got the word from his agent: Paramount wanted to hire him for a single appearance in a short film, one of those one-reel wonders that played between the feature films in those days. Filming was to be done on Easter Sunday (probably to utilize stages and equipment otherwise reserved for more important productions). Realizing how anxious his client was, Marty Martyn agreed to pick up Gwyllyn in Santa Monica and take him to the job. "I was so nervous arriving at Paramount," Dad recalled, "I nearly passed out."

17

The short was to be a brief musical set in a swanky nightclub called the Café Esplanade. A selection of singers—June Kilgour, Billy Daniels, and Bill Roberts—and specialty dancers—Dorothy Dayton and Stanley Brown—would perform one after the other. Gwyllyn would portray the nightclub's master of ceremonies and introduce the acts. The part paid $25.

Dad's nervousness did not end when the work began. He was sure his makeup was too heavy, and he thought the way they had styled his hair—slicked back like Rudolph Valentino's—looked terrible. The tuxedo they had put him into was so tight he couldn't breathe. In my father's diary he recalls: "Because it was Easter Sunday the wardrobe department was closed and the assistant director looked all over the place and the only outfit he could find was the tux that had originally been made for Marlene Dietrich for the film *Morocco*." The director, Herbert Moulton, who headed the short subject division at the studio and who may have preferred to sleep late on Sundays, showed little interest in Gwyllyn or anything else about the short film.

They shot Dad's opening speech. The director called for a second take. Gwyllyn spoke his lines again, trying not to think about how his hair looked. Moulton mumbled, "Print it," and they moved along.

They worked all day and into the evening. The studio commissary was closed on Sunday, so everyone was given a box lunch at noon. Dad ate his Easter dinner, a hunk of roast chicken and some potato salad, sitting on a little wooden bench near the set. Looking around at the phony nightclub, watching his fellow "stars" perched on benches eating greasy cold chicken out of a cardboard box, it was hard for him to believe this first job in movies could lead to anything. On the other hand, there was nowhere to go from here but up.

Ted Lesser later offered my father a studio contract for $35 a week. Gwyllyn was eager to take it, but Marty Martyn insisted he turn it down. The offer specified voice and extra work, and Marty said it was a dead end. "He felt the studio would never take me seriously if I began showing up as an extra. He was sure that something better was going to come when the short subject came out."

The short was released on July 29, 1937, under the title *Night in Manhattan*. Gwyllyn, uncredited, appears nervous, shifty-eyed, and skinny. It looked like someone had rubbed so much pomade into his hair that it would not have moved in a hurricane. None of the other performers came off much better. In his diary Dad noted: "Today I saw myself on the screen for the first time in my life and from what I saw it will probably be my last. I looked awful!!!"

As he suspected, his debut in movies did not bring Hollywood running to his doorstep. It was back to looking for theater jobs and working with his hands. For a time he was employed by the Atlas Glass Company installing windshields.

A great loss came to the Ford household in mid-November 1937, when Hannah's mother, Caroline, finally surrendered to the ravages of diabetes. She had lived with Gwyllyn and his parents all his life, and he loved her like a second mother. Caroline had always told him he was going to become a famous actor someday, and in his grief the young man swore to Hannah that he would make his grandmother's wish come true.

One more Community Players production opened on December 10, 1937, at the Miles Playhouse — *Judgment Day*, with Dad in the lead as the blustery Russian general Rakobski. A friend notified him that he was coming to that night's performance with a man from Twentieth Century Fox Studios. This man, it turned out, was Tom Moore, a one-time silent movie star (and the former brother-in-law of the queen of Hollywood, Mary Pickford) now working in the casting department at Fox. Moore was impressed and then some. He and Gwyllyn had a long talk after the show, and when Moore returned to the studio the next day he sent off a memo to Fox casting director Lewis Schreiber: "If Mussolini had walked on that crowded stage he could not have had a more electrifying effect," Moore wrote. "He received tremendous applause after each exit. . . . I don't think he's handsome but personality sticks out all over him. . . . Lew, don't pass this fellow off lightly, because if you do I have a feeling you will regret it."

It was quite an endorsement, and Schreiber naturally brought Dad in for a screen test at Fox. But Schreiber was unimpressed with the results and took pleasure in telling Moore how wrong he had been. "I not only didn't get a job," Dad said, "I damn near cost Tom his."

But Moore remained a believer in my father's talent and potential. He would bring him back to the studio two more times, trying to convince executives of his discovery. Marty Martyn, meanwhile, continued to push Dad at the other Hollywood factories. As Dad recalled it, "I was rejected by every studio in town."

Homer Curran found Dad a second professional stage job, though from an acting perspective it was no more promising than the first. It was for the West Coast tour of Clifford Odets's smash hit *Golden Boy*, and Dad would again work as stage manager while pausing in his duties to say exactly two lines in the third act: "Knockout!" and "Lombardo's stiff." Following three weeks of rehearsal in Los Angeles, the production headed to Santa

Barbara for two "tryout" performances at the Lobero Theatre. The first show was scheduled for April Fools' Day.

"Actors are a very superstitious breed," said my father, remembering that night. "So there was already a feeling of uneasiness among some in the cast. The curtain went up and everything went smoothly until we got to the second scene. The actor playing the boxer's immigrant father in the play, Joe Greenwald, said his line—'A good life, ah, is, ah, possible . . .'— and suddenly collapsed dead of a heart attack. I rushed onto the stage immediately. He was lying in the arms of one of the other actors. He was already dead. God, what an experience."

The show was shut down for a week until a replacement—Lee J. Cobb from the original Broadway production—could be found. Dad's one happy memory of the unfortunate tour with *Golden Boy* was the unlikely friendship he developed with much older character actor Louis Calhern (perhaps best remembered for playing Marilyn Monroe's sugar daddy in *The Asphalt Jungle*). Calhern was a skilled, self-assured journeyman actor who glided with ease between work in movies and the theater. He took a liking to my father—he nicknamed him "Hatrack" on account of his 138-pound slender frame—and offered him uplift and advice based on his long years in the acting trade.

One night after a performance the two were sitting backstage, and Gwyllyn began to complain of his encounters with the people in Hollywood:

> I told him, "I know I'm no Errol Flynn. My nose isn't right, and my mouth's not really centered, but some girls think I look all right. Gosh, Louie," I said, "am I really too homely to be in the movies?" And Louis said, "Hatrack, forget about the studios. You're too talented to be begging them for crumbs. What you need to do is go to New York and get a part in a decent play. That's where you belong. And then the studios will come begging to you."

Dad took the advice to heart. Once more he turned to Homer Curran for help, and Curran came through. A play called *Soliloquy* written by a man with the odd name of Victor Victor was headed for Broadway after some West Coast tryouts. Gwyllyn could again stage manage and act a small role. By the time they went into production he had also been asked to understudy the lead, played by John Beal.

Hal Clifton accompanied Gwyllyn on the cross-country train ride to New York in early November 1938. Hal, said my father, wanted to share in the glory of his debut in New York (Donna, Dad's girlfriend, unhappily stayed behind in Santa Monica). Hal paid for their rooms at the luxurious St. Moritz Hotel on Central Park. Opening night was to be Monday, December 28. My father was convinced that finally his time had come.

Gwyllyn would long remember the thrill of those first days in Manhattan, walking down Broadway and seeing marquee after marquee with the brightly lighted names of theatrical legends appearing in shows that season: Alfred Lunt and Lynn Fontanne in *The Seagull*, Laurette Taylor in *Outward Bound*, Tallulah Bankhead, Ethel Barrymore, and on and on.

Even more thrilling was seeing for the first time the Broadway theater where Dad would be working in his own show. From his room (number 2223) at the St. Moritz he wrote to Hannah in an excited scrawl that he got to meet stars Jack Benny and Sophie Tucker in the lobby. Louis Calhern and his actress wife, Natalie Schafer, took him to a formal birthday dinner for aged actor Otis Skinner at the Players Club, where Gwyllyn was awed to sit alongside Walter Huston and the "Yankee Doodle Dandy" himself, George M. Cohan.

Unfortunately, the play that had brought Dad to New York proved a less than wonderful experience. The show had been plagued by problems in all its tryout performances. *Soliloquy* was the story of a murderer with a guilty conscience, with the audience hearing the voices inside his mind. The prerecorded "voices" often didn't work right, and there were missed cues, as the man at the record player couldn't always hear what the actor onstage was saying. Sometimes Gwyllyn would have to grab a microphone backstage and speak the lines live. "It was a major flop," he remembered. "We opened and closed in two days. Frankly, I don't know how we managed to go that long."

Hal Clifton had to return to his theater work in Santa Monica, but Gwyllyn chose to stay in New York and look for another job. Nothing worked out, however. In New York he was no longer the bright star of the Santa Monica theater or the young hopeful with a show opening. He was just another out-of-work actor among thousands of experienced pros looking for a break. His savings dwindled. He was embarrassed to ask his New York friends for help and ashamed to wire home for money.

"By Christmas Eve I was down to my last fifteen cents," Dad remembered. "New York's a wonderful place to be on Christmas Eve, but I wasn't feeling very cheerful. I walked around till it was very late, listening to Christmas music coming out of the shops and churches, feeling pretty low. It was late by then, and I was very hungry. I went to an Automat and got a piece of pumpkin pie for a dime. That left me a nickel. I looked at the nickel and thought, The hell with it, and got a scoop of ice cream to go on the pie. Then I walked back to the hotel and went to sleep."

Soundly defeated, he left New York by train on New Year's Day, 1939. He returned home using the ticket Hal had left him and went back to work at the Atlas Glass Company in Santa Monica. He resumed his still apparently chaste romance with Donna. She had begun to talk about the future and marriage. Perhaps, she was saying, it was time to give up the acting and settle down.

One morning that spring (it was May 20, a Saturday), Gwyllyn was busy washing his father's car when he got a call from Tom Moore, the man from Twentieth Century Fox who stubbornly believed in him. Tom asked Gwyllyn if he could come into the studio right away. "Tom said he was up for a small role in a new picture at Fox and he couldn't find anybody else to do the scene with him in a test. I told him I looked like hell, hadn't shaved. He said it didn't matter; I was just going to feed him lines off-camera. I couldn't say no—Tom had tried to do so much for me."

Gwyllyn got to the studio as soon as he could and found his way to the soundstage where Tom was waiting for him. They were going to do a scene from a script titled *Heaven with a Barbed Wire Fence*. Tom told him he was to play the part of a security guard at the top of the Empire State Building chatting with the story's protagonist, Joe Riley, an innocent young man about to leave New York for Arizona.

They rehearsed it once, and then Tom played the scene for the camera. Much to my father's surprise, the director of the test then asked the cameraman to film my father—for intercutting purposes only for Tom's test. Gwyllyn felt more at ease than he had during any of his previous on-camera experiences, knowing that there was nothing at stake this time. He acted with a low-key naturalness, improvised a line or two, smiled and laughed when either of them flubbed a line and had to start over. Whether or not Tom had deliberately engineered the circumstances of the test scene as a way of getting my father to relax in front of the camera, the resulting test won people over. Free of makeup, his hair loose, wearing an old leather jacket, he looked and acted entirely unlike the nervous, pomaded man who had appeared in *Night in Manhattan*.

On Monday Tom Moore showed the test to Sol Wurtzel, the Fox executive in charge of producing the studio's low-budget productions. Wurtzel was impressed. His next B picture was scheduled to begin shooting in exactly seventeen days, and he did not yet have a lead actor.

Seventy-two hours later my father returned to the offices of Twentieth Century Fox and signed his name on a contract for $150 a week with a two-week minimum to play the role of Joe Riley in *Heaven with a Barbed Wire Fence*. It had all happened so fast and so unexpectedly that the only thing Dad was sure of was that he owed Tom Moore a great debt of gratitude.

There was much to do in the two weeks before filming began: memorizing his part, going to the studio for wardrobe fittings and tests. But most urgently, Gwyllyn needed to find a new name.

It was a time-honored tradition in Hollywood to change a screen actor's unusual or awkward-sounding real name to something shorter, smoother, or more glamorous. Marion Morrison became John Wayne, Archie Leach was changed to Cary Grant, and Spangler Brugh became Robert Taylor. Although he was proud of his distinctive Welsh name, which had stood him in good stead on assorted playbills and theater marquees for many years, Dad was not surprised when the studio insisted on a change. "People had frequently told me it sounded like a girl's name . . . or that it always looked like a spelling error."

Many suggestions were made, but Gwyllyn got involved, insisting he could rename himself and retain a continuity of identity that way. He found what he wanted in the name of a place out of his childhood, the rural Canadian village of Glenford, where his father had been born, with an extra *n* added for good measure.

He would be now—and forever after—known as Glenn Ford.

2

"Somewhere over the Rainbow"

Sol "Solly" Wurzel had worked at Twentieth Century Fox since the time it was still just plain Fox, before it had merged with Darryl Zanuck's upstart Twentieth Century in 1935. In those seven years he had produced no fewer than eighty movies, including various musicals, mysteries, comedies, dramas, and assorted entries in the Mr. Moto and Charlie Chan series. With the possible exception of a pair of Will Rogers vehicles directed by John Ford, not one of those eighty films Wurzel made would ever be hailed as a classic. Solly was not expected to make classics, only to oversee an assembly line of briskly entertaining product made on a tight budget and intended for the lower half of a double bill. In 1939 alone he was responsible for fourteen releases. One of these was *Heaven with a Barbed Wire Fence.*

It was an unusual project in that *Heaven* did not fit into one of the typical B-picture genres like mystery, crime, western, or comedy. It was a sort of odyssey, or "road" movie, before Kerouac—or Hope and Crosby— coined the term. More unusual still for a Hollywood B movie, it contained elements of tragedy and social criticism.

Joe Riley, the hero, leaves New York to claim twenty acres of Arizona land he intends to cultivate. Along the way he meets and travels with a band of odd and troubled characters, including a streetwise drifter who shows him the ropes, a half-Spanish girl on the lam from the immigration authorities, and a homeless former professor. By journey's end, the girl has been nearly gang-raped by hoboes, the drifter loses a leg after being shot, and Joe's Arizona acres turn out to be a plot of dry dirt. A happy ending could not be denied, however; Joe marries the girl to save her from the law, and the couple looks to a hopeful future turning their dry acres into bountiful farmland.

The principal screenwriter of *Heaven* was Dalton Trumbo, then commencing his long and distinguished—and sometimes notorious—career. Ahead lay epic assignments, Oscars, blacklisting, and a term in prison as one of the Hollywood Ten. Scene-stealer Raymond Walburn, a specialist in dithering blowhards, played the professor, Ward Bond was a would-be rapist, veteran Marjorie Rambeau was a saloon keeper, and Jean Rogers—Flash Gordon's "Dale Arden" in the series—was the leading lady. In the role of the tough young drifter was a young actor from New Jersey also making his film debut, Nick Conte, who in a few years would be known as Richard Conte.

Directing the film was yet another movie star—or at least he had once held that title. This was Ricardo Cortez, a well-known leading man in the silent movie days and in the early talkie years at Warner Bros. His real name was Jacob Krantz. By the late 1930s he was trying to make a new career as a low-budget director.

Low-budget meant no time or need for rehearsals. Since many actors under studio contract were often scheduled to finish a film one day and begin a new one the next, it was not unusual for cast members to meet their director and each other on the first day of shooting. That was the case on the June morning when Gwyllyn—that is, Glenn—first reported for work at the Fox lot on Pico Boulevard in Los Angeles. Hurried through makeup and wardrobe, he joined the crew and his fellow cast members on the soundstage. Trying to hide his nervousness, he stood around making small talk with the other actors. At last, flanked by flunkies, strutting and glowering like a summer stock copy of Erich von Stroheim, Ricardo Cortez arrived.

The director stopped before the line of gathered actors and looked them over, then barked, "Which one's Ford?"

"Mr. Cortez?" my father said, clearing his throat. "Uh . . . I'm Glenn Ford."

"Yes, that's right," said Cortez. The director backed up and raised his voice to address the entire cast and crew. "I want you all to know," he began, "they have stuck me with this guy in the lead. I didn't want him. I wanted a real actor for this thing and not some unknown amateur. I'm disgusted, but there is nothing I can do, so I ask you for your patience as we put up with him."

My father stood there, almost sick with anger and humiliation. Before he could speak, Cortez clapped his hands and barked some orders, and everyone went to work. Mortified but determined not to walk out on the biggest opportunity of his life (which he was sure was exactly what Cortez had wanted), Glenn swallowed his pride and took his place on the set. Any hope for a reprieve from his director was quickly dashed. Cortez treated his "star" with contempt and cruelty throughout the first day and the next and then for every day of the two-week schedule. "That's the stupidest expression I've ever seen," Cortez would shout at him, day after day. "That's how a fairy would say it. . . . Christ, what did I do to deserve a no-talent like you on my picture?"

"It was the worst experience I would ever have in the movie business," Dad would remember. "Every time I looked up I saw pity in the eyes of the other people on the set. The cameraman, Eddie Cronjager, was very kind, and he'd whisper, 'Don't let the jerk get to you.'"

Since Dad was not an important figure at the studio, there was no one willing to stand up for him. Tom Moore sympathized but told Dad to get through it. It was still a big break, and the studio would probably offer him a star contract afterward.

Every night after work he would go home a bundle of nerves. "I never told my mother and dad what was happening. I would just go off by myself and build things as if I were a demon, hammer and saw in hand. In the morning I would wake up with my fists clenched."

In the end it hardly seemed worth it. When he got a look at his performance and appearance in *Heaven*, he thought he came off as bad as in *Night in Manhattan*. Cortez's "Stroheim" act had destroyed his concentration, kept him on edge and unfocused in scenes he was sure he could have done much better.

Ricardo Cortez's directorial career did not last much longer, but Dad's anger with him would last a lifetime. Decades later, in the late 1950s when my father was one of the top box-office stars in the world, we were having lunch at the Bel Air Country Club. Someone was talking loudly at another table, and Dad's ears pricked up when the loud voice was heard to say, "Didn't you know that I'm the man who discovered Glenn Ford?" It was, yes, Ricardo Cortez. Dad quivered and pushed back his chair, saying he was going to go over and "punch the phony bastard in the nose." He sat down again when he got a look at Cortez, then a shrunken and long-unemployed old man. "I made a vow," he would tell me, "after the experience on *Heaven*, if in the future I ever got any power as an actor, I would never, never permit anyone to abuse anyone on a set like that."

Fox did not, as predicted, offer a contract to my father after *Heaven* wrapped. Dad decided to return to the theater and give up on the movies for good, if movies hadn't already given up on him. Then Tom Moore, who was still looking out for him, arranged to get him an appointment with a prominent agent, Milton "Gummo" Marx, who had once been one of the immortal Marx Brothers until he put performing aside to become a talent agent, eventually joined by another brother who wanted out of the act, Zeppo. By the late 1930s he and Zeppo had a thriving agency whose clients included stars such as Barbara Stanwyck and Robert Taylor, starlet Evelyn Keyes, and many top directors and writers. Dad hesitated. Was it worth the effort of another humiliation or failure? But in the end he agreed to go talk to the agent and hear what he had to say.

Gummo was willing to take a chance on a young actor who had already nabbed a lead part in a movie, even if Fox had passed on a long-term contract. "We'll get you something, baby," Gummo told him. "Leave it to me."

Dad and Gummo Marx were helped by a fortuitous incident. When Dad was midway through shooting the principal photography on *Heaven*, a casting director at Twentieth Century Fox, James Ryan, was tasked by the studio's executive committee with finding an unknown actor to play a gag on a retiring executive who was leaving the studio after twenty years. At Al Levy's Tavern on Vine Street in Hollywood my father, dressed as a busboy, dropped a tray full of dishes in the midst of the toastmaster's solemn tribute to the guest of honor. Dad began shouting an abusive and libelous tirade against the guest and his friends. The studio executive knew every actor in the business, but he didn't know my father because he was not yet established. This practical joke was witnessed by many members of the industry, and Dad became notorious for pulling it off.

When, after some weeks, Gummo landed an offer for his new client, it came from Columbia Pictures vice president Ben Kahane, who had been in attendance on that day, remembered Dad, and admired his spunk. The offer was for a seven-year contract.

"Seven years! Wow," said my father.

"Or six months."

"Six months? Didn't you say seven years?"

"Maybe six months, maybe seven years, leave the details to me," said Gummo.

It sounded like an old Marx Brothers routine. The agent finally explained: Columbia offered a standard agreement, with all the options in the studio's favor. If they wanted you, you couldn't leave them for seven years; if they got sick of you, they could fire you after any six-month period, including the first.

"I see," Glenn said. "Well, what's the pay?"

"A hundred dollars a week," said Gummo.

"A hundred! Gosh, that's fifty dollars a week less than I got for my first picture."

Gummo explained how the contract worked: $100 a week; if he survived the first option, a raise to $125; by the second year, $200; and so on for the next seven years.

"Seven years is a long time," my father said thoughtfully.

"You can do seven years standin' on your head," said Gummo. "Let's go sign the contract."

Columbia's earliest Hollywood headquarters was a ramshackle storefront on Gower Street and Sunset Boulevard. An assortment of other small, underfunded movie companies did business in the immediate area, most of them—including Columbia for a time—specializing in cheap westerns. It was a crossroads that insiders called "Gower Gulch" due to the preponderance of real-life cowboys who clustered around the street and offices looking for work as actors, extras, or stuntmen. Buoyed by success, Columbia began to buy up the surrounding fly-by-night entities and their soundstages, until Columbia dominated the area.

Stigmatized by its low-class origins on Gower Gulch and not helped by the reputation of its brutish production head, Harry Cohn, Columbia had always been in the shadow of the more important "majors," the brotherhood of the big studios: MGM, Warner Bros., Paramount, RKO, and Fox. Cohn accepted that he could never match the others for the number of stars and big pictures they offered but instead sought to make a very few carefully produced box-office smashes and Oscar contenders, most of these the work of his most valued employee, producer-director Frank Capra.

When big names came on the Columbia lot, top directors such as Howard Hawks and Leo McCarey or stars like Cary Grant and Katharine Hepburn, they were generally borrowed from another studio or signed for a single film (Jean Arthur was one of the rare exceptions, a long-term

Columbia asset). Cohn never had much luck creating big stars for his studio. When Dad began there in late 1939, a majority of Columbia's roster of releases were run-of-the-mill, and Cohn's ace in the hole, Frank Capra, had made his last picture for the studio.

On September 1, 1939, seated next to Gummo Marx and leaning over the desk of Columbia vice president Ben Kahane, Glenn Ford signed his first long-term Hollywood contract. Kahane, sliding the contract into his desk drawer before the ink had dried, said, "Glenn Ford . . . Glenn Ford . . . it doesn't have much sparkle. . . . Sounds very ordinary to me."

Dad took a breath. He guessed that Kahane was about to call for another name change.

"His real name's Gwyllyn," said Gummo. "With two or three *l*'s."

"Sounds like Gwendolyn," Kahane muttered.

According to my father, the exec glanced out his window and saw the sign on the corner of Gower Street. "What about Gower? Glenn Gower . . . hmm . . . no. . . . What about . . . Gordon Gower? John . . . maybe . . . Johnny Gower? That's not bad."

Gummo said, "Ben, the kid's first picture is coming out, and it says 'starring Glenn Ford.' Plus, he's been mentioned by that name in the columns a couple of times."

Kahane sighed. "All right, Glenn Ford. Fine. As long as it passes muster with Harry."

Harry was Harry Cohn, of course, a notorious figure in Hollywood, known for his vicious temper, foul mouth, and general crassness, though no one could deny that he was a showman. Dad's new boss had been born into terrible poverty in a rough New York neighborhood, and he still had a kind of kill-or-be-killed mentality. He was the boss, and he let everyone know it. He'd been quoted as saying, "I kiss the feet of talent," but he once told my father, "Actors are like cattle. I graze 'em and breed 'em, and I can eat 'em."

Dad recalled the day he formally met Cohn for the first time. Summoned for an appointment, he sat down and waited in Cohn's outer office; after a while he was then admitted to the inner office and more waiting, a conscious intimidation tactic used on all visitors. After an hour he was finally admitted into the mogul's private chamber. It was a massive room with a huge desk on a raised platform at the far end and lights aimed at the visitor's face, the whole setup copied from the Roman office of Italian dictator Benito Mussolini.

To Dad, Harry Cohn would always be both friend and nemesis, a man instrumental in Dad's great success to come, but one whose antagonistic behavior and bad decisions could drive my father to the point of angry and even violent confrontations with him. He would love the man and hate him—sometimes both in the same day.

The studio wasted no time getting their money's worth out of their new contract player. By early October Glenn had received the script for his first Columbia picture, a crime drama called *My Son Is Guilty*. It was the story of a veteran New York cop (played by silent screen cowboy Harry Carey) who is forced to shoot and kill his criminal son (Bruce Cabot). Glenn was cast as Barney, a friend of the son's former girlfriend. Filming took exactly two weeks.

Dad remembers *My Son Is Guilty* with fondness for one reason: it introduced him to actor Edgar Buchanan. He was the burly man with the squinty look and sandpaper-tinged voice who would become one of those familiar characters audiences loved, seen in scores of movies and as "Uncle Joe" in the 1960s TV series *Petticoat Junction*. He and Dad hit it off as if they had known each other for years, and their warm friendship lasted for decades.

As he was beginning his contract with Columbia, Dad celebrated another momentous event. On November 10, 1939, he became a naturalized citizen. He felt affection for his Canadian birthplace, but he had lived in America since he was a child. Hannah had completed the process earlier in the year, and Newton's formal citizenship was imminent. "The citizenship was essential to me," Dad told me, "not only because of my love for this country but for practical reasons as well. A few years earlier I had lost a job with a government-sponsored radio station because I wasn't a citizen, and with the war in Europe escalating, citizenship seemed more important than ever."

Dad's second Columbia production began filming just days after the first one "starring Glenn Ford" ended. In *Convicted Women*, a lurid exposé of corruption and murder in a women's prison, he played a reporter and the romantic interest for sweet-faced twenty-five-year-old actress Rochelle Hudson. The studio thought they looked good together and planned to promote them as a team, but audiences never responded to the three films in which they appeared. "Rochelle was a great girl. She was fun to work with and very professional," Dad recalled. "It's too bad we made such lousy pictures together."

These were B movies, second-echelon productions meant to give audiences another sixty or seventy minutes of entertainment for their ticket price. Although some B movies turned out to be terrific entertainment, most weren't—they were made quickly and rushed out the door as soon as possible. Glenn's second Columbia film finished shooting on December 12. His first was already playing in theaters two weeks later.

Following a break for the holidays, Glenn began filming *Men without Souls* in January. It was another prison drama, this time with Glenn behind bars as a man framing himself for a crime so he can seek revenge on the corrupt guard who killed his father. Rochelle Hudson again played his worried girlfriend. There were now hints, in Dad's brooding performance, of the tough, intense screen presence he would bring to later films. He got a brief mention in the *Hollywood Reporter* review of *Men without Souls* when it opened in early March 1940. "Glenn Ford is excellent as the kid," said the review. "His work is the pivot on which hangs the picture's credibility and a bow is due [to director] Nick Grinde for capitalizing on Ford's inherent talent."

The studio seemed fixed on putting Glenn into grim exposés. His next assignment was *Babies for Sale*, about the illegal adoption market. He played a righteous investigative reporter who falls for a pregnant young widow, played by Rochelle Hudson (their third and final pairing).

On Saturday, April 6, while Glenn was at the studio making *Babies for Sale* and waiting to do his next scene, a studio messenger appeared to tell him there was an urgent call from his mother. Picking up a soundstage phone, he heard Hannah on the line shouting that Newton was gasping for air and suffering a blinding headache. The doctor had been called but hadn't arrived yet. Glenn told her he was on his way home to where the family now lived at 614 7th Street in Santa Monica.

Newton was unconscious when Dad arrived, having suffered a coronary occlusion. Nothing could be done, the doctors said. Glenn and Hannah were at his bedside when he died three days later. Newton Ford was laid to rest at Woodlawn Cemetery on 14th Street, fifteen blocks south of their home and just a few feet from the grave of Hannah's mother, Caroline Mitchell. The passing of his father at the age of fifty always haunted Glenn. He was convinced that he too would die young, and at that moment he determined to pack as much living as he could into what he was certain would be a short life.

"Things had been going so well until then," Dad remembered. "Just the week before I had told Dad that he could quit that damn tram job. It was terrible to lose him, but especially so at that moment, just as our money worries were easing up."

With Caroline and now Newton gone, the Ford family was reduced to two. Increasingly, Hannah would focus on her son as her pride and joy and the center of her universe. Throughout her life she worshiped everything about her boy and could never find fault in him.

In the late spring of 1940, Glenn was promoted up from the "B depths" for a comedy-drama titled *The Lady in Question*, a remake of the 1937 French film *Gribouille*, about a middle-aged family man, Andre, who helps acquit Natalie, a young woman accused of murder, then helpfully invites her to move in with his family. British actor Brian Aherne topped the cast as Andre, with Irene Rich as his wife. Evelyn Keyes (a year after her break as one of Scarlett O'Hara's younger sisters in *Gone with the Wind*) played the daughter. Glenn was cast as Andre's son, Pierre, an aspiring astronomer who eventually makes "the lady in question" his betrothed.

The film is most memorable because of the twenty-two-year-old actress cast as Natalie. Her name was Rita Hayworth. She and my father would make movie magic together—but not yet. *Lady's* gentle comedy was light years away from *Gilda's* erotic noir melodrama—although, ironically, both films had the same director, Charles Vidor, a tough Hungarian who on occasion could be a martinet.

Rita was on the cusp of stardom but had not quite yet made her breakthrough. She had been in movies since the mid-1930s, and Columbia had been pushing her for several years, mostly in cheap B movies, occasionally on loan to other studios. Rita, at the time of *The Lady in Question*, was married to a sometime car salesman named Edward Judson who was twelve years older than his wife. It was no great love match. Dad, who befriended Rita, felt that she used the overbearing Judson as a shield against other male predators. For all the beauty and sexual self-confidence she exuded, Rita was a very shy and vulnerable woman.

When it came time for Rita to do a kissing scene with my father, she had great difficulty. Each time their lips would come together her body would visibly stiffen. Director Vidor would yell "Cut!" and "Try it again . . . not so stiff, Rita!"

Dad told me, "She kept pulling back, almost cringing. We tried it several times. I said, 'What's the matter? Is it me?' She said, 'No, no, I'm sorry. It's just so hard for me to do things like this in public.'"

Exasperated, Charles Vidor led the two actors off the set and escorted them across the street to Naples restaurant.

"Two double martinis," the director ordered.

"Vidor made sure we drank them," Dad recalled. "Rita and I had never tasted martinis. . . . I guess we liked them, because we agreed to have a second round. Vidor then took us back to the set, got the cameras running, and had us do the scene. The kissing went easily this time."

One day Glenn and Rita were on the set chatting when it suddenly occurred to him that he had actually met her long ago when they were both young teenagers and Rita—as Marguerite Cansino—was part of her father's dancing troupe. "I asked her, 'Do you remember a time the Cansinos were going to perform on that gambling boat, the SS *Rex*, many years ago? It was anchored off the coast in Santa Monica bay. You were all dressed up in your costumes, and you took the Venice tram down to board the water taxi in Santa Monica?' 'Oh yes,' Rita said, 'I remember that night. Why? Did you see us perform?' I told her, 'No, but the young man who drove the tram that took you all to the water taxi was me.'"

Their friendship began, and on-screen together for the first time, Glenn and Rita proved to be an attractive couple with a pleasing chemistry, although it was nothing like the powerful heat they would generate some years later.

Shortly before filming ended on June 22, 1940, Gummo Marx brought Dad some exciting news. David L. Loew and Albert Lewin, who had recently formed an independent production team, were looking for a young actor to cast in their upcoming film version of Erich Maria Remarque's novel *Flotsam*. The author of *All Quiet on the Western Front* had written a moving account of Europeans displaced by war and their struggle to keep love and hope alive in the face of Nazi occupation and pursuit. Glenn was being considered for the role of Ludwig, a persecuted young refugee.

Dad was thrilled to hear about the particulars of the production. The stars were Fredric March and Margaret Sullavan, two of the more distinguished and skilled names in the movies. The director was John Cromwell, whose previous credits included *The Prisoner of Zenda* and *Of Human Bondage*. My father went to a meeting at David Loew's beach house in Santa Monica. Nervous already at this important job interview, he became thunderstruck when he realized both March and Sullavan were there waiting to read with him.

"I managed to read as ably as I could in front of these two legendary actors," he recalled. "March started teasing. He'd say, 'Margaret, doesn't he remind you of a young Hank Fonda?' Sullavan, of course, had once been married to Hank Fonda. But it was just in fun. Later, when I was getting ready to leave, March patted me on the back and said, 'Congratulations!

We all agreed you'll be perfect in this part.' I mumbled, 'Th-thanksss, Mr. March,' and then I drove home in a daze."

Dad was troubled to learn that he would have to seek Harry Cohn's permission to appear in *So Ends Our Night,* as the film was to be called. When the time came for the discussion, he nervously entered Cohn's massive office and gave the boss his pitch, explaining what an important movie it was and how good it would be to work with such notable costars. Then he waited, expecting one of Cohn's abusive, four-letter responses, but the mogul simply nodded. "OK, do it," Cohn said. (Unknown to my father at the time, Columbia would be paid directly for their contract player's services and would pocket the considerable profit over Dad's measly salary.)

Shooting on *So Ends Our Night* began in August 1940 at the Universal Pictures lot. An epic production compared to Dad's two- and three-week shoots at Columbia, *So Ends Our Night* would take two months to complete. Although shooting this A-budget film was complicated and often exhausting, Glenn felt a greater sense of creative fulfillment. It helped to no end that both Margaret Sullavan and Fredric March treated him with respect, like a peer who belonged in their company. Once, after a good day's work, Sullavan presented him with an expensive necktie as a show of her appreciation, a gift Dad prized and wore for many years as a good-luck charm.

During his Universal sojourn, Dad was delighted to get to know a true legend, perhaps the most famous and acclaimed actor in the world at the time: John Barrymore. The "Great Profile" had a dressing room directly beside Dad's own on the Universal lot. Barrymore was a notoriously decayed character at this point, long past his Broadway heyday. My father felt sad to see him in such a state. Dad remembered:

> John would always call me "M'lad," inviting me into his room for a drink. He would tell me, "I only have two friends in this goddamned town, Haig & Haig!" [the name of a famous Scotch whisky]. We both laughed at W. C. Fields, who was also working on the lot, because he thought he was fooling everyone when he came to work with his booze hidden in milk cartons.
>
> John gave me one piece of career advice. He said, "Never turn down a chance to play the villain. They were always the best parts."

Dad's performance in *So Ends Our Night* was a genuine breakthrough, and the accolades began to circulate in Hollywood long before the film opened to the public. Offers began coming to Columbia from other studios and producers eager to cast the hot new star. The high-class release began with a premiere at Grauman's Chinese Theatre. Glenn did a publicity tour, appearing at a black-tie premiere at the Lincoln Theatre in Miami with special guests Lucille Ball and Desi Arnaz, Damon Runyon, Jack Dempsey, Sinclair Lewis, Sophie Tucker, and Paul Whiteman. The *Miami Herald* covered the premiere: "It was as much as anything a coming out party for a fine faced youngster with flowing locks and deep, dark eyes, who came to see and hear himself proclaimed a star of new and greater promise. It was Glenn Ford's first major dramatic part and it's no exaggeration to say he walked away with the picture and with the hearts of the assembled audience, which remained to cheer him and sing his praises into the fading night."

On January 30, upon arriving in Washington, D.C., Dad wrote a letter to Hannah:

> I got the surprise of my life when about a thousand kids met me at the station and just about tore my clothes off getting autographs—I did so want to sign all the pieces of paper and books they shoved at me. We then went to a big cocktail party at the Mayflower Hotel—Wally Berry and Lana Turner were there and I met the Senators and I don't know who all. Tomorrow is terrific from morning to night—I will meet the President in person. . . . Darling, I think we're in the "big time" now—this is what we have dreamed about, you and I and Dad, if only he were here with us how proud he would be—but somehow I have a feeling he knows everything that is going on—and is still proud—All my Love—Gwyllyn.

So Ends Our Night was screened for President Roosevelt, who was most interested in the subject matter, and Glenn was soon among a group of Hollywood celebrities invited to lunch at the White House in celebration of Mr. Roosevelt's Annual Birthday Ball. He was mightily honored to be in such exalted company. Glenn Ford, who had not yet voted, registered as a Democrat after he returned to Los Angeles and then declared his allegiance to FDR. "I was so impressed when I met Franklin and Eleanor Roosevelt," Dad recalled. "They were both larger than life. He said he really admired *So Ends Our Night*, and I was thrilled when I got back to Los Angeles and found a beautiful oversized photograph of him personally autographed to me. It always held a place of high honor in my home."

Dad was brought to New York for *So Ends Our Night*'s premiere at Radio City Music Hall. On this trip he stayed at the Warwick Hotel at 65 West 54th Street, and in the first days of February 1941 he patiently sat for more than twenty-six newspaper and magazine interviews. The press seemed entranced by the new star, admiring his boyish grin and natural modesty. He was the antithesis of the typical slick Hollywood playboy, they decided. He savored strawberry nut sundaes with whipped cream and hated nightclubs.

On a visit to his first upscale restaurant, the famous Stork Club on East 53rd Street, Dad was so excited to be there that he asked for a book of matches as a souvenir, proof that he had actually been to the club. Sherman Billingsley, the owner, gave him a whole box to take home.

The publicity tour was capped by the first extensive article on my father in a movie magazine. The January 1941 *Modern Screen*, one of the most important film magazines at the time, published a two-page story by Sylvia Kahn with ten photos of my father's work on *So Ends Our Night*. He was really proud of this and bought many copies to give to friends and relatives. The beautiful Priscilla Lane was on the cover, and not long after Glenn would be dating her sister, actress Rosemary Lane.

Instead of lending his new star to one of the rival studios for a prestigious production and for a profitable fee, Harry Cohn, following his own logic, decided he would keep Dad for himself. Cohn had another young male star under contract (whom he shared with Paramount Pictures), William Holden, who had come to fame in the film version of Odets's *Golden Boy* in 1939. Holden had been a hit in *Arizona*, a big-budget Columbia western starring Jean Arthur. Cohn had his staff cook up another horse opera as a follow-up, this one called *Texas*. Since Jean Arthur wasn't available, Cohn cast Claire Trevor in the girl's role and decided to team up Holden with the new kid on the block, Glenn Ford.

Texas would follow the picaresque adventures of two Civil War veterans, who cross paths with stagecoach robbers, a boxer, stampeding cattle, and Claire Trevor. The film would be shot on location in Calabasas, thirty miles northwest of Hollywood, and at the Columbia Pictures ranch, a forty-acre parcel of land at the eastern edge of the San Fernando Valley in Burbank, where sets were built to represent frontier Abilene, Kansas, and Windfall, Texas, circa 1866.

Directing the film was fifty-year-old George Marshall, a twenty-five-year veteran moviemaker whose films included *The Ghost Breakers* with Bob Hope, *Destry Rides Again* with Marlene Dietrich and Jimmy Stewart, and *Pack Up Your Troubles*, starring Laurel and Hardy (in which Marshall also acted, playing a vicious chef). Marshall would mold *Texas* in the style of *Destry*, with lots of rowdy slapstick mixed with action and a tearful twist at the end. Marshall told a reporter, "I feel that laughs have a rightful place in Westerns. . . . People do not go to the theaters to read drab history books, but to be entertained."

There were plenty of laughs on Marshall's set and quite a few thrills too. Dad had to watch his step with a director who didn't believe in stuntmen when a healthy young actor could do the job just as well. But he came to adore George Marshall, and they would become best friends. George was a tough-looking bird; in fact, he looked like a vulture, bald and fierce faced. He didn't exactly resemble a matinee idol, but he was a world-class carouser, always with a few ladies on his arm. He was an outrageous character, and Dad enjoyed his company very much and learned a lot from him both on and off the set.

Another friendship started on that film. The two young costars, Glenn Ford and William Holden, were less than a year apart in age, worked at the same studio, and were roughly appropriate for the same sort of roles. Both had shining futures and might well have been wary of each other as rivals, but it didn't work out that way. "Bill was a strange, rather fantastic character," Dad remembered. "I liked him immediately, and we came to really care about one another, friends for life." Their personal rapport was evident on-screen, where they enjoyed each other's company as boisterously as in real life.

This was my father's first western, a genre with which he would become identified for much of his career. He took to the requirements of a cowboy role with ease. He sat handsomely astride his horse and handled guns and lariats with finesse. "I felt very much at home on a horse. Right away I couldn't wait to make another western." But the filming "was a rough, exhausting job, Bill and me riding, fighting, and shooting in nearly every scene." Dad further explained:

> At times things got very dangerous. For one take of a stampede we had these five hundred imported longhorn cattle charging. It felt like an earthquake with all those cattle moving around us. Suddenly, the herd took an unexpected turn, crashing into the camera car at the center of the action. Our assistant cameraman, George Kelly, was knocked from his perch. He was about to fall under the hooves. I was on horseback a few yards away. There was no time to think about it. I spurred my horse and went forward into the cattle and grabbed Kelly by the belt. He climbed up behind me on the horse, and we got the hell out of the way.

In another scene George Marshall's directorial methods were just as dangerous. Marshall became exasperated by the weak reaction to gunfire Dad and Bill Holden were showing. "I guess Bill and I didn't look scared enough," my father recalled. "So George hauled out a .30-06 rifle and started firing it at us. I knew what real bullets sounded like, and these were flying within two feet of us. We both nearly lost our lunches, he so scared the hell out of us. But George got the reactions he wanted."

Dad looked forward to working with George Marshall again. They would collaborate on eight film projects in the years ahead.

With his tenure at Columbia now paying him $200 a week, Dad felt he could afford to move Hannah and himself to a more comfortable residence. He found a home at 519 Ocampo Drive in the prestigious Huntington section of Pacific Palisades. The handsome Spanish-style house, built a decade earlier, featured adobe walls, a red tile roof, four spacious bedrooms, and lush landscaping.

America was not yet at war in the summer of 1941, but there was an air of uncertainty in the land, and many people were sure the United States would soon be dragged into the conflict already raging in Europe. Although he had received a Class 3 deferment from the draft because he was his mother's sole support, my father had a deep patriotic desire to serve his country. On September 1, 1941, he enlisted in the Coast Guard Auxiliary.

Three nights a week and most weekends Dad would drive to San Pedro to take part in training and maneuvers with his unit. Occasionally, someone would take notice of the movie actor in their midst, or a newsman would show up wanting to take some photographs of Glenn in uniform. Dad would shun the attention. "I wouldn't let any pictures be taken. I wasn't in the Coast Guard to call attention to myself. I just wanted to blend in with the other guys." After December 7 and the Japanese attack on Pearl Harbor, Glenn's Coast Guard duties would be considered essential, as there was widespread fear of an enemy attack along the California coast. He took the work very seriously and would eventually be awarded the Coast Guard's Asiatic-Pacific Campaign Medal for his service.

Inevitably, Glenn's life and work separated him from his old haunts and friends in the local theater community. His long relationship with Donna had faded and died through the previous year. As a young bachelor movie star he had no trouble finding new female friendships. In those free-wheeling days he went out with a bevy of young ladies, many of them beautiful starlets and famous names, including Laraine Day, Brenda Joyce, Rosemary Lane, model-actress Jinx Falkenburg, and "hillbilly" comic Judy Canova. In the interest of good international relations, Glenn had some evenings out with Brazilian bombshell Carmen Miranda and French star Michelle Morgan. Dad fell hard for a young gal working at Paramount by the name of Patti McCarthy, who was Dorothy Lamour's secretary. A. C. Lyles, the venerable producer at Paramount Pictures, told me that my dad and Patti were, for a brief time, very serious about each other and made a handsome couple.

One of Glenn's more intense relationships begun at this time was with actress Evelyn Ankers. Evelyn was a tall, Chilean-born blonde with limpid green eyes. She had been filming *The Wolf Man* at Universal when she and Glenn met (she would go on to be the studio's "scream queen" in other horror flicks). Evelyn and Glenn went out for several months, and he grew very fond of her, even bringing her home to meet his mother. Evelyn was ready to settle down, but Dad was not.

On one occasion when my father was out of town on location, Evelyn met and began dating actor Richard Denning—at first secretly, but they would later marry. Evelyn and Richard's daughter, Dee Dwyer, recently told me a cute story about how the matter was resolved. One night Denning insisted on putting Evelyn in his car and driving over to Dad's house on Ocampo Drive. He instructed Evelyn to go inside and talk to my father about his intentions. Denning gave her fifteen minutes, and if she didn't come out within the appointed time, he said he would drive away and accept the fact that she loved Dad best. Evelyn went in the house, she and Dad talked, and she came out in a timely fashion and drove away with her future husband.

A few weeks after completing *Texas*, Glenn was rushed into an inconsequential B movie costarring with *Blondie*'s Penny Singleton in *Go West, Young Lady*. It didn't matter what my father thought of it: he was on payroll and making films as fast as Harry Cohn could assign them. *Go West, Young Lady* did give my father the opportunity to romance another young lady—Ann Miller. Ann was just beginning her dazzling dancing career, and as a young girl who had just turned eighteen she was attracted to Dad, an "older man." I doubt their affair was intimate, but it certainly was affectionate. Annie, one of the sweetest ladies in show business, became a dear and close family friend.

My father met a venerable actor in the cast who would become a lifelong friend—Charlie Ruggles. Charlie's career had started before my father was born, and on this film he and Dad bonded. Charlie would often join Dad and Edgar Buchanan and others in their gang for Wednesday night poker parties. Some players came and went, but the core group was always the same, writers Doug Morrow and Norman Krasna, director Rudy Mate, actors Bill Holden, Broderick Crawford, and Robert Walker among them. The location of the game would rotate from house to house, with the wives preparing the food and serving the refreshments. It was a tradition that continued well into the late 1950s.

My father's eighth film was *The Adventures of Martin Eden*, based on a semiautobiographical novel by Jack London (*Call of the Wild*, *The Sea-Wolf*, etc.). It was the story of an aspiring writer and his harrowing experiences as a seaman under a sadistic captain. As a great fan of Jack London's work, Dad was thrilled at the chance to bring one of his novels to the screen. Playing the title role of Martin Eden was akin to playing the author himself.

The studio financed a week-long jaunt up the California coast to Oakland so Glenn could soak up the atmosphere in London's old haunts. Of course, a studio photographer went along to pursue all possible pre-publicity for the film. Dad described the experience:

> I was able to visit the London ranch in Sonoma County and met his widow, Charmian. She was around seventy but still vital. She was no pushover when it came to her husband's legacy and had her doubts about Hollywood. I told her how much I had always loved her husband's books, which was the absolute truth, and that I very much wanted to make a film that would give his story its due. I also told her that it was my first important starring role, and I would be trying to do as good a job as possible.

Dad appears to have charmed Jack London's widow. "She said I had his exact coloring, and my hair covered my forehead at just the same spot as her husband's had." To help Dad with his characterization, Charmian let him listen to some rare cylindrical recordings of London's voice. When he was leaving she presented him with many of Jack's personal items, including an autographed first edition of *Martin Eden*. (From the stories Dad told, it appears that Charmian wanted to present him with more than that, but my father was intent on only pursuing the nuances of Mr. London's character, not those of his widow.)

Filming of *The Adventures of Martin Eden* took up the month of November 1941. At Columbia's Burbank ranch the crew built a huge lagoon where they could shoot all of the "seagoing" scenes aboard the SS *Lorelei*, and at one section of the water's edge, art director Lionel Banks created a vintage version of the San Francisco waterfront.

The film, though strong in places, did not live up to Dad's or Mrs. London's high hopes for it. A John Ford or William Wellman could have done something memorable with the material and the capable cast, but Columbia B-picture director Sidney Salkow was not up to the task. As a contract player, with a few notable exceptions, my father was denied the opportunity throughout his career to work with the top directors in the business, and this had—and continues to have—a negative effect on his standing and reputation.

The happiest result of the film's production was a full-scale world premiere in the birthplace of its star. Glenn, Hannah, and Columbia representative Leo Politt traveled to Canada. They were greeted by large crowds in Montreal and then in Quebec City, where Glenn shuttled to dual premiere screenings at the Capitol and Empire Theatres. On March 7 they were escorted to another event, this one at the old family settlement in Portneuf, where they were greeted by dozens of relatives and old family friends. "I still can't really believe he's famous," Hannah said to a Canadian journalist covering the local lad's triumphant return. "To me he's still just a nice youngster with Sir Galahad manners and a healthy dose of the Marx Brothers."

Glenn was back at the studio in Hollywood by the second week of March. Strolling across the lot one day, he ran into Joan Crawford. The legendary MGM star was on loan to Columbia to star in *They All Kissed the Bride*. She was a last-minute replacement for Carole Lombard, who had died in a plane crash in January while on a war bond–selling tour. Glenn and Joan recognized each other and exchanged warm greetings.

Dad had been quoted by a reporter saying, "Joan Crawford had the most beautiful eyes of any actress in Hollywood," and Joan had obtained his phone number, called him, and thanked him for the compliment. Soon they were going out together, dining and dancing at the favored Beverly Hills nightspots. Some evenings Joan would invite him for dinner at her Brentwood home. She was the most dazzling, glamorous woman he had ever known, and a woman well known for her aggressive sexual appetite. "We had a brief affair," he recalled, smiling. "We enjoyed each other's company very much for a while. I wouldn't call it a love affair. She was too powerful a presence for that. I don't think she wanted that. She was very much sufficient unto herself."

His favorite memory of Joan Crawford was not exactly romantic or glamorous. "One evening we had gone up to her bedroom with a bottle of Champagne. Joan said teasingly, 'Well, you can make love to me . . . if you can get my girdle off.' She was serious. So I began struggling. It was so tight it took quite a while, and she didn't help me at all. Finally, I got a good grip and stretched it off of her, until it snapped . . . and almost threw me across the room!"

The fling burned out quickly. Crawford found someone else soon enough, marrying Phillip Terry a few months later. Dad was soon to meet someone new as well.

The Harry Cohn assignments didn't slow down: My father's eleventh Columbia film was *Flight Lieutenant*. It was a convoluted drama about father and son pilots, the disgraced older airman regaining his honor by saving his son's life in the melodramatic climax. Veteran star Pat O'Brien would receive top billing in the role of the old ace to Glenn's young pilot.

"We shot most of that one at the Alhambra Airport about twenty miles east of Hollywood," my father recalled. "The place had been taken over for the war effort, and there were strict security procedures in effect. Our cameras could not shoot any aircraft while they were taking off or landing. Even stationary planes could not be photographed without supervision. You never forgot we were in the middle of a war, even if the fighting was thousands of miles away."

Warmhearted, avuncular Pat O'Brien was an all-around swell guy. Dad enjoyed working with him very much, and the two became fast friends. That friendship would soon have a great significance in my father's life— and in mine too.

In April, a few days after completing *Flight Lieutenant*, O'Brien joined a group of stars aboard a specially appointed train known as the Hollywood Victory Caravan, departing from Union Station in Los Angeles on a twelve-city, three-week train tour of the country to promote the sale of war bonds. There were many famous movie stars on board, but one particular member of the caravan whom Pat befriended was a twenty-nine-year-old movie actress and dancer Fred Astaire once declared to be "in a class by herself." Her name: Eleanor Powell.

3

"Love and Marriage"

My mother was born Eleanor Torrey Powell on November 21, 1912,
to Clarence and Blanche (née Torrey) Powell in Springfield,
Massachusetts. They were an old Yankee family, in the New
England area for many generations. Capt. Thomas Powell had come to
what was later to be known as New York from Shalford Essex, England, in
the 1630s. His son purchased a fifteen-square-mile tract of land from three
Indian tribes in 1695 called the Bethpage Purchase, which today includes a
large portion of Long Island.

On my mother's side of the family there is a line to Charles Martel
(literally "Charles the Hammer") and his grandson, Charlemagne, the
eighth-century saviors of Christendom. She was also descended from a
passenger on the *Mayflower*, Richard Warren, who was one of the forty-
one signers of the Mayflower Compact, the first governing document in
what was to become the United States of America—in all, quite a pedigree.
In those early days both sides of my mother's family were prosperous and
influential, but by the turn of the twentieth century there was no pomp,
only poverty, and Mom and Grandmother had to survive in very humble
circumstances.

Clarence and Blanche were married in Springfield, Massachusetts, and
less than three months later Blanche, then just fifteen, gave birth to a
daughter. The marriage ended in divorce one year later, but for many years
Blanche would lead Ellie to believe that her father had died just after she

was born, since divorce was a shameful thing to many people in those days. Blanche had no means of support and took jobs as a hotel maid to support herself and her little daughter.

Eleanor began taking dance lessons at the age of seven to overcome her extreme shyness and immediately revealed a tremendous natural ability. By age eleven she had left school, and at age twelve she made her professional debut as a dancer in Atlantic City, New Jersey. In the fall of 1927 she and Blanche went to New York, where my mother found work in nightclubs and vaudeville. In her first month there she was invited to dance at a charity event and met the legendary dancer Bill "Bojangles" Robinson. Bill recognized her talent and they became friends. It wasn't long before the pair was invited to dance together at private parties in the grand homes of New York's social elite.

It must have been quite a sight to see this fifty-year-old black man with his fifteen-year-old protégée in tow as they danced for the Astors, Vanderbilts, Whitneys, and other wealthy New Yorkers during the closing years of the Roaring Twenties. Mom recalled that for these events she and Bill were required to enter the mansions from the back—the service entrance— and never through the front door.

Segregation was the rule of the day, and Negroes were regarded with disdain—good enough to perform for the enjoyment of the white upper class, perhaps, but not worthy of the same respect accorded the white entertainers. My mother was offered the opportunity to be treated differently from Bill Robinson, but she declined. Where Bill went, so did she, and I'm certain she learned more lessons about human nature and the world around her than she could have ever known as a pupil back in Springfield, Massachusetts. Blessedly, she passed these lessons on to me.

On January 30, 1928, my mother made her New York stage debut at the age of fifteen. Eleanor, now the family breadwinner, studied and rehearsed with a steely determination, perfecting all the various dance styles, but it was tap that became her calling. She developed a unique style that blended ballroom, ballet, and jazz technique. Her precision and speed were startling, her sense of rhythm breathtaking; these traits, combined with her prettiness and ebullient personality, made her a star. Soon, she was wowing audiences in stage reviews produced by Billy Rose, Flo Ziegfeld, and George White. She appeared in the chorus of some early silent films while in New York, but it was White who took her out to Hollywood, where she appeared in *George White's 1935 Scandals*, starring Alice Faye. The *New York Times* review of the film called Eleanor's tap solo "miraculous."

Louis B. Mayer, the mogul of MGM, took notice of the young dancer and signed her to appear in a big-budget Metro musical, *Broadway Melody of 1936*, casting her as Irene Foster, the ingénue opposite the studio's young heartthrob, Robert Taylor. When the film opened audiences were completely taken with Eleanor's wholesome, sunny personality and her amazing dancing talent. At MGM a series of glossy musical features followed, including *Born to Dance, Broadway Melody of 1938, Rosalie,* and *Honolulu.* Eleanor Powell became one of the most successful and beloved of Hollywood performers. She was Louis B. Mayer's pride and joy at MGM. (I have the original incorporation papers that in 1923 formed what was to become MGM Studios, as well as a photo of Mayer inscribed to my mother: "You are my lucky star!") The production numbers the studio created for her were breathtaking, and her self-choreographed dance routines were talked-about sensations in their day. She was a perfectionist as a dancer, and experts on dance and the movies usually agree that her only peer was Fred Astaire. She was, in fact, paired with Fred Astaire in what is regarded by many as the quintessential Hollywood musical, *Broadway Melody of 1940*, in which Eleanor and Fred danced spectacularly to the tune of Cole Porter's "Begin the Beguine."

Settled down in Hollywood after many years on the road and living in hotels, Eleanor and her mother had established a relaxed home life in a Beverly Hills house they rented from Marion Davies, 727 North Bedford Drive. It boasted five bedrooms and bathrooms, with quarters for a maid and butler and an apartment for a chauffeur over the double garage. The servants included a masseuse, who was always on call to help Mother relieve the leg cramps she suffered at the end of her twelve-hour days in front of the movie cameras.

Nearing her thirtieth birthday in 1942, Eleanor had begun to think about making changes in her life. She was still a very big star, but she wondered how long her popularity would continue, with the mood of impending crisis in Europe increasingly at odds with MGM's rosy spectaculars. Sure of her talent as a dancer, she equally believed that she was not skilled enough to hold an audience's interest as an actress alone. She had no desire to overstay her welcome on-screen and did not want to see a decline in the quality of her movie vehicles. But there was something else missing from her life that transcended all of those professional considerations. She had worked nonstop as a performer since she was a little girl, and now she felt it was time to concentrate on having an equally fulfilling personal life. She wanted to get married and have a family.

Let us return to that Hollywood Victory Caravan, the star-packed train that kicked off its twelve-city visit on April 26, 1942, on its cross-country tour to sell war bonds to support Army and Navy Relief agencies. As my mother would recall it, many of those movie actors and actresses who were on this tour were very freewheeling personalities, rowdy and uninhibited, both the men and the women. There was a considerable amount of drinking and revelry taking place, on and off the rails, with twenty-two stars (including Cary Grant, Joan Blondell, James Cagney, Merle Oberon, Claudette Colbert, Laurel and Hardy, Bing Crosby, Desi Arnaz, Charles Boyer, and Bob Hope) indulging in numerous sexual escapades and partying in each other's sleeping compartments. In an uncharacteristically bawdy remark, Mom recalled that Merle Oberon bedded so many participants that "she had the Santa Fe logo imprinted on her backside."

My mother had been brought up by her mother to maintain a strict moral code and was still a virgin at twenty-nine (this was probably due to Blanche's own teenage indiscretions in Springfield). Normally, Grandmother would have accompanied Eleanor on a trip like this, but she had not been able to go. Eleanor felt isolated and intimidated during the long stretches between stops until fellow war bond salesman Pat O'Brien befriended her. The conservative, Catholic, and happily married Pat played protective dad to Eleanor. The two would sit together in the club car and play gin rummy and talk about the news, work, and movies they had seen. A film that Eleanor spoke of with enthusiasm was the newly released Jack London story, *The Adventures of Martin Eden*. She had gone to the showing with her mother and had fallen in love with my father's character on-screen.

"Oh, yeah, *Martin Eden* with Glenn Ford," said Pat. "I just finished a picture with him."

"Really?" said Eleanor. "He was wonderful in that film."

"Glenn's a great guy," Pat told her.

"What's he like?" asked Eleanor.

Pat raved about his new friend. "You should meet him, Ellie. I think you two would like each other."

Eleanor had no objection. And one day in May, with the tour completed and everyone back in Los Angeles, she was invited to Pat's house in Brentwood for a party celebrating the Victory Tour. Pat invited Glenn, who initially begged off, busy studying a script for his next picture. But Pat insisted. "Glenn, there's somebody coming I want you to meet. It's a young lady."

Dad would remember that first glimpse of Eleanor Powell:

I saw her from across the room. She was wearing a lavender cocktail suit, I remember. She had a wonderful figure, gorgeous legs, of course. But I had only seen her in black-and-white movies, and in person I was struck by her coloring, her chestnut hair, worn in soft waves to her shoulders, this glowing complexion, and beautiful cornflower blue eyes. And when she smiled I was just captivated.

I don't remember what we said. The party was crowded and boisterous, and at the end of the day we only had a few moments alone.

At that time Dad was seeing singer Dinah Shore, and she was his date a week later when they attended the Navy Auxiliary Relief Ball at the Coconut Grove, which was in the Ambassador Hotel on Wilshire Boulevard in Los Angeles. In those days each studio would send a delegation to events like this to show solidarity with the war effort and to support the troops and their causes. Dad was with the Columbia tribe, and Mom was with the MGM group. Public occasions like these generated good publicity for the studios, and attendance was a requisite for most players under contract.

There was a patriotic stage show, and afterward the hotel orchestra played and everyone danced. Among those on the crowded dance floor was Eleanor Powell. She and Glenn exchanged hellos as she swept by his table in a cloud of Jungle Gardenia perfume, dancing in the arms of her date, the young MGM actor John Carroll. "She looked spectacular," Dad recalled, "very classy and understated in her style, not overdone like so many of the girls who could only think about getting the attention of the photographers."

With Dinah Shore's permission he eventually got up and cut in on Carroll for a dance with Eleanor. The two swayed around the palm-encircled dance floor to the romantic strains of "Moonlight Serenade." They had another dance. Almost at once it seemed clear to them both that they were drawn to one another. They agreed to meet for dinner the following week.

It was a hectic time for Glenn to try and get to know Eleanor. He was in the midst of starting a new film, *The Desperadoes*, learning his lines, packing for a trip to the film's location at Kanab, Utah, and expecting to be gone for a month and a half. But that first date—an early dinner they had together at Musso & Frank Grill in Hollywood—convinced them that they wanted to continue seeing each other. Eleanor promised to write to him in Utah, and Glenn said he would try and call her whenever he could.

The Desperadoes was a conventional western in most ways, but it was also another important milestone in Glenn's career, as he was headlining with Randolph Scott in what was—for Columbia—an expensive superproduction, the studio's first Technicolor feature. Harry Cohn approved an elaborate location shoot, resulting in a magnificent-looking film, with Kanab's towering and flame-colored rock formations beautifully captured by cinematographer George Meehan under the direction of Charles Vidor.

During the three weeks the company was on location, with temperatures in excess of 120 degrees in the canyons, Dad had a riding accident. Hannah heard about it over radio station KCEA at home. "Glenn Ford—now on location in *The Desperadoes*—will be in a cast for two or three days!" She was soon fielding concerned calls from Glenn's female friends (Eleanor and Joan Crawford included). My grandmother Hannah, always practical about furthering her son's career, was very keen on Joan and encouraged Dad to write to her in answer to the wire she had sent him.

When Dad returned to Los Angeles in late August, despite his mother's preference, he rushed to reunite with Eleanor. They began an avid courtship. They went out nearly every night of the week, most often getting together after work for quiet early dinners. They settled on a favorite spot, Don the Beachcomber, a popular Hollywood Polynesian-style restaurant. On the weekends they would stroll arm in arm around Hollywood, haunting music stores and buying each other records or taking leisurely drives up the Pacific Coast Highway in Glenn's 1941 black Cadillac coupe. They would park on Old Ox Road near Malibu and talk for hours.

They were a couple made for gossip column headlines, Glenn the handsome "playboy" actor who had been linked with numerous beautiful and available actresses and Eleanor the sweet musical star whose private life was considered squeaky clean and "dull" by tabloid standards. (Eleanor's mother had kept older wolves like Clark Gable, band leader Abe Lyman, and Al Jolson at bay, and though Ellie had once had a light romance with Jimmy Stewart, up to this time she had dedicated herself to her work and couldn't have cared less about men and dating.)

Eleanor was also three years older than Glenn and earned—at $3,400 a week—ten times Glenn's Columbia salary, differences that were a bigger obstacle in those more traditional days. But they managed to nurture their friendship, and along the way it became much more than a friendship. In late 1942, dressed in their best, they were pictured in numerous movie magazines on intimate dates at the chicest nightclubs: Ciro's, Trocadero, Mocambo, and the Coconut Grove. They had fallen in love.

It was an exciting time in Glenn Ford's life. He was becoming an important movie star, he was in love with the dazzling Eleanor Powell, and he was feeling increasingly determined to take a more active part in the war effort. Dad and my mother were at the official opening of the USO's Hollywood canteen on October 3, 1942, and on December 13 Dad entered the Federal Building in downtown Los Angeles and enlisted in the United States Marine Corps.

His impulsive move took Columbia by surprise. Dad was in the midst of making a war melodrama, *Destroyer*, costarring the great Edward G. Robinson, with the always provocative Marguerite Chapman as the female lead. The film was directed by the prolific if undistinguished William Seiter. Studio executives had to beg the Marine Corps to delay Glenn's start of duty until the film was completed in March. The Marine commander, recognizing the film's (and Glenn's) value as war propaganda, agreed.

Destroyer was shot in nine weeks on four stages at Columbia Pictures studios. The story wasn't much (a new Navy destroyer locked in combat with a Japanese sub), but in Robinson, Dad had a good friend who was also a neighbor off-camera, and they would work together again thirteen years later, this time with Glenn top-billed.

After filming was completed, on December 22, 1942, Glenn and Eleanor went Christmas shopping in Beverly Hills. Despite the chilly day, Glenn suggested they go have an ice-cream soda at Martha Smith Fine Candies and Ice Cream on Beverly Drive. Glenn recalled:

> We sat down at one of the tiny wrought-iron tables. We ordered chocolate ice-cream sodas—I don't know why, because I hate chocolate. . . . From my overcoat I took out a small velvet box and opened it in front of her. I remember it was a half-carat diamond in a platinum setting with two smaller diamonds on either side of the bigger stone. It was a simple choice, but I knew she would not like anything terribly ostentatious; besides, that was all I could afford. I don't recall what I said, but I was a hit. I was about to slip the ring on her finger when she suggested we give the moment more meaning by doing it three days later on Christmas. So we waited, and on Christmas Day we went to the little St. Augustine's Episcopal Church in Santa Monica where I had gone to Sunday school as a teenager. We went to a pew, and I knelt down beside her, and I finally asked for her hand and put the ring on her finger.

Like many thousands of other young couples in those years, Glenn and Eleanor had to adjust their plans, their lives, to the unpredictable and dangerous times. They both knew that anyone who entered the military during that world war faced an uncertain future. But like so many others, they took the need for self-sacrifice to heart. Eleanor respected Glenn's decision and loved him all the more for it.

Glenn knew he was potentially giving up his career just when it was really taking off. "Bill Holden went into the Army Air Corps around the same time I joined the Marines," Dad recalled. "We talked about it, and we were both convinced that our careers, which were just getting established, would likely be forgotten by the time the war was over and we got back to Hollywood . . . if we got back."

Glenn's Columbia paycheck would stop, although Harry Cohn had agreed to pay him a retainer of $100 a month. To economize, Dad had moved with Hannah from his spacious home in Pacific Palisades to a small two-bedroom apartment at 137B South Camden Drive in Beverly Hills.

On March 22, 1943, Glenn arrived at the Marine base in San Diego to begin boot camp. At the time of his enlistment he had been offered the opportunity to join the Corps as an officer, due to his previous service in the Coast Guard, but my father declined. He didn't want any perception of preferential treatment because he was a movie actor, even though he rightfully could have taken the commission. He elected to join the Marines as a private. It was a tough routine, but Dad said he was familiar with the regimen and discipline from his Coast Guard training, and anyone who worked in the movies was used to getting up for work by dawn. He even liked the base cuisine, which included plenty of hearty meat and butter, items strictly rationed among civilians. "I'm having the time of my life," he wrote to his mother.

Also stationed at the base was Tyrone Power, who befriended Glenn and encouraged him to lend his talents to the radio broadcast *Halls of Montezuma*, which aired from San Diego every Sunday evening. When Glenn's glossy Technicolor western *The Desperadoes* opened, there was a screening at the base. Glenn feared an antagonistic reaction from his fellow Marines, who made mincemeat of anyone among them who showed signs of egotism. He sat during the screening, waiting for the merciless ribbing, but *The Desperadoes* and its down-to-earth star were treated to raucous applause.

Dad did well in boot camp, earning a Rifle Marksman Badge and a Marine Corps Basic Badge with Expert Bayonet bars; he was named "Honor Man" of the platoon by his tough drill instructor. He was promoted to sergeant by the time he finished boot camp and awaited assignment at Camp Pendleton in Oceanside, California. Glenn and his platoon settled into one of the dozens of two-story barracks that dominated the big plot of military real estate.

You will not find this film listed in any Glenn Ford filmography, but Dad appeared in a film in 1943—*Guadalcanal Diary*. During the week of June 7 he worked as a member of a Marine raider outfit in battle sequences for the Twentieth Century Fox picture. He was just atmosphere in these scenes, but I have some great photos of him with a determined look on his face charging up a beach into combat with bayonet fixed. To make it all the more ironic, not only was he an "extra," but he was also working for Fox, a rival to Columbia Pictures, where he expected to resume his contract after the war.

At the time my father would never have guessed that this minuscule acting job in *Guadalcanal Diary* was as close to real combat as he would experience. I can remember very clearly sitting in my father's bedroom as a young child looking at the picture of him with that bayonet. More than once he set up his Bell & Howell 16 mm projector and showed me war footage and described the details of certain battles. The battle of Tarawa was one I remember.

"Look son, there's Daddy!" He would point himself out to me as I sat on the edge of his bed wide-eyed in amazement. He had many black-and-white war films. I later discovered that he never participated in any of these battles, but I guess he felt he needed to make me think he was a war hero.

On June 10, 1943, Louella Parsons's *Los Angeles Examiner* column announced, "Eleanor Powell Retires from Screen." "Turning down a renewal of her MGM contract and an upcoming film assignment opposite George Murphy," the columnist wrote, "Eleanor feels that marriage and a career do not go together." Eleanor had also turned down a four-week engagement at Radio City Music Hall in New York City that would have earned her a weekly salary of $10,000. She wanted to stay in California to be near her fiancé. She reasoned that if she did not stay close and he was eventually sent overseas and possibly killed, she would regret those lost four weeks for the rest of her life, no matter how much she earned.

Many of my mother's fans dismissed her own public statements and believed that it was my father who had insisted on her retirement, and they held it against him for many years. In fact, she had to assure my dad that the surprising news was true when they saw each other for dinner in San Diego a few days after Parsons's column appeared. Eleanor explained that she had a few more obligations to the studio, including some personal appearances to promote her latest film, *I Dood It*, costarring Red Skelton, and then she would be done for the time being.

Destroyer opened in August, and Dad received very good notices and some mentions of his current service. "Glenn Ford," said the critic in the *Hollywood Reporter*, "gives his best screen performance to date as the hero. His work should keep his memory fresh in the minds of fans until peace comes and he returns from the Marines."

Eleanor and Glenn began making plans for their wedding as best they could in between Glenn's stints at Camp Pendleton. Under the circumstances of wartime, they decided that a simple ceremony would be best, held at Eleanor's home and with a minimum of fuss. Her house, beautifully decorated by Eleanor and her mother and with some luxurious art and elaborate wall and ceiling carvings installed by the owners, Marion Davies and William Randolph Hearst, was a more than elegant setting for the intimate event. Glenn was granted a ten-day marital leave so the couple could enjoy a proper honeymoon before the new groom returned to the Marine base.

Glenn and Eleanor were wed on Saturday, October 23, 1943. Eleanor wore a cream-colored satin gown and held a long spray of white orchids. Glenn was in impeccable dress uniform. They looked very much the beautiful movie star couple. The Reverend Ray Moore of the First Methodist Church of Santa Monica performed the ceremony. In attendance were Stebbie Delson, Eleanor's secretary and dear friend, who served as matron of honor, while Ned Crawford, an old friend of Glenn's from the Santa Monica little theater days, was best man. The two beaming mothers, Hannah Ford and Blanche Powell, flanked their offspring. Filling out the rest of the room was a host of photographers from Columbia and MGM and select periodicals. Mr. and Mrs. Ford posed for their official wedding portraits standing amid banks of pale chrysanthemums. The hired pianist played "Sweet Leilani" as the couple danced for the first time as husband and wife.

The newlyweds boarded a train for San Francisco and on arrival checked into room 223 of the St. Francis Hotel, overlooking Union Square. They did what most just-marrieds do on their honeymoon. Occasionally they left their hotel room to stroll around the city, eat at the exclusive Persian Room, and enjoy the live band on the St. Francis's Starlight Roof, one of the city's legendary rooftop venues for dining and dancing. "People recognized us and stared," Glenn recalled. "I felt like they were expecting me to be as good a dancer as Eleanor, and of course I never was."

When Glenn returned to Camp Pendleton, Eleanor, realizing that it was not as easy as she thought it would be to live without her large MGM salary coming in, decided to accept a one-shot offer to make a film, *Sensations of 1945*, for independent producer Andrew L. Stone. Besides providing a useful paycheck, the film would be done very quickly, unlike the elaborately rehearsed musical extravaganzas she made at Metro; and she would play an adult role and not her typical sweet innocent. After all, she was over thirty now and a married lady.

Glenn, meanwhile, had to deal with the disappointment of being unable to play the role of Chopin opposite Paul Muni in Columbia's production of *A Song to Remember*. Harry Cohn had attempted to get his star released for three months in order to make the film, but this time the Marines would not hear of it.

As soon as she could get free, Eleanor headed south to find a residence close to Glenn's base camp. In La Jolla, a picturesque beachfront community that was a thirty-minute drive from Camp Pendleton, she found a house to rent, a small guest cottage on the grounds of an estate on Dunemere Drive. It was a lovely, idyllic address, surrounded by ruby-colored bougainvillea, with a great ocean view and delicious sea breezes. The rent was $60 a month. It was there at the cottage, when Glenn could manage to get leave, that they enjoyed home life as a married couple for the first time. On a budget of $35 a week and with no staff or servants, Eleanor took on a new role, that of housewife—cleaning and cooking meals, or attempting to cook them. (About the only dish she could take pride in making was, as she liked to describe it, a "wonderful pot of beans.")

In June Glenn was back in Los Angeles on leave for a three-day weekend. My parents were having breakfast one Saturday morning, June 17, when my mother announced she had some news. She was pregnant. Always a very precise person, Eleanor further declared that the baby had been conceived in La Jolla on May 1, Glenn's twenty-eighth birthday.

Within a few days the newspapers were spreading the word of the pregnancy, and headlines read: "Glenn Ford and Eleanor Powell Await Stork." There were pictures of the expectant couple smiling for the camera and gleeful quotes. In Eleanor's scrapbooks she had copies of the announcement in various languages and papers from around the world. Eleanor was certainly delighted by the news, but Glenn had mixed feelings, thinking they had not yet had much time to themselves as a married couple. He worried about his obligations to the Marines—he was scheduled to begin Officer Training School that summer, and there was still the looming prospect of being shipped overseas.

Another surprise development occurred that made his concerns about the military moot, however. A couple of weeks after the weekend in Los

Angeles, Dad was laid low by acute abdominal pains. On July 31 he was diagnosed with duodenal ulcers and transported to the U.S. Naval Hospital in San Diego's Balboa Park. He had long suffered from recurring epigastric pain, but this time it was serious enough to warrant a hospital stay, with six weeks of complete bed confinement. The severity of the condition lessened by the end of the hospital stay, but the ulcers remained, and he was in and out of medical care for the next five months. The doctors finally recommended a medical discharge for my father. He would remain on medication for the ailment for many years.

Dad was discharged from the Marine Corps without the combat duty or the military glory he had desired, but he had served his country earnestly and would be forever proud and grateful of his time in the Marine Corps. On December 7, 1944, Sergeant Glenn Ford received his final mustering-out payment of $100 and a set of X-rays of his ulcer along with his honorable discharge.

Glenn's sudden return to civilian life put the Powell and Ford families into temporary confusion. For a while the newlyweds went back to living apart, as Eleanor moved back into the house with her mother and Glenn moved into Hannah's current apartment on Camden Drive. It seemed the newlyweds were still more used to taking care of their mothers than of each other.

Glenn and Ellie went out to dinner on his first night home, eating at Don the Beachcomber in Hollywood, their old favorite. Ellie was abuzz with excitement and happiness at having her husband back, but Glenn was in a decidedly mixed mood. "I had contacted Columbia to tell them I was going to be a civilian again," Dad recalled. "Harry Cohn said that they had nothing ready for me at that moment. It was just too short notice. And until they had work for him he said I would not be going back on my contractual salary."

To Dad it sounded like his worst fears confirmed. The world had moved on, new people had entered the movies in the time he had been away, the audience had found some new favorites. "I don't think Columbia wants me back," he told Eleanor. "Maybe I'll go join some of my old Santa Monica friends and get a job at Douglas Aircraft until something turns up."

Eleanor knew that her savings could keep them afloat for some time to come, but she knew better than to mention it then. She understood Glenn's pride as an actor who had achieved a certain status and as a man who wanted to be the family breadwinner.

In the weeks after his discharge, Glenn waited for word from Columbia, with growing distress. He and Eleanor spent some of that time looking at houses, trying to find the perfect place to raise a family, rather than both living with their respective mothers.

In mid-January Glenn's friend Jerry Asher, a prominent publicist and magazine writer, invited him to join him for lunch at the Warner Bros. studio commissary. They were finishing their meal when a woman approached them. "You're Glenn Ford, aren't you?" she asked. The woman was Catherine Turney, a screenwriter. She said, "I wonder if you'd mind stepping over and saying hello to Bette Davis?" Dad recalled the scene:

> I said I would be delighted. She took me over to where Bette and her entourage were dining in the exclusive Green Room. I went in and said hello. Bette looked at me thoughtfully for a moment and then shook her head. She said, "No . . . you're too young." I didn't know what to say to that.
>
> She said, "I've never seen you on-screen. I've heard you're an excellent actor. It may be you'll look too young to play opposite me."
>
> She took a long drag of her cigarette, still sizing me up. "I'll tell you what. This weekend come back to the studio and wear a tweed jacket—something rugged, with brown leather elbow patches, you know what I mean? Oh, and a pipe, do you smoke a pipe?"
>
> I told her I did. "Okay! Bring your pipe and a tweed coat. We'll see what happens!"
>
> And with that she turned back to her lunch, and I was dismissed. I backed out of the Green Room and asked Jerry Asher what had just happened. He said Bette was looking for an actor to play her husband in *A Stolen Life*. She didn't like the studio's choice, and she was producing this picture herself and was taking charge of the casting, and they needed to make a decision right away. "It looks like Bette wants you for her leading man," Jerry finished.

A Stolen Life was to be a remake of a 1939 British film starring Elisabeth Bergner and Michael Redgrave. In Catherine Turney's Americanized adaptation, the story concerned the Bosworth sisters, wealthy identical twins, one a selfish playgirl, the other an earnest aspiring artist. The more aggressive twin steals the other's man and marries him. Then, after a boating accident that leaves the playgirl dead and the artist sister dazed, the latter assumes the dead girl's identity and pretends to be her brother-in-law's wife. It was highly melodramatic nonsense, but the script allowed for a tour de force performance by Bette Davis, playing her two polar opposite character types—the aggressive virago and the mousy spinster—in a single movie.

It was the one and only time Bette Davis would serve as her own executive producer. She was taking the job seriously and becoming involved in all decisions for *A Stolen Life*. Warner Bros. preferred to cast the lead from its roster of contract players. Not only was Glenn Ford too young, eight years Bette's junior, but he was not under contract to the studio and would cost it more. The studio executives did what they could to discourage testing Glenn, including floating the rumor that he had been discharged from the service suffering from shellshock! But they should have known from past experience that Bette Davis was not easily thwarted. She herself arranged for the screen test on a Sunday afternoon, with *A Stolen Life*'s director, Curtis Bernhardt, personally directing the test.

It was on the next day, Monday, February 5, 1945, that I was born. My mother had gone into labor on Saturday, and Dad had rushed her to Cedars of Lebanon Hospital on Fountain Avenue in East Hollywood, arriving at four o'clock Saturday afternoon. My father stayed in her room throughout the night. He didn't eat, bathe, or shave, and by Sunday morning he looked like a haggard wreck. It would be a nerve-racking weekend. He left the hospital Sunday morning, swung by his apartment, picked up his clothes, and went directly to the studio for the test. After the test he rushed back to the hospital to be with my mother.

If he had tested as the young, confident Glenn Ford, clean-cut as he looked in all of his early films, he never would have gotten the part—or perhaps the films and the success that followed. Years later I would tease him that his big break in becoming a movie star was because of me. Had it not been for me taking my time coming into this world, thereby causing him such anguish, his career might have been different.

The doctors had advised a Caesarean section, but Mother refused. At last, after thirty-two grueling hours of labor, at eighteen minutes past midnight on Monday morning, my mother finally gave birth. My parents had been told to expect a girl, so there was some surprise when I arrived, a healthy, crying boy—8 pounds 14½ ounces and 22½ inches. They named me Peter (from the Bible) Newton (after my paternal grandfather).

Because the delivery had been so difficult, Eleanor followed doctor's orders and remained in the hospital for a week after my birth. Dad made sure her sixth-floor room was filled with bunches of aromatic pink carnations, her favorite flower.

Meanwhile, there were negotiations to be conducted for Dad's return to the screen in a major Warner Bros. production. Bette Davis had forced Warner Bros. to accept Glenn Ford, and now Warner Bros. had to pay a pretty penny to Harry Cohn to borrow him from Columbia. Still miffed at the way Cohn had treated him when he was discharged from the Marines, Dad decided he would play tough with Harry, demanding that Columbia renegotiate his salary first.

Glenn sought Eleanor's counsel, often many times a day, on this contract while she was in the hospital. She was more experienced in such things and bolstered his confidence in his demands. Eleanor would later teasingly say that she gave birth twice—once to her son and again to her husband's contract.

Cohn was furious to be challenged by one of his minions, but he was a businessman above all. Betting that *A Stolen Life* would be a hit and raise the actor to a new standing, he agreed to loan Dad to Warner Bros. and to boost his salary to $1,000 a week when he returned to the home lot. It was a victory for both Mom and Dad.

Eleanor came home with me on February 12, to her mother's house on Hillgreen Drive in Beverly Hills, which had been purchased from director King Vidor in 1943. Dad was in the highest of spirits. His wife and newborn child were home safe, and he was about to embark on an exciting assignment and had a new and improved contract at his home studio. For mother and baby's arrival he went out on a shopping spree, buying presents of all sorts. But what he was most anxious to buy was a new home for his burgeoning family.

In mid-February my father placed this ad in the *Los Angeles Times*:

> ACTOR—Honorably discharged Marine
> DESIRES 2–3 BEDROOM HOUSE OR
> APARTMENT for wife and infant son.
> Up to $300 in Beverly Hills—CR 6-6775

Too soon, Dad had to leave us and start work on *A Stolen Life* at the film's Laguna Beach location with Bette Davis. In the days since he had accepted the offer to work with her, he had heard plenty of stories about her imperious ways, how she could eat up a director or costar and spit him out before breakfast. When Dad arrived at the Plantation Motel in Laguna, he wondered what he was getting into and double checked that he had packed his ulcer medication.

As they began working the next day, he was pleasantly surprised to find Bette a helpful collaborator who was watching out for his best interests. Director Curt Bernhardt immediately began coaching Glenn to say his lines in a clipped, faster style. Bette quickly told him to knock it off. "I want that natural way he speaks," she told the director. "That's one reason I liked him for the part!"

Glenn would drive back to Beverly Hills from Laguna whenever he had some time off, and he made sure to get back to attend my christening on April 22 at the First Methodist Church in Santa Monica. Dad took rolls of photographs of me, posed with my mother and both my grandmothers. When he was away my mother would write to him every day on her powder blue stationery, giving him detailed accounts of her day. One morning, she wrote him, Harry Cohn arrived with his wife, Joan, and their infant son, bringing along some very expensive gifts for me. The letters were also full of heartfelt sentiments and romantic statements of love. "No wife in the world worships her man more than I," she wrote. "You are my heartbeat."

At long last, the *Stolen Life* company returned to Burbank for the interiors and studio-based shooting. The work was complicated and slow. Because the story required Bette to appear in some scenes as both twin sisters, elaborate special effects photography was needed. Bette and Glenn had to shoot the same scene in multiple versions for matching and superimpositions (the exposure of more than one image on the same film strip done in the lab). To Dad's relief, he and Bette meshed perfectly. Bette was so pleased with her costar that she threw him a birthday party on May 1 at the Hollywood Canteen, where Glenn and Eleanor were photographed sharing birthday cake with a horde of starstruck servicemen.

During the week of June 16 the company had to go on location again, this time for a week near the windswept bluffs of Monterey and Carmel in California, shooting the first romantic moment shared by Glenn and Bette's characters, and the finale, where the couple is reconciled on the rocky cliffs overlooking the pounding surf.

On the last day at the location Bette asked Glenn to celebrate by having dinner with her at the Pebble Beach Golf Course clubhouse. They had a luxurious meal, enhanced by a couple of bottles of wine. Afterward they went for a stroll out on the moonlit grounds. Bette led him to a manicured plot of ground on the eighteenth green, overlooking the Pacific, glistening in the light of a full moon. Glenn recalled:

Suddenly Bette reached up and held me and planted a kiss on my lips. I was startled. In the back of my mind I had sometimes thought Bette had been interested in more than my acting prowess, but we had gotten to be friends, and nothing like that had happened before—she knew I was enjoying a happy marriage with a new baby at home. I honestly felt I had never done anything to provoke her.

While I stood there not knowing what to say she started to unbutton her blouse. Later I would hear that this was what she did when she wanted to seduce someone, exposing her breasts. She was a very attractive woman and had breasts that were absolutely unbelievable. But I was very much in love with my wife at the time, and I simply wasn't interested.

I told her, "I'm sorry, Bette, I just can't."

She said I was stupid. She said, "You'll never regret the things you did. You'll only regret what you didn't do."

There was a very awkward moment as we stood there before she covered her breasts again. But she took it in stride and never mentioned it again. We remained on very friendly terms for the rest of the picture.

Dad's work with Bette Davis had been not just a great professional opportunity. He had learned much from the great star and had been able to talk about the craft of acting with her in a way he had never done before. He explained:

One of the things Bette would say to me was, "The really interesting people are not the wishy-washy handsome men and beautiful women. It's the characters who are different, who have unique problems to overcome, and for whom the audience can feel sympathy and great interest."

Our talks crystallized many of the ideas I had been formulating before I went into the service. Even then I was getting tired of playing conventional nice guys. I was only too eager to get a chance to play someone more complicated—characters that were both good and bad.

Glenn was to have that chance in his very next role—in a film noir called *Gilda.*

4

"Amado Mio"

Rita Hayworth once said, "Men went to bed with Gilda, and they woke up with me." She was speaking of the distance between that larger-than-life erotic creature she created on film and the more human, life-sized, fragile person she was in reality. Glenn Ford would be one of the few men in Rita's life with whom she retained a lifelong intimate friendship, a person she could trust and love without disappointment on either side. They had met as teenagers, he had befriended her when she was an innocent young starlet before the birth of the Love Goddess, and they had collaborated in her creation of the immortal Gilda. He knew well the sweet, sometimes troubled, and lonely woman who was Rita off-screen. Glenn recalled:

> She was the most beautiful, glorious creature then. Film posters cried, "There was never a woman like Gilda"—and they were right. There has never been anyone in the history of movies that had such a magical presence on film. She was delightful and sexy, and she moved with such grace and glamour. We had worked together when we were both coming up in the business, and then she had zoomed to the top.
>
> I can remember when I was at Camp Pendleton [the Marine Corps base near San Diego], and every young Marine there had her picture pinned up in every locker and on every wall. I would see her in those very sexy pinup poses in slinky lingerie and think how different her image

seemed from the very shy brunette I knew when we were making *The Lady in Question*.

Gilda came from an original story by E. A. Ellington, adapted by Jo Eisinger and scripted by Marion Parsonnet. It had gone through considerable transformations along the way to production, from a tough gangster story set in Reno, Nevada, to the exotic and erotic final entity set in Buenos Aires and involving an interesting mix of Nazis, police spies, and international adventurers. Producer Virginia Van Upp would write much of the final script, revising scenes and delivering new dialogue long after filming had begun. Columbia's top contract director, Charles Vidor, was put in charge of the set, the cinematographer was to be the very talented Rudolph Mate, and art direction was by Stephen Goosson and Van Nest Polglase. The opulent wardrobe for Rita was designed by one of her favorites, Jean Louis. The colorful cast featured the epicene George Macready as the villain, with Joseph Calleia (as Detective Maurice Obregon) and Steven Geray (as Uncle Pio) in strong supporting roles.

Gilda starts on the Buenos Aires waterfront, where a young American drifter, Johnny Farrell (Glenn's character), is doing well in a nocturnal game of dice. A bit later, though, he is mugged by a stranger for his winnings but fortuitously saved by an elegantly dressed man wielding a sword-cane. The man, Ballin Mundson (Macready), offers Johnny a job working as his personal lieutenant at an opulent gambling casino. One day Mundson returns from a trip with a new bride, Gilda.

Johnny and Gilda, as it happens, are former lovers but say nothing to Ballin of their tempestuous past. Ballin is secretly involved in an illegal cartel with a group of criminal Germans, a man is murdered, and Ballin tries to escape but apparently dies in the attempt. Johnny blames Gilda for Ballin's death, and the two enter into a twisted, sadomasochistic relationship. Johnny eventually sees the error of his ways, professes his true love for Gilda, and begs her forgiveness. Ballin then reappears and must be dispatched before the couple can head off into the South American sunset.

Filming began at Columbia Pictures studios on September 4, 1945. Much had happened in the lives and careers of Rita and Glenn since they last worked together, but they quickly rekindled the easy rapport they had enjoyed while making *The Lady in Question* five years earlier. "We just got along so well and became the closest friends right away," Dad remembered. "We were both fairly new parents—her daughter, Rebecca, was only two months older than my son—so we had a lot of the same problems and joys, and we each did a lot of bragging about our kids. We traded complaints about Harry Cohn. I would tease her about her new sexpot image. We had a lot of laughs. But it was clear that she was not very happy underneath it all."

Rita's marriage to Orson Welles was in turmoil. She had been very flattered to have won the attentions of the great genius of the theater and film and had fallen in love with him. They had married and had a child. Despite the fact that both of them were extraordinary individuals, Rita expected to have an ordinary, old-fashioned marriage, full of love and devotion. But Orson was mostly in love with Orson, and he devoted the majority of his time to his ambitious creative pursuits: acting, producing, directing, and writing. That left only a small window in his schedule for his beautiful bride. They fought, separated, reconciled. Rita suffered, aware that Orson was conducting numerous affairs behind her back. It was a vulnerable time for her. Many days she would come to the studio upset, on the verge of tears. The friendship with her costar would deepen as she turned to Dad for understanding and sympathy.

Brief love affairs between costars are considered almost inevitable in Hollywood. Rita was vulnerable and starved for affection, and my father felt protective toward her. "You couldn't help but fall in love with Rita," Glenn would say. "She was such a lovely person but so miserable. I lent a sympathetic ear, and she trusted me because she knew I cared for her and wouldn't let anyone hurt her. You wanted to do whatever you could to make her feel less unhappy."

Indeed, the erotic tension and passion between the characters they were playing seemed to spill over into real life. And director Charles Vidor seemed to be encouraging just that, coaching them with outrageously explicit suggestions about what Johnny and Gilda wanted to do to each other. "His instructions to the two of us were pretty incredible," Glenn remembered. "I can't even repeat the things he used to tell us to think about before we did a scene."

Glenn had once resisted the advances of Bette Davis in deference to his marriage, but in the embrace of Rita Hayworth his resolve weakened. It was hard to keep their affair a complete secret. Grace Godino, Glenn's friend from the Santa Monica Players whom he recommended to Rita as her stand-in at the studio, recalls, "Glenn and Rita fell in love, you could see it in the way they looked at one another. But this was a different era, and people were much more discreet about such things. But we could see the sparks were definitely there."

It did not take long for Harry Cohn to suspect that something was up between his two stars, a situation that made him very agitated. Harry had his own tortured relationship with the actress he had nurtured into his studio's greatest asset. Insiders knew that Cohn endlessly lusted after Rita, but she would have nothing to do with him physically, and in return he treated her cruelly and resentfully in their professional dealings. It was one more burden Rita had to endure for no greater sin than being beautiful and desirable.

Cohn learned that Glenn and Rita did not go home after work but hid out together in Rita's dressing room until later in the evening. One day the studio boss summoned Glenn to his office to talk about it. Glenn described their meeting:

> I went to see him. He was very unpleasant. He demanded to know what Rita and I were up to—he knew exactly how long we were in the dressing room together. When I told him we were rehearsing and just having a couple of drinks at the end of the day, he snorted that he wasn't going to keep the studio open all night anymore, and we were to go right home after work.
>
> The situation became ridiculous. We found out that Harry had planted listening devices in the dressing rooms. We were both furious. But then we decided to play a joke on Harry. Just for Cohn's microphones we acted out a scene like we could never have gotten away with in the movie. I'd start groaning, "Oh, Rita . . . come on, baby, give it to me!" And Rita would moan back, "Oh, Glenn, that's great . . . yes, yes!" Rita would repeat the refrain from the song "Amado Mio" from the film, "Love me forever and let forever begin tonight."
>
> Harry never picked up on our mischief. Sometimes we'd have to rush out of the dressing room because we were laughing so hard and didn't want the microphones to pick it up.

For all his concerns and suspicions, Cohn could only have been pleased with the way *Gilda* was turning out. Charles Vidor, Rudolph Mate, and the various craftsmen were creating a sumptuous movie in which the sets and costumes shimmered as if in a bright dream. Everything seemed to click into place. When songwriters Allan Roberts and Doris Fisher were assigned to the film and told to come up with a Latinesque song and a burlesque-type number, on the spot they delivered the film's two terrific musical interludes, "Amado Mio" and "Put the Blame on Mame." Working with her trusted choreographer, Jack Cole, Rita's every dance move became breathtaking perfection. As an actress Rita had gone far in a few years, from the tentative performer she had been to a charismatic star. And Glenn, too, seemed to have matured for the film; he was grittier and more commanding than he had ever been.

Like some of Hollywood's best-remembered films, *Gilda* was a kind of happy miracle, a film in part made up as they went along. As in the making of *Casablanca*, there was sometimes no idea where the story might go on a given morning. Did Johnny and Gilda hate each other or love each other? Virginia Van Upp's continuing rewrites and new pages often delivered only hours before filming forced the actors to stay spontaneous and fresh. The unique sense of sexual tension and perversity that runs through the film was pinpointed in provocative, memorable lines of dialogue with subtle innuendo.

Director Charles Vidor was an Old World sophisticate (born Vidor Karoly in 1900 in Budapest) and knew exactly how to bring out the unusual elements not quite spelled out in the script, including a possible homosexual attraction between Johnny and Ballin. (When I asked about this, my father could not recall any explicit discussion of the homosexual implications between his character and Ballin, saying only, "I guess different viewers see different things.") Vidor seemed particularly enthusiastic when directing sadomasochistic game-playing scenes like the one where Glenn slaps Rita hard across the face. Vidor was "very much a sadistic personality," my father recalled, who particularly enjoyed demeaning defenseless crew members and supporting actors, cursing and insulting them when their work did not rise to his expectation.

Absent any use of four-letter words, nudity, bedroom scenes, or other explicit behavior permitted today, Glenn and Rita became in *Gilda* one of the most passionate, erotic pairings ever seen in movies. Was their sexual intensity on-screen a reflection of the relationship developing off-screen? Or might it have been the reverse, life imitating art—Rita and Glenn inspired off-screen by the passion of their cinematic alter egos?

Between Glenn and Rita there was no thought of a serious or continuing relationship. On Glenn's part . . . well, it wouldn't have been easy for any man to have turned away from Rita Hayworth, even one supposedly happily married. But Rita had turned to Glenn at a moment of loneliness and insecurity. Her marriage to Welles wouldn't last much longer, but it didn't help matters that he heard of her fling with Glenn, either through gossip or some admission by his wife.

One late night, about a year after *Gilda* completed production, a ferociously drunken Orson showed up in the driveway of the house Eleanor shared with her mother, a bottle in one hand and a revolver in the other, screaming various threats in his highly theatrical voice, calling for Dad to come out and tell him where his wife was hiding. Needless to say, my mother, who already suspected that Dad was having an affair with Rita, was very upset about this looming showdown between her husband and another woman's husband armed with a gun. She called the police, but by the time they arrived, Orson had lurched off and disappeared.

Glenn blithely tried to explain away the incident, but it puzzled my mother, and for the first time in the marriage she was troubled by her husband's behavior. Outwardly, life went on, and Glenn and Eleanor kept their image as one of Hollywood's happiest couples. Privately, the seeds of doubt and deception had been planted.

As with so many films now beloved as classics, in its day *Gilda* was overlooked and undervalued by the critics. When *Gilda* opened at Radio City Music Hall on March 14, 1946, it was looked upon as just another glossy melodrama, less coherent than some.

The *New York Times*' Bosley Crowther wrote, "This reviewer was utterly baffled by what happened on the screen. . . . [I]t simply did not make sense. . . . The details are so mysterious and so foggily laced through the film that they serve no artistic purpose." Other experts in the newspapers called the film "a boring and confusing production," "trash," "dime novel stuff," and "junk." Some even came down on Rita Hayworth's dance numbers as a "questionable display." Somehow, in this condescending atmosphere, Glenn managed to come out fairly unscathed. *Variety*'s observer wrote that "he's a far better actor than the tale permits. . . . [H]e's able to give a particularly credible performance."

Audiences—women in particular—responded very favorably to Glenn's new, rougher style on-screen. He had become more muscular during his time in the Marines and was a much more believable tough guy than he had been in *Martin Eden*. He was very credible in the kind of hard-boiled part that also served the careers of Robert Mitchum, Burt Lancaster, and other stars of the new style of dark melodrama catching on in the postwar period. Nice guys were "out" in the movies, hard-edged heroes were "in." Glenn's performance as the hard-bitten, morally ambiguous Johnny Farrell was just what audiences were looking for—as Glenn liked to say, "I became a star when I slapped Rita Hayworth."

Gilda opened on April 25, 1946, and was an instant hit, earning a profit of $3.75 million in its initial release, a big return in those days of two-bit admission prices. It became one of the most popular films of the year. Then *A Stolen Life* opened ten weeks after *Gilda*, on July 6. Reviews were mixed, critics chiding the over-the-top plot of twins and amnesia and impersonations. Still, most had a good word for Bette Davis's surprisingly restrained dual performance and also for Glenn, who—according to *Variety*—had to weather a preposterous plot and inane lines but managed "through sincerity and sound histrionic sense to master these situations."

Gilda and *A Stolen Life* were like a one-two punch, and audiences now saw Glenn in a new light as a strong and romantically exciting screen presence. Despite the fact that he had been making movies for nearly eight years and had starred in quite a few, he was discovered anew. More and more these days Glenn found himself constantly stared at, followed by autograph hunters and surprisingly young fans. The Bobby Soxers of America, a nationwide youth organization comprising nearly ten thousand female teenagers, voted Glenn "Man of the Year" for 1946, displacing previous favorites like Frank Sinatra and Van Johnson. (Perhaps as a result of his newfound cachet with college-age girls, the satiric *Harvard Lampoon* also bestowed an award on Glenn as "Least Talented New Find.")

Thanks to the terms of his new contract with Columbia and the money he was paid for *A Stolen Life*, in September 1946 Glenn and Eleanor decided to buy a large home, an estate big enough to shelter not only their immediate family but Glenn's mother as well. They were drawn to a place in the hills above Sunset Boulevard in Beverly Hills. This two-story, twenty-room English country–style house, built in 1936 for composer Max Steiner (who wrote the music for *Gone with the Wind*, among other famous films), sprawled over an acre of land at 1012 Cove Way (the address has since been renumbered). The gated, parklike grounds included a mammoth side yard with towering pines and California pepper and eucalyptus trees. A bridge led to a pathway climbing a small rock mountain about thirty feet tall to a seating area. At the base of this rusty red lava rock outcropping was a small fish-filled lake fed by a pumping system that, when activated, sent gallons of water down the face of the butte in a glorious waterfall. There was also a separate backyard, behind the house, laced with walkways bordered by manicured box hedges with a central fountain surrounded by legions of colorful rose bushes. The detached three-car garage at the rear of the property had a chauffeur's apartment on top.

The asking price of $215,000 was far above their budget. Glenn said, "In about two years, if I get all my salary jumps, I could afford it." Eleanor told him, "I'll go back to work and help pay for it." Dad, who didn't like the idea of his wife contributing financially, agreed it was the only way to get their dream house before someone else claimed it first.

We soon moved into our new home, which was located in the very bosom of Hollywood aristocracy. Nearby neighbors included Charlie Chaplin, David O. Selznick, and Jennifer Jones (who lived directly across the street). Fred Astaire was just up Summit Drive near Mom's friend Mary Pickford, and Harry Cohn lived around the corner.

We were just a few blocks north of the Beverly Hills Hotel and only a couple of minutes from the heart of the Beverly Hills commercial district with its fine shops and restaurants. But the neighborhood was quiet and countrylike. Cove Way was unpaved in those early days, and dozens of quail rushed out of the way of our car when we went to and from town. The deer came down from the mountains in the evenings and became fixtures grazing on our lawn or drinking from the little lake.

When *Gilda* and *A Stolen Life* took Dad's stardom to new levels, young women discovered our address, and they materialized as often as the deer, hopping the low fence that bordered the property and banging on the door, day and night. "Is Glenn Ford here? Can he come out and talk to us? Can he sign my autograph book? Please! PLEASE!" They were a constant, mostly harmless, but still disconcerting presence in our life in the big new house that would be a family home for the next twelve years.

For my father the house was a strong confirmation of his rising status in the film industry, even if the financing needed his wife's tap shoes to help make it happen.

Mother oversaw the house, with its formal dining room painted in pink, white, and baby blue, dominated by an Italian crystal chandelier. For casual dining they made a roomy breakfast nook in the den with a gingham-clad table and upholstered window seat under a rack of beer steins and English hunting prints. The most unusual room on the ground floor was left just as Max Steiner had left it. In a style we could call Hollywood Chinese, it contained delicately carved and lacquered tables, a bamboo-framed mirror, porcelain Asian figurines, and stunning, hand-painted, burnished gold-leafed wall panels depicting traditional scenes of Chinese life that hid the many sheet music storage closets. It was in this room that Steiner had written his Oscar-winning scores.

A winding staircase in the entry led to the second-floor bedrooms. Glenn and Eleanor each took one of the large bedroom suites at either end of the hall that ran the width of the house, with my grandmother Hannah and me in smaller rooms in between. In those more formal times, it was not unknown for married couples who could afford the space to maintain separate bedrooms, although it was less common to have the husband's mother stationed midway between them. My mother's good nature kept her from wanting to challenge Hannah or engender bad blood with her mother-in-law; however, in time she would view Grandmother as more of a guard or gatekeeper than a mother-in-law.

My mother's boudoir was pure, femine elegance, with dusty rose walls and a brocaded chaise. On the wall above the headboard of her bed she proudly hung a large gray frame with three portraits of me that she said gave her comfort because I was looking down on her while she slept. Across from her king-sized bed was a wood-burning fireplace flanked by her mahogany Federal-style antique writing desk and chair and her mahogany glass-fronted perfume cabinet. She had a massive bay window that looked out over the side yard—later to be the site of a small mosaic-tiled swimming pool. My mother's large adjacent dressing room was fully mirrored, behind which were concealed a fur safe, many closets, and banks of drawers. The bathroom, all in shades of pink, displayed a large bathtub as well as shower with an etched René Lalique door depicting a maiden and fawn in a meadow.

Dad's suite was in sharp contrast: huge, very country-squire masculine in shades of dark red and hunter green, paneled in a dark chestnut wain-scoting and with a deep green shag carpet. In the corner near the door, which accessed the long deck that looked out onto the backyard, was a gun closet in which Dad stored his many rifles, shotguns, and pistols. When I was six a ritual began whereby I was required to shoot every armament in his arsenal into targets he had hung among the trees at the back of the property. And there was a wall safe near his bathroom door hidden behind the wood paneling. A well-stocked walk-in bar stood across from his walk-in closet.

In years to come my parents added an Olympic-sized swimming pool and cabana with a spacious workshop where Dad renewed his skills as a carpenter and Mr. Fixit. Later still he would turn over some of the side yard to a private vegetable garden and a chicken coop that he and I built together; we (or, rather, I) raised and tended numerous chickens. The eggs that we didn't eat were taken to the studio for my father's friends or shared with the neighbors.

Our little "farm" was unique for the time, especially in Beverly Hills. In 1970 my father wrote a gardening book about the experiences of raising me and the chickens and other fanciful stories—*Glenn Ford: RFD Beverly Hills*. Dad was an early environmentalist, and our family seemed to be the original "Beverly Hills Hillbillies."

One afternoon not long after we had moved in, my father was standing at the Cove Way entrance, looking over his new real estate. A car driving by suddenly pulled up and stopped, and the window went down. It was Louis Calhern, Dad's old pal and acting mentor from the early repertory days, when success for Glenn Ford was as yet very uncertain. "Hello, Hatrack!" the senior actor shouted to him and pointed a thumb at the imposing house and lush grounds. "Looks like things worked out all right, didn't they?"

My dad laughed. "Not bad, Louie, not bad."

Dad's first film after *Gilda* was an aviation drama called *Gallant Journey* in which he was to play the real-life forgotten hero of early aviation, John Montgomery, who in 1883—years before the Wright brothers took off at Kitty Hawk—successfully designed, built, and flew a glider plane. The film traced Montgomery's early struggle to perfect a lighter-than-air craft, his various setbacks, his tragic end after crashing in one of his aircraft and dying in the arms of his devoted wife. The assignment had appealed to Glenn for two reasons—after playing the tough, cruel Johnny Farrell in *Gilda*, *Gallant's* noble tragic hero would show his versatility. Even more appealing was the fact that the film was a pet project of director William Wellman, whose list of film classics included *The Public Enemy*, *A Star Is Born*, *The Ox-Bow Incident*, *The Story of G.I. Joe*, and the famed air-war movie *Wings*.

"I had really loved *Wings* when I was a kid and was a big aviation enthusiast," recalled Glenn. "I really looked forward to a chance to work with Bill Wellman." Wellman was known as "Wild Bill" for his dynamic personality and unpredictable behavior on a set. If things were going well, he could bowl you over with his enthusiasm, but if you disappointed him, you could really catch hell. Luckily, he and Dad got along very well. With a man of Wellman's vast experience you did well if you followed his lead. "Wild Bill could be temperamental," Glenn recalled, "but I was eager to please him. He appreciated actors who strove for naturalism in their performance, as I tried to do, to make things realistic and believable."

Filming was done largely on location at Lasky Mesa in the western hills of the San Fernando Valley and farther north in the coastal town of Del Monte near Monterey. It was a tough shoot. Wellman worked with speed and intensity, pushing his crew and actors all the time. Near the end of the shoot Glenn caught the flu and suffered, but he refused to take any time off. "I think I really earned his [Wellman's] respect during the final week of shooting. He knew I was working through a high fever to get my final scenes completed."

Everyone felt they had made a solid and historically significant motion picture. But when edited together and screened for studio officials, *Gallant Journey* proved underwhelming. There were striking scenes and some thrilling aerial footage, but the central story line, which was supposed to be a compelling biographical drama, played out as plodding and redundant. Reediting attempted to refocus the plot on the marriage of John and his wife, Regina, but Glenn and leading lady Janet Blair lacked on-screen chemistry. As a last attempt to adjust the film's allure for audiences, the publicity simply played up Glenn's popularity with females. "If he excited you in *Gilda*," the ads declared, "wait until he thrills you with Janet Blair in *Gallant Journey*."

To coincide with the dedication of a nearby park in John Montgomery's honor, the premiere of *Gallant Journey* was held in San Diego on September 4, 1946. Glenn and Eleanor were flown down in a small private plane to attend the festivities. As they headed for the theater an overzealous autograph seeker accidentally poked Glenn in the left eye with a fountain pen. His eye became inflamed, and Glenn had to wear a dressing over it when he appeared at the New Spreckels Theatre for the premiere. It was one more unfortunate development in a disappointing sequence of events.

The *New York Times* described *Gallant Journey* as "curiously ill-constructed . . . a limp and aimless tour." And the critic for *PM Magazine* wrote that "Montgomery's story . . . as Glenn Ford enacts it, was of a tedium seldom surpassed."

No wonder the studio decided that for Dad's next film it was a wise bet to put Glenn into another tough guy role like the one in *Gilda* that had excited so many ticket-buyers. *Framed*, a noir tale with echoes of *Double Indemnity* and *The Postman Always Rings Twice*, was the story of a ruthless blonde femme fatale (Janis Carter, a B-movie actress getting her chance in a bigger production) who tries to lure an innocent mining engineer into a nefarious plot involving embezzlement and murder. The screenplay was by Ben Maddow, an eccentric but talented writer who would later script the classic John Huston film noir *Asphalt Jungle*. The director was Richard Wallace, a veteran filmmaker who handled the production with moderate skill. In supporting roles the studio cast Karen Morley, Barry Sullivan, and (at his urging) Glenn's favorite supporting player, Edgar Buchanan. Filming was done at the studio and the Columbia Ranch and around the mountain resort of Lake Arrowhead ninety miles east of Los Angeles.

Framed was Dad's first solo, over-the-title billing, and he lived up to this honor with a terrific performance, one of his most underrated. As the seduced and corrupted mining engineer he revealed a new maturity and subtlety. In one especially effective, wordless sequence he awakens in a cheap hotel room suffering from a hangover, "blanked out" and looking ravaged, enacting his confusion and misery in an uncompromising, unflattering light.

Production ended on the last day of October 1946, and Dad looked forward to a long vacation; his next film was not scheduled until after the year-end holidays. But the studio interrupted his time off with an unexpected request to report to a federal courtroom.

It seemed that Charles Vidor, one of Columbia's top contract directors for many years, had decided he wanted to abruptly end his association with the studio. Having recently married Harry Warner's daughter Doris, he expected a very lucrative offer from his new father-in-law, the production head of Warner Bros., a larger and more prestigious place of employment than Columbia at that time. As a point of pride as well as a business decision, Harry Cohn had no intention of letting Vidor out of his long-running contract without a fight. Vidor had now filed suit against Columbia, trying to terminate his contract and collect a large sum for damages for Harry Cohn's exploitation and verbal abuse.

Glenn thought the whole fight was a little ridiculous, but he agreed to testify in court as requested. He had had his arguments with Cohn but felt that Vidor was an opportunist and a hypocrite, since Vidor treated people on his sets to every bit as much of the same verbal abuse as Cohn. In the courtroom Charles Vidor tried to make his case that he had been wounded by Cohn's foul mouth. Cohn's various obscene expressions were entered into the record, causing some in the courtroom to laugh and a couple of the more fragile female spectators to flee the room.

Columbia's vice president, Ben Kahane, then testified that Cohn used various four-letter words and obscene phrases so freely and without thought that no one could take them personally. When Harry Cohn referred to someone as a son of a bitch, Kahane explained, he often meant it as a compliment. Cohn's defense team then put actor Steven Geray on the witness stand to tell of the four-letter tongue-lashing he had received from Vidor on the set of *Gilda*. Glenn followed Geray to the stand and gave a similar account of Vidor's demeanor, adding that the harsh language was "addressed mostly to the little people on the set who couldn't answer him."

After a lengthy deliberation Judge Harrison ruled against Charles Vidor. "The court," he explained, "finds that Harry Cohn was accustomed to and in the habit of using obscene language in talking to Mr. Vidor and others. Such language was not intended by him as insulting or used for the purpose of humiliating the plaintiff and the plaintiff so understood that. Mr. Cohn and Mr. Vidor inhabit a fictitious, fabulous topsy-turvy temperamental world that is peculiar to their way of life. . . . Let them be judged by those people of decency who inhabit their world of fantasy and fiction."

And so Vidor was thwarted, and the mogul and the director were directed back to the studio and back to cursing at each other as before.

In September 1946, Glenn Ford, now husband, father, home owner, and established member of the Beverly Hills community, took his first step into politics—a local step, but he wanted to be heard. He was elected to a three-year term on the Board of Directors of the Screen Actors Guild (SAG). In the same election Ronald Reagan was elected third vice president, and later, on March 10, 1947, Reagan would replace Robert Montgomery as guild president.

This was another sign that Glenn had joined the elite in his craft. The opportunity to mix with these other actors and actresses gave him confidence, and he began to form a point of view and hone his political awareness. He and the SAG board didn't always see eye to eye on issues regarding the guild, and in those early days my father, like Reagan, was a staunch Democrat. He found comfort with the company of friends like Henry Fonda, Montgomery Clift, Edward G. Robinson, Gregory Peck, and Lee J. Cobb, who all expressed a decidedly left of center outlook. However, my mother, a conservative Yankee, while not in any sense political, mixed more easily with Robert Taylor, publicist Hedda Hopper, Mary Pickford, Marion Davies (and her "secret lover," William Randolph Hearst), and of course her former boss, Louis B. Mayer, all of whom subscribed to a much more conservative political point of view.

While the domestic agenda was the only thing my mother controlled in our household, in time her political prodding led my father to look anew (as did Reagan) at a different political party and philosophy. He embraced the notion of limited government. In later years my father and Reagan became good friends, and Dad supported Reagan unconditionally as our nation's president.

But back to the present. In order to help pay for our new home on Cove Way in Beverly Hills, my mother had offered to go back to work. For the first time in years Mom was putting on her dancing shoes. She seldom thought of herself as a star any longer, but, luckily, a lot of other people still did, and when she announced her comeback she had no trouble booking a nightclub tour, set to begin in Buffalo, New York, before continuing on to Chicago, Washington, D.C., and Ohio in the spring of 1947. I can still recall sitting on my mother's quilted bedspread and watching with fascination as she moved about the room gathering and packing the collection of bright, sparkling costumes she wore onstage.

On February 5, 1947, after a little party for my second birthday, Mom kissed us good-bye and with her mother, Blanche, who returned to her old role as companion, secretary, and wardrobe mistress, headed off to Union Station to catch the streamliner train for Chicago, on the way to Buffalo. For the women left behind—Gussie (my nurse), Agnes (the cook), and Grandmother Hannah—she bequeathed a near encyclopedia's worth of detailed instructions for the care and feeding of baby Petie.

My father was not happy about his spouse going off on that extended tour. But his own work schedule kept him from accompanying her, and Mom's earnings for the tour—averaging $5,000 a week, far more than Glenn was then being paid—made it possible to afford the family's wonderful home. The two stayed in close touch through constant back-and-forth telegrams and long-distance phone calls; when she wrote she always used her blue stationery, as she knew Glenn would recognize her letters in the mailbox and open them first. They communicated so often that the phone bills amounted to hundreds of dollars. Some nights Eleanor arranged for Glenn to call her backstage, and she would keep him on the line to listen through the receiver to her entire act.

Mom's stage tour was successful. She had sold-out shows everywhere, danced at a benefit in front of twenty thousand people at Chicago Stadium, and in Washington, D.C., performed for President Truman and visiting dignitaries, including Gen. Dwight D. Eisenhower. Although she remained devoted to her roles as wife and mother, it was plain that she was looking for more than just money from her revived career in show business. She wanted her husband to see her in the same glamorous light in which he viewed his sexy costars, those actresses he worked with all day and talked about at the dinner table. A letter she wrote to her husband from the road made this quite clear:

> I did 14 numbers during the evening and still had to beg off. Isn't that wonderful, darling? I thought I was all washed up. I'm so proud, Glenn, not for myself but for you. I want you to be so proud of me. You know when you play opposite Rita Hayworth and people like that—Bette Davis, etc., I feel in my heart, Oh! Golly, he admires them so, and I want that same feeling from you. Not just as your wife, but as a top performer. I want those people you play opposite to look at me and say, "She really is tops." Not for me but for you. I want to shine in your eyes, not only as a wife and mother but in your profession also. I want to be the sun, the moon, everything to you.

Glenn wrote back with declarations of pride and love. "I promise you could not miss me more than I miss you," began a letter that reached her in Chicago. "Twenty-six more days and I will be able to touch you—I love you."

Glenn had begun work on his next production a few weeks after the New Year. *The Man from Colorado* was a western set in the wake of the Civil War. Glenn played Col. Owen Devereaux, a veteran of the war left mentally unhinged by his violent experiences. After he returns to Colorado Territory he becomes a federal judge, appointing his best friend, Del Stewart, as his marshal. Devereaux's megalomania and sadism—hanging innocent men and burning a town to the ground—eventually lead to a confrontation with Stewart, and the by now entirely insane judge is killed.

Glenn had worried about taking on such an unsympathetic part but had finally agreed with Eleanor that it was a very strong role and a challenge for him as an actor. My father had never played such an intense and menacing character before, but, recalling John Barrymore's advice years before never to turn down the part of a villain, he took the chance. Dad was pleased, however, that he would again be working with his old pal William Holden, whom Columbia managed to borrow from Paramount. Location filming would be primarily at the Corrigan Ranch, located thirty miles northwest of the Columbia lot.

After taking Harry Cohn's side in the legal dispute with Charles Vidor, Dad learned once again that Cohn was an unreliable and exasperating ally. *The Man from Colorado* had been scheduled to be directed by Edmund Goulding, the well-respected director of *Grand Hotel*, *The Razor's Edge*, and *Nightmare Alley*. But Goulding left the film in preproduction, and Cohn immediately assigned another director. The replacement? Dad's nemesis, Charles Vidor. "That was my thanks for testifying on behalf of the studio," Glenn recalled. He could laugh about it later, Glenn would say, "but at the time I didn't think it was funny."

Vidor was predictably unfriendly to his courtroom foe. He all but refused to speak to him directly, and every one of his instructions on the set had to be relayed through an assistant. "Tell Ford he needs to sound more believable, . . . tell him that line lacks intensity," etc.

Traditionally, the director was king on the set, and Glenn was reluctant to pull rank, but the situation was untenable. He called Cohn and insisted that Vidor be replaced. At first Cohn said he didn't "give a shit" how Vidor was treating Dad, but later the mogul agreed to fire the director because he was working too slowly. Indeed, Vidor had declared that the forty-eight-day schedule for a complicated Technicolor production like *Colorado* was too short by twenty-five days or more.

Ironically, Vidor was proven right, as the production would need ninety days for completion. The third director on the job was an employee from the B division, Henry Levin, and the problems were not over. During the staging of the Glory Hill fire at the story's climax, a gasoline line leaked, and an unexpected blaze spread in all directions. In no time there were flames all across the set, and people were screaming and rushing everywhere in panic. Glenn and Bill Holden were among those trying to contain the blaze until the fire trucks arrived. Dad came away coated in black soot, with burns to his arms and hands.

Eleanor returned from her national tour close to the end of filming. There was a happy reunion, and things seemed to be returning to normal, with Mom throwing herself into the role of mother even more fervently than that of wife. She felt guilty that she had been away for three months from me, her precious child, and she was determined to indulge my every whim.

One morning a call came from the studio after my father had left for work. It was Harry Cohn himself.

"Have you been keeping an eye on that husband of yours?" said Cohn, in his usual pleasant style.

"What do you mean, Mr. Cohn?" asked my mother.

"You know this dame Adele Jergens?"

The voluptuous Columbia contract player was a busy actress, bouncing around the Columbia lot, and at the time she was appearing in a film for S. Sylvan Simon appropriately titled *I Love Trouble*.

"I don't think I've ever met her, Harry."

"Well, your husband's getting to know her pretty well. I don't want any scandals at my studio. So keep an eye on him."

When Glenn got home from the studio that day he found Eleanor in a fury, her eyes red from crying. She told him about her conversation with Cohn.

"He's crazy! I barely know Adele!"

"Why would he say it, then?" Mom was understandably suspicious.

"You know Harry! He thinks every actor on the lot is sleeping with his actresses because that's what he'd like to do! You know how he treats Rita."

Whatever had or hadn't happened with Adele Jergens, Glenn was incensed at Harry's outrageous intrusion into his home life. After doing his best to calm his wife but reducing his own anger not at all, Glenn rushed out of the house, got into his car, and roared off to find Cohn. Cohn had left the studio. Dad considered driving directly to Cohn's house, which was just around the corner from ours, but instead waited until morning and then headed directly to his studio office. He burst through the inner door, a couple of startled secretaries too slow to block him. Slamming the door behind him, he charged toward Harry's big desk.

"What . . . what the hell's going on!" Cohn cried.

Glenn recalled what happened:

I saw this small wooden baseball bat on his desk, a gift or a prop or something, and I reached down, grabbed it up, and slammed it down on the corner of the desk. It hit so hard it splintered apart. I waved the hunk of wood in his face and screamed at him, "I'm going to shove this up your ass!"

Harry Cohn looked stricken. He was a tough bastard, but I had taken him completely by surprise, and I was blazing with anger. I said, "Don't you ever call my wife again, you understand me, you son of a bitch!" I tossed the bat on the floor and stormed out. He got his breath back by then and told me the old cliché: "You're finished! You'll never work at this studio or anywhere else in this town again!" I yelled back over my shoulder, "Big deal. . . . Go to hell!"

Cohn could have ended Dad's movie career then and there. Dad had been too angry, he said, to weigh the consequences. But if Cohn held a grudge against every person with whom he had a violent argument, he would soon have been reduced to making only cartoons. Glenn Ford was one of the studio's most valuable assets and was just completing one of the most expensive productions in the studio's history. Above all, Cohn was a sharp businessman.

The confrontation became the stuff of studio legend. Mogul and movie star eventually made up and even occasionally laughed at the memory of the baseball bat brawl. "I don't know what had gotten into Harry to do that to me," Glenn would say. "Maybe he was trying to punish me for having Vidor taken off of *Colorado*. Who knows!" Or maybe Harry knew that Glenn was not the chaste husband that had been sold to the public, and he was warning him to be careful with his image and career.

Eleanor chose to forget the incident, or pretend that she did. She was only too conscious of the temptations in the movie colony. What could she do? She could be an accusing, nagging spouse or a dutiful wife and mother, putting her faith in God and her husband. She chose to go on believing in her marriage and praying that her husband would do the same.

The Ford family, October 1916—Patriarch Joseph Ford (age 83) seated right, grandfather Roland Ford (56) seated left, father Newton Ford (21) standing above, and baby Gwyllyn (5 months) in Roland Ford's arms. This photo was taken at the family compound in Portneuf, Quebec, Canada.

Gwyllyn's first professional portrait sitting at age three in Quebec City, Canada, at the studio of Montminy & Cie., June 1919.

Gwyllyn with Hannah and Newton in the backyard of their home on 14th Street in Santa Monica, July 1929. Gwyllyn is a proud member of Troop 13—the Black Cat Patrol.

Gwyllyn's first portrait-sitting as an aspiring actor at the Fred Carter Studios in Santa Monica, November 1936. This photograph was taken during the rehearsals for the little theater production of "The Royal Family."

Right: A young man full of himself as he is about to board the train to New York City to appear in his first Broadway play, "Soliloquy," November 1938. This photo of his protégé was taken by Harold Clifton.

Gwyllyn, now Glenn Ford, with costar Jean Rogers in his first feature motion picture, Twentieth Century Fox's *Heaven with a Barbed Wire Fence*, June 1939.

A bicycle built for two is what gets Glenn Ford and Rita Hayworth around the Columbia studio lot in their first costarring role together, *A Lady in Question*, May 1940.

Glenn Ford chats with actors Claire Trevor and William Holden (standing right) during a break in the filming of *Texas* with director George Marshall (seated in wagon), June 1941. This would be the first film pairing of Glenn and Holden and the first of many between Glenn and director Marshall.

Dad is dating Joan Crawford during this time as they walk hand in hand at the Columbia Pictures studio when she was appearing in *They All Kissed the Bride*, March 1942. They look very sweet together in this public outing but their relationship was to have some torrid moments behind closed doors.

Glenn Ford and Rita Hayworth rehearse their lines on the set of *Gilda* with Glenn's dialogue director, Harold Clifton, November 1945.

Top left: Glenn at Camp Pendleton, California, as a Marine, May 1943. He shares a moment of reverie with a photograph of his future wife, Eleanor Powell, in a frame to his right in his barracks.

Bottom left: The wedding of Glenn Ford and Eleanor Powell, October 23, 1943. In attendance were their immediate families, a best man, a maid of honor, and Dad's minister, as well as the thirteen invited guests pictured here.

Dad, Mom, and I pose for a fan magazine photographer in a family portrait, November 1947. It wasn't too many weeks after this photograph was taken that Dad was in Lone Pine, California, reunited with Rita Hayworth on the film *The Loves of Carmen.*

Dad relaxing with Bill, our German shepherd, in the China Room at 1012 Cove Way, June 1948. This was the home we shared as a family for twelve years. Bill was accidentally killed by our neighbor, Charlie Chaplin.

5

"Trouble in Paradise"

What is happening to Glenn Ford at Columbia?" asked Sheilah Graham in her Hollywood column. "After *Gilda*, Glenn was the hottest property in town. Since then his pictures have not been important."

It was something my father worried about in those years after he had made his breakthrough only to see himself thrown into one less than spectacular movie after another. He would complain about the quality of some of his assignments and often suggested projects he thought would be more worthwhile. But Harry Cohn once said, "I've never met a grateful performer in my life," and he felt that Dad should be grateful for his contract and the work.

It was frustrating to see the peers of his generation, the other major male stars of the postwar years, begin to appear in major hits and award winners—Gregory Peck in *Gentleman's Agreement*, Kirk Douglas in *Champion*, and Dad's old friend Bill Holden in *Sunset Boulevard*, the kinds of films and performances that got talked about and led to better opportunities. In my father's day, when almost all stars were under long-term contract to a studio, a performer had little control over his or her destiny. You took the assignments you were given and did the best job you could, hoping the executives knew what they were doing. A star could protest and complain, but the studios held all the cards; if you gave them too much trouble, you were suspended and sent home without pay. Glenn's films after *Gilda* had been a mixed bag. All were pretty good entertainment, and some of his performances were excellent. But the films did not have that extra something—a great story or script, an inspired director, to make the world sit up and take notice.

"Back then," he told me, "we could only complain so much about the parts that were handed to us. Look, I was glad to be working and well paid. But you still hoped to do good work. And, of course, in the picture business you never really know for sure what's going to be a hit or acclaimed. A lot of the things I screamed and hollered that I didn't want to do turned out to be the things that were right, and the things I was sure would be great for me turned out to be disasters."

I fully believe that despite my father's triumphs he was never secure in feeling that his good fortune as a working actor could last. He had come from a blue-collar background, and any "higher" education he had was achieved through his own wits and desire to learn. He was like a kid who somehow found his way into the candy store when the door was ajar; he wanted to fill his pockets with the goodies before he was shown the door.

In his later years he was quoted as saying, "I *need* to work—today, tomorrow, next year—whether I need the money or not. What really still amazes me most, though, is that I'm paid for doing what I like to do the best—act and ride a horse." Not everything he said in interviews was false publicity. He loved to act, and that simple pleasure, paid or not, in laudable projects or not, was his most joyous fulfillment. All the rest was just icing on the cake.

Dad's next assignments, harmless and pleasant entertainments, were hardly the sorts of pictures that would elevate anyone's status. *The Mating of Millie* was a romantic comedy about an independent-minded woman who conspires to marry a coworker so she can legally adopt a young orphan boy. It was Glenn's fifth pairing with perennial Columbia leading lady Evelyn Keyes.

Evelyn would recall her longtime costar as more aloof than he had once been, disgruntled by the script, spending less time joking around on the set, and retreating to his dressing room instead. "It wasn't that he was ever rude or snobbish," she would recall, "it's just that he seemed to prefer his own company most of the time. He wasn't a prima donna at all. He was always a marvelously generous actor to work with, and when he was in the mood he could go back to being his old charming self."

When Columbia first presented my father with this light comedy he told Harry Cohn that he would rather take a suspension than work with such tripe. But Cohn had his way, knowing that my father and mother had just bought a new home and that Mom was out on the road earning money dancing again. My father backed down and took the assignment. Indeed, Dad and Evelyn would reprise their roles in a *Lux Radio Theater* broadcast on January 3, 1949, for CBS.

The follow-up to *Millie* seemed even less promising: *The Return of October*, a sentimental whimsy about a teenage girl who comes to believe that a racehorse has been inhabited by the spirit of her recently deceased uncle. Glenn would play a stuffy young psychology professor who becomes fascinated by her delusion. Again a light comedy, this time shot in color, and, as with *Millie*, it was not the best career step. However, Dad wasn't averse to comedy, and Eleanor was on the road again on another dancing tour—this time for two and a half months.

Playing the girl was a sparkling, fresh-faced eighteen-year-old named Terry Moore, making her film debut. *The Return of October* was really a vehicle to introduce Columbia's new young female costar. (Terry Moore had done radio under the name Helen Koford. She changed her name to Jan Ford some months before being cast in this film. Now, costarring with Glenn Ford, she abandoned all these names and reinvented herself as Terry Moore. Some might know her today as the onetime Mrs. Howard Hughes.) Terry remembered the filming sixty years later:

Glenn was so wonderful because he took the time to teach me things, and he was so patient with me. And the director—Joseph Lewis—was just awful. He was terrible to me, he would pick on me. He was so insecure. If Glenn forgot a line, he wouldn't say a word, but if I did, he would rage. Glenn hated to see him being mean to me. And eventually the director was replaced.

Gosh, I was enamored of Glenn. But I knew he was married. I thought it was so wrong to have a crush on a married man; it made me terribly nervous. When we were working it was okay, but when I would see him at the studio I would run and hide! But really, I knew that Glenn thought I was a child, and I *was* still a child, and the furthest I ever got with him then was a French kiss. We were doing the scene where I back him into the fence and kiss him. And he called me a child, so I thought, now *really* kiss him. And so I stuck my tongue in his mouth. And he really went crazy! Is that a riot? But I was mad at him for calling me a child.

Production ended on *The Return of October* on Halloween night, 1947, with Glenn looking forward to an overdue rest and vacation. Eleanor, still on her nightclub tour, was playing the Club Cairo in Washington, D.C. He planned to join her at the tour's completion in Detroit just before Thanksgiving.

But Dad's idleness didn't last long. Columbia put him right back to work. After the lightweight *Millie* and *October*, at least the new project came with a literary pedigree and the earmarks of importance. It was to be an adaptation of Prosper Mérimée's novella *Carmen*, the source of the opera by Bizet, already subjected to a half dozen film versions, including silent movies with Theda Bara and Dolores del Río as the leads. This time Mérimée's temptress would be played by the sex symbol of the day and Columbia's reigning queen—Dad's old friend and lover Rita Hayworth.

The old warhorse story would reunite Rita with her *Gilda* costar. The doomed affair of Carmen and her lover, Don José, had much the same in-flamed passion as that which existed between Gilda and Dad's character in the earlier film, or so the studio believed. The tempestuous Spanish gypsy Carmen was a perfect role for Rita, but was Glenn Ford—the dark hero of urban film noir, the cowboy, the romantic comedian—the right man to play the costumed Spanish dragoon in this period piece? Dad had his doubts. He was even more dubious when the studio assigned the director, his practiced tormentor, Charles Vidor. "I went to Rita and told her that I didn't think this thing was right for me. But she insisted. I think she felt a need to have a friend doing this with her, and she wouldn't take no for an answer."

Dad's trepidations mounted as he went into preparations for the new role. His costumes were to be snug military jackets and skintight pants, an unforgiving wardrobe that, for the first time, would have him on a strict diet throughout shooting. ("No liquor, bread, potatoes, or dessert. The outfits didn't allow for an ounce of fat.") Even more disconcerting were the long curls he was required to sport for the role.

On November 14, 1947, Glenn headed off to Lone Pine in the Sierra Nevada for more than a month of location filming. He had urged Eleanor to return to California and join him, but she was unable to cut short her tour. She was not pleased to learn that while she was on the road busily working, Glenn and Rita had been thrown together in another motion picture. In letters to her husband written after she found out about the Lone Pine location, she warned, "Glenn, I don't trust that hussy, you know

I'm jealous of her," referring to Rita. As it turned out, Mom's suspicions were not unfounded.

At Lone Pine, Glenn and most of the cast and crew settled into the Dow Villa, a rustic, fifty-five-room hotel that had been built in the 1920s to accommodate large caravans from Hollywood. Dad was relieved to discover that Charles Vidor had gotten over his grudge and was on his best behavior, but the shooting was not without its discomforts. Grace Godino, on hand as Rita's stand-in, recalled, "We shot in very wild terrain, and the temperatures were seldom above 35 degrees during the day. We had to work with mules, riding on steep mountain trails, and they were not very cooperative. They hated the wind and the cold weather, too. In the midst of a shot they would come to a sudden stop and refuse to budge, no matter what the trainer or Charles Vidor shouted at them. We wasted so much time each day because of those darn mules."

Rita was again at a dissatisfied, lonely point in her life. In the time since *Gilda*, she and Orson Welles had sustained a reconciliation of sorts and had made their only film together, *The Lady from Shanghai*. By the time *Carmen* began shooting, however, the marriage was finally kaput, and, as far as Rita was concerned, there was no looking back. Now in cold and desolate Lone Pine, she once more turned to her costar for support and comfort. The love affair that had drifted to a friendly end at the conclusion of *Gilda* now sprang back to life in full bloom.

Rita had accepted that Glenn was committed to maintaining his marriage and family. "I'm no home wrecker," she would say. Hollywood stars had their own mores, and by those standards these were two "dear friends" who were keeping each other happy on a lonely, distant location. This time, however, the friendship had more serious consequences. During an evening of unguarded passion between Glenn and Rita, she became pregnant. She said nothing about it to Glenn at the time, and he did not learn about it until much later. By the time she became aware of her condition, filming on *The Loves of Carmen* had ended, and Glenn and Rita had gone back to their separate lives. Rita left Hollywood for Europe in the company of her friend Leigh Leighter for a long vacation that included a visit to the American Hospital in Neuilly, France. When she returned she was no longer "with child."

Glenn learned this after the fact. He would speak about it many years later and with great sadness; however, Dad and Rita would remain good friends.

As the spring of 1948 began, the Ford family was finally back together on Cove Way. Glenn had been given nearly two months to recover before his next assignment. Mother had returned to her maternal duties after her dancing tour, so in late March my father took the opportunity to take a trip to New York for a three-week working vacation at the behest of Columbia Pictures. He wanted to go alone, he told Eleanor, to clear his mind; he didn't intend to do anything other than read, rest, and give a few radio interviews. But I think he was contemplating the status of his marriage after another affair with Rita. There was a chill between my parents, and Mother increasingly focused her attention on me rather than her husband.

Keep in mind that I was conceived six and a half months after my parents married and born just two months after my father was discharged from the Marines. My father had returned home to share an apartment with his mother, while his pregnant wife lived with her mother. He had never enjoyed a traditional household, and there certainly was little opportunity for intimacy in our hectic one.

Unfortunately, when I was born my mother turned the obsessive work ethic that made her a great dancing star into a challenge to be as perfect a mother as she was a dancer. In this she succeeded, but at a great cost to her marriage and ultimate happiness.

So Dad left for New York alone and stayed at the Waldorf Astoria, Room 2506, enjoying the Easter parade and some Broadway shows. He especially liked Henry Fonda in the play *Mr. Roberts* and told Mom that actor Phil Silvers sent his love. From the first day of filming *The Man from Colorado* (February 24, 1947) until the last day of filming *The Loves of Carmen* (February 24, 1948), exactly one year, he had enjoyed a scant two months of freedom from the camera.

My father had met some interesting if not unsavory characters during his rise to stardom. Those sorts of people seem to attach themselves to people of wealth and power. Whether they were associated with the mob or, as Dad used to call them, your average "gunsel," they had a way of getting things done for you should the occasion arise. Dad made the acquaintance of a fellow who used to be a bag-man for a racket that ran money from a Tijuana race track to launder in Los Angeles. Through this estimable citizen Dad was introduced to the plight of William "Bill" Rhinehart while vacationing in New York.

Bill had spent twenty years in a New York correctional facility and was about to be paroled. He needed a sponsor, a job, and a home; my father, always a man with a spirit of adventure, assumed the responsibility. Bill accompanied Dad back to Los Angeles from New York, got set up in a residence, joined the Screen Actors Guild, and became my father's stand-in (the person who takes the stage in lieu of the working actor for lighting and blocking purposes). Bill became a very grateful quasi member of our family and worked with Dad for more than ten years until he passed away.

We now had our own in-house bodyguard. He ran errands for us, took me places when John, our butler, wasn't able to, surreptitiously accompanied our family in the public forums, and traveled with my father on location to ensure my father's safety and well-being.

In May, Dad began working on *The Undercover Man*. This was a story based on the Treasury Department agent Frank Wilson's successful 1931 prosecution of "Scarface" Al Capone on income tax evasion charges. Robert Rossen was producing, and Joseph H. Lewis was assigned to direct. Rossen wanted the film to have a realistic, semidocumentary style, following on the success of recent groundbreaking crime films like *Kiss of Death*, *Call Northside 777*, and *Naked City*, films that garnered a lot of attention for their authentic big-city locations. The strong cast featured Nina Foch and James Whitmore making his movie debut after much work on the Broadway stage.

However, Rossen's idea of making a film in the new "neorealist" style was thwarted from the start by Harry Cohn's budgetary restrictions. Instead of shooting on the streets of Chicago (like Twentieth Century Fox's *Call Northside 777*, for example), everything was done in Los Angeles and at the studio, with only brief outdoor work at Lockheed Airport, a local hardware store, Union Station, and a playground in North Hollywood. The film turned out to be a good, tough thriller, thanks to Joseph Lewis's imaginative staging, but Columbia's cost-cutting measures left the picture an also-ran compared to more innovative contemporary productions.

The Undercover Man wrapped in mid-July, and in early August 1948 Glenn began filming his next assignment, *Mr. Soft Touch*, a Damon Runyonesque story about a gambler, a social worker, and a bunch of underprivileged kids. This was Glenn's sixth and final teaming with Evelyn Keyes. Percy Kilbride (of Ma and Pa Kettle fame) and John Ireland were very good in supporting roles, but the film wasn't satisfying as comedy or drama. The film was shot quickly and on a tight budget, but the public took an interest in the latest Ford-Keyes pairing, and it grossed $1.6 million, for a tidy profit. Once again Harry Cohn had made money while my father marked time. But he had only one more picture on his studio contract.

Dad's final picture for Columbia, *Lust for Gold*, began shooting in October 1948. It was an intriguing fact-based story about the legend of the Lost Dutchman gold mine in Arizona's Superstition Mountains. The project showed the influence of John Huston's *Treasure of the Sierra Madre*, a huge critical success that year. Both stories dealt with prospectors, greed, and violence in the wilderness. Glenn was cast as ruthless Jacob Walz, who schemes and murders to become the sole possessor of the gold mine. When his ownership is challenged by an equally scheming Julia Thomas (played by seductive, smoky-voiced Ida Lupino) and her husband (Gig Young), a romantic triangle develops; the conflict is resolved when Julia murders her mate. An earthquake then brings unexpected justice to the greedy murdering couple, a roaring landslide burying them alive.

The whole story was presented as a flashback, with an opening sequence in modern times, the tale told by a young descendant. Originally, Dad was intended to play two roles, Jacob and his present-day descendant. "I talked them out of it," my father recalled. "It was a gimmick, and I always felt you want an audience to leave the theater wishing to see more of you and not less."

Declining the dual roles was just the first of Glenn's clashes with the film's producer, S. Sylvan Simon. The two men never saw eye to eye. At their first production meeting Glenn startled Simon by reminding him of a meeting they had had a dozen years before when Simon was at Warner Bros. The producer told the young Gwyllyn Ford that he lacked the looks required of a leading man. Their relationship never recovered from that awkward moment.

Lust for Gold was to be directed by George Marshall, which augured well for Dad, since the two men worked amiably together. George brought high spirits and lots of laughs to his sets as well as great storytelling skills. But George didn't get along with Sylvan Simon either. Simon had been a director for many years before donning a producer's hat, and he could not keep himself from interfering on the set, buzzing around with suggestions and countermanding Marshall's directions with cries for extra takes or different camera setups. After only a few days of filming George told Sylvan to "take the job and shove it," and he quit the picture. Simon—without needing much encouragement—took over the direction.

In late November the production moved on to Arizona locations, beginning shooting at Wild Horse Mesa, a forty-mile trek from Phoenix. It was another grueling shoot on rough terrain, and one day they were hit with a blinding dust storm. Ida Lupino proved a real trouper in the rough locale and impressed my dad as an actress. He told her, "The two really fine actresses I've worked with are you and Bette Davis." She in turn told a visiting reporter that Glenn Ford and Richard Widmark were her favorite costars. This was quite an endorsement, since Ida had worked with just about everyone in her nearly twenty years in movies.

Even so, *Lust for Gold* turned out to be a strong drama, with intense work by the two leads and an especially uncompromising performance by my father. For those young students of film who might not be totally familiar with my father's work, I would commend his performance in this almost forgotten film. But there is no question that it wasn't in the same league as *Treasure of the Sierra Madre*.

Glenn's films had gotten piled up in the Columbia releasing schedule, and as a result several—*The Loves of Carmen, The Return of October, The Man from Colorado*—began hitting theaters with little pause between them, all before Christmas. Glenn believed in not overstaying his welcome on-screen, making the audience hungry for more of you, not less, and he didn't think much of the studio's tactic of inundating the public and critics with his pictures (and it didn't help matters that none of the pictures were "must-see" productions).

The critics were unimpressed by the lot. "Downright absurd," wrote Howard Barnes in the *New York Times* of *The Loves of Carmen*, "a generally silly and pretentious production." *The Return of October* had moderate reviews and equally moderate success. *The Man from Colorado* was a poor mix of history, cowboy shoot-'em-up, and mental illness melodrama, according to the *Christian Science Monitor* critic. Glenn's intense performance as an insane lawman went unappreciated.

Dad's contract at Columbia was now up for renegotiation, and he was determined to do better for himself, both financially and in terms of the quality of his films. He turned to the man who had represented my mother at the height of her success, agent Johnny Hyde, now a vice president at the William Morris Agency, signing a three-year representation deal with the Morris office just before the completion of *Lust for Gold*. Eleanor was on the road working, but in a torrent of letters and phone calls between Glenn, Eleanor, and Johnny the constant theme was, What should Glenn do?

Glenn did not want to leave Columbia if he didn't have to, despite his complaints about the studio, but he strongly considered working as an independent, as many of his friends in the business were doing with great success. He was torn by his attachment to the many people he had worked with at the studio. "It was like a second family for me there," he would say. "You spent so much time with these people, and really their only goal was to present us actors in the best possible light." But Eleanor was pushing for him to cut his ties with Columbia. "We don't need Cohn," Eleanor said in one letter, and the consensus was that Glenn could do better in every aspect (scripts, directors, and pay) anywhere else—or as an independent. But he was nervous about the decision.

All three agreed that Glenn needed a substantial raise in salary, but, of equal importance, they wanted an iron-clad promise of better stories and scripts. Harry Cohn, always a tough bastard in contract negotiations, was the wild card. Eleanor reassured Dad, "Don't worry at all. If Harry doesn't come through, we will do something else. You've got to hold out for better stories."

Cohn and Johnny Hyde had numerous noisy confrontations in the process of discussing a deal. But in the end Cohn recognized that Glenn Ford was one of his studio's prime assets, and he gave in to many of Hyde's demands. Under the negotiated terms, Glenn would sign for another seven years and receive between $85,000 and $100,000 for each picture he made. He agreed to star in seven films, but he would not be available to Columbia for the first four months of each year so he could pursue other studio offers. His films would be budgeted at no less than $600,000 each (for those days, the price of a solid if not epic-sized A picture). He was guaranteed equal billing and equal likeness in all advertising for his films. Harry Cohn would not budge on the length (seven years) or number of films (seven films) Glenn had to make to fulfill the contract.

The important projects Cohn assured my father were his to choose from included *All the King's Men*—Robert Penn Warren's fictionalized story of Huey Long, the populist governor of Louisiana who was assassinated (with Dad earmarked for the role of the reporter who observes the governor's rise and fall); and the Broadway smash comedy *Born Yesterday*, which Cohn had bought specifically for another reunion of Glenn and Rita Hayworth. Both of these prestigious and high-profile projects were certainly the kind Glenn had in mind for the future, although neither was to be—not for him, that is.

After much deliberating Glenn swallowed hard and put pen to paper, getting back in bed with the devil that was Harry Cohn and inking a new seven-year deal on December 16, 1948. Security and practicality trumped any risk taking, and once again Glenn took the safe but, as it turned out, possibly less rewarding career decision. Cohn was delighted. Columbia had reclaimed one of its major stars through 1955 (that's what Cohn thought, anyway), although that was also not to be.

Thinking back on that fateful decision to stay at Columbia, the little studio that was always somewhat in the shadow of mighty MGM, Warner Bros., and Paramount, my father had mixed feelings. "I might have gotten slightly better scripts elsewhere—who knows? But Columbia was in stable financial shape at the time, and also I had learned over the years how to deal with Harry Cohn's nonsense. I didn't want to have to start from scratch with any of the other Indian chiefs in town."

When mother came back from her latest nightclub tour in late December, the family was together again for the Christmas and New Year's holidays. Having no film work scheduled before May, my father took the occasional guest-starring role on a radio program. Radio was still the primary form of home entertainment in those days before television took over, and movie stars were paid well for their airwaves participation. Such work also gave actors a chance to try atypical parts or work with other stars they might not otherwise encounter. For instance, on February 4, 1949, Dad starred with Vincent Price and the wonderful Claudette Colbert on *The Ford Theatre* in an adaptation of *No Time for Love*, a comedy Claudette had made years before as a film with Fred MacMurray. And later that same month Glenn appeared on Dupont's *Cavalcade of America*. Playing the title role in this radio play, *Valentine for Sophia*, timed for the Valentine's Day celebration, was Patricia Ryan, the twenty-seven-year-old star of a popular children's series called *Let's Pretend* and an actress considered to be of great promise. In the radio play Ryan portrayed a girl suffering from blinding headaches, and, strangely, the actress was herself stricken with a terrible headache during the live performance. She muttered her last line and rushed home, that night dying of a cerebral hemorrhage.

My mother went out on the road again at the end of that winter. She had been thrilled to receive an offer to make a four-week tour of the British Isles; she opened at the Empire Theatre in Glasgow, Scotland, for one week, followed by a three-week engagement at the legendary London Palladium. My father was about to begin work on a film under the terms of his new contract, and once again their careers would keep them apart for weeks at a time. "Understand your opening a big success," Glenn telegraphed her at the Dorchester Hotel in London. (That was an understatement—there had been rave notices, and all performances sold out in advance.) "So very happy for you, my love."

Just before Eleanor was to return from England, Glenn wired her that she should stop in New York City on her way home and meet him. He was being sent to New York to do research for his latest film project. To my father's surprise, Columbia was loaning him out to another studio, something they hadn't allowed since *A Stolen Life* was made at Warner Bros. And the studio was Eleanor's alma mater: the gold standard of Hollywood studios, Metro-Goldwyn-Mayer.

Veteran MGM producer Pandro Berman had been a longtime fan of my father's and had tried to get him for a major part in *Ziegfeld Girl* with Lana Turner in 1941. Now Columbia agreed to loan Glenn—at a tidy profit to Harry Cohn—for a medical drama called *The Doctor and the Girl*, the story of a young physician, his difficult relationship with his doctor father, and his romance with a young female patient. Charles Coburn would play the father, and playing "the girl" was a fresh-faced young beauty and charming new MGM star named Janet Leigh.

The film would have been a simple production made on the backlot under the recently departed Louis B. Mayer, but the ambitious new production chief, Dore Schary, insisted on obtaining some gritty realism by shooting the picture on authentic locations in New York City. Dad was sent ahead to conduct research at Bellevue Hospital, Columbia-Presbyterian Medical Center, and other proposed locations that would be used in the film. Mother stayed with my father for a week before coming home. They both made their first television appearance at this time on a CBS program called *We the People*.

The location shoot in New York proved exciting for Dad. Director Curtis Bernhardt (who had last worked with Glenn on *A Stolen Life*) chose not to acquire the permits usually required by the local authorities when a big production was shot on New York's streets. Bernhardt decided the documentary flavor that Schary sought could be better obtained by shooting scenes on the fly, just simply hitting the streets and mixing with real people. Bernhardt and cinematographer Robert Plank would film with a camera hidden inside a truck, and Glenn would simply carry on as though he were a part of the actual street scene. In this way they shot scenes in Times Square and Greenwich Village and at the entrance to Bellevue Hospital. Glenn loved the unpredictable aspect of location filming and felt that it added a vivid edge to *The Doctor and the Girl*. "It was never as easy as being at the studio, but I always felt it was well worth any trouble in the long run."

Janet Leigh was a recent discovery with little acting experience. Former screen queen Norma Shearer had seen her picture on the desk at her father's ski lodge in the Sierra Nevada and decided Janet was meant for the movies. Near the end of production Janet gave Dad a signed copy of that very same photograph with the inscription: "To one of the nicest people I've met in the career this picture started." "Janet was a lovely girl and so easy to work with," Dad would recall. "I was very impressed with how quickly she had learned her craft. So many girls were discovered because of their looks, but it took real ability, brains, and ambition to turn that break into a lasting career, as Janet did."

Seeing how well they worked together, Curt Bernhardt encouraged the two to improvise and play with some of the scenes. It gave their footage a refreshing spontaneity. "When a director had the confidence to let the actors have some space," said my father, "and not overrehearse every breath they took, you got something on-screen that looked more like real life, and you had a better chance of making the audience believe in what they were seeing."

Now and then the fun the two stars were having before the camera threatened to spin out of control. "In this one scene," Janet said in one interview, "Glenn had to carry me up two flights of stairs—it was supposed to be our wedding night. We were in high spirits, ad-libbing. . . . Climbing up those stairs, Glenn kept whispering, 'I don't think I can make it.' And the more he struggled, the harder we laughed. I laughed so hard I actually wet my pants. I should've been embarrassed, but that made me laugh even more."

Loan-outs were lucrative for Columbia, and Glenn's next film was another one, this time to RKO for an adventure story of mountain climbing in the Swiss Alps titled *The White Tower*, a Technicolor production costarring Italian actress Alida Valli, Lloyd Bridges, and a trio of distinguished character actors, Claude Rains, Oscar Homolka, and Sir Cedric Hardwicke. It gave Glenn his first trip to Europe—a first-class Atlantic crossing aboard the RMS *Queen Mary*—with location work on Mont Blanc, a high peak in the French Alps, and in the village of Chamonix. And there was opportunity for a weeklong visit to Paris before the filming began.

The director was Ted Tetzlaff, an old acquaintance whose long-ago good deed had made him a treasured memory for my dad. Glenn greeted him warmly on the first day of shooting.

"Good morning, Mr. Tetzlaff. Remember me?" But the director didn't have a clue what Dad meant.

"Good morning, Glenn, have we met before?"

"Yes, indeed," Glenn said, "and I never forgot you for your kindness that day to a kid who was so nervous I could hardly breathe."

Tetzlaff looked blankly at Glenn.

"You were the cinematographer the first time I was in a film—*Night in Manhattan* in 1937 at Paramount."

The two became fast friends on this film and would work together again soon on another European location.

Glenn tried to insist that Eleanor accompany him on this first-ever European adventure. To Glenn's dismay, his wife was not interested in leaving home. She had been on the road a great deal recently; back home now, she wanted only to resume her role as homemaker and mother. Glenn protested that I would be well cared for by two grandmothers and the household staff, but to no avail. My parents fought about the upcoming trip for quite some time. Mom wouldn't budge. Dad remained angry about the situation right up to his departure. I was only four years old but unwittingly held responsible for their disagreement.

Movie stars become used to nonstop adulation and undivided attention from everyone in their orbit. Anything less than that can prove traumatizing. Mother had left home on the day of my second birthday and then stayed on the road for thirty-four weeks of the next two years. She left me and, more importantly, her husband behind. After her first dancing tour she needn't have kept working, since she had earned enough money for the down payment on our home, but she did. She wanted to prove her worth to her husband, but she also felt compelled to perform to please her fans. Whenever she was home, she tended to me so earnestly, often to my father's exclusion, that it became a real problem in our little family.

In my father's mind—and it saddens me to say this after many years of thoughtful consideration—I had become a formidable competitor, even at my young age, a rival stealing away his wife's affections. My father was worshiped by his mother; he was all she had in life. My mother had not known other men—my father had conquered this dancing queen absolutely. But then I arrived, a rival for my mother's attention and devotion, which she gave to me freely and fully. In frustration, Dad would naïvely seek the love for which he yearned through casual peccadilloes. This fed a cycle of hurt and longing between them.

I missed my father and my mother when they left home for long periods, but I was left in the care of Gussie, my nurse, and David, the houseman. I'm sure, living in that big mansion at that early age, I wanted for nothing materially. And it may be that my parents were happiest when they were apart. The letters between them were always full of professions of love, new hope, and happy expectations, but these were rarely realized when they were together.

Dad made the long Atlantic crossing by ship and then made his way to Paris. He was accompanied by his ever-faithful dialogue director and old friend Hal Clifton. The thrill of visiting the fabled French city for the first time was tempered by not being able to share it with Mother. He was not angry anymore, just lonely and sad, as his letters home made clear. From the Prince de Galles Hotel on August 8 he wrote, "Dearest . . . I would do anything to be able to hold you in my arms this morning. Just to be able to touch you would be the most wonderful thing in the world. How is little Peter and Bill [the family's new German shepherd dog]? Please tell him his Daddy misses him very much. . . . We need to get all the work done and get home soon. . . . [T]hat is all that is important to me right now, just getting home to you! I miss you, my wife."

The White Tower was an unusual, colorful story concerning a dangerous mountain ascent. Carla Alten (Alida Valli) is a young woman determined to conquer the mountain that claimed her father's life a decade earlier. She enlists two old friends to accompany her, an experienced local guide, Andreas (Oscar Homolka), and Nicholas (Cedric Hardwicke), a British naturalist. They are joined by Hein (Lloyd Bridges), a disillusioned French writer (Claude Rains), and a reluctant American former bomber pilot named Martin Ordway (Glenn). The dangerous climb results in two fatalities and a love affair between Carla and Martin, who go off into the alpine sunset together.

In Chamonix, just south of Mont Blanc, Glenn and his costars took a crash course in mountaineering, with local experts teaching them the methods of climbing and the use of pitons, crampons, and other devices. A second unit crew had already done extensive filming on the mountain with skilled climbers doubling for the actors, but for closer shots Glenn, Valli, and the rest would have to do some tricky, dangerous moves without any fakery.

Indeed, my father came close to losing his life on this film. For a few nervous hours back in Hollywood there was uncertainty whether some of the cast and crew might have suffered the same fate as the seven mountain climbers who perished in a severe storm and ensuing avalanche on the face of Mont Blanc. On August 17, 1949, a cable arrived at RKO: "Film Stars Escape—The RKO film studio today made public a cable from its *White*

Tower unit which reported that location scenes near Chamonix had been destroyed by an avalanche. The stars of the film, including the Italian actress Valli, Glenn Ford and Claude Rains, escaped by five minutes."

The cast developed a good rapport, but Dad had a knack with friendships, and he embarked on a lasting one with Sir Cedric Hardwicke. On days off Glenn rented a convertible MG sports car, and he and Sir Cedric made sightseeing trips through the spectacular countryside. Dad enjoyed following the zigzagging mountain roads at breakneck speed, though his driving made Sir Cedric howl in terror.

There was only so much of the story's eventful climb that could be shot with the stars on location; the higher altitudes were too difficult and dangerous. An elaborate mountain set was built back at RKO Studios in Hollywood, the mock Mont Blanc made of canvas, wood, and plaster, rising forty feet high on Stage 14. Despite the best efforts of skilled studio craftsmen, the soundstage mountainside never really matched up to the real footage from location. Still, Dad was having good luck on his loan-outs; *The White Tower* was a strong, unique film, beautifully photographed in color, full of exciting moments, and well acted by a terrific cast. Howard Barnes in the *New York Herald Tribune* called my father's performance "his best to date," and many other critics agreed.

6

"It's Only Make-Believe"

Glenn began the new decade of the 1950s with, by his own reckoning, one of the worst decisions of his career. Harry Cohn had paid an unprecedented $1 million to obtain the movie rights to the hit Broadway comedy *Born Yesterday*, the story of a bellowing junk merchant, his tough but soft-hearted tootsie, and the writer who tutors and falls in love with her. From the beginning Harry had earmarked the part of the writer for Glenn Ford and imagined Rita Hayworth for the role of Billie Dawn. But when the film was finally ready to go into production, Dad turned it down. "The other two characters were so strong, so boisterous; I felt that third part would just be swamped by those two showy parts. Bill Holden took the part, and I saw how wrong I had been. Under the direction of George Cukor and with Bill's great performance, that part was every bit as important and an integral part of a film that really enchanted audiences."

Instead of appearing in an Oscar-winning comedy classic, Glenn entered the decade starring in a prison melodrama, *Convicted*, a second remake of *The Criminal Code*, a 1931 production with Walter Huston and Phillips Holmes. In the updated version Glenn played the man sent to prison for accidentally killing a politician's son, with Broderick Crawford as the sympathetic prison warden. Filming began on December 12, 1949, and ended on January 19, 1950. It was a well-made film if a little old-fashioned, but it was no *Born Yesterday*.

In January Glenn began work on a short-lived radio program for NBC, *The Adventures of Christopher London*, about a globe-trotting private investigator. At NBC's broadcast studio at Sunset and Vine in Hollywood, Glenn would record two episodes per session twice a month. Everything was done efficiently and without fuss, and Dad was delighted with the minimal time required and the $50,000-plus salary he earned for his efforts.

To commemorate my fifth birthday my parents took me to Beverly Ponyland, a small but well-known local amusement park that boasted horse rides around an enclosed ring. These sorts of family occasions were not spontaneous but arranged photo opportunities to create publicity for the various movie magazines of the time. Often, a press crew from *Photoplay*, *Movie Stars Parade*, *Modern Screen*, or some other fan magazine would come by our home, and we would gather together, make statements to the reporters about how much fun it was to be the Ford family, then pose by the swimming pool or other places in the yard, happily smiling as the photogs snapped our pictures. As soon as the press people departed, we'd return to our real lives. As a youngster I never had the pleasure of being with either of my parents on a celebratory occasion without it being documented by the press.

Most weekends at home were spent doing either chores to "toughen me up" per Dad's instructions or photo layouts for photographers and film crews; I had little time to be with friends or to see a movie. Dad and I had graced the cover of *Movie Stars Parade* in January 1949, and now I smile to look at it, because I'm holding a fishing rod while seated next to him. I actually never did go fishing with my father until I was twenty-three—there were no camping trips, no sitting by the campfire, nor any other ordinary father–son bonding adventures. Once again, for my fifth birthday, we were back in *Movie Stars Parade* (the May issue) in an article titled "Spree for Two." It was a sweet story about a father and son having the time of their lives, documented by thirteen photos of the happy day—no friends or birthday cake, but I guess it must have been swell.

Dad's next film was no more groundbreaking than *Convicted*. A story of espionage in the final days of the Civil War, it went into production as *Beyond the Sunset* but was released with a title intended to be more provocative, *The Redhead and the Cowboy*. Glenn played a cowboy with allegiance to neither side in the Civil War but who becomes drawn into a dangerous web of intrigue involving Confederate spies and Union army intelligence agents as well as a love affair with a duplicitous saloon hostess. The female lead—as the Rebel secret agent—went to flame-haired beauty Rhonda Fleming. The person who had steered Glenn into stardom, Tom Moore, had ended his career as a talent scout at Twentieth Century Fox and was hoping to resume his acting career. Glenn wrangled a small role for him in *Redhead*, more than happy to help the man to whom he owed so much. Direction was undertaken by a former movie actor named Leslie Fenton, recommended to Glenn by Bill Holden after Fenton had directed him in *Streets of Laredo* at Paramount. The movie was shot partially on location in picturesque Sedona, Arizona.

Fifty-some years later Rhonda Fleming recalled for me her experiences making the film:

> Your dad was an excellent, underrated actor. He made it look so easy. . . . Glenn was very comfortable to be with. And very much a gentleman. And generous with a scene—he never tried to take over. He was very likeable and, I thought, very sexy. I think he was very attractive to women because he had that boyishness about him.
>
> We filmed in Sedona, which I loved, so beautiful. I loved shooting outdoors. But I had a terrible accident on the film, and I've paid for it the rest of my life. There was a scene, running up a hill. A stunt girl would have done it, but they thought it would be good if I could do it. And it was Glenn who said it to me, "Rhonda, if you can do this instead of the stunt girl, we could have the camera much closer." He didn't mean anything, I don't mean to say that at all; it wasn't his intention for me to risk getting hurt. And so I said I would see if I could "raise the horse up," and I sat on the horse and I raised him up. I said, "Fine, I can do that." But I never practiced on a hill. And maybe the horse on flat ground was fine, but when you go up the hill somebody should have told me you don't raise them up that much, you just barely do it. And so we were running uphill for the camera, and the horse went up and over. It knocked me out cold. I suffered a lot of damage from it. I didn't know how much damage.
>
> I came to and, you know, being a kid, you say, "I'll be okay." And nobody even said to me, "Look, let's take you to the hospital, get you checked out." They were all so shocked. But I absolutely have suffered the rest of my life from that fall, my neck and back. By the grace of God I didn't end up in a wheelchair.

Rhonda would remain Dad's friend until his passing. They dated briefly in later years, and I think they were quite attracted to each other, but they were both in other relationships. Never has there been a better friend to my father and our family.

Glenn then returned to his home studio of Columbia to make *The Flying Missile*. From a story by playwright N. Richard Nash, *The Flying Missile* told about the development of a guided missile that could be launched from the deck of a submarine. Glenn would play submarine commander Bill Talbot, who battles to see the new technology brought to fruition even as he faces several dangerous obstacles, including a dire injury to his leg. In preparation for his role, Glenn went on a twenty-four-hour submarine cruise on the USS *Baya*. "Twenty-four hours was plenty!" Glenn recalled. "Conditions on the sub were much more claustrophobic even than I had imagined."

Filming began on July 11 at the guided missile training center in Point Mugu in Ventura County on the California coast and in the nearby town of Oxnard. One of the locations was the Naval Hospital in San Diego's Balboa Park, where Glenn had been treated prior to his discharge from the Marines. The film received extraordinary cooperation from the Department of the Navy. Despite some exciting footage, though, the film was not very good. Harry Cohn himself, never one to mince words, told Glenn, "It stinks."

If my father's new contract could not guarantee masterpieces, it did allow him more flexibility. The nonexclusive options permitted him to pursue opportunities with other studios, and in September 1950 he began a lucrative and promising five-film arrangement with Darryl F. Zanuck and Twentieth Century Fox, starting with the life story of Ben Hogan, the legendary golf champion.

The winner of four U.S. Open Tournaments among nine major championships, Hogan had come close to losing his legs as a result of a terrible car accident in early 1949. His win at the U.S. Open a year later, after months of grueling therapy, was called one of the greatest comebacks in the history of American sports. Zanuck assigned Frederick Hazlitt Brennan and Casey Robinson to construct a screenplay that would tell the story with an emphasis on the relationship of Ben and his long-suffering wife.

Zanuck originally had pushed for Montgomery Clift in the lead role, but the Hogan family had demanded casting approval, and Valerie Hogan insisted on Glenn Ford, who, she said, had a "quiet sincerity" that would be perfect for the part. In fact, Hogan was considered by many to be a cold fish, admired more than liked, obsessive and a perfectionist. He lacked the sort of genial charisma that fans and columnists enjoyed in their sports heroes. "I felt I understood Ben," Dad recalled, however. "I could be uncomfortable in crowds, too. I just had to call on that part of me to play him."

With the Hogans' blessing and Glenn's, producer Samuel Engel cast Fox contract star (and Oscar winner for *The Razor's Edge*) Anne Baxter as Valerie. The rest of the cast would be sprinkled with real-life figures from Ben Hogan's world, playing themselves on-screen, including sportswriter Grantland Rice and renowned golfers Sam Snead, Cary Middlecoff, and Jimmy Demaret. Curiously, the fictional role of "Chuck Williams," a golfing competitor with a drinking problem (played by Dennis O'Keefe), was clearly based on Demaret. Directing chores were assigned to a reliable if not spectacular Fox contract man, Sidney Lanfield. Glenn noted in his diary that eleven years earlier on *Heaven with a Barbed Wire Fence* Zanuck had paid him $125 a week, but on this film he was guaranteed $12,500 a week, which was more than Hogan ever made as a pro golfer.

My father had been an enthusiastic golfer for years, and so it was a definite thrill for him to get to work with the legendary Hogan.

> In order to make me look like a believable champion when I was playing golf on-screen, Ben agreed to spend a month, four hours a day every day, for several weeks coaching me before the cameras rolled. We set up a driving range and canvas targets at the rear of the Cove Way house. For the film Ben lent me a set of MacGregor clubs and had me soak my hands in vinegar and salt to toughen them up. And he taught me how to duplicate his techniques. He was determined that I would not disgrace him in the movie. By the time we began filming I looked pretty great, although I still couldn't hit the ball like him. Ben was on the set throughout the filming and standing behind the camera asking for retakes any time I didn't rise up to his standards.

Glenn's practiced imitation of Hogan's style was highly credible and hailed by golf aficionados. But it did end up having a debilitating effect on Dad's personal enjoyment of the game. "It was weird, but when I tried to remember my own style of play, I kept mixing it up with Ben's. And after the movie, people expected me to play as good a game as Hogan did. Finally, I just gave up and didn't play at all anymore." At the end of production Ben gifted Dad with the MacGregor clubs my father used in the film.

Prior to its opening, the film's original title, *The Ben Hogan Story*, was changed to *Follow the Sun*. "Ben was crushed when they changed the title," Dad recalled ruefully. "I wasn't that crazy about it either. There was a line in the picture about following the sun as the Hogans crisscrossed the country in their old Buick going from one tournament to another, and they took it from there."

As a tribute to Hogan, the film was premiered on March 23, 1951, in Ben's hometown, Fort Worth, Texas. Glenn and Dennis O'Keefe headed the Hollywood contingent, confronting thousands of noisy fans who crowded the festivities at the Worth, Hollywood, and Palace theaters. Although, predictably, a movie about a golf pro did not light the world on fire, Dad's portrayal of Hogan was excellent, nuanced and underplayed, true to the real character. The *Hollywood Reporter* critic wrote that the star was "very much the Hogan we know from the links—a stoic . . . more interested in playing a good game than being a good fellow. Yet, thanks to Ford's persuasive playing you like Hogan and root for him."

As soon as Dad finished work on *Follow the Sun*, Zanuck had him start the second film in the Fox deal, another true story (sort of) released as *The Secret of Convict Lake*. It recounted the 1871 escape of twenty-nine convicts from a Nevada prison. Most died or were captured as they trudged through the icy peaks of the Sierra Nevada, but a handful, pursued by a posse, made it safely to a small settlement near Monte Diablo Lake in Mono County at California's central eastern border. This outpost was inhabited only by women, including the sympathetic Marcia Stoddard, who were waiting for their men to return from a journey. The convicts, who had laid siege to the outpost, were discovered by the men returning home to their women, and the ensuing shootout became a local legend. Monte Diablo Lake was renamed Convict Lake.

In the Twentieth Century Fox version, cobbled together by several writers, including an uncredited Ben Hecht, the escapees are led by James Canfield (Glenn), an innocent man framed for murder and robbery who narrowly avoids the hangman by participating in the escape, and Johnny Greer (Zachary Scott, past master of sneering villainy), a cutthroat who believes Canfield will lead him to the spoils of the robbery. As it turns out (with the sort of amazing coincidence that Hollywood scriptwriters were fond of), Marcia (Gene Tierney) is engaged to the man who earlier framed Canfield. After many twists and turns the bad guys are confronted by the men returning home, a battle ensues, and the villains are killed, although the good guys (and gals) are saved.

The film was directed by the well-regarded Michael Gordon, who had last coaxed an Oscar-winning performance from Jose Ferrer in *Cyrano de Bergerac*, but this would be the last film he would direct until *Pillow Talk* in 1959 because of his refusal to testify before the HUAC hearings. The stark black-and-white photography was by Leo Tover, who also shot *Follow the Sun*. The rugged exteriors were filmed in the Sierra Nevada town of Bishop, California (with some second-unit material shot in and around Durango, Colorado), with interiors on Fox soundstages.

Glenn remembered the picture mainly for the discomfort he felt during filming due to a serious viral infection in his left eye that required him to wear an eye patch when not on-camera. He suffered under the intense studio lights. On the brighter side, there was the pleasure of getting to work with the great Ethel Barrymore in one of her last performances as one of the women in the besieged community. "She had a wonderfully dry wit," Dad remembered, "and I tried to be in her presence as much as possible."

He also befriended beautiful Gene Tierney, who was married to Oleg Cassini at the time but was an adventurous soul like my father. Dad wrote in his diary: "It's the walk. She walks and all you can think of is following her. She's got the original come-hither sway." The diary hints that Gene "hithered" and "swayed," and Dad followed. "I was a fan of hers for a long time, a gorgeous, sculpted beauty and a real pro." Tierney had a strong role in this picture, and she played it well. My father lamented, "I wish I could have worked with her again."

Reaction to *The Secret of Convict Lake* when it opened in late June 1951 was mixed, most critics praising the performances while finding the story's plot unbelievable.

So far Dad's Twentieth Century Fox films hadn't been earthshaking, but *The Green Glove* was a change of pace that for different reasons dramatically upended his life.

The Green Glove was a collaboration between Benagoss, a short-lived U.S. company, and France's Union Générale Cinématographique, with additional financing by United Artists in exchange for the U.S. distribution rights. The screenplay was by Charles Bennett, famous for writing several of Alfred Hitchcock's British suspense classics in the 1930s, including *The 39 Steps* and *The Man Who Knew Too Much*. A suspense thriller set in postwar France, the story concerned a former American paratrooper and a female tour guide attempting to return a jewel-encrusted religious relic (the gauntlet of the title) looted by the Nazis during the occupation. Rudolph Maté, known as a brilliant cinematographer, would direct, with Claude Renoir behind the camera. Glenn's old friends George Macready (from *Gilda*) and Sir Cedric Hardwicke were cast as a sinister German and the saintly Father Goron, respectively. Young Geraldine Brooks, in films since 1947, was cast as *The Green Glove*'s leading lady and Glenn's love interest.

The important thing for Glenn was that he was returning to Europe. The deal called for $125,000 plus first-class travel and accommodations for two for weeks in Paris and the South of France. It was not the only time, Glenn would admit, that he accepted a picture offer mainly because it provided a paid visit to another part of the world. He said in an interview at the time, "I'm only doing three pictures a year from now on. One of them will be in Europe. I want to travel and see the world. When I was a kid my father subscribed to the *National Geographic* magazine. That made me want to go to faraway places."

But when Glenn boarded the *Queen Mary* for another Atlantic crossing, only a little more than a year after he had returned from filming *The White Tower* in Europe, once again he sailed without his wife. Eleanor, mother and homemaker, had again insisted on staying home with me. Glenn didn't make a scene about it this time, instead inviting his mother to accompany him to Europe. Hannah, fifty-eight years old now, would get to see England, her ancestral home and a place she had not seen since she was a child. She could be reunited with her brothers Edward and Sam Wood and for the first time meet her younger sister Dorothy, who had been born after Hannah went to live in Canada.

On arrival in London there was a tumultuous family gathering. Hannah's siblings and their families all came down from Lancashire and swarmed into the Ford suite at the posh Hotel Savoy. Hannah was thrilled to show off her movie star son to her British relatives. Explained Glenn: "It was just a wonderful time, to see how happy it made Hannah and to meet these relatives I had known only by name. We sat around and everyone told the old family stories. I was so pleased to have fulfilled a promise I had made to Mother years before."

Hannah was happy to stay behind in England in the company of her relatives while Glenn headed to Paris to begin work on *The Green Glove*. Before leaving the Savoy, Glenn received a letter from Eleanor. It was a heartfelt, deeply emotional communication and gave evidence of her great love for him, but it also made reference to the strains the marriage had suffered:

> We grew so close together the last few weeks before you left that I don't
> even want to leave the house. I love to go in your room and sit in your
> chair and imagine seeing you sitting behind the desk. Sometimes I hear
> your footsteps. . . . I smell your clothes, look at your pipes and think of
> you and wonder what you are doing. Oh Glenn, we were pulling apart
> so . . . we have so much to catch up on—seven lost years—remember
> darling how happy I was in La Jolla? I am so afraid you will change. Don't

let anything happen to this. Oh, sweetheart, we must be a unit from now on, it is so important to Pete.

A dramatic, poignant letter: what did my mother mean by those "seven lost years"? That was about the duration of their entire marriage—had Mother come to think of all those years together as somehow "lost"? Did she really need to go all the way back to their weeks in La Jolla, at the very beginning of the marriage, to reclaim a "happy" time? And my father, when I asked him decades later what exactly she meant by the "seven lost years," could not or would not explain.

Geraldine Brooks was a beautiful twenty-five-year-old with a crown of auburn hair and sparkling green eyes, prominent cheekbones, and full, soft lips. She had been born to a theatrical family—her parents were both costumers for Broadway productions—and had grown up in the sophisticated atmosphere of New York stage folk. She was a talented young newcomer to movies, having gone under contract at Warner Bros. after World War II and made a very good impression in a series of supporting roles. She was no naïve starlet but a sharp, free-spirited, worldly, and alluring young woman. When I asked my father to describe her, he gave this one-word response: "Irresistible."

Some of the blame for what happened next could be fixed on their surroundings. *The Green Glove* company had gathered in Paris, a romantic enough setting, and then moved on to the French Riviera. It was apparently while filming in the sensuous environs of the Mediterranean that their romance developed. The company was based in the resort city of Nice. Glenn and Geraldine were lodged at the Negresco, a regal old hotel facing the beach and the blue Mediterranean waters. They began seeing each other for meals and cocktails in the hotel, then took long walks through the city and excursions up the coast and to the villages in the surrounding hills. Many evenings they were seen walking hand in hand among the other couples on the Promenade des Anglais.

Being so far away from home and from the reporters and columnists who staked out the Hollywood scene, Glenn must have felt there was less need for discretion. Or perhaps he was smitten enough with the beautiful Geraldine that he didn't care what people saw. In any case, the affair did not go unnoticed. They were constant companions on the set and after work. When the production gave them some time off, the couple went touring around in a snappy red MG sports car the company had put at Glenn's disposal. They spent a long weekend in Vienna, taking a plush suite at the stately Sacher Hotel, with the outlines of the Vienna State Opera House visible from the window and a soft rain falling day and night. Glenn would sometimes tell friends a story of that weekend—how he and Geraldine had planned to go see the sights of Vienna but never left the hotel. "Gerry had really wanted to go to a nightspot and enjoy a romantic Viennese waltz," he'd confide. "Instead we found some waltz music on the radio and just danced in the hotel room, in the dark."

Glenn's previous affairs had been on-set liaisons and passing fancies, nothing more than pleasurable perks of the movie star trade (although my father's intimate friendship with Rita Hayworth was in a category all its own). The relationship with Gerry Brooks had flared into something else. This time he found himself falling in love.

Both knew they were playing with fire, risking their valuable professional standing in the picture business if a scandal erupted. Those were the days of Ava Gardner and Frank Sinatra, not to mention Ingrid Bergman and Roberto Rossellini and their child out of wedlock. Adulterous celebrity affairs caused uproars of outrage among the press and public. Reluctantly, the couple debated breaking off their romance. Glenn would always remember being torn up by his conflicting passion and guilt, afraid of the consequences of pursuing the relationship, the potential damage to his career and the end of his marriage.

Whenever they would agree to cool things down or when Brooks outright rejected him, my father would go off to a distant part of town and a dark bar and drink. One night he had been drowning his troubles so deeply that he decided the only solution was to escape from the scene and enlist in the French Foreign Legion. He found his way to a recruiting station and demanded the enlistment forms. He signed them and then asked for a cot to sleep on that night before heading off into the Sahara. The next morning cast and crew looked frantically for him. His old friend Sir Cedric Hardwicke thought of where he might be. They found him still asleep at the Legion headquarters. There were intense negotiations, and after much discussion the Legion discharged Glenn, and he sheepishly returned to the work of completing *The Green Glove*.

Professional considerations prevailed, and the situation settled. Brooks had to return to New York for a stage part. Glenn was due back in Los Angeles to start another film. The separation cleared both their heads. The fire that had blazed in Europe would cool down in time. And *The Green Glove* turned out to be one of Geraldine Brooks's last films. She would remain in New York for years, working on Broadway and in television, and acting very rarely after marrying writer Budd Schulberg in 1964. She died of cancer in 1977 at the young age of fifty-one.

"I cared for Gerry very, very much," Glenn reflected many years later. "We remained close friends through the years. . . . She was dying of cancer the last time I saw her. She had lost all her hair. I told her she still looked beautiful."

Glenn returned to the house on Cove Way, back to his wife and son but still in the grip of a strong emotional entanglement with Geraldine Brooks. Eleanor received him with something short of complete enthusiasm. She had learned of his romance with yet another costar thanks to the Hollywood gossip mill. Evidently, she was the last person in town to learn of it. Her husband's adultery was one thing (cheating movie star husbands were an industry tradition), but what hurt much worse was her perception of the seriousness of the affair, something Glenn did little to deny. She was still deeply in love with her husband no matter what happened, but she could no longer believe he felt the same. It was a humiliating blow.

A breakup was still unimaginable to Eleanor. Her religious values discouraged divorce. And like many parents in those days, Eleanor believed it was better for a child to be raised within a problematic marriage than to suffer through a divorce and live in a single-parent home. It became the terrible irony of the years ahead: while Mother saw her child as the essential reason to stay married, Dad increasingly blamed their marital problems on her relationship with that child—me. I was seven years old then, too young to understand what was going on but old enough to know that our time as a happy family had been sorely compromised and was ending.

My father had seen little of Rita Hayworth after they finished filming *The Loves of Carmen*. These were the years of her European "adventure" and marriage to the Moslem playboy prince Aly Khan. There were occasional postcards scrawled with brief holiday or birthday greetings, signed just "M" (for Margarita), and a couple of letters with more heartfelt messages, one of these concluding with the line, "Glenn I always know that you are there for me when I need you." But Rita's life had become an endless round of travel and empty socializing in the café society haunts of the Old World. She felt increasingly anxious, bored, and lonely, a spectator to her own life.

Rita had had a child with Aly Khan—a beautiful daughter, Yasmin— but the marriage was obviously unstable. One evening, late at night in Europe, Rita called Glenn long distance, and my father listened to her choke back tears as she confessed she was miserable. He tried to console her as best he could from many thousands of miles away. She was determined to leave her husband and return to Hollywood and make her first movie in four years.

This friendship, this relationship, also worried Mother, and Glenn may have had something to do with plans announced by Harry Cohn for Hayworth's long-awaited comeback feature, which was to be another just-as-long-awaited pairing of Rita and Glenn. What a reunion that might have been, if things had gone according to the original plan. Cohn had purchased the rights to the best-selling but controversial novel about U.S. soldiers stationed in Hawaii at the time of Pearl Harbor, *From Here to Eternity*, authored by James Jones. The novel, with its profanity and sexual subplots, was considered unfilmable by others in Hollywood, but Harry and producer Sylvan Simon were certain they knew how to get it made without losing its raw power in the process. For the roles of Sergeant Warden and the adulterous base commander's wife, Karen Holmes: Glenn Ford and Rita Hayworth. The steamy, love-hate relationship between the sergeant and the married woman had clear echoes of Johnny and Gilda. All they needed was a good script.

Unfortunately, Sylvan Simon dropped dead of a heart attack at age fifty-one in the spring of 1951, and the project was left dangling for months. Harry Cohn continually told my father the part in the film was his (of course, followed by the phrase, "But I need you to do this piece of shit first"). By the time the film finally went into production in March 1953, it would, of course, star Burt Lancaster as Warden and Deborah Kerr as Karen and go on to earn many awards and huge box-office success. There's no denying that *From Here to Eternity* became a classic with Burt and Deborah, but I'd like to think that Dad and Rita would have done equally well if given the chance. Once again, it was a missed opportunity for my father.

When the RMS *Queen Elizabeth* landed in New York bearing Glenn, Hal Clifton, and Hannah from Europe, after finishing *The Green Glove*, Dad was expecting to join Rita in a new film as Harry had promised. Glenn knew Rita had returned from Europe and was staying at the Beverly Hills Hotel, three blocks from his home. He was anxious to see her again. *Eternity* wasn't ready, nor was what Columbia was calling *The Hayworth Story*, which Harry's minions had been working on for the past months. So, after two months of cooling his heels, Glenn took on another film for MGM to fill the time.

MGM was having its own troubles on a feature in production called *Young Man in a Hurry*. Russell Nype, amidst a ten-week break from his lead in a successful New York stage play opposite Ethel Merman, *Call Me Madam*, flew out to Hollywood to star in the MGM film, but he and the producers didn't see eye to eye on the interpretation of his role. On September 11, after twelve days of shooting, he quit and went back to Broadway. MGM had only five days of film without Nype in the shots that they could use and a cast and crew sitting idle on the payroll—things were desperate.

So it was back to the old routine: Dad took a film for the money and not the prestige. Directed by Mitchell Leisen, who was imported from Paramount, and with a modest script by Arthur Sheekman, *Young Man in a Hurry* was ill-destined from its inception and intended all along as a second feature on a double bill. But Glenn, after signing a generous offer from MGM, started work two days later, on Thursday, September 13, and completed the job in six weeks. This light comedy was eventually released as *Young Man with Ideas*, costarring Ruth Roman, Nina Foch, and Denise Darcel.

At least this gave Harry Cohn time to cobble together Rita's comeback, the third Ford–Hayworth costarring vehicle that Columbia had been referring to as *The Hayworth Story*. The actual title would be *Affair in Trinidad*, another thriller slavishly trying to re-create the *Gilda* magic with a similar story of intrigue and torrid, slightly sadomasochistic romance in an exotic tropical setting.

Virginia Van Upp was drafted to put together the "Gilda-esque" script for Glenn and Rita, but she was having troubles with the story. Van Upp was at a difficult time in her life, with a growing alcohol problem, and the script she concocted under tight deadline was inadequate. Other writers— James Gunn, Berne Giler, Oscar Saul—submitted hasty revisions. The results remained highly uneven—it was as though they put all the ingredients of *Gilda* into a hat, tossed them in the air, and then pieced them together in random order.

The story went like this: on the Caribbean island of Trinidad, nightclub chanteuse Chris Emery's (Rita) husband is murdered. Police suspect his powerful and mysterious associate, Max Fabian (Alexander Scourby). The dead man's brother, Steve (Glenn), arrives in Trinidad to investigate the murder. He believes that Chris is a suspicious character in cahoots with Fabian and treats her brutally, yet he can't help falling in love with her. Chris is actually working undercover with the police to gather evidence against the villain, who is, in fact, leader of a spy gang. In the end, Fabian is vanquished, Chris reveals her good intentions, and she and Steve go into a clinch.

Years later my father made an observation about the hazards of launching a film with a makeshift script. "I've learned to be mighty wary when they tell me the script they're giving me 'isn't in shape yet' or 'we're gonna fix it.' *Gilda* was an exception. Never does an unfinished, weak script work on-screen, but we never seem to learn. Today a solid script before shooting starts is more vital than ever."

Affair in Trinidad was a shabby knockoff of *Gilda*, as everyone seemed to agree. Dad knew it was second-rate material, but he knew that Rita needed to work as soon as possible, and for her sake (and the money) he was prepared to soldier on. But then word came from Rita's camp: she found the script highly unsatisfactory and refused to appear in the film. A few days later she escalated her threat, saying that due to poor treatment by the studio she was walking out on her contract. My father suspected that Harry Cohn had probably insulted her as well behind the scenes, reigniting their long-running enmity.

The battle dragged on, as both Rita and Harry refused to budge on their positions, with my father caught in the middle. Cohn threatened to sue her if she didn't start work by a certain date. Rita told him to go ahead and sue. Dad watched other good film offers come and go while *Trinidad*'s production start was announced and then postponed several times, but finally the crisis was over. Harry promised certain schedule changes and a massive rewrite by a respected scenarist.

None of these promises were kept, however, as *Affair in Trinidad* began filming on January 25, 1952, with a budget of $1.2 million and Vincent Sherman assigned to direct. The script wasn't the worst of it. Being in close contact with Rita for the first time in years, Glenn was disturbed by the changes he saw in his old friend. "I don't know if it was a depression about her failed marriage, or the feud with Harry, or just the passage of time, or maybe illness, or everything," my father wrote in his journal, "but she had changed. She was still beautiful, still a marvelous girl, but the flame did not burn as bright. There was a tiredness about her now, a sadness in her eyes. She was unhappy a lot of the time. Those of us who loved her tried to bring her out of it but without a lot of success."

Shooting lasted eight weeks and went smoothly but with little cheer or enthusiasm. Rita's disdain for what she was doing affected everyone. Cohn wanted to rush the postproduction to capture the audience he was sure was waiting for the comeback of the "Love Goddess." And so, only three months after the last take had been recorded, VIPs and press reps were invited to a gala preview. Rita herself, however, refused to attend the event, causing Cohn some embarrassment. The studio boss begged Dad to convince his costar to show up.

My father remembered:

I called Rita. She was very reluctant. I said, "Come on—it can't do any harm to see it." She finally agreed, if I would be her escort. We arrived at the studio and went to Projection Room One. There was Harry, Vincent Sherman, and a bunch of other people. We took our seats, and they started the picture. I could tell she was not enjoying herself. She would grip my hand, and hers was shaking. She didn't like what she was seeing, not just the picture but her own image, I thought. She looked older, maybe that was it, or part of it.

Then, about halfway through the picture, she began to fall apart. She was crying and whimpering, pressing her head into my shoulder. She whispered, "Please, please, Glenn, take me out of here!" I tried to calm her, but she had to leave. She got up and started rushing out to the aisle. Harry Cohn saw her and called out, "Where are you going?" Rita didn't say anything, just kept going. He called after her, louder this time, "Wait! Where are you going? You can't do this!" And Rita shouted back at him, "I'm getting out of here! You son of a bitch, how could you do this to me!"

I hurried out of the projection room and caught up with her. She was a wreck. I took her outside, and we drove to the Fox and Hounds Restaurant in Santa Monica, a place we had gone to together many times. She was still upset, even after the long drive, still crying off and on. We had a drink, and she began to get worked up again. She yelled for someone to bring a phone to the table. I knew who she was going to call, and I tried to talk her out of it. "Call Harry tomorrow," I said. "No," she said, "the bastard's not going to get away with this."

She managed to reach Harry at the studio and began berating him. I couldn't make much sense of the things she said to him. They were all vague complaints and threats. One thing she kept saying to him: "You're using up my life. . . . You're using up my life." What did it mean? She couldn't—or wouldn't—explain.

In later years my father and other friends of Rita's would speculate whether her depression and erratic behavior had been early signs of the mental disease that would consume her life in the 1970s. For now, it seemed only the behavior of a disconnected woman for whom *Affair in Trinidad* only poured oil on the flames.

Rita was not the only one who was troubled. Glenn had been pleased in 1948 to sign a second but nonexclusive contract with Columbia. Yet Cohn's film offers to him continued to be disappointing.

Convicted and *The Flying Missile* in 1950 and now *Trinidad* were not what Glenn had in mind, not what Harry Cohn had promised as prestigious projects. Adding to Glenn's angst, during the first week of shooting *Affair in Trinidad*, United Artists made a claim for his service based on a two-picture deal that Columbia had made when lending Glenn out for *So Ends Our Night* in 1940. Glenn was concerned that he was going to be forced into some horrible film, Rita was driving him crazy, he had troubles at home, and all he could think of was how he might break his contract with Columbia and get on with his life.

Providence fell upon him in a strange way when *Affair in Trinidad* was released in late July. The reviews were predictably negative, but it is what else he saw in the newspapers that buoyed Glenn's hopes. The newspapers were full of ads heralding the picture, and Columbia's art department had constructed the promotions and advertisements that were splashing across the globe to show Rita full figure and glamorous with Glenn as a small figure in the background. Glenn grabbed a newspaper and drove to Columbia to demand an immediate audience with Cohn.

"I want out of my contract," Glenn said.

"What are you talking about?" Cohn responded. "You owe me four more films."

"I did," Glenn replied in the past tense as he spread the newspaper on Cohn's desk. "Under my contract you have to give me equal likeness and billing in all advertising of my films."

Finally, Dad had the upper hand on Harry Cohn. A month of negotiations followed, after which Glenn was able to get his remaining film commitment to Columbia cut in half (from four to two films) and a year shaved off his contract. He'd be free from Columbia by the end of 1954.

On the whole, *Affair in Trinidad* was drab in comparison to *Gilda*, but, even so, audiences remained interested in seeing the two stars together, and the film was a hit at the box office, taking in $2.7 million.

My father continued to care for Rita and would always try to be there for her when she needed a shoulder to cry on or a friend she could trust. But I think he also had a feeling that Rita's problems were overwhelming. Later in the year, plans were made for Rita to star in *Miss Sadie Thompson*, a Technicolor update of Somerset Maugham's tropic melodrama, *Rain*.

The company would be on location in Hawaii for two months. Rita tried to convince Glenn to take the part of the Marine sergeant in the film so she would have a trusted pal on the distant location. Although two months in Hawaii with Rita Hayworth sounded awfully tempting, my father had other projects lined up, and the part was a supporting role and not an interesting one from his point of view. My father begged off; Aldo Ray would take the role. Rita was very hurt, but trouble and hurt seemed to stalk poor Rita.

Instead, Glenn agreed to make a film with MGM's British division, and due to the delays with *Trinidad* his makeup had barely been removed from that film before he was heading to London to shoot *Terror on a Train*, under the direction of *The White Tower*'s Ted Tetzlaff. The script read like a taut little thriller, and it was another appealing sojourn in a European capital, another possible adventure and respite away from wife and child. The film costarred a relatively unknown French actress, Anne Vernon, in her second American film.

Glenn left Pasadena, California, on the Super Chief on March 29, 1952, heading for New York and the awaiting ship that would take him to Europe. He didn't like to fly and had a clause in all of his film contracts specifying travel by car, rail, or ship. After an overnight stay at the Sherry-Netherland Hotel and dinner at Danny's Hideaway on East 45th Street (a steak joint favored by celebrities and New York insiders), he boarded the French ship *Liberté* for the trip across the pond and then stayed at the famous Dorchester Hotel. Unfortunately, the London weather was miserable that April, and the filming of *Terror on a Train* (aka *Time Bomb*) dragged on for weeks.

The rather blunt title told the premise: a time bomb is planted on a freight train already loaded with explosives. Maj. Peter Lyncourt of the Royal Canadian Engineers (Glenn, with the rare chance to play a citizen of his native country) is in the midst of marital discord with his French wife, Janine. He is tasked with trying to locate and defuse the bomb while the train sits in a dockyard near a crowded neighborhood. In the way of movie logic, the major manages to explode the bomb safely and repair his marriage, all within the seventy-two-minute running time. Most of the exterior filming was done in and around the Hammersmith & Chiswick goods yard.

On one of his last days in the British capital Dad bumped into a fellow American in the same business who was on his way to Cornwall to join the beautiful Gene Tierney and director Delmer Daves to make *Never Let Me Go*. It was the "King," Clark Gable. Dad had met Gable only a few times in passing, but far from home they felt like old buddies. Gable invited him to dinner, and a raucous night followed. My father found Gable to be a wonderful down-to-earth guy. "He likes vodka and onions," Dad wrote home. "Both of us got very drunk. But we were still able to walk. Barely."

Spring in London had been uncomfortably cold, and Glenn was relieved to head back to California in early June. Back on Cove Way in Beverly Hills life went on. I was growing up, a schoolboy. As the only child of two stars I had many advantages, not the least of them to be thrown constantly into the company of men and women of the movie business whom the rest of the world could know only as larger-than-life figures on the silver screen. Fred Astaire was our charming, unassuming, always perfectly dressed neighbor around the corner. (Fred told me, "Your mother is a much better dancer than me"!) Another neighbor, brooding James Mason, filled in as my babysitter when I was younger and no one else was available. Dad and Mr. and Mrs. Mason had their issues, though—James and his wife, Pamela, had many cats, and we had our dog, Bill, a German shepherd. When Bill would get off our property, he often would head to the Masons' home two blocks away and grab one of the cats. He would bring it home, and in the morning we'd discover the poor animal (usually expired) on the front lawn. To say the least, this did not please the Mason household, and many arguments ensued about our dog. (Bill discovered raccoons too, and I bet I was the only kid in the neighborhood whose Davy Crockett hat had three tails.)

Some mornings when I came downstairs past the den to the kitchen, I would find some of Mother's old vaudeville pals like Sophie Tucker, Al Jolson, Jack Benny, and Eddie Cantor sitting around the table having breakfast and laughing and singing. Mom's friend Mary Pickford—one of the very first superstars in the history of the movies—would invite us for visits to Pickfair, her massive estate on Summit Drive at the top of our hill. When I was very young I would sit on the knee of "America's Sweetheart," and she would tell me whimsical stories about the exotic game animals whose heads were mounted on the walls of her home. Frank Buck never had better stories in his book *Bring 'Em Back Alive*.

The neighborhood was alive with activity, and there were always people dropping by to visit. A knock on our front door in the evening might mean Bill Holden or Barbara Stanwyck arriving for dinner or Lana Turner or Ava Gardner stopping by to visit us.

Not every association with our famous and talented neighbors was a happy one, and I suppose, unbeknownst to him, Mr. Mason did get his revenge. One evening, Bill, our dog, chased Charlie Chaplin in his car on a rainy night. Somehow Bill got tangled up in the wheels of Charlie's car and, sadly, was run over and killed. For a while I was frantic with grief over my poor canine friend. Chaplin may have made millions laugh in his day, but at that moment I despised him.

I learned how to play tennis from champion Pancho Segura on the court of the Beverly Hills Hotel. Johnny Weissmuller, the movie's greatest Tarzan and the Olympics' greatest swimmer, who had met my mother at Atlantic City in the late 1920s when she first started in show business, gave me swimming lessons in our pool. Memorable birthday parties (ineluctably staged for publicity—see *Movie Stars Parade*, August 1952), horseback riding with Dad and Bill Holden and his boys (covered of course in *Modern Screen*, April 1950), and an all-day outing to Buckaroo Town to enjoy carnival attractions (*Movie Life*, December 1950) were a few of the family events chronicled by the press. I was taught the rudiments of the game of golf by Ben Hogan when he trained Dad for the film *Follow the Sun* (*Screen Stars*, April 1951), and for three years I even appeared weekly on Mom's television show (*The Faith of Our Children*, 1953–55).

Yes, I enjoyed opportunities and advantages that other little boys might have only dreamed about, but I never asked for any of it. However, I was not going to grow up spoiled or develop into a "Beverly Hills brat" if my father had anything to do with it. From the time I could walk he made sure I knew the meaning of discipline, and he would go to some lengths to teach it. I often wished he had not felt compelled to go as far as he did.

7

"Fire and Rain"

I don't want to leave the impression that my father was simply a disciplinarian, without kindness or humor. At times he was relaxed and full of fun. There were the Sunday mornings following services at Beverly Hills Presbyterian Church, strolling along the grassy parkway on the northern side of Santa Monica Boulevard. We would pass under the wide canopy of a leafy ficus tree on Beverly Drive, and my dad would stop and ask me if I wanted some chewing gum. Then he'd reach up and harvest a stick of Wrigley's right off one of the branches. My dad had a magician's hand and would palm things very expertly, but at a tender age I fully thought that there was a "gum tree" from which one could pick sticks of gum.

I recall when I was even younger sitting at the dinner table, where, despite the formality, my father would call out Richard the Midget, who lived under the dining room table. Dad would throw his voice into a high-pitched squeak, rap under the table, and have Richard pay a visit, to my delight. I knew Richard was always there, but I could never see him unless Dad summoned him.

There were very few children living in our rural neighborhood when we first moved there. Scott and Winters McComas were among the first I remember when their parents moved in next door, and they became my lifelong friends. After church on many Sundays they would come over to my house, and we'd enjoy one of Ellie's pancake breakfasts and have famous pancake-eating contests. Mom would make dozens of silver-dollar pancakes topped with pure maple syrup and butter, adorned with sausage or bacon, juice, and milk. The opportunity for publicity was too tempting, so this moment was captured in *Movie Stars Parade* in the story "Sunday Kind of Fun" (July 1951). Yet these were happy times; I wish all the times had been as happy.

As I grew older those fun times seemed increasingly few and farther apart. Most of the time my father was just not around, and when he was, he was often distracted or exhausted. When making a movie he was so preoccupied when he got home at night that he hardly seemed to recognize any of us. My mother was asked about her husband's preparation for his films, and she said, "Glenn's a different person with every part he plays. I can hardly wait to read his next script—so I'll know what kind of man I am married to!"

She was only half kidding. My father took his craft very seriously. After dinner and some desultory conversation with my mother and Grandmother Hannah he would retreat to his bedroom for the rest of the evening to memorize his lines for the next day's shooting. My father had developed his own technique for this, reading his lines into a tape recorder and then playing them back repeatedly in order to commit them to memory. He would have music playing—often a soothing recording of quiet Hawaiian music, his favorite soundtrack. No one was allowed to make any noise or disturb him when he was locked in his bedroom. He had a small red light installed above his door like the one outside the soundstage door at the studio that, when lighted, signified "Do Not Enter—Work in Progress." When the light was lit, you did not dare go near the door, let alone knock on it.

In 1946, after my father had established himself in Hollywood as a movie star, he returned to his alma mater, Santa Monica High School (SaMoHi), and created a tradition that continues to this day—the Glenn Ford Award. This award is given annually by the drama department to the student who shows the most promise or in some way has achieved distinction. Coupled with the trophy today is the Glenn Ford Scholarship, benefiting from a tax exemption for charities.

In 1956 the award was won by a young student named Ken Smith. Ken would become an integral member of our family, and among his tasks was an occasional job keeping a watch on me when my parents were away or out on the town. Ken's main interest was in all things electronic. He was an electronics genius and installed all of my father's stereo, recording, and ham radio equipment throughout the house. Dad even had him install stereo speakers in our swimming pool.

One thing Ken created was a phone patch system in my father's room. With the flick of a switch my father could activate his secret audio-taping system and record any and all phone conversations to and from the house. My mother and I didn't learn of its existence until many years later, but this was after my father had secretly recorded hundreds of hours of phone conversations. There were no secrets in our house, and this was definitely a violation of privacy, but now, many years later, being able to listen to myself, my mother, and various famous people sharing the intimate details of their lives and careers with my father on the phone (even a former president of the United States) is a bittersweet privilege. Most of these voices have now, of course, been silenced.

My father got to know President Richard Nixon very well during his presidency and afterward. I have many recordings of Richard the "White House Tapes" Nixon unknowingly being taped by my father. President Nixon, Mom, half of Hollywood's Golden Age performers, and I are preserved on those tapes for posterity. Some of the conversations are intimate, and some are sensational, but I think it would be best never to share them with the public.

When he began his professional career in the film industry, Ken changed his name to Ken Wales. He acted in seven movies with my father and later became a producer. Among others, he was the associate producer with Blake Edwards on *The Party* and *The Revenge of the Pink Panther* as well as the producer of many other projects, including an inspiring 1994 television series, *Christy*.

Some nights my father did not come home at all, or he came home very late, well after my bedtime. Later I would hear about his "homes away from home," the bachelor pads and party houses belonging to friends like Columbia makeup man Bob Schiffer, who co-owned a two-story Normandy-style apartment building in Beverly Hills. At Schiffer's place old pals like Glenn Ford, Bill Holden, and others were welcome any time to drink, play poker, or entertain a new lady friend. Columbia helped too: in earlier days Harry Cohn had set up a small penthouse suite (number 54) at Columbia's expense for his two roving young bachelors, William Holden and Glenn Ford, at the fabled Chateau Marmont on Sunset Boulevard.

I don't know how much my mother knew of such activities, though she had her recurring suspicions. In June 1952 things reached another crisis point. There was a blowup over something. Dad moved out or was thrown out of the house. This time the press got wind of the brewing troubles in the Ford household, and on June 21 the papers reported that Glenn and Eleanor were separated.

Louella Parsons—not called the "Queen of the Hollywood Gossips" for nothing—managed to get my mother to talk fairly candidly about the crisis. "I don't know where Glenn is living or where he is. I've never been so unhappy," Louella quoted her crying into the phone. Parsons also got through to Ellie's mother, Blanche, who said that her daughter was in "hysterics" and had been put to bed with a sedative. "They had quarreled," said Blanche. "I can't deny to you that there is serious trouble."

My father had gone only as far away as a bungalow at the Beverly Hills Hotel just down the hill from our house. In a few days my parents' tempers calmed, and, with the newspapers still pushing their story of a separation, my father returned home. "It was nothing serious," Eleanor reassured the press. "Just what two people go through now and then in a long marriage. We're working towards resolving our problems."

But it was serious. While Mother wanted things to work out, I think she knew that she and my father could never put all the pieces back together. These were stressful years for her, trying to maintain her optimistic outlook, remaining a loyal wife and perfect mom, trying to keep her sometimes humiliating private life separate from her beaming public persona. If she was still performing, it might have been easier to take her mind off her personal concerns, but she had hung up her tap shoes for good in 1950 after a cameo appearance in the Esther Williams musical *The Duchess of Idaho*. Instead she began devoting more time to her church work. She began teaching my Sunday school class at the Beverly Hills Presbyterian Church on Rodeo Drive.

Noting how warmly the kids responded to Eleanor's personality and instruction and knowing what a delightful screen presence she was, the Reverend Clifton Moore, a local Presbyterian Church leader, came up with an idea, a way to spread the Word to a much larger audience: Eleanor could teach her class on local television. Mother enjoyed the idea of expressing her spirituality and perhaps inspiring young minds in the process, talking to many more people than would ever come to the church. She agreed to host the program. Los Angeles television channel KRCA offered studio space and air time every Sunday afternoon between 1:30 and 2:00.

The Faith of Our Children went on the air for the first broadcast in October 1953. Ellie was wonderful on the program, communicating the same bright spirit and goodness she had conveyed in her MGM musicals but now with a higher purpose. The show was a great success and found a large audience almost from the start. The program became one of my mother's proudest achievements. It was the first weekly religious show to be broadcast west of the Rockies, and during its run of three and a half years my mother won two local Emmy Awards for best female personality (1954 and 1955), while the program itself won three for best children's program (1955, 1956, and 1957). It would also attract many high-profile weekly guests from stage, screen, and sports, including, on occasion, Glenn Ford.

The show became my own entry to my parents' world of performing, as Mother had me appear with her on a regular basis as a member of her TV classroom. I enjoyed being on the stage and acting and began to think I might look into a career in the family business. One of the other youngsters appearing regularly on the program was my good friend Jack Stillman, the son of a producer who would work with my father on *The Americano*. In time Jack became a "legendary" bisexual porn star rechristened Jack Wrangler, which is quite a circuitous career trajectory from his start portraying a shepherd in the religious plays on *The Faith of Our Children*!

My father continued to work, work, work. I wish I could say all the films he made became classics, but my father felt it was better to stay actively employed and keep his name on the marquees than sit around and wait for the perfect opportunity, which rarely came his way.

In August 1952 Glenn reached an important milestone, making his first film as an independent actor with script, director, casting approval, and—for the first time—a percentage of the profits. It was a western for Universal Studios, *The Man from the Alamo*, based on a true story about a man who leaves the legendary Texas fort just before the final battle in order to warn his family and other townspeople of an imminent attack and then must defend his reputation against charges of desertion. Costarring with Glenn were Julia Adams, Victor Jory, Hugh O'Brian, Chill Wills, and Neville Brand. Assigned to direct on the Universal backlot and Agoura Hills locations was Universal contract director Budd Boetticher, a longtime friend of Dad's. "I had known Budd when he was just starting out in pictures," my father recalled. "He was just an assistant director at Columbia then, but I knew he was going to do all right in the business. He had been a bullfighter previously, of all things. I liked him very much, and we worked well together."

Actress Julia Adams, *Alamo*'s leading lady, told me what she remembered of my father and of the film:

> Glenn was very generous and kind. I was relatively new to all of this, and I appreciated that very much. He was such an interesting screen actor to watch. . . . He was always very "present," and you could feel him communicating with you in a scene. He and Budd worked well together. I enjoyed Budd very much. He was colorful and interesting and a lot of fun to work with. He made the set very alive. There was great energy in his direction, and every scene had a kind of spark to it. And you needed someone to keep your energy level up on that location, out in Agoura. It was ferociously hot. I remember one time standing there to do my close-up, and my nose started to bleed from that burning sun. It was a tough location. Any chance we had we crawled over to the shade or an air-cooled room.

Boetticher encouraged the actors to do their own riding and fighting when possible for the sake of greater realism and impact on-screen. Glenn loved to ride and was not about to defer to a stuntman in an action scene if he could get away with it. "I always felt that using doubles and taking only long shots in the tough scenes and stunts is cheating the public," my father explained once. "If a guy can't do some of the stunts, he shouldn't accept the assignments. Understand, you can be a damned fool and try to do things that are too tough for you."

Or you can have bad luck. On September 15, in the third week of filming, a chase scene was being shot on some hilly ground between Glenn and actor Victor Jory. Glenn was galloping at a good clip when two other riders veered sharply into Glenn's mount and forced him straight into a tree at high speed. Glenn was knocked unconscious and rushed to St. Joseph's Hospital in nearby Burbank. "It was a terrible thing to see," Julia Adams recalled. "Glenn was a very good rider, and with Budd's encouragement he was really riding hard that day. The horse lost its footing, and Glenn got slammed. We were all alarmed and concerned and very happy when it wasn't a more serious injury."

"I cracked three ribs and got some serious deep bruises," my father remembered. "Well, you're bound to get a few bumps making action pictures." Yet the injuries were serious enough to shut down production for over a month while my father healed. "Naturally," he recalled with a grin, "as soon as I returned to the picture, the first scene I had to do was that same gallop that had put me in the hospital."

Despite the effort, *The Man from the Alamo* did not have much impact on first release—the mainstream critics had no interest in applauding a

Universal backlot western. But it has stood up well over time, and a lot of people have caught up with it on television and say what a fine film it is. Boetticher has developed a cult as a filmmaker. With limited resources, Budd did a great job of capturing the chaos of the fierce Alamo battle and made the wagon train shootout a thrilling set piece. My father's performance was a fine one, balancing the hero John Stroud's strength and determination with vulnerability. His wordless reaction to the destruction of his family and home is heartbreaking.

Less than a week after completing *The Man from the Alamo*, Dad was headed to Mexico to make *Plunder of the Sun*. This was a production of Wayne-Fellows (later Batjac), that is, partners Robert Fellows and actor John Wayne. The Duke personally chose Dad to do this film and paid him $125,000 to star in the adventure story based on a novel by David Dodge, author of *To Catch a Thief*. Dad would play Al Colby, an American insurance adjuster stranded in Havana. At the instigation of an exotic beauty and her elderly husband, Colby sails to Mexico on a quest for priceless Aztec riches hidden somewhere near the town of Oaxaca. Along the way he meets an assortment of colorful characters, including a lusty alcoholic blonde and various ruthless villains. To direct, Wayne gave the reins to John Farrow (father of actress Mia Farrow), a tough Australian whose previous work included suspenseful melodramas and film noirs like *His Kind of Woman*, *The Big Clock*, and *Where Danger Lives*. Rhonda Fleming was originally scheduled to be the female lead, but after the riding accident on *Alamo* the start date of *Plunder* had to be delayed. Rhonda had another commitment, so Patricia Medina was cast in the role.

My father found himself on a grand tour of Mexico, as filming locations were scattered over assorted regions of the country: in the city of Veracruz on the Gulf Coast, in Oaxaca far to the south, in the village and Zapotecan ruins of Monte Albán in the southern mountains, and in the Churubusco studios in Mexico City. Patricia Medina told me years later:

> I don't remember any difficulties. Oaxaca was not a dreamy location. Not a comfortable place at that time, and no one spoke English. It was a little easier for me because I spoke Spanish. Farrow had a reputation for being difficult. I heard that he didn't like one of my early tests for the part, so I told him he better get someone else, and I think he thought, Well, she's a tough one, and he liked me more after that.
>
> I was a little frightened of Glenn to begin with. He wasn't one of those actors who made small talk or liked to discuss a scene beforehand. A lot of actors, you know, they like to be together and talk and laugh. I can't say

that we ever had any social discussion in all that time down there. Diana Lynn, who was playing the drunk, said the same thing. She said to me, "Do you talk much with Glenn? He doesn't say anything to me." Not a talkative actor. An introvert.

But maybe he was only shy with women. My husband, Joseph Cotten, worked with him and got along with him very well. And later he came to dinner at our place, and he was delightful. I decided that he was an actor who only liked to concentrate on work when he was on the set.

The film benefited immeasurably from the locations, especially the scenes at the stark ruins of Monte Albán. Farrow's camera crew vividly captured the exotic settings with glistening black-and-white cinematography. My father did very well with the sort of tight-lipped tough-guy part that Humphrey Bogart had once owned, Patricia Medina was a knockout, and Irishman Sean McClory (a John Wayne/John Ford stock company favorite in those days) was an amusing and shamelessly scene-stealing fey villain in a platinum blonde-dyed hairdo. Unseen for decades, held in limbo by the John Wayne estate, *Plunder of the Sun* was finally released to cable and DVD several years ago and has been rediscovered by old movie fans as a memorable and stylish thriller.

There was some time off for Christmas and New Year's celebrations, a trip to New York, where Glenn and Eleanor met with press and appeared on some popular radio programs, then back to work for Glenn with another film at Columbia, his second to last.

As a *Saturday Evening Post* serial by William P. McGivern about a lone wolf cop's vengeful crusade against corrupt superiors and a powerful crime boss, *The Big Heat* was a good enough story to make Harry Cohn pay $40,000 for the film rights. But there was nothing about the property's journey to the screen as a modest A-budgeted production that led anyone involved to believe they were making something special. Not even when the legendary Fritz Lang was hired to direct did they expect anything out of the ordinary. Lang's stock had fallen considerably since the days of his silent masterpieces, *Metropolis* and *Dr. Mabuse*, or even his notable Hollywood films *Fury* and *Scarlet Street*. According to my father:

Fritz Lang came out of the old German studio system, where the director was like a dictator, barking commands and making people jump. He had a pretty nasty reputation in some quarters. There were people in Hollywood who had worked with him who hated his guts, especially some of the crew guys down the line. I mean, there were stories of people throwing lights at him and threatening to kill him for the way he treated them. So I head into this picture wondering how bad it's going to be. And then Fritz and I met and had a couple of cocktails, and he couldn't have been sweeter. He treated me with great respect. A wonderful friend, and I learned so much from him. We're talking about one of the real geniuses of the movie business.

The original plan had been for Jerry Wald to produce *The Big Heat* as a veritable tribute to the old Warner Bros. gangster films of the thirties with a cast including George Raft, Paul Muni, and Edward G. Robinson. Wald was then replaced by Robert Arthur, who was best known for Abbott and Costello comedies, and the project was reslated as a vehicle for Columbia's own Glenn Ford. Sydney Boehm, the ex–crime reporter who had scripted Dad's earlier crime picture, *Undercover Man*, was assigned to write the screenplay adaptation.

The story begins with the suicide of a big-city police sergeant, Tom Duncan. Investigating the incident, fellow detective Sgt. Dave Bannion discovers that several local politicians and top cops are on the take from Mob boss Mike Lagana and that Duncan's widow, Bertha, hardly grieving, is blackmailing Lagana to keep her secrets. Duncan's mistress, a B-girl, is murdered after she tells Bannion secrets about the Mob. Bannion is warned off the case, but the determined cop confronts Lagana in person. In return he is marked for death. A bomb in his car kills his young wife instead.

Suspended from the force for disobeying orders, Bannion begins a private pursuit of Lagana and his lieutenants, including the sadistic Vince Stone. Stone's sexy moll, Debby, speaks to Bannion, and Stone punishes her by hurling a pot of boiling coffee in her face. Badly disfigured and seeking revenge of her own, Debby helps Bannion uncover the crimes of the bad guys and gets back at Vince in kind but at the cost of her life. Bannion is reinstated on the force and reunited with his young daughter.

Censorship was still in force in Hollywood in the early 1950s, and violence was monitored just as sternly as sexuality. *The Big Heat*'s script contained a number of unusually violent and code-challenging scenes, including an opening suicide, brutal murders, and a sadistic disfigurement or two. There was a lot of concern over how much of this would have to be cut or toned down, but Fritz Lang was adamant that the scenes of violence and cruelty stay as written—they were his favorite parts of the script. He would find a way, he said, to shoot it all but in a style that would get everything past the censors.

A strong cast was put together. Supporting Glenn as Detective Bannion, the widower detective, was Alexander Scourby—the bad guy in *Affair in Trinidad*—as the slippery crime boss Lagana, Jeanette Nolan as the cold-as-ice Bertha Duncan, and Jocelyn Brando as the doomed Mrs. Bannion (the lovely Jocelyn entering the movies in the footsteps of her celebrated brother Marlon). In an early career highlight, playing the cruel gangster Vince Stone was twenty-nine-year-old Lee Marvin. And in the part of Debby Marsh, the gangster's moll turned tragic avenging angel, was Gloria Grahame, giving perhaps the most memorable performance of her career.

My father watched with enthusiasm and admiration the way Fritz Lang crafted the film, putting his actors and camera in place with the precision of an architect. There was no improvisation with Lang, my father would explain. "He had in his mind what he wanted to see to the exact inch." After so many films in which the director's only goal seemed to be to get the job done, my father found Fritz Lang a more stimulating collaborator. At the end of a day's work they would often go out together for a meal or a drink or drop by the house. I can still remember seeing Fritz and my father at the bar at home, drinking martinis, deep in conversation. I must confess that my first taste of alcohol was at the tender age of eight when at the encouragement of both men (who were no doubt inebriated) Fritz mixed my first martini (shaken, not stirred, with olives). My mother was furious with my father over this coming-of-age experience.

The finished film, as many will agree, is memorable. Scene after scene plays with a stark, relentless ferocity; the dialogue is eminently quotable (like Debby's famous quip to the corrupt cop's widow, "We're sisters under the mink"), and the scenes of violence retain their power to this day, including the suicide by gunshot in the opening scene, the hot coffee thrown in Gloria Grahame's face by Lee Marvin, and Glenn Ford's anguished attempt to reach his wife inside the bombed car. I am hardly alone in calling it one of the great titles in the film noir canon; *The Big Heat* is the film of my father's that has grown the most in stature since its first release.

I must say that my father was always modest about his own contributions to these films, whether they turned out great or forgettable—though in my opinion he added considerably to them all. "Whenever I began to feel like big stuff," he liked to say, "I just thumbed through the old movie magazines and looked at the pictures of people who were tops ten or fifteen years ago and who are now forgotten. You really get to thinking when you see those onetime favorites. That's how I keep my feet on the ground."

Appointment in Honduras was definitely forgettable. Benedict Bogeaus was an independent producer with RKO distribution doing some good work at the time but mostly on very restricted budgets and with mostly faded movie stars or B-listers like Ronald Reagan and John Payne. Why my father or his agent signed on to an unprepossessing production like *Appointment in Honduras* at this time in his career is now hard to understand, but it may have had something (if not everything) to do with the fact that Bogeaus offered Dad 15 percent ownership of the finished product.

The old-fashioned exotic adventure plot involved an American adventurer, Steve Corbett, on a mission to bring money to embattled revolutionaries in war-torn Honduras. Traveling through the jungle with a group of misfits, including an unhappily married couple, Corbett and company encounter menacing soldiers, crocodiles, bats, burning villages, and pestering ants before the mission is accomplished and Steve wins over the unhappy wife. Ann Sheridan was cast as the dissatisfied spouse, Zachary Scott as her oily husband, and Rodolfo Acosta (Ann's lover off-screen) as a mysterious native. Jack Elam, Stuart Whitman, and Robert Brown filled out the supporting roles. To direct, Bogeaus hired French-born Jacques Tourneur, a highly skilled filmmaker responsible for the best of the Val Lewton horror movies of the 1940s (*Cat People, I Walked with a Zombie*) and Bob Mitchum in one of his iconic roles in *Out of the Past*, but by then Tourneur was on a career slide and headed for television work.

Since it was on a limited budget, the production got no closer to Honduras than Pasadena, California. Most of the tropical jungle scenes were filmed at the Los Angeles County Arboretum & Botanic Garden in Arcadia, a 127-acre site of lush, cultivated vegetation and meandering streams, already a backdrop for numerous jungle dramas and Tarzan pictures.

Ann Sheridan had been in movies since the 1930s, when Warner Bros. had promoted her as the "Oomph Girl," a word coined to describe her supposedly indescribable sex appeal. In the 1940s she had starred with James Cagney and Humphrey Bogart. She was a tough-talking Texas lady who had had affairs with Errol Flynn and other lady-killers and had her own reputation as something of a man-killer. She was at loose ends at the time of *Appointment in Honduras*, bitter about Hollywood and talking of relocating to Mexico with Acosta.

Unfortunately, my father and his female costar took an instant dislike to each other almost from the first hour of production. On the first day of shooting, before they even were formally introduced, Ann strode up to

Glenn and said, "I hear you're tough on your leading ladies. Well, we'll see about that." This did not set well with Dad.

Sheridan had taken this film as part of a settlement with RKO shortly after Howard Hughes purchased the studio in 1949 and removed her from the cast of *My Forbidden Past* because Hughes didn't like her. Dad wasn't ready for any shenanigans from Ann Sheridan. Sheridan, who was not pleased that RKO had stuck her in this iffy film, was quoted by a visiting reporter as saying that her costar had manhandled her during a scene in which they were supposed to be struggling. ("I was black and blue for two days," she supposedly said. "Glenn looks the gentle sort, but, honey, it's always the gentle sort who are roughest with the women.")

A full-on feud began that lasted throughout the filming. The producer sided with Glenn in his disgust with Ann's scene-stealing antics and generally bad attitude, but Zachary Scott, Glenn's old friend from *The Secret of Convict Lake*, did not see it that way and sided with Ann. This made things even worse; in front of the camera together they could barely keep from hissing at each other, while Tourneur kept muttering "Sacrebleu!" and calling for another take.

The one bright spot from Glenn's point of view was making the acquaintance of Stuart Whitman, playing one of his many tiny roles on his slow climb to stardom. At the age of twenty-seven Whitman was trying to build a career while taking care of a wife and newborn baby. Glenn heard about his struggle. Whitman told me later:

> He came up to me on the second day of filming. He said, "Hey, you got a hundred dollars?" I was flustered that he was even talking to me, and I mumbled, "No, Glenn. What do you need a hundred dollars for?" He said, "I was talking to my bookie, and I've got a sure thing." I said, "No, I've got no money to spare at all." After a moment he smiled at me and said, "Aw, you're covered." The next day he came in and walked over to me. He handed me six hundred dollars, took a hundred back from it, and said, "You won!" It was incredible. Who else would do something like that? So he became my dear friend.

Appointment in Honduras was released in October 1953 and quickly became a favorite pincushion for critics. John McCarten in the *New Yorker* wrote, "The program didn't say who played the ants, but they were the best actors around." My father could think of nothing to say about the picture when I asked him except to remark, "Not one of my best, but it made me some money."

Oddly, my father's very next picture was another Latin American adventure tale, RKO's *The Americano*, produced by Robert Stillman (the father of my childhood friend, the aforementioned Jack "Wrangler" Stillman). Budd Boetticher would be directing again, and the cast was to include Cesar Romero, Arthur Kennedy, and the gorgeous Spanish singer-actress Sarita Montiel. For this go-round Dad would receive $125,000 and 20 percent of the movie's profits.

The story concerned a Texas cattleman who agrees to bring three of his prize Brahman bulls to a wealthy rancher in Brazil, a journey plagued with man-eating piranhas (instead of marauding ants), hostile gauchos, robbery, murder, lynching, and a villainous rancher, relieved only by a beautiful *dona da fazenda*. Unlike the old-fashioned, penny-pinching *Appointment in Honduras*, *The Americano* intended to follow the trend toward exotic location filming, with Hollywood in the mid-1950s trying to lure audiences away from their television sets with big-screen attributes. Not only that, but *The Americano* would be shot in the new true stereo 3-D process.

Filming would take place largely on the wild Mato Grosso plateau, an area of more than 348,788 square miles in the middle of Brazil, encompassing primordial rain forest, winding rivers, treacherous swamps, and great expanses of fertile grazing land. Interiors would be shot at the Companhia Cinematográfica Vera Cruz studio in São Paulo.

This would be the longest, most remote trip Dad had yet undertaken for a film. My father insisted that my mother should accompany him to Brazil, and to ensure that she'd go with him this time, I was included. Mother undoubtedly had trepidations about heading off to the wilds of South America and taking her young child along. But she also knew that her decision to stay at home on other similar location jaunts of my father's had contributed to their marital difficulties. She was pleased to hear him say that if they couldn't all go together, he would tell the producers it was no deal. At this point, if it meant a chance to repair their marriage, I think she would have gone along on a journey to Jupiter. I was eight years old by this time, and the filming was to take place during summer vacation anyway. It was settled: the Ford family was headed to the jungles of Brazil.

In the third week of June, my mother, my father, and I took the Southern Pacific streamliner to New Orleans, stayed overnight at the Roosevelt Hotel, had dinner at Antoine's in the French Quarter, and the next day boarded the SS *Del Mar* for a two-week cruise to Brazil.

The long, slow journey took us across the Gulf, through the Caribbean, past Venezuela and the Guyanas, and down and around the endless coastline of Brazil to our destination. We lost all sense of time onboard. I would wander about the ship, swim in the pool, and mingle with the crew, one of whom taught me how to play his harmonica. This was not a cruise ship as we know them today but rather a floating means of transportation with only ninety passengers aboard. At night everyone dressed very formally, and we sat in the place of honor at the captain's table. Aside from periodic gawking and requests for autographs, the other passengers mostly left my parents alone. And for the first time in a long while I think they really did rediscover the happiness in each other's company that they once had known. I can remember seeing them strolling on the decks holding hands and embracing. I felt happy for them, for all of us.

In Brazil I got my first real view of my parents' stature as cinematic deities. Of course I knew they were famous and was long aware of the way people deferred to them or stared at them or made a fuss about them when they were glimpsed in public. But in South America I witnessed frenzied crowds wherever they appeared. It was nearly impossible for any of us to sightsee or even step outside the hotel without a crowd starting to gather and surround us.

Although it had been over a dozen years since Mom had starred in a movie, the crowds were even more excited by Eleanor Powell than by Glenn Ford. There was an item about our whereabouts every day in the local papers. At some places, when we arrived there would be huge floral arrangements with giant signs reading: "Brazil greets Eleanor Powell!" My father was pleased to see Mom as the object of such adulation again, but perhaps he found it a little disconcerting too—it had been a long while since he had thought of himself as secondary to his wife in the screen star hierarchy. Her notoriety attracted a few wishful Latin lovers besides.

Although the ship landed in Rio de Janeiro, we were there only a few days before we traveled to the historic city of São Paulo. The Hotel Florida at the beach resort of Guarujá became the film company's headquarters for most of its stay in Brazil.

In the mornings, after Dad left for work, my mother would take me down to the hotel's beach. Groups of local people would gather around, with my mother swiftly becoming the object of attention for many young Brazilian men. One of these gentlemen began bringing her large bouquets of flowers, every day returning with more and more flowers, finally coming up to her quite seriously with a formal proposal of marriage. "I kept pointing to my wedding band," she would say, "but I couldn't get rid of him." My mother thought it was a cute story, but I know my father was not amused.

Then one of the gossip columns reported a rumor that the famous Hollywood dancer Eleanor Powell was having a romance with the man who had been assigned as our guide and local facilitator, a good-looking aspiring actor by the name of Mario Sergio. It was nonsense, but my father was not amused when a photo of Mom and me in this fellow's sports car speeding down the empty beach one early morning was published on the front page of the newspaper. My parents had some marital strife about it. On orders from my father, Dad's stand-in and bodyguard, Bill Rhinehart, who was in Brazil with us, took the young actor aside and threatened to "eliminate" him if he ever spoke to my mother again. Needless to say, no more flowers were sent to the room, and car rides on the beach ceased.

It wasn't long before things also began going wrong on the set of *The Americano*. For starters, key members of the crew did not show up as scheduled. The start date for filming came and went as the producer tried to round up everyone needed. By the time all were finally accounted for, the area was hit with many days of torrential rain. Then, with filming at last under way, it was discovered that Sarita (aka Sara) Montiel could not speak English, and she had no experience on horseback, which was exactly where most of her scenes took place. More schedule changes, more delays.

To make matters worse, many of the cast and crew took ill, including my mother, my father, and me. On one of the first nights in Brazil I found a big worm in my string beans, and we were all afraid to eat anything after that. We were told that we might have swallowed parasites, as they were endemic, and, sure enough, one after the other—all three of us—suffered severe digestive difficulties. A five-day stay on a ranch where Dad was filming added to my difficulties, as I returned home bitten by red ants and infested with ticks. I also remember that on the day I played a small role (my first time on-screen) I had to plunge into some water, and I emerged with leeches clinging to me—shades of *The African Queen*. I vividly remember that evening my father used his lighted cigar to burn the leeches off my legs and torso.

The heat, the humidity, the bugs, and the loose bowels plaguing cast and crew made the production a virtual nightmare for all involved. After two weeks of shooting, the director only had about a reel of usable footage in the can, ten minutes or so. A screwup with the banks left the local crew unpaid and ignited a nasty rebellion and threats of violence. RKO, having invested in the picture in return for distribution rights, suddenly pulled their funds out. The production shut down on September 8, and we found ourselves stranded in Brazil. My father fronted the money for our family, Hal Clifton, Bill Rhinehart, and a few friends in the American cast (including Cesar Romero and Arthur Kennedy) to sail back to the United States. Within a few days we were back aboard the SS *Del Mar* headed for America.

It was supposed to have been a wonderful time for the Ford family, a working vacation, but it had ended as a disaster. Everyone was ill, exhausted, short-tempered. My father felt embarrassment for what had happened. My parents were barely on speaking terms. And, as happened so many times in the past, somehow I was the one who was made to feel the blame, but this time I acted out my anger. A warning was posted by the ship's captain that no one should use the ship's pool one afternoon because the crew was going to empty it to change the salt water. Some young friends and I decided we would enjoy the pool despite this admonition. As the water level sank, the agitation inside the pool buffeted us from side to side in a dangerous way. A crew member told my father that I was in the pool, and he came and angrily plucked me out. As punishment, he would not allow me to join my friends to see *The Greatest Show on Earth*, the movie they were showing that night in the ship's theater. I was furious. Alone in one of the ship's lounges while the movie was playing, I took out my pocket knife and slashed a red leather banquette. My father was understandably horrified when he found out, and he paid for all the damages. Normally, I would have been severely punished for such behavior, but we were all so weary and beaten down after all we'd been through that he decided to forget it ever happened. Under the circumstances, it was a wise decision.

It would be nearly a year before *The Americano* went back into production. Producer Bob Stillman claimed he tried to restart the film several times, but Glenn Ford was never available. My father regarded the film as an albatross. When Stillman finally filed a $175,000 lawsuit against my father, Dad decided he had better find the time to finish the picture, and production resumed in June 1954—not in Brazil, thankfully, but at a 325-acre dairy farm in Corona, a picturesque rural area in Riverside County southeast of Los Angeles.

Along with the change in scenery came a largely new cast, Frank Lovejoy replacing Arthur Kennedy and German-born (but this time English-speaking) Ursula Thiess instead of Sarita Montiel. Abbe Lane, the voluptuous singer and actress, signed for a supporting part and contributed two sensuous musical numbers. Typical of the film's misguided thinking, however, both her songs were sung in Spanish, though the character was a Portuguese-speaking Brazilian.

A new director was also on board; Budd Boetticher had been replaced by William Castle, a talented man known for keeping things moving fast and under budget. He would later be responsible for a slew of exploitation-type horror films, including *The Tingler, Macabre,* and *Homicidal.* The almost entirely new version of *The Americano* was completed by the end of August and released the following February to mixed notices and double bills. It was all aggravation and wasted effort.

But the experience of *The Americano* would prove to be a valuable lesson for my father. He had been given talent and luck, he realized, but too often in the last ten years he had wasted both in working simply for the paycheck. He had watched his friends and contemporaries making the important films and winning acclaim and awards. Now and in the years ahead he became determined to make a kind of fresh start, to look for challenges as an actor and for worthwhile film projects in which he could take pride.

The Big Heat had been one of a handful of good choices. Fritz Lang's film had surprised the studio by making over $2 million at the box office, a solid return in those days, and Columbia was eager to reteam Glenn Ford, Gloria Grahame, and director Lang. The project: *Human Desire,* a remake of *La bête humaine,* Jean Renoir's gritty French drama of the 1930s starring Jean Gabin and based on a novel by Émile Zola. Recent Oscar winner Broderick Crawford would join my father and Gloria Grahame as the villain of the piece.

In the Americanized adaptation by Alfred Hayes, a Korean War vet named Jeff Warren has returned to his job as a brakeman for the railroads. He becomes involved with a sexy temptress named Vicki and her violently jealous, physically abusive husband, Carl, who has killed his wife's boss in a rage. Seducing Jeff, Vicki pulls him into a web of lies and risk from which he narrowly escapes at the end of the story, leaving Vicki and Carl to their miserable self-destruction.

The production began filming on December 14, 1953, on locations at the Santa Fe railroad junction in Reno, Oklahoma. For Glenn, the film was a delightful return to the world inhabited by his own father, long ago an engineer with the Canadian Pacific. Climbing into the engine for the first day's shoot, Dad fondly recalled the stories his father had told him about the great iron horses of the past. Glenn delighted onlookers with his easy command of the huge machine.

Once again, my father found himself in awe of Fritz Lang, who seemed to have a kind of laserlike ability to reveal the dark desires and inner anxieties of the characters and who knew how to motivate his actors to convey these emotions. Lang also seemed to relish the location work and the giant railway engines and cars he got to order around like a commandant. The machinery and mechanical movements were great props for his visual ideas, reminiscent of the relentless, huge machinery in his old silent masterpiece *Metropolis*.

Gloria Grahame played a seductive woman with an adventurous sex life, which wasn't far from Grahame in real life. Although she enjoyed a reputation for going to bed with her leading men, she and Glenn had had a merely pleasant but distant working relationship in *The Big Heat*. The chemistry between actors working in a movie, however, often seems to reflect what is occurring in the story line being filmed. In *The Big Heat* Gloria was the damaged moll, and Glenn was the righteous recent widower; there were no romantic sparks between them. But in *Human Desire* Gloria was a femme fatale seductress, on- and off-camera. Like their characters in the movie, Gloria and Glenn engaged in a brief affair, which lasted, as my father put it, "the time it took to shoot the movie."

Like *The Big Heat* and a few others of my father's films, *Desire* has continued to grow in stature through the years. It was the final collaboration between him and Lang. They talked about doing a western together and even had a script idea at one point. It never came to fruition. This was the caliber of director, Dad realized, he should have been working with more often, someone who could push him to greater heights.

When *Human Desire* ended, so did my Dad's second contract with Columbia. The long association with Harry Cohn had been a mixed bag through the years. The studio had kept Dad busy and before the public for more than a decade, but there was no denying that Cohn had forced him into more than his fair share of mediocre films and that he had suffered from cautious budgets and poor creative decisions.

With Glenn Ford coming on the market again for the first time in years, he and his representatives at William Morris were determined to make the best deal possible, one that would finally allow him to fulfill his potential as an actor and a star. Yet Cohn was eager to continue working with Glenn, and he made a suitably larger financial offer for his future services. Harry guaranteed that my father would have the starring role in the forthcoming *Picnic*, but Dad had heard Cohn's promises before and didn't trust him on that score. Cohn poured on the salesmanship, however, and who knows, in the end perhaps he liked and appreciated Dad more than he cared to let on.

On March 4, 1954, Dad signed his third agreement with Columbia, a new nonexclusive pact that would run for five years, committing my father to one film a year and setting him free to do any other work at other studios. In addition, he would earn more money and have more say in the choice of scripts, directors, and costars.

The first film under the 1954 agreement was *The Violent Men*, with Dad top-billed in a powerful cast that included Barbara Stanwyck and Edward G. Robinson and notable support from Dianne Foster, Brian Keith, and May Wynn. The Harry Kleiner screenplay was derived from the Donald Hamilton novel *Smokey Valley*. It was a combustible melodrama about an honest rancher battling a corrupt cattle baron, with subplots galore concerning the cattle baron's evil, adulterous wife and the love affair between the rancher and the villain's young daughter. *The Violent Men* reunited Dad with director Rudolph Maté, who was in fine form with this tempestuous western, ruggedly staged and shot with a brilliant use of color and widescreen. Not only had Rudy been the cinematographer on *Gilda*, director of *The Green Glove* and now *The Violent Men*, and producer of *The Return of October*, but, best of all, Rudy was a semiregular in Dad's poker club.

The Violent Men was filmed in Old Tucson, Arizona, at the Columbia Ranch, and in Lone Pine, California, on the slopes of snow-covered Mount Whitney, where the spectacular fire scenes were shot. Both Robinson and Stanwyck were accomplished veterans whom my father had admired long before he'd ever become a part of the movie business, and he felt gratified to be working with them. "Just marvelous actors, both," he would say. "Barbara was so good, so real, one of the best actresses I ever worked with. She was tough, hard-working, very professional, but a real woman."

From notes in my father's diary I believe he was smitten by Barbara. A few years before making *The Violent Men* she had divorced her second husband, Robert Taylor. Barbara and my father had a measured romance during the making of this film. They were both lonely and shared moments of common understanding, which is the only way I can describe it. A romance perhaps not exactly, but certainly they established a bond. In 1965, when Barbara Stanwyck signed on to play the matriarch on the TV series *The Big Valley*, it was mentioned that the plot and setting of *The Violent Men* had been the show's inspiration. After her death Barbara Stanwyck did not have a funeral and has no resting place—her ashes, at her request, were scattered in Lone Pine. As for my father, *The Violent Men* also remained one of his favorite films.

Perhaps my father was happiest making westerns. He was once quoted as saying:

> If I could do whatever I wanted to for the rest of my life, I wouldn't do anything but westerns. I love 'em, and I believe they're underrated. They call for a different kind of professionalism. I've seen professional actors go to pieces on a western. You're on the Mojave and the sand's blowing and it's hot and the horses are giving trouble. The actor's got to ride to the camera and say three lines, and he cannot make it.
>
> No foreign country can make a western. In Spain, it's not a western. It's got to be done where it happened. . . . The public knows a real western and God help anybody who tries to fool 'em. . . . Westerns are a man's world.

8

"Rock Around the Clock"

The *Violent Men* wrapped up in May, and after my father attended to the matter of finishing *The Americano* for Jack Stillman and RKO, he was tempted by an offer from the most prestigious and luxurious of all the dream factories. Dore Schary, MGM production head, had asked my father many times to join the studio, but there was always a conflict or other commitments. Now, with just a one-film-per-year responsibility to Columbia, Dad felt it was time to give MGM a try.

Dad had come to Dore's rescue when he filled in for Russell Nype on *Young Man with Ideas* three years earlier—Dore appreciated that. Dad agreed to do one film at MGM before making any long-term commitment so that he and the studio could get a sense of each other before they planned for the future.

When my father arrived at MGM in the fall of 1954, it was a rather different place from the one my mother had known when she began working there nearly twenty years before. The times had changed, and with them the appetite of moviegoers. Box-office receipts were down; television was blamed for keeping audiences at home with its less grand but free entertainment. The great names that had once been synonymous with MGM had faded or been allowed to slip away.

The group portrait taken at the studio's Silver Jubilee (its twenty-fifth anniversary) in 1949 had featured an array of fifty-eight famous faces under contract, but now, six years later, only four of those faces remained. Not only the stars and featured players but many of the longtime personnel behind the scenes had been trimmed from the payroll. Even the once mighty, invulnerable mogul himself, Louis B. Mayer, had been made redundant, replaced by Schary.

Schary was a different sort of showman from Mayer, with different ideas and ambitions. The studio would continue to make pure entertainment such as *The Tender Trap*, *Seven Brides for Seven Brothers*, and *Singin' in the Rain*, but Dore's real interest was in more serious fare, dramatic and realistic filmmaking and, as often as possible, a movie that espoused a message or a cause. Schary would readily give the green light to mature and hard-hitting projects that old Louis B. Mayer would never have dreamed of authorizing.

Interrupted Melody was the first project that Schary offered to Dad, a biographical subject with music, the life of opera star Marjorie Lawrence, an Australian-born soprano who brought theatrical flair and innovation to her productions around the world. Lawrence had contracted polio at the height of her fame, been nearly destroyed by depression, and then in her wheelchair returned to the spotlight in triumph. The film had originally been prepared for Greer Garson, but that grande dame of the studio was now too old for the part, and her contract with Metro had ended. The role had been bequeathed to Eleanor Parker, a leading actress since the mid-1940s who had increased her stock with dramatic, Oscar-nominated work in *Caged* and *Detective Story* while showing her flair and sex appeal in recent lighter fare like *Scaramouche*. It was Parker who asked the studio to pursue Glenn Ford for the role of Lawrence's caring doctor husband. Indeed, Parker was insistent and even willing, if necssary, to sacrifice her top billing.

While the film was clearly focused primarily on Marjorie Lawrence and not her husband, Glenn liked the subject. It was something different for him, a chance to do a plush Technicolor musical, introducing himself to a fresh sector of the moviegoing public. He had worked before with the assigned director, Curtis Bernhardt, and producer Jack Cummings, now a family friend, had produced Eleanor Powell musicals years before and was highly esteemed by her.

Filming got under way on September 15, 1954, on the Culver City lot, with some location work in Santa Monica and El Segundo (doubling for the Florida coast). "I had it easy," my father remembered, "compared to Eleanor Parker. She had to do all those opera arias, in different languages, Puccini, Bizet, Wagner. For logistical reasons they had to shoot all of those scenes back to back, so she really had an enormous amount of rehearsal and memorization."

Director Bernhardt revealed that he was in over his head, Parker recalled, as soon as the filming of the musical scenes began. "He didn't know where to put the camera or where to have us stand. They shut down for a few days and found an actual opera director who knew how to stage those scenes properly."

"I watched them filming these beautiful opera house scenes," Dad said, "and I was so impressed with Eleanor. She worked very hard to make the singing seem real. Even when you are lip-synching to a record you really need to sing out loud to make it look believable on film, no matter how well you sing. Eleanor did it all-out, had great stamina, and she was wonderful."

Interrupted Melody was a sort of tryout for Glenn and MGM, and both parties declared satisfaction with the result. Schary had a pet project all ready, so there was only one weekend between the completion of *Interrupted Melody* and the start of an unusual film that broke ground for my father and the studio and started a movement in Hollywood. That film was *Blackboard Jungle*.

It is hard to understand nowadays, when there are few taboos on subject matter and everyone has seen and heard it all, how shocking *Blackboard Jungle* was in the 1950s. No one had ever dared to present such an uncompromising account of juvenile delinquency and violence within the walls of a modern American high school. In many people's minds, teenagers were still the adorable innocents of MGM's Andy Hardy movies, with nothing taking place in their lives more dramatic than pining for a date on Saturday night with the girl next door. *Blackboard Jungle* took that pleasant cliché and exploded it like a bomb.

The story came from a novel by Evan Hunter, who had worked briefly at the Bronx Vocational High School in New York. A young, idealistic war veteran starts his first assignment as a teacher in a tough, poverty-stricken neighborhood. He soon finds that the school is a place of anarchy and simmering violence, the classrooms filled with unruly and threatening hooligans who hold their fearful teachers in contempt. Clinging to his ideals about the value of education and the American Way, the teacher fights an uphill battle and risks his life to inspire the apathetic students and defeat the violent delinquents.

Louis Mayer would have thrown up his hands. But for Schary—who had earlier produced *Crossfire*, the first Hollywood film to broach the

149

subject of American anti-Semitism—*Blackboard Jungle* was just the sort of newsworthy, controversial material he embraced. Dad was immediately excited. "I didn't have any doubt that this could be a great picture," he recalled. "If done right and without any punches pulled, I thought it could have a real impact. I'm not big on message pictures as such. But this was highly dramatic material that also revealed a reality and a problem that had not been seen in motion pictures before."

Pandro Berman, *Blackboard Jungle*'s producer, had delayed the start date of his film until my father had finished *Interrupted Melody*. The director and screenwriter was Richard Brooks, a talented and tough former reporter, an ex-Marine, and a protégé of John Huston's (and, not incidentally, the author of the original novel upon which *Crossfire* was based). He and Dad had to get along. My father recalled:

> I had never met Brooks, but I knew his reputation, and I was familiar with some of his work as a writer on *Key Largo* and the prison picture *Brute Force*, which was very strong. When I read his script for *Blackboard* I knew we were in good hands. It was a great piece of work, maybe even better than the book.
>
> Dick was full of good ideas, and we discussed all aspects of the picture together. I remember that the studio or Pan Berman was giving some thought to doing the picture in color, and Brooks told them absolutely not, that we needed black and white to convey that depressing neighborhood the kids lived in. We also talked about the casting of the boys for the classroom. Dick Brooks wanted to avoid using any of the sort of clean-cut young actors who might be in the MGM stock company. He wanted people that looked like they had come straight off the streets. He didn't care if they could act or not in some cases, if they had this realistic look.

Berman and Brooks assembled a strong ensemble. The actors were a real mix, from every sort of background and level of experience, including gorgeous contract starlet Anne Francis as the teacher's wife, Broadway actor Richard Kiley as the fragile teacher Mr. Edwards, who has his cherished record collection destroyed by the delinquents, and my dad's old touring company pal and booster from the 1930s, Louis Calhern, as the most cynical of the burned-out instructors.

To play the tough students in Dad's class, Brooks picked a mixture of fresh faces: Rafael Campos, Paul Mazursky (Paul would go on to be an acclaimed writer-director of such films as *Bob and Carol and Ted and Alice*), Jamie Farr (later famous for his role as the cross-dresser Klinger on

TV's *M*A*S*H* but back then going by his real name, Jameel Farah), and Vic Morrow, whose intense style seemed to recall the early Marlon Brando in *The Wild One*. Playing the toughest of the school kids, Vic was a New York Method actor who seemed to stay in character long after the day's work was done. One day I was with my mother, and we got to meet him. Vic was wearing his juvenile delinquent costume. I thought he looked very cool and asked my mother if I could get a leather jacket just like his. Mom looked horrified and said, "We'll ask your father."

Making his fifth feature film in the role of the African American kid who evolves from alienated delinquent to become the teacher's ally was Sidney Poitier. His extraordinary performance would launch his career as a leading man in major Hollywood productions. Dad and Sidney worked well together, and they became friends; Sidney was a frequent guest at our house during the years ahead.

Sidney Poitier speaks fondly of my father to this day, I am proud to say. Recalling those *Blackboard Jungle* days, Sidney told me:

> I had been an admirer of his work. He was a genuine American movie star. And there was more variety in his body of work than in comparable actors. He was deft at comedy, drama, westerns, love stories. The man had great range.
>
> We had never met before starting the picture. And when I met him I found that he was a very nice man. I spent a lot of time with him, one on one, and he was a lot of fun, this guy. He was an actor whom I liked, and I was very happy to have the opportunity to work with him. He was the kind of actor who made you believe almost everything he did. He had a wonderful natural quality. You could hardly see him acting, he was just so good at it. As a young actor coming along, I tagged him as someone from whom I could learn.

Interrupted Melody finished shooting on Saturday, November 13, 1954. The filming of *Blackboard Jungle* started on the following Monday. Just before the cameras rolled, Richard Brooks rushed into my father's dressing room and led him out by the arm. My father recalled:

> I said, "Where are we going?" He said, "I'm taking you to the studio barber to get a haircut." I said, "I just got a haircut." He said, "Glenn, this character, this young guy on his first day at school, he's just gotten out of the service. Your hair isn't right for the role." We got to the barber, and I got into the chair. Brooks told the barber to cut it short. I had thick, wavy, dark hair then, and I always wore it pretty much the same in my pictures,

with the exception of *Loves of Carmen*, where it looked ridiculous. I said, "All right, but not too short."

But every time the barber finished trimming it Brooks told him to cut some more. I said to him, "What's the idea?" He said, "I mean you have to have a Navy haircut, a real wartime haircut." I looked at Dick Brooks's head. He was well known for his own haircut, which was a close-cropped military buzz cut like you got on your first day in boot camp. I said, "You mean a haircut like yours!" He smiled and said, "Something like that." I said, "If you want this character to have your haircut, Dick, you play him!" We argued back and forth, with me losing a little more hair each time. I told him if they cut any more I was going to look less like a New York schoolteacher and more like I had just escaped from Devil's Island. Finally, I gave up. "Okay, the hell with it. Cut it."

And so I got the short haircut I wore in that picture. And as Dick Brooks never failed to point out, I got to like the way it looked, and I ended up wearing my hair short like that in most of the pictures I made from then on.

Brooks's original hopes of shooting the film on location at a real city school had been thwarted—no board of education would have anything to do with *Blackboard Jungle*. The novel was already notorious among the school systems of America. Instead, it had to be filmed almost entirely on Metro soundstages. Most people who see the film would agree that a convincingly gritty sense of the New York slums was achieved by the MGM set designers. And by shooting in the controlled studio environment, they were able to make the film with a concentration and speed that might not have been possible on location.

Dad was a disciplined professional, but it took a little time to adjust to Brooks's directorial methods. In the classroom scenes, the dramatic heart of the film, Brooks wanted a raw, improvised quality, which would be aided by the lack of experience of many of the actors playing the students. Brooks did not want to make the school kids (some of whom were well into their twenties in fact) learn the conventions of rehearsing and performing for the camera: "The more we rehearsed, the worse they got," he would recall. So he encouraged them to move and talk freely within the framework of the scenes. My father had learned to hit his marks for the camera when speaking or moving and then make that appear to be natural and realistic—and he was pretty good at it. But when they started filming, some of the "kid" actors spoke their lines too soon or too fast, or they talked right over him, or they turned away or moved in another direction than he had expected. My father recalled:

I went to Brooks privately with the problem. I said, "Every time I start to say a line they're climbing all over me. I don't see how this is going to work." Brooks said, "Forget the way we rehearsed it. From now on just play it right through, whatever they do. If they walk past you, let me worry about it. We'll change the angle, or you can follow them. From now on you just play it as though it were actually happening." I said, "You think it will work?" Brooks said, "I have no idea! But let's find out."

Later Brooks would applaud my father for taking a chance with him, saying, "Instead of carping about 'Well, they need to be in the right place and give me my cues,' he agreed to accommodate their inexperience. It was an unusual way for him to work, but with his vast experience he was able to adjust."

The excitement and challenge of making *Blackboard Jungle* reawakened something in my father. He was always a skilled performer, but in this film you can see him digging deeper with zest. Maybe it all started with that short haircut or being around so many first-time actors, but there is something sharp and raw and flexible in his performance. He conveys the teacher's humble decency and determination with an immediacy that is very alive; it's brilliant, nuanced acting, one of the screen's great portrayals of an everyday American hero, if I may say so, comparable with Gary Cooper's Sergeant York or Jimmy Stewart's Mr. Smith.

"I think Glenn's whole career changed at that time with that picture," Brooks said later. "He was seen in a different light afterwards. He became a leading figure for the 1950s. He became someone who could take a stand in a movie, rather than just someone in an insipid love story. In *Blackboard Jungle* Glenn began to reveal elements of his own personal character that were utilized in the development of his movie character, essentially a decent man who stands up for what he believes."

There was one element of *Blackboard Jungle* that would have a lasting impact over and above its stature as a classic film. I am referring to the song heard over the opening credits and later in the movie: Bill Haley and the Comets' "Rock Around the Clock." I happened to have a personal connection to this ingredient of the film, so indulge me while I recount it in some detail. After all, it is not every day that a nine-year-old boy gets to influence music history.

We were a very musically aware family. My mother, of course, was a singer and dancer. She had recorded with Tommy Dorsey and many other well-known musicians, and she had grown up loving the music of all the great early jazz and big band leaders. Her personal record collection included people like Art Tatum, the Ink Spots, and Fats Waller—she played the latter so much that the vinyl had literally worn away.

My father had a broader taste, and his own collection included everything from classical to folk to Hawaiian ukulele recordings. Growing up, I was exposed to this range and variety of music, and at a very tender age I had developed an ardent interest in music. By the age of six or seven I was already able to identify the work of different classical composers and popular singers and big bands.

I have already mentioned that, in our home in Beverly Hills, we had a room that was called the China Room, which had been the study of composer Max Steiner when he had owned the house before us. I would often visit that room, looking at it as something of a sacred shrine, a piece of music and film history; later, when my mother sold the house, I rescued many of the Chinese panels from the demolition crew, and I still have many of them on display in my home today. It was a perfect room in which to listen to music, and in good times we would all retire there after dinner to enjoy whatever anyone wished to play on the record player, my mother doing her knitting and my father relaxing or reading.

By the fall of 1954, when *Blackboard Jungle* was in production, I was a precocious fifth grader who spent a good part of my time shuttling between the Beverly Hills Music Shop and Wallach's Music City at Sunset and Vine, keeping up with all the latest recordings and bringing home everything I liked. I didn't have many close friends, and music was my passion. I was very much into the new sounds of rhythm-and-blues, or "race music," as it was then called. I listened to the Midnighters with Hank Ballard and the wonderful ballads of Johnny Ace. I can remember when I excitedly made my mother and father listen to my newly purchased record of Willie Mae "Big Mama" Thornton singing "Hound Dog" long before it became a hit for Elvis Presley. I liked to think of myself as most likely the only "black" white kid living in Beverly Hills at the time.

That style of music was catching on with white recording artists as well and beginning the gradual blend with country-and-western and hillbilly and Tin Pan Alley into the amalgam that would come to be known as rock and roll. One of the records I bought during the fall of 1954 was "Thirteen Women (and Only One Man in Town)" by a raucous white band called Bill Haley and the Comets. Earlier I had purchased my first Bill Haley record, "Crazy Man Crazy," and I knew he and his group were on to something. I was looking forward to hearing their new release.

I was disappointed to find that I didn't much care for "Thirteen Women." I turned the record over to play the B side. More often than not, the B side of a record was inferior, mere filler. So I wasn't expecting much when I set the needle down on the phonograph and listened to those now-familiar opening bars of "Rock Around the Clock" (the composition credited to James E. Myers, aka Jimmy De Knight and Max C. Freedman, and recorded on April 12, 1954, released the following month). My eyes opened wide and my foot started tapping as I heard that irresistible recording for the first time. How Decca Records could have thought that this was not the A side of the release was a mystery to me.

One day toward the end of the filming of *Blackboard Jungle*, Richard Brooks, who lived about a mile away from us, came by the house after work, as he did on a number of evenings while they were making the picture. He and Dad began to discuss the need to use some musical recordings in the film that would reflect what these high school kids would be listening to in real life. Naturally, my father suggested that his son, Peter, had the most up-to-the-minute records in town, and he asked me to select what I thought was the best from the latest additions to my collection. My father and Dick Brooks followed me into the China Room and listened to "Rock Around the Clock" and a couple of other records (including, to the best of my recollection, Big Joe Turner's version of "Shake Rattle and Roll" and "All Night Long" by the Joe Huston Orchestra). Brooks asked if he could borrow them. He brought the records to the studio the next day and played them in his office for assistant director Joel Freeman and others on his staff. Everyone agreed that "Rock Around the Clock" was the best choice, the perfect choice for the movie.

MGM purchased the film rights to the recording from Decca for $5,000, with the contract stipulation that they could use it just three times within the film. It has been written that for $2,500 more MGM could have bought outright ownership of the recording and probably made millions from it by now.

"Rock Around the Clock" was the first "rock song" used in a motion picture. By July 1955, seven months after Richard Brooks first heard my 78 rpm copy of it at our house, "Rock Around the Clock" was the number one record in the nation and stayed at the top of the charts for eight weeks, selling eight million copies. The music ignited an interest in the new American music that would ultimately lead to a rock-and-roll explosion in the United States to Europe and across the globe. "Rock Around the Clock" became a symbol of a new spirit of youth and unbridled freedom and helped change the culture of America and much of the world forever. Music impresario Dick Clark called it "The National Anthem of Rock and Roll."

B*lackboard Jungle* completed principal photography in just twenty-nine days, and on Thursday, January 13, 1955, my father went to a screening room at MGM to see a rough cut of the picture. Dore Schary, Pandro Berman, Richard Brooks, and Dad's agent, Bert Allenberg, from the William Morris office were also present. There were great expectations for the film, but with so many unusual elements, the ugliness and violence in the story, the untested actors involved, Brooks's at times improvisatory direction, there was no way of knowing how well it would come together. The final cut was still a few weeks away, and there was no music track. Even so, the movie was powerful, and my father was thrilled with the film and his performance. He came home and took my mother and me out to a celebratory dinner at the Brown Derby in Beverly Hills, our favorite haunt.

A couple of weeks later the film was completed and a sneak preview scheduled for February 2, a Wednesday night, at the Encino Theatre on Ventura Boulevard in the San Fernando Valley. As an early treat for my up-coming tenth birthday, my father asked me if I wanted to go. Of course I did. I was anxious to see whether they had used any of those records of mine that Brooks had borrowed. I had pestered my father about it, but he had never seen the film with the music added, and all he could say was he understood we'd hear one of my records somewhere during the movie, but we'd probably have to listen close.

We got to the Encino along with Pandro Berman and Richard Brooks and crept into the back of the theater just as the picture was about to begin. The theater grew dark, the curtain was raised, the screen lit up. We saw the familiar roaring lion of the MGM logo. An empty blackboard appeared, and with it came another familiar sound: a drum beat and the voice of Bill Haley counting out, "One, two, three o'clock, four o'clock rock!" I let out a gasp and grabbed my father's arm. There it was—*my* record, as I thought of it, played loud the way I always did at home and not just heard on a jukebox playing in the background of some scene, as I expected, but right from the start, the whole record, playing over the credits and then weaving through the first minute of the film as the characters are introduced and the kids in the school yard snap their fingers to the beat. Wow.

I loved the whole movie and thought Dad was great, of course, but I couldn't stop thinking about that credit sequence and the music I loved playing front and center. There wasn't a happier kid than me in the whole world just then.

Dad's two completed MGM pictures, *Interrupted Melody* and *Blackboard Jungle*, were set for a simultaneous release in March 1955, but first he had to settle some contract details with MGM. On February 4, 1955, my father entered into a five-year agreement with MGM taking effect on March 7. My father agreed to make five films for MGM every two years. The total: twelve films. As a surprise nod to Dad's new status on the lot, he was assigned ex–MGM star Clark Gable's former dressing room, which was the nicest on the lot.

With Dad now in MGM's stable, the studio sent him on a cross-country publicity tour to promote the two new films. In those days it was still common to travel long distances by train; my father loved train travel and that long, leisurely way of seeing the country. He made stops along the route in select major cities, where studio representatives would make sure there were photographers and local press ready to chronicle his visit. My mother and I stayed behind.

One evening he pulled into Kansas City, where he was to change trains before continuing east. Who was waiting for him on the platform when the train pulled in? None other than William Holden, his close pal since the days of *Texas* in the early 1940s. Bill was in the Midwest working on *Picnic*, in the starring role that Harry Cohn had promised to my father two years before. A mutual friend, Columbia publicity man George Lait, had found out that Glenn would be passing through Kansas City on the train and brought Holden to the station to surprise him. The two actors headed back to the exclusive club car to try and wangle a drink. My father recalled the incident:

> We had the whole car to ourselves, except for a very elegantly attired waiter. The bar was closed, but we convinced him to open up and pour us a couple and a couple more. Bill and I in those days both took pride in being able to hold our liquor. In fact, we looked down at people who couldn't, the ones who got loud and obnoxious.
>
> We were shooting the breeze, reminiscing, and suddenly Bill says, "Say, I just remembered. Some character gave me a couple of marijuana cigarettes. Have you ever had one?" Neither of us had ever tried the stuff; it wasn't our scene. Bill said, "Shall we see what they're like?" I didn't even smoke regular cigarettes, but sitting there in the club car, enjoying a drink with Bill Holden, I said, "Sure, why not." Then Bill said, "But let's agree, if either one of us starts doing anything crazy, we'll stop." I guess neither of us had any idea what the stuff would do to you when you smoked it. I agreed.

He got out these spindly hand-rolled cigarettes, and we both took turns lighting and puffing and trying to keep it lit, which wasn't easy. The thing kept going out. But we kept at it. We smoked both of them and sat there. I said finally, "Do you feel anything, Bill?" Bill said, "Not a thing." We sat there, doing nothing, just staring out the window. We both thought it was a nothing experience. But I don't think either of us moved for over an hour, and then we both started feeling extremely hungry for a big steak dinner. We were stoned and didn't know it. I also lost track of the time, and I nearly missed my train.

Both of Dad's Metro productions did well, but of course it was *Blackboard Jungle* that became the international sensation, very much in the way that *Gilda* had made waves a decade before when Dad was at Columbia. Reviews for the film were terrific, and my father got some of the best notices of his career. *Variety*'s critic wrote: "Ford is so real in his performance, under the probing direction of Richard Brooks, that the picture alternately has the viewer pleading, indignant and frightened before the conclusion is brought about with a hackle-raising classroom fight in which Ford and Poitier find themselves as allies and the teacher subdues a knife-wielding Vic Morrow." The *Hollywood Reporter* agreed: "Glenn Ford proves what a great actor he can be. One of the best performances of the year."

Not everyone was pleased with MGM's new film about a teacher battling the problem of juvenile delinquency in an American high school, however. There had been expectation that the film might cause some controversy, but no one was prepared for the vehement reaction from certain quarters.

First came condemnation from educators and the teachers' unions, which felt that the school environment was sensationalized, showing lurid and violent situations that were unlikely or downright inconceivable, and that the portrayal of cynical and alienated teachers on-screen was highly insulting. More alarming were the politically tinged attacks on the movie and its makers. Those were the days of the cold war, the blacklist, and Senator Joseph McCarthy, and an array of columnists and politicians came out gunning for the film, declaring that *Blackboard Jungle* was nothing less than anti-American propaganda and giving comfort to America's enemies at home and abroad. My father even received hate mail and death threats because of his sympathetic relationship with Sidney Poitier's character in the film. My father took these letters, many of them from outraged southerners, to heart: he and my mother became very active in the Urban League. My mother did her part to further promote racial understanding by having a young black singer named Darlene Powell (no relation) perform prominently on her *Faith of Our Children* TV show every week. This too was greeted by some with howls of protest.

Of course, my father, who was as patriotic and devoted to American ideals as anyone could be, and Dick Brooks, who had done some time fighting for his country as a U.S. Marine, thought this was all bullshit, the squawking of small minds and political opportunists. The United States was certainly strong enough to stand up to self-examination, and in any case, *Blackboard Jungle's* ultimate message was positive and pro-American. Can anyone forget the moment when my father's character, defender of civilization and democratic ideals, holds out the American flag as his weapon to defeat the switchblade-swinging delinquent?

Either audiences shrugged off these protests or else they proved the truth of the old showbiz saying, "There's no such thing as bad publicity." In any case, the *Blackboard Jungle*, which cost $900,000 to produce, grossed a whopping $9 million on its general release in 1955. According to Evan Hunter, author of the book, the proceeds of the film saved MGM from bankruptcy. I'll leave that proclamation for historians to debate, but in the summer of 1955, before the film was released, MGM was not flourishing as it once had been.

Dore Schary was so happy with the way the film had turned out and so pleased with my father's performance that he had the studio rush to find a follow-up with some of the same ingredients as *Blackboard Jungle*. The first film Dad would make under the new contract was *Trial*, based on a *Harper's* magazine article and subsequent novel by Don Mankiewicz (who was the young son of Herman Mankiewicz, the screenwriter of *Citizen Kane*). Like *Blackboard Jungle*, *Trial* confronted provocative topics: racism, mob mentality, the threat of Communism.

The story was about an earnest young law professor named David Blake who interns for a wily, flamboyant attorney named Barney Castle. Castle is defending Angel Chavez, a poor Mexican teenager charged with murdering a white co-ed at a local beach, though the boy declares he is innocent. Outspoken local racists stir up a would-be lynch mob, but violence is contained, and the case goes to trial as scheduled. As the plot develops, Blake finds that Castle is deliberately trying to lose the case. Blake makes the shocking discovery that Castle is the organizer of a Communist cell and wants Chavez to be martyred so the local Mexican community will be motivated to join the Communist Party, supposedly paving the way for racial and economic equality. The proceedings end in a wild melee as Blake exposes Castle and the furious "subversive" attorney loses his mind.

Dad agreed with Dore that the part of David Blake was ideal for him. It had much of the same qualities of earnest decency, intelligence, and civic-mindedness of the schoolteacher in *Blackboard*. Once more he would confront a difficult and dangerous contemporary social problem and come out the hero, not through derring-do or might but through intelligence and moral courage.

Producer Charles Schnee gathered together a talented production team, including director Mark Robson (*Champion* and *Home of the Brave* among his strong previous work) and cinematographer Robert Surtees (his credits at MGM included *The Bad and the Beautiful* and *Mogambo*). Dad's castmates included Dorothy McGuire as the sympathetic staff worker, Rafael Campos (fresh from the gang in *Blackboard Jungle*) as Angel Chavez, and the powerful Mexican actress Katy Jurado as Angel's mother. The role of the duplicitous, charismatic attorney, Barney Castle, went to Arthur Kennedy, who would give a scene-stealing performance in the film. He was rewarded with an Academy Award nomination.

As with *Blackboard Jungle*, *Trial* was filmed very quickly. Exteriors were shot at the Santa Monica City Hall; a house in the same neighborhood filled in as the home and front yard of Mrs. Chavez. It was a neighborhood from my father's childhood, and the house they photographed was actually one that he remembered from his paper route as a kid. He told Dorothy McGuire, "I used to throw the *Evening Outlook* on this porch every evening for years." The "Free Angel Chavez" rally in the film was shot at the huge Shrine Exposition Hall in downtown Los Angeles. Over two thousand extras were hired. Assistant directors had to comb the vicinity, including the nearby USC campus, dragging dozens of students off to help fill up the space in the massive setting.

Although not quite in the same league as *Blackboard Jungle*, *Trial* was an unusual and powerful film and a daring one. It confronted more than its share of hot-button issues with a complex and unpredictable story line and an assortment of strong characterizations. Completed in mid-May, *Trial* was released nationally on October 7, 1955. Reviews were mixed— some found the film too frantic or thought it had bitten off more social issues than it could swallow—but the majority was in agreement with the *Hollywood Reporter*, which called the film "exciting, compassionate and intelligent" and said that "every American should see it." Of my father's performance, *Variety*'s Jack Moffit wrote: "Glenn Ford shows a combination of audience-winning dynamic personality and technical perfection that tops even his great work in *Blackboard Jungle* and *Interrupted Melody*. He is now firmly established as one of the screen's truly great actors."

At the end of the year, both *Blackboard Jungle* and *Trial* appeared on many "ten best" lists. An Academy Award nomination went to Richard Brooks for *Blackboard Jungle*'s screenplay. There had been a great deal of hopeful speculation that Glenn Ford would be nominated as best actor, but it didn't happen. He would never be nominated by the Academy despite a long list of distinguished performances. Richard Brooks, who did not win in his category, blamed the shutout on the film's controversial reputation. The Academy was just not ready to stir that same brouhaha up all over again at awards time.

My father was not complaining. In fact, he was feeling on top of the world. After such a long period of modest hits, missed opportunities, and a number of inconsequential and unworthy vehicles, he had in one year at MGM turned it all around.

His marriage, on the other hand, was not doing as well. My grandmother Hannah had lived with us almost from the day Mom and Dad were wed. My mother had for years graciously accepted the circumstances of having her mother-in-law living down the hall midway between herself and her husband. My mother could not remember a day when she had been completely alone in the house with Glenn (her own mother, Blanche, came to the house rarely, mainly for holidays). And don't forget that Grandmother Hannah was, at all times, Glenn's number one fan and always, no matter how sweetly, ready to side with her son in any argument.

After Dad finished shooting *Trial* my mother suddenly announced that she wanted Hannah to move into her own residence. Curiously, my father did not put up much of an argument. Not that Hannah went very far away. Dad found out that our next-door neighbor Charlie Chaplin, who was living in Europe now, another victim of the Hollywood blacklist, was willing to sell his very large garage, which was across the street from his home and on a separate lot adjacent to our home. This structure had a large guest or chauffeur's apartment on the second floor. Dad turned Chaplin's garage into what he called a rumpus room. It was actually a vast space with a pool table and a hideaway bed and a workshop for Dad in a divided corner. He would retreat to this workshop whenever things got heated between my mother and him. Hannah moved into Chaplin's refurbished second-floor apartment, fulfilling the "eviction notice" from my mother.

The remaining three of us continued to live under the same roof, and to the press and public and even some family friends everything appeared normal. Mom and Dad still appeared together at public events, and the family posed for publicity photographs and did a good job of keeping its problems hidden from the world. We had all been trained very well in the Hollywood system, where image and illusion were more important than reality. Even as a preteen I was instructed never to talk about family strife to friends or the press.

My mother had kept up her illusions for so long that she believed them. She clung to the notion that love would ultimately triumph, like it did in the movies. She would give up on that false hope one terrible evening in 1956, when all the bottled-up tension and resentment within the marriage, fueled by too much alcohol, blew up in our faces.

My parents were having a party at the house, and there was a lot of drinking among the adult guests. A few of my young friends and some of the guests' kids were corralled in the den watching television while the adults were in the living room. A pal of my father's named Jack Holland, a movie magazine writer, became extremely drunk, wandered into the den, stood in front of the television, and wouldn't move. I asked Mr. Holland if he would move so we could see the screen, but he wouldn't. So I got up and went out to find my father.

Dad was in the living room with my mother and the adult guests. I quietly explained to him about Holland blocking the TV, which all of us kids were watching. My father responded angrily to my complaining about his friend and seemed to act as if I was the troublemaker about to ruin his evening. He had been drinking too much, which didn't help. He instructed me to go to my room, at which point my mother got involved, and a big argument broke out. My father marched me upstairs, and my mother followed after him. The argument continued inside my room.

When I tried to plead my case my father grabbed me, shook me, and threw me down. My mother came forward to stop him, and he backhanded Mother, and she flew across my bed. I threw myself on her to protect her, but by then my father had rushed out of the room. Mom and I were both shocked, because nothing like this had ever happened before. I know Dad didn't intend to act violently, it just happened, a flash of drunken pent-up temper. But my mother didn't wait for an explanation. She told me to pack some clothes in my overnight suitcase, and she grabbed some things herself, and the two of us left the house in the middle of the party and went to stay at my grandma Powell's house.

My mother was now ready to seek a divorce, but, to hear her version of the events, she backed down when my father threatened to get the best lawyers in town, leave her broke, and take full custody of me. How exactly she thought he could get custody of me I don't know, since the divorce courts favored mothers and since her behavior as a parent was exemplary—especially compared to his.

One of the problems was that I was not yet fourteen, which is the age of consent in California, so I could not choose which parent I would prefer to live with. Mother was afraid that my father would take me away from her; furthermore, my mother had no means of support other than Dad's income. Mother knew nothing about legal questions or lawyers or divorce laws.

My mother was a rather unsophisticated person when it came to money. For instance, I don't believe she had ever even written a check or lived on a budget in her life. It's not that she couldn't, but it was never asked of her. She had left the conduct of her daily affairs to her mother before her marriage and to her husband, his business office (to which he paid a hefty 15 percent of his income), and attorneys after the marriage. My father was the breadwinner and had a powerful position in the company town in which we lived. So my mother was reluctant to throw down the gauntlet. She stopped thinking about divorce for the time being. But from her perspective, from that point on the marriage was over.

Dad probably worried about his image as a nice guy and losing his standing with audiences if a messy divorce revealed his many peccadilloes. He also viewed divorce as a sign of failure, a blow to his masculine pride. But I also believe he still loved my mother and did not want to face the prospect of a permanent breakup. He was willing to let the situation slide and hope for a miracle. As for me, during my whole life I never understood my father's true feelings toward me. His friends told me he said he loved me, but he never said those words to me personally, and more times than not he treated me as though he didn't.

We stayed at Grandmother Blanche's house for a few weeks. The house on quiet Hillgreen Drive was a small but charming two-bedroom English cottage with the requisite three birch trees out front. A few years earlier Grandmother had met and befriended a young student at USC. She had invited him to take the spare bedroom in exchange for helping her around the house. The arrangement was mutually beneficial, because in a short time Harlan James Juris became "Uncle Jim"—Grandmother's caregiver and friend. Many times throughout my life Jim acted as a surrogate father to me.

9

"Glory Days"

After a three-film absence, my father returned to his old "home" at Columbia Pictures to make another western. And *Jubal* turned out to be a fine film, a large-scale color and widescreen production shot on location in the rugged and spectacular landscape in and around Jackson Hole, Wyoming.

The director and cowriter was Delmer Daves, a very talented and highly educated (Stanford Law School grad) Hollywood veteran whose previous work included *Broken Arrow* with Jimmy Stewart, *Dark Passage* with Bogie and Bacall, *Destination Tokyo* with Cary Grant, and countless scripts dating back to the early talkies. Daves and my father made three pictures together—all westerns—and all three were among those my father considered among his most satisfying films.

Unlike most Hollywood directors, Daves actually had firsthand knowledge of the West and of Native Americans from his childhood experiences living in the wilderness areas and among the Hopi and Navajo. "Adult" westerns were thriving in post–World War II America, and they were no longer only about stagecoach robberies or Indian battles. The best of them dealt with the human condition in all its complexity. *Jubal* was a parable of adultery and betrayal.

My father played Jubal Troop, a drifter taken in by a benevolent rancher, played by Ernest Borgnine. The rancher's wife is a restless cheater who sets her sights on Jubal and seeks revenge when he spurns her. Several subplots involving pacifist sheepherders, a love interest, played by Felicia Farr in her first film, and a jealous former lover of the rancher's wife, played by the ever-brooding Rod Steiger, made this an unusually intricate and emotionally charged story.

The company was housed at the famous Wort Hotel in downtown Jackson Hole. The hotel's Silver Dollar Bar (which was named quite literally, since the bar contained in its design over two thousand vintage silver dollars) was a popular hangout for the movie crew as well as the tourists and locals who congregated there. There was plenty of drinking and revelry at the bar and quite a lot of action at the hotel's illegal casino. Wall-eyed character actor Jack Elam, who specialized in playing sniveling bad guys, became addicted to the gaming and is said to have lost his entire salary at the tables—he probably wasn't the only one.

Ernie Borgnine shared some memories about making *Jubal* with my father:

> Oh, that was a beautiful location, gorgeous. And we had a ball on that one, we really did. It was a very dramatic serious picture, but we were all having a ball. Delmer Daves was one of the finest directors I ever worked with in my life.
>
> I'll never forget, we were just starting the picture. Delmer, Glenn, and I were walking down the road leading up to this ranch house. And Glenn kept shaking his head. Delmer said, "What's the matter? Why do you keep shaking your head?" And Glenn said, "I'm frightened, I tell you." Delmer says, "Why? What the hell are you frightened about?" And Glenn said, "Can you guess?" He's very upset now. "I'm frightened . . . of him!" And he points his finger at me. I said, "What? What the hell are you frightened about me?" And finally he said, "Well, Jesus, you just won the Academy Award and everything else." And I said, "What? You, a guy with all your credits—you can't be serious. Afraid to work with me?" But it was a put-on. He was just putting me on!

Glenn's fondest memories of *Jubal* had to do with the young actress who played his love interest. "Felicia was just lovely," he recalled. "Very pretty and smart. I was very fond of her. There was something between us, but let's just leave it at that. She married a great guy [Jack Lemmon], and I know they were very happy together."

My dad described an incident with another costar, Rod Steiger, that he found rather revealing. Rod had been a devotee of the Method, a type of acting taught by Lee Strasberg and practiced by Marlon Brando, James Dean, and others. Glenn recalled:

One day we were set up ready to shoot, and Steiger wasn't in his place ready to shoot the scene. We figured he was still in his dressing room, but we heard what we thought was him behind a wagon. Eddie Saeta, our assistant director, found him behind a wagon gagging himself to throw up in order to get into the character he envisioned for his role.

That was Rod Steiger, a fine actor but a real strange fellow. When I was a young actor I followed Spencer Tracy's advice, "Learn your lines, hit your mark, don't bump into any props, and do the scene." That's all a good actor needs to know in my opinion. "Doing nothing well" is my definition of a good actor. One of the great misconceptions about this business is that you get in front of a camera and "act." That's the very thing an actor should *not* do. Be yourself—people need to identify with you. If they're not able to, you're in trouble.

On location, it seemed, there was as much high drama off the set as on. My father found himself in the middle of one crisis involving two locals. As director Delmer Daves's son Mike recalled for me:

We were all having an early breakfast before starting work. Suddenly the waitress who served us came running out in tears. She had had some kind of big blowup with the cook. The cook was very threatening, and Glenn got in the middle of it. The cook drew a knife. We were at the door watching this, and it was pretty dramatic stuff—this wasn't some movie. The guy looked ready to lunge at him with the knife. But Glenn had his Marine training, he could certainly handle himself, and he was at the top of his game. He argued him down, made him drop the knife. His force of personality really dominated this cook. It certainly left an impression on me.

It was back to MGM for Glenn's next assignment—*Ransom!*—a kidnap drama adapted by Cyril Hume and Richard Maibaum from a television episode of *The United States Steel Hour*. The studios had begun to switch their attitude to television, and now it was "if you can't beat 'em, join 'em." The big-screen versions of small-screen dramas like the Oscar-winning *Marty* proved that audiences would pay to see some shows that had already been offered free of charge in their living rooms. Most of the action of *Ransom!* took place in a family's suburban living room, and Dad would be backed by another fine supporting cast headed by Donna Reed and Leslie Nielsen (at the start of his career, with real stardom in the *Naked Gun* movies still decades away).

The story recounted the kidnapping of a child and how the parents are affected by the ordeal of negotiating for his return. In the film's most memorable scene, the child's father, Glenn's character, goes on television waving the ransom money and declaring that it will be used as a bounty to find the kidnappers if anything happens to his son. At the time it was filmed some pundits said this highlight constituted one of the longest sustained close-ups in movie history. My father topped Lionel Barrymore's courtroom speech in *A Free Soul* and Luise Rainer's Oscar-winning telephone scene in *The Great Ziegfeld*. He was on-screen for the entire close-up, running some 650 feet of film and covering more than three minutes of dialogue, with Dad speaking directly into the camera.

The plot twists in *Ransom!* were more contrived than sensible, but the film carries an emotional wallop, and Dad's performance is outstanding, particularly in the gripping television scene—his sense of desperation and anger boiling over—and again in his reunion with his kidnapped son, played by ten-year-old Bobby Clark.

Clark recalled working with Glenn Ford and the challenges of that final scene:

> My goodness, what a wonderful performer he was. He was so sweet to work with. He was right there, always. He was kind to work with me off-camera when he didn't have to do that. After his stuff was all done he could have left, and an assistant would have had to feed me lines. But he insisted on being off-camera to read the lines to me. I was very impressed with him and learned a lot.
>
> He would give me great advice about motion picture acting. He explained that you needed to hold back something from the audience, don't give them everything you knew about the character, let the audience sit on the edge of their seat and do some of the work, make them participate.
>
> For that last scene together we didn't rehearse it much. We were sort of on the same page and wanted it to be natural. We didn't want much direction; it seemed to just come out of both of our souls. That guy *was* my dad in the scene.

It was no coincidence that once again my father was playing the decent, strong-willed Everyman taking a brave stand against injustice. The critical and box-office success of *Blackboard Jungle* prompted MGM to craft vehicles for my father with the same type of character and story and thematic elements. Even the western the studio lined up for him next, *The Fastest Gun Alive*, was an unusually thoughtful character study with a serious underlying "social message."

Being a major star under contract at a major Hollywood studio was comparable to reigning like a potentate in a utopian village. In his permanent MGM dressing room—number 5, really a three-room suite with a bed, bath, and more—everything was provided and everything was complimentary. Increasingly, it became his sanctuary, his home away from home, and Dad would stay overnight if he worked late or if there was trouble at home. No doubt it was also the convenient site of late-night rendezvous best kept secret from Mom—and the public.

MGM in those days was a full-service plant. One could dine in the beautifully appointed commissary. Do you need a shoeshine or a haircut? Just go to the barbershop (that's where he took me when I was a kid). An oil change or a car wash? See the head of the transportation department. For medical needs the studio physician was always on call. If you wanted clothes for that special party, stop by the wardrobe department. Supplies like wood, nails, and hardware for work at home—those were available from the mill. Why buy a certain book or furniture when it was there for the asking from the property department?

Ransom! was released on January 20, 1956, and met with great success from the moviegoing public. The buzz in town was that Glenn Ford was a shoe-in for an Oscar nomination. However, when the Academy Award nominations were released on March 6, Dad was again conspicuous by his absence. Edwin Martin of the Copley News Service complained publicly: "Glenn Ford, who gave performances of Academy stature in four films, *Interrupted Melody*, *Blackboard Jungle*, *Trial* and the recent *Ransom!*, was not even mentioned."

Jack Moffitt of the *Hollywood Reporter* said it all at the end of his review of *Ransom!*: "From the start to finish it is Glenn Ford's picture. We talk and rightly so, of the importance of 'new' faces. But what of a man like Ford, who for almost twenty years has with patience, perseverance and humility struggled to make something out of every lousy script this town could throw at him? During the past year, he has given four performances that can be reasonably called historic. People talk about his 'lucky breaks.' But luck had very little to do with it. Every fragment of that triumph has been honestly earned and unremittingly worked for."

Although I know in my heart that my father was disappointed never to be honored with an Oscar nomination or award, I never heard him complain aloud.

The Fastest Gun Alive featured Glenn as George Temple, a seemingly timid married man and shopkeeper who is also an expert with a six-gun. Once,

George tells people, he was a deadly gunslinger. A crazed bandit played by Broderick Crawford, roaming the West to confront anyone who challenges his own claim to be the "fastest gun," hears of George's skill with a pistol and comes to town to spur a showdown. But, it is revealed, the fearless gunman George claims to be was actually his father. Long ago he failed to save his father from a fatal attack, and ever since he has lived with a crippling guilt complex.

Directed by Russell Rouse and written by Rouse and Frank Gilroy, *The Fastest Gun Alive* was an original, riveting story that managed to borrow the beloved clichés of familiar westerns—with a strong nod to *High Noon*—while turning many of those conventions upside down. This was one of the best "adult westerns" examining the nature of courage and violence and responsibility. Both the hero and villain were psychologically damaged, driven figures.

The character Glenn was playing had to have a credible quick-draw, and my father, who hated fakery in a role, began working on his technique far in advance of the filming. "I had two teachers I used," Dad recalled, "Rodd Redwing and a gun expert by the name of Carl Pitti. We actually got them both parts in the picture so I could turn to them for advice. I trained mainly on a single-action Colt. And with all modesty I have to say I got pretty damn good at it."

My father did take this part of his performance very seriously. He would come home many days and want to practice his quick-draw, and I was drafted to be his opponent in imaginary showdowns. Well, this was some serious fun for a boy. We'd go out into the yard, face off, and blast each other over and over, using blanks of course, until Mother broke up our gun battles with a call to dinner.

My dad loved the second chance to work with Brod Crawford, who was a unique, larger-than-life character. Have I already mentioned that Crawford was a world-class drinker who didn't let a little thing like making a movie get in the way of his nonstop alcohol intake? He was apparently bombed during most of his waking hours but managed to deliver a memorable performance anyway. I heard it said that once in a while during a take and with the camera rolling Brod's eyes would suddenly roll to the back of his head, and he would take a brief nap. "We were good pals and went out for a drink or two," my father admitted. "Brod knew how to have a good time, let me put it like that. We had some very crazy adventures, but luckily the next day nobody could remember exactly what happened the night before."

Another member of the cast was the wonderful actor and dancer Russ Tamblyn (perhaps best known as the leader of the Jets in *West Side Story*);

it was the first of three pictures he appeared in with my dad starring. Russ offered these memories of my father and working on *Fastest Gun*:

It was a contract assignment, and I didn't really want to do it because it was a nothing part. Except that they said I could do my own dance number. And I learned later that Glenn tried to get it cut out of the movie! And I can understand why. Most westerns might have a little musical interlude where some dance hall girls come out and do a couple of kicks. And I guess I was supposed to do a little folksy number. They didn't know I would go all over the barn with the thing. Alex Romero and I worked out the choreography. And Glenn just flipped out. "Hey, this is a little western here, and this guy is coming in and doing a Donald O'Connor all over the walls!"

They *did* cut the number out. But at the first sneak preview they forgot to cut out the line in the credits: "Russ Tamblyn dance number choreographed by Alex Romero." So a lot of the people in the preview audience complained, "Where was the dance number?" So they put it back in! But it was funny too, because Glenn told me he really loved dancing and dancers, and of course he was married to Eleanor Powell. And I remember once I was doing a little dance and he told me, he remembered how sometimes in the morning he would hear this banging from the kitchen, and he would go in there and Eleanor would be in there tap dancing while she was making breakfast. I thought that was a cute story.

Glenn was always on top of it. One way you could see that was to watch how he made a scene work even when the person he was working with wasn't very good. In that picture he was working with Jeanne Crain. And I thought she was really wooden. She was absolutely gorgeous, but I thought she just stood there and read her lines. And Glenn was playing this complicated character, a very problematic cowboy, you know, and he had to carry the scene. I asked him afterwards one time, after a scene with her, "God, Glenn, how can you keep a straight face?" He said, "It's hard. It's hard." ·

One thing I got from him was about makeup. I said, "Glenn, you don't wear any makeup, do you?" He said, "Yes I do. I've got a little under my chin." And he explained he wore black, dark makeup under his chin to firm up the jaw. I thought that was smart. I think I started to mimic him a little bit. I even started combing my hair forward the way he did.

The Fastest Gun Alive is one of those pictures that catch people by surprise when they stumble upon it. It doesn't have a major reputation as a western classic, but almost everyone who happens to come across it playing on television sometime always ends up saying what a terrific movie it is.

This was a heady time in my father's career. In some ways he was on top of the world. We didn't see him much at home, but at least family life was calm.

In many ways his next film for MGM would be his most ambitious, high-profile production yet. He met his costar for the first time at lunch in the MGM commissary on June 7, 1955, and had lunch again with him and some of the other members of the cast in September, hosted by Jack Cummings, the man who had produced six of my mother's films. In the interim Dad and his costar got together for several dinners to get to know each other better; it was important to the studio, and to my father, that he like this man, the young star of, among other films, *A Streetcar Named Desire* and *On the Waterfront*—Marlon Brando.

My father was well aware of Brando's growing legend in the American acting pantheon, and he looked forward to going mano a mano against such a phenomenon in the film version of the smash Broadway comedy *The Teahouse of the August Moon*, to be produced by Cummings and directed by Daniel Mann.

Dad would play U.S. Army officer Captain Fisby, assigned to bring the benefits of postwar democracy and free enterprise to the quaint Okinawan town of Tobiki, with unexpected and farcical results. In Brando MGM made an unexpected casting choice for the role of Sakini, the captain's sly, hustling local interpreter and go-between with the Okinawan community. But after several years of groundbreaking and often grueling dramatic parts, Brando was as eager as my father to extend his range and show his lighter side, first in the musical comedy *Guys and Dolls* and now in the droll *Teahouse of the August Moon*.

This film would entail another long journey away from home—to Japan. Dad invoked his no-fly clause once again, this time not only because of his fear of flying but because he felt that the slow trip across the Pacific would give him valuable time to rest, read, and prepare for his work. On March 13, 1956, Dad sailed on the SS *Cleveland*, which stopped in Hawaii before continuing to Japan.

Once again he traveled with old friend Hal Clifton and his stand-in, Bill Rhinehart, all three seated nightly at the captain's table, along with another Hollywood luminary onboard, mogul Samuel Goldwyn. "I spent a good portion of the voyage playing gin rummy with Goldwyn," my father remembered wryly. "He was a lousy player and I beat him every time, much to his dismay. But he would never give up, so we had to keep playing forever."

On arrival in Japan a studio car drove them to the city of Nara. "We stayed at the Nara Hotel, a beautiful hotel built of cypress. I had never seen any place quite so beautiful, and the Japanese people were delightful, polite, and gracious. I decided this was the loveliest place anyone could ever go to make a movie. In fact, the movie was getting off to a bumpy start in Japan, as the whole country had been deluged with recurring torrential rains. Cast and crew were waiting for a letup."

Also in the cast were Eddie Albert, Harry Morgan, and Dad's longtime friend Louis Calhern. "That first evening I met up with Louis Calhern in the hotel's bar," Dad recalled. "Louis was his usual witty self, but when we were supposed to go have dinner he begged off, saying he was too tired. We made plans to do some sightseeing in Kyoto the next day. But he didn't show up and begged off every invite, staying in his room until he finally had to appear on the set."

Louis's wife had recently left him, and he was very depressed. Since arriving in Japan he had only wanted to be left alone and to drink. The depression seemed to lessen when they began working on the film, and Louis seemed to revert to his old amusing, elegant self. He still called Glenn "Hatrack" and still offered bits of wise advice just as he had twenty or so years before when Dad was a naïve young actor and Louis was even then a seasoned, seen-it-all pro. But about three weeks into filming, Calhern suffered a heart attack and died suddenly at age sixty-one. Whether it was connected to his drinking or to the stress in his life, no one could say. There was a lot of confusion and red tape about sending the body back to America, and Dad put himself in charge to make sure Louis's body was properly transported to the U.S. Army hospital in Osaka. Dad took the loss very hard, feeling a long and sentimental connection to the venerable actor, and Calhern's death put a damper on the location filming. The cast and crew didn't linger in Japan much longer because of the rainy weather anyway; they only shot about 30 percent of the film before giving up and coming back to the United States, where they restaged scenes at the studio.

The relationship between my father and Marlon Brando had started out warmly enough, but once they began working together it chilled to a smiling but barely disguised animosity. They got along fine on the surface and spent time together playing chess between takes and even did some sightseeing together, but it was clear they were never going to be on the same wavelength. My father recalled:

We'd drive back to the hotel every evening. Marlon would invariably bring up his favorite subject at the time, psychiatry. He'd say to me, "Glenn, you have got to go to a psychiatrist. It will free you of all your problems." And he would launch into all the destructive incidents in his life that he had worked out on the shrink's couch. I finally told him that as a matter of fact I had gone to a psychiatrist once years ago. Marlon got very excited and asked me to tell him exactly what had happened. I explained that I had sat there in the doctor's office and for fifty minutes the doctor told me all his problems, and then at the end of the session he pulled from his desk drawer a movie script and asked me if I thought I could show it to the studio. Marlon was very disappointed in this story.

When Brando wrote about the making of *Teahouse* in his autobiography, he went on and on about all the ways that Glenn Ford tried to upstage him. I had to laugh when I read that—and feel a certain pride. Here was Marlon Brando, who had perfected every possible way of stealing any scene that he was in, complaining that low-key, naturalistic Glenn Ford was giving him competition.

Actually, these two very different types of actors got into a certain unspoken rivalry on the set, both approaching each scene with some sly strategy that would top the other man. Both of them had an expertise in how a shift in relation to the camera could alter the impact of a performance, how it could make the audience turn away from one actor on-screen and concentrate on another. Dad liked rehearsal; Brando didn't. Brando was often late to work, didn't know his lines; Dad regarded that as selfish behavior. My father told me that Brando seldom memorized and preferred improvisation for fear of losing the realness of a situation, and, yes, he did have a reputation of being the worst ad-libber in town.

Dad admitted there were moments when he took advantage of Marlon, using some of the improvisatorial techniques he had picked up throughout his career and honed, especially, while making *Blackboard Jungle*. "In the beginning where I first address the villagers," my father explained, "I started throwing lines at Marlon that weren't in the script. I was reacting to what the people in the town were doing, playing off these characters. And it threw him. He hadn't expected to contend with that from me. It was a bit of dirty pool, I guess."

Director Daniel Mann finally had enough of the two actors and their one-upmanship. "Fellas! What are you doing!" he shouted at them one day. "You're acting like you're both a couple of twelve-year-olds instead of professionals with great talent and integrity." Mann would say in a later interview that the two stayed competitive to the end. "We survived it, but it wasn't easy."

When asked, my father was not shy about declaring the winner in the battle between himself and Marlon Brando. "Frankly, I plucked Marlon's feathers," Dad told me. "I'm not bragging—maybe I just had a better hook on my character." Columnist James Bacon was not the only commentator to write: "No one had stolen a movie from Marlon [Brando] before but Glenn Ford stole this one." His opinion was echoed by others, including columnist Hedda Hopper: "Glenn Ford's performance was magnificent; he stole the picture."

Many years later Mann praised Glenn's performance. "This was high comedy," said the director, "and he maintained a very delicate balance. He could have appeared to be very foolish, but he played the American officer with a great sense of integrity. The audience accepted that he was a good man, and so they could laugh at his fumbling and confusion without losing respect for him." None of the conflicts, however, are evident in the finished film. *Teahouse* was perfectly translated from the stage to the screen, and the two leads, one way or another, worked wonderfully together. "The year's best in comedy-drama," wrote the critic for the *Los Angeles Times*.

An interesting situation occurred when Metro closed down the production due to the poor weather in Japan and ordered everyone back to the States. I never knew exactly why my father loathed flying. I believe the claustrophobic nature of air travel bothered him, but upon arrival in Honolulu when he completed the first leg of his journey home, MGM wired him and begged him not to travel farther by ship. My father had left Japan on May 30 and arrived in Hawaii on Sunday, June 3. The production team, his costars, and the crew had flown back to America ahead of him, had assembled quickly, and were waiting to start work.

The film was severely behind schedule and over budget by this time, and producer Jack Cummings frantically pleaded with my father to take a plane for the sake of the film's schedule. Dad wanted to be a team player, so despite his apprehensions he boarded a plane on Sunday, June 4, in Honolulu so he could be home quickly and start work the next day. Then the unbelievable happened. Far out over the Pacific Ocean one of the plane's engines failed, a second engine conked out as it approached the mainland, and two other planes had to escort the craft to safety from four hundred miles out. The airliner just made it to Los Angeles International Airport, though as it touched down on the runway it spun around several times. Nobody was hurt—but my father vowed to never, ever fly again.

The good news for MGM was that during its initial release *Teahouse of the August Moon* grossed an astounding $5.6 million. The film was honored by many U.S. critics as among the year's best, Glenn and Marlon were both nominated as best actors by the Golden Globes, and the script and director were nominated for the top awards by both the writers and directors guilds that year.

But it was back to Columbia, at the end of 1956, for Glenn's next collaboration with Delmer Daves: *3:10 to Yuma*, costarring Van Heflin and Felicia Farr, based on an Elmore Leonard story, the first one to be filmed (the hardboiled author is still going strong as I write this, fifty years later).

The plot was simple and focused: an outlaw is captured, and an ordinary, struggling rancher agrees to guard him until he can be transported to jail on the afternoon train of the title. The clock ticks toward an inevitable showdown with an outlaw gang. What made *3:10 to Yuma* an unusual project for Glenn Ford was that in this one he would not be playing the stoic hero. That role, Dan Evans, would go to Van Heflin. Glenn chose instead to play against type as the villain—the leader of the stagecoach-robbing desperadoes, Ben Wade.

But this was no ordinary villain. Ben, as portrayed by Glenn, would be a sympathetic, seductive, and ultimately even noble outlaw. Dad had successfully played villainous characters before, notably in *The Man from Colorado* and *Lust for Gold*, but those performances were relatively melodramatic by comparison to the subtle, nuanced, very human villain of *3:10 to Yuma*.

The taut script was masterfully filmed by Daves on Arizona locations. Dad and Van Heflin played off each other beautifully in the battle of wits that ensues as Wade tries to undermine Dan's determination to get him on that train. Most of the action took place between the two men sitting alone in a small hotel room.

Felicia Farr was once again the leading lady of a Glenn Ford film. The supporting actors included Henry Jones, Richard Jaeckel, Ford Rainey, and the portly Robert Emhardt as Mr. Butterfield, owner of the stagecoach line. But it was a lesser-known member of the cast—Robert "Buzz" Henry, playing one of Wade's henchmen—who was destined to play a role in the Ford family's future.

Our family had fallen into a routine at home. My mother's television show was not on the air any longer, and she and my father, when he wasn't working, threw themselves into charity work. When Dad was at home, he worked around the house, which was a way of working at just being "Father." I was in the seventh grade in my second year at the exclusive and private Buckley School in the San Fernando Valley. Record collecting, reading, dreaming about girls, and escaping from real life in the world of movies were the extent of my ambitions.

We continued doing countless photo layouts and other public appearances at the behest of both the Columbia and MGM publicity departments. The publicity mill concocted magazine articles about our happy family: "The Marriage Gossip Didn't Wreck" (*Screen*, February 1956), "Hotter Than Hot" (*Movieland*, April 1956), "Private Property No Visitors" (*Movie Mirror*, May 1956), "It's Fun to Fight" (*Photoplay*, May 1956), "You Can Be Happy in Screenland" (*Picturegoer*, May 19, 1956), "Hollywood's Greatest Untold Love Story" (*Motion Picture and TV*, August 1956), and of course "Happily Married" (*Photoplay Annual*, 1957).

There were some genuinely happy times for us. Dad and I went to a few ball games together. He bought a Lambretta motor scooter, and I'd jump on the back some evenings with him. We'd drive down to the Beverly Hills business district, and he would buy a newspaper from the fellow selling them on the corner (such people still existed back then). I'd visit the studio with him on special occasions, like when *Forbidden Planet* was filming. It was a closed set (it was really "sets," as it was filmed on many stages), which meant that no visitors were allowed. I "met" Robbie the Robot and saw the space ship up close, and one of the special effects people showed me everything that surrounded Dr. Morbius and Altair IV. This was one of the perks of being a movie star's son. I even got to miss a day of school for that trip.

Another proud moment for our family was a nod from the black community for the work my father had done in *Blackboard Jungle* and *Trial* and my mother for her television show. They were both honored by the Los Angeles Urban League on February 15, 1957, when the Urban League held its Third Annual Ball at the Beverly Hilton Hotel—my father was chairman. He and actress Dorothy Dandridge accepted awards that evening. I had been taught at a very young age to be color blind when it came to race, and for this and more I honor my parents.

In May 1957 Elvis Presley came to MGM to make *Jailhouse Rock*. Since my "Rock Around the Clock" record had made such a splash at MGM,

Dad thought I should meet Elvis. Pandro Berman (who produced *Blackboard Jungle*) was producing *Jailhouse Rock*, and he set it up. We went to MGM and watched him shoot a scene and then visited him in his dressing room. Apparently, Elvis was a big Glenn Ford fan, and we had a nice visit with him and his "boys."

A few weeks later Dad brought home an autographed photo and nearly every record that Elvis had made at that time (RCA only—none of the earlier and precious Sun labels, unfortunately). After that first meeting Dad went back to the studio a few times and had lunch alone with Elvis. He took a liking to him and told me he was a very warm and pleasant fellow. Dad wasn't wild about Elvis's music and didn't know if as a singer he'd amount to anything more than a passing fad, but he thought that with diligence and determination Elvis could be a fine actor.

Don't Go Near the Water took Glenn back to MGM and reunited him with Anne Francis in their first teaming since *Blackboard Jungle*. Gia Scala, Earl Holliman, Keenan Wynn, Fred Clark, Eva Gabor, Russ Tamblyn, Jeff Richards, and Mickey Shaughnessy rounded out the cast. This little gem of a film was directed by Charles Walters, following *The Tender Trap* and *High Society*.

The story was about a landlubber public relations operation run by the U.S. Navy on a South Pacific island during World War II. The William Brinkley novel had brimmed with laughter and sentiment, and the screenplay by Dorothy Kingsley and George Wells only enhanced these qualities. It grossed a respectable $4.5 million when the counting was done, and my father won a Laurel Award as best actor in a comedy role from the Motion Picture Exhibitors.

Shot entirely in Los Angeles, it was a very pleasant film for Dad to make, but probably his good memory of the making of this film is due to making the acquaintance of a woman he would almost marry in the future—Eva Gabor.

10

"Singin' the Blues"

Many Hollywood movies have a long and circuitous history before they finally come to life on-screen, and *Cowboy* was one of them. It was based on a memoir by Frank Harris about a daydreaming Chicago hotel clerk who decides to join up with a tough cattle driver and his outfit and learns to be a real man of the West. John Huston purchased the film rights in the late 1940s, hoping to star in the picture with his father, but Walter died in 1949, and the project was abandoned for a while. Huston then resurrected the film in the early 1950s with Spencer Tracy as the intended lead and Montgomery Clift as the young dude. By June 1954 Clift was out, and there was discussion with Columbia about my father playing the younger part. By 1956 it looked like it might be Gary Cooper and Alan Ladd, but the project was again shelved, until Delmer Daves went to Harry Cohn and pitched the idea that Glenn Ford could play the veteran cowboy; Cohn agreed. Dad insisted that the irrepressible Jack Lemmon—who was courting Felicia Farr—was the perfect choice to play Frank Harris.

Glenn invited Jack to have lunch with him at the Naples Restaurant up the street from the Columbia lot, telling him about the picture and the part. My father recalled:

Jack was flattered but told me he couldn't do it. He said, "The last time I rode a horse I was about eleven years old, back in New England where I

178

was born, and it was an English saddle. And I didn't like it! And there's no time for me to learn how to ride before this picture starts shooting." I said, "Don't worry about that. I'll get you a good horse." We were having cocktails, and I ordered us another round and then another one after that and told the waiter to keep them coming. After each drink I would press my case for Jack being in the picture, and each time he was a little more open to my suggestion. Jack claimed later that I was pouring my drinks into the potted plant behind me. Many drinks later Jack decided he could ride a horse after all and he wanted to be in this picture very much. The only problem he had on his mind by then was figuring out how to stand up without falling down and how to find his way back to the studio.

In due time, the *Cowboy* cast and crew checked into La Fonda Hotel in Santa Fe, New Mexico. Jack had forgotten about his aversion to horses until the first day of shooting. As often happens in making movies, scenes were shot out of chronological order, and Jack's first day's work called for a sequence that actually took place at the end of the movie, when he was supposedly transformed into a hardened cowboy now respected by the other cowboys. It meant literally jumping into the saddle from day one. Unfortunately, as Jack recalled it, Glenn's promise of finding him a "good" horse had been forgotten. The wranglers put Lemmon onto a quarter horse named Sunday who instantly broke into an uncontrollable run and knocked down three members of the crew.

Jack had to remain on horseback for nearly the entire first day. What began as discovery in the morning progressed to agony by late afternoon. He looked with awe at his fellow actor's skill as a horseman. "Glenn was superb. I've never seen a guy sit in a saddle like he did. His body didn't even move."

By the time the day was over, Jack Lemmon couldn't even get off the horse, he was in such pain. Three men were needed to lift him down from the saddle. The all-day riding had torn open the flesh on Jack's backside. He was taken in hand by some of the tough cowboy extras and stuntmen. They took his pants down, and someone poured a bottle of booze onto the split skin. They told him that would toughen him up as Jack screamed in pain. "It toughened me up all right," Jack recalled. "I had to wear a Kotex every day for two months while I was on that friggin' horse. I was never off the damn thing long enough to let it heal. I wanna tell you, by this time I could have killed Glenn Ford with my bare hands!"

After location work in Santa Fe, the filming was done at the Columbia Ranch in Burbank, where a facsimile of the El Paso stockyard was erected complete with functioning cattle cars. A key dramatic sequence involved

Glenn and Jack stuck in one of the cars among the cattle and Glenn having to save Jack from being trampled and gored by the angry longhorns. Director Daves set up three cameras to shoot through the slats in the cattle car. Injections of sedatives were given to the cattle to keep them from becoming uncontrollable, with representatives from the Humane Society in place to make sure that nothing harmful happened to the beasts. Meanwhile, the two humans, Glenn and Jack, found themselves very much in harm's way.

Daves had decided that the scene could not be shot with stunt doubles, as he wanted the camera close to the action. Jack Lemmon was carefully positioned under a fallen cow that he was supposed to be trying to coax back upright. Glenn, meanwhile, was in place on top of the two-by-fours of the cattle car, waiting for his cue to jump in and help Jack, who had become trapped.

Lemmon, scared to death as he recalled it, surrounded by restless cattle with giant horns and heavy hooves, took hold of the fallen steer's horns so they wouldn't stab him when the animal rose up. When the steer did not appear to be moving as expected, a prop man leaned through the wooden slats and zapped it with a cattle prod. Suddenly, Lemmon found himself literally airborne as the steer came to life as though shot out of a cannon. The other cattle stirred nervously, and suddenly those horns and hooves were in motion all around Jack. He described the scene:

> Glenn screamed for them to get me out of there. He couldn't come down to help me, as he would have had to jump right into the horns. It was very hairy—nobody knew what to do. And I remember looking up and seeing Del Daves with a look of panic on his face. And I'll never forget, still thinking like a director, Del waved his arms at the cattle and yelled, "CUT!" Not at the cameras, but at the fucking steers!
>
> When he could find a clear space, Glenn jumped down to help me. And a moment later a steer kicked backwards, and the hooves shot right through the two-by-fours exactly where Glenn's leg had been a moment before.

Despite the risks, pain, and physical exhaustion, both Dad and Jack managed to look back on the filming of *Cowboy* as a largely enjoyable, sometimes thrilling experience. "I learned a lot," said Jack. "That was still fairly early on, and Glenn did help me a helluva lot. I leaned on him a little. I depended on Glenn a lot more than he thought. And he was a very giving actor, whether it was with a kid who had one line or the lead opposite him. He's one of the better screen actors I've ever worked with, without any question. And a terrific guy, personally."

Cowboy ended Dad's collaboration with Delmer Daves, though they remained good friends afterward. The three westerns they made together, I believe—and many agree with me—stand up as some of the best ever made. "It was always a lot of hard work doing a picture with Del," mused my father, "but it was always worth it. I can't tell you why Del and I worked so well together. We just had good chemistry right from day one. Del was like Fritz Lang. He knew exactly what he wanted to get from every shot he made. Very precise, very well prepared. I owe a lot to Del for helping me achieve my goal of portraying a real cowboy, not an actor pretending to be a cowboy."

My father had enjoyed incredible success during the mid-1950s, a virtually uninterrupted run of first-rate films—critical hits, big box-office winners, a few stone-cold cinema classics, a series of memorable and varied performances. This period culminated in 1958 with Glenn Ford being named the number one box-office star in the world by the Motion Picture Exhibitors of America. When you stop and think about what his big-name competition in Hollywood was in that year—John Wayne, Cary Grant, Marlon Brando, Gregory Peck, Gary Cooper, Burt Lancaster, Bill Holden, Jimmy Stewart, Robert Mitchum, Elvis Presley, Jerry Lewis, Marilyn Monroe, Elizabeth Taylor, and so on—I think one could call that a hard-won competition. My father was very proud of his achievement.

At the same time, it must be said that the films with which he closed out the decade were not quite in the same league as the ones that preceded them. Starting with *The Sheepman* in 1958, however, they were all first-rate entertainments. This comic western reunited Dad with the man he always called his favorite director: George Marshall. They had not worked together since George had walked off the set of *Lust for Gold* back in 1949. But my father often said he had never enjoyed making any picture more than *Texas*, his first one with George in 1941. Now, with the clout to pick his directors, he returned to a man he considered a mentor, a friend, and one of the most talented and entertaining characters in the movie business. Dad and George would make no fewer than five pictures together in the next four years, four alone in 1958 and 1959.

The Sheepman, a hilarious western from a superb script by William Bowers, would be followed by *Imitation General*, a wartime comedy-drama with Glenn masquerading as a dead general to boost morale at the front, the romantic comedy *It Started with a Kiss*, and the blackly comic *The Gazebo* and *Cry for Happy*.

Bill Bowers had written Dad's earlier film *Convicted* (1950), and he would also write *Imitation General*, another offbeat western. *The Sheepman* lured actress Shirley MacLaine away from Paramount and reteamed my father with Leslie Nielsen, who had had a modest, third-billed role in *Ransom!* Mickey Shaughnessy was also back working with Dad, and Edgar Buchanan was pulling his usual scene-stealing maneuvers in a comedic take on a serious subject (at least in the 1880s) about sheep and cattle grazing on the same range, with my dad and Leslie Nielsen representing the hostile beef and mutton camps, respectively.

The Sheepman was so popular with audiences that MGM immediately gave Dad and George Marshall the go-ahead for *Imitation General*. Actor Dean Jones was in the cast of that film and recalled the working relationship of the star and director:

What a fun experience that was. George, God love him, was a character. He was a hoot. I grew to love George Marshall. The relationship he had with Glenn was just tremendous. I had so much fun watching them, and I learned so much. I had never seen any director, in my three years I had been at Metro, operate the way George worked with Glenn. It was remarkable. They would be doing a scene from the script, and right in the middle of it, George would say, "Cut!" and yell to Glenn, "Right there why don't you say something like such and such" or "Go around and do such and such."

He would just stop Glenn while they were rolling film and toss him a new line or a new idea. And Glenn would nod and say, "Okay! No problem at all."

There was no rehearsal, just do something new. And George would say, "Let's roll." And the camera would turn again, and Glenn would throw in the new line. This is what they did all the time, back and forth to each other. Sometimes it brought a whole new life to a scene.

It was electrifying to watch them, the way they could bounce things back and forth. I had been directed by other directors, including some great and famous ones, like Vincente Minnelli. Minnelli would line up everything the way he wanted it, not a hair should be out of place. I remember, I was passing by the stage, and I saw Minnelli on the set, long before the scene was to be shot, concentrated, adjusting an ashtray to just the place where he wanted it on the table. With George Marshall, though, it was less like you were shooting a movie than being at a fun party. And between George and Glenn there was a creative freedom like I had never seen before.

Robert "Buzz" Henry, who had worked with Dad on his last two westerns for Columbia, played a small role as a tank commander in *Imitation General*. By now he had also become my father's stunt double. Dad often claimed he did all his stunts, and while many times he did—especially riding horses—Buzz often doubled for Dad over the next ten years on the more difficult "gags," as the stunts were called.

Buzz became another surrogate father, insofar as my dad designated him to teach me about the birds and the bees as a part of my coming of age. Other fathers and sons have one of those sit-down awkward conversations, I suppose. In my case, it was during a late-night outing with Buzz and a bunch of cowboy stuntmen viewing a series of stag films in an East Los Angeles movie theater. I was almost thirteen years old, and I did have a vague idea of what went on between a man and a woman sexually, but sitting in the dark watching a big movie screen—women cavorting with animals and naked men doing things I can't describe—boy, did I get educated. And it was terrifying.

Believe me, stuntmen live in a separate universe, but the stag films put a new light on the meaning of Dad's film *The Sheepman*. Seeing what these women were doing with livestock on-screen . . . I remember that someone, not in our group, got up in the middle of the film and relieved himself against the theater wall near where I was seated. After the film was over, Buzz and the boys thought it was a swell idea to complete my education by taking me to a whorehouse to experience the delights of lovemaking myself, first stopping at a bar on the way. I knew that I needed to get back to the safety of my own bed in Beverly Hills as soon as possible, but I could only achieve this retreat from stuntman heaven with great difficulty, as they had been instructed by my dear father to bring me back "bred." I'm sure the stuntmen were in fear of their jobs, had they failed, but I reassured them that my introduction to the pleasures of sexual bliss would have to wait, and Dad would forgive them.

This particular outing was not as well covered by the press as most of the other high points of our lives. The very week after this adventure, for example, I participated in a four-page feature layout for the *Saturday Evening Post* (January 4, 1958) titled, "I Can Always Escape," which pictured my father and me building something in his workshop. The caption under the photograph read: "The author and his son, Peter, 12, at work in the workshop of the Fords' home in Beverly Hills." "What balances your life," Glenn was quoted, "is not only play but hard manual work."

Boy, did he get that right! Except that, around our house, I did all the work under the watchful eye of the trail boss—my dad. It's a good thing they didn't ask me about the "happy life" I was really living or what had transpired with Buzz and his buddies the week before. But of course I was trained to be guarded and would never have said anything to compromise our carefully crafted public image.

Torpedo Run was Dad's first war movie in years. Dad played the commander of a submarine in the Pacific on the trail of the Japanese fleet. Just as the western had gone "adult," the World War II movie had evolved from the gung-ho stories of the 1940s to a more somber presentation, with my father's Lt. Cdr. Barney Doyle a troubled and war-weary figure.

A huge water tank on a soundstage stood in for the Pacific in this film, and Dad, Ernest Borgnine, and thirty other actors squeezed (and I do mean squeezed) into a submarine built by the studio down to every possible detail. For the film's dramatic evacuation scene, the conning tower set was lowered into the water tank, and the water was allowed to enter the structure and rise up around the actors playing the sub crew. The actors were using authentic World War II U.S. Navy breathing devices called Momsen Lungs, which proved to be problematic. Actor Dean Jones, playing a member of the crew, explained to me:

> This was 1958, and this equipment had been lying around in some storeroom since World War II ended. They had been packed for all those years with some sort of preservative, a fine powdery substance, and when you sucked in air through the lung, a little bit of that powder would come into your throat. It became very difficult not to start coughing. Some of the actors inhaled too much of the powder and started to gag. And as the water came up over our heads inside this small space, one man really panicked. He began flailing with his hands as he was trying to get ahead of everyone to the escape hatch. And in the process he pulled some of the breathing tubes out of some actors' mouths, and there was an all-out panic. It became a very desperate situation for a while.

Torpedo Run has never been considered to be in the same class as such better-known submarine dramas as *Run Silent, Run Deep*, *Das Boot*, and *The Hunt for Red October*, but I have to say that through the years my father would often run into or receive letters from Navy veterans who told him that *Torpedo* was their favorite and the most realistic submarine movie they had ever seen.

In February 1958 Harry Cohn died of a sudden heart attack. He was sixty-six years old. Harry's name would always set off a mix of emotions for my father. Harry was argumentative, offensive, and often wrongheaded and had made many mistakes in managing my father's career. But he was the man, more than any other powerful figure in Hollywood, who had believed in my father as a movie star. There is the famous old joke attributed to Red Skelton about the large crowd at Harry Cohn's funeral: "Give the public what they want, and they'll come out." But Dad marked Harry's passing with a great deal of sorrow and respect.

As it happened, *Torpedo Run* had wrapped on May 22, 1958, and my father was scheduled to go back to Columbia for his next film per his contractual obligation. With Harry Cohn's passing, however, the studio was thrown into turmoil. Cohn had been trying to talk Dad into doing a drama called *The Last Angry Man*, but Dad, preferring another western, had refused. Paul Muni was to be the costar, playing a stronger part that Dad felt would smother his character. The studio had Dad's part rewritten to build it up, but Dad still didn't like the script, and, having sworn that he'd never start another film with the "we'll make it better later" promise, he refused again. Maybe Cohn and Dad would have worked something out if the mogul had lived, but the new management—namely, Sam Briskin—was angered by Dad's stubbornness.

On June 4, for the first time in eighteen years, after making thirty films for Columbia, Glenn was sued for $676,876 (the preproduction costs for *The Last Angry Man*) and put on suspension. The studio tried to get an injunction to stop Dad from working at any other studio, which caused Dad to lose work for the next nine months while MGM and Columbia resolved the dispute. It was an unfortunate turn of events for everyone, and Dad wouldn't work again at Columbia for three years.

Yet Dad had been earning good wages with MGM, and although he was unemployed for a while, he didn't suffer. Because of his hilarious and endearing performance in *Teahouse of the August Moon* he was being offered a wider range of material than ever before—as many comedies as dramas and action films. Except for this one forced hiatus, the late 1950s and early 1960s were very busy years for my father, making three and even four films in a single year.

Many of these films were elaborate productions that entailed distant and lengthy location trips. Work kept him away from home for months at a time. When he was away I would miss him and wish he were home with us more often. But then he returned, and after a few days when we would all be together again, the old tensions would resume. And still it seemed that I always was caught in the middle, even if I had nothing to do with the disputes between my parents. I would be punished for the slightest infraction in a most effective way—I called it psychological torture. My father never struck me or was physically abusive. However, one of Dad's methods of discipline was to call me into his bedroom, close the door, sit me on the edge of his bed, and verbally berate me about whatever I had done wrong, or what he perceived I had done wrong, until I broke down in apologetic tears. Ironically, that became the key to my freedom: I learned that if the crying came quickly enough, I could avoid Drill Sergeant Ford's further humiliation of my already insecure and vulnerable psyche.

Of course, I would emerge a basketcase from these ordeals, head to my room, and wait for my mother to find me there and coddle me with love and attention—which further incurred my father's wrath. If Mother was going to spoil me, in his eyes, then he would have to be the one to discipline me; he was determined that I not end up "sissified." In my mother's eyes, contrarily, I could do no wrong. In my father's eyes, I sometimes felt, I could do nothing right.

In Peter Ustinov's 1962 film adaptation of Herman Melville's *Billy Budd*, Billy asks, "What was his crime?" upon seeing another man being flogged.

> "Any one of many possible reasons," Dansker the sail-maker replied. "You mean you don't know what he did?"
> "Flogging," Dansker replies. "The only answer to every problem. I warrant even the culprit himself doesn't know! It was just . . . his . . . turn."

In retaliation for my mother's seeming overindulgence of me, my father would assign me more and more chores, which seemed increasingly daunting as the years went on. On most Saturdays I had to stay at home and take care of our huge property, doing things like chopping up trees for the fireplaces and painting, raking, digging, or planting any number of things on our property. I was very unhappy a lot of the time and wondered why my father was so hard on me.

There were times, days, when my father and mother seemed to be getting along. I couldn't know all that went on out of my sight, arguments and such, but I could sense when things had turned sour again—as they inevitably did. Dad didn't want the marriage to end, but neither did he want to repair the damage that had been done. He was gone most of the time, and he was having affairs.

At last, my mother had enough. Characteristically, she was more concerned for my welfare than her own—she didn't want me to witness any more of the coldness and hostility that too often filled the house. She began seeing lawyers.

First there was Jerry Geisler, the legendary "celebrity lawyer" famous for defending Robert Mitchum, Errol Flynn, and Lana Turner in their various legal difficulties. Geisler was a tough, take-no-prisoners type who wanted Mom to file against Glenn on charges of adultery and essentially blackmail him with scandalous threats unless he made a very generous settlement. Again, my mother feared the effect of a messy divorce on her family and would have nothing to do with Geisler's plans, even if it meant accepting a more modest financial arrangement. She settled on another attorney, Robert Neeb, during the period of time when my father could not work due to the *Angry Man* problem.

Dad's inactivity had made him stir-crazy. He still was receiving his MGM salary, but nine months at home with nothing much to do had provided opportunities for mischief and further estrangement among all of us.

As he was preparing to leave for Spain on my fourteenth birthday to make his first film since *Torpedo Run*, my mother announced her intention to seek a divorce. She made it clear this was not just another disagreement that would blow over. She had her lawyer, she would get a legal separation, a divorce would follow.

My father told her they would talk about it when he got back from Europe, but he must have understood that this time it was serious. On a long trip to the filming location he had plenty of time to think. He took a train to New York City with a stay-over at the Plaza Hotel, then boarded the RMS *Queen Elizabeth* to Southampton, England, then traveled by train to London with a four-day rest at the Connaught Hotel, where he met up with his buddy Bill Holden for drinks and a night on the town and, I'm sure, some marital soul searching.

Then it was off to Paris by ship across the English Channel and rail to the "City of Lights." A few days in Paris—staying at the George V—turned into two weeks when Glenn received notice that the arrival of co-star Debbie Reynolds was delayed and the picture would start late. He eventually arrived in Madrid by train on March 5 but already had been gone from home for a month. The communications between him and Mom had been few and terse.

Dad's friend and favorite director, George Marshall, was once again directing him in *It Started with a Kiss*, his first film with Debbie Reynolds. That rowdy father figure dashed out to greet Glenn when he arrived at the lobby of the Palace Hotel in Madrid, shouting, "Glenn, where the hell have you been?"

"I've been in Paris, George. I didn't want to sit around Madrid waiting for the picture to start when I could be in Paris."

"But Glenn, we had work to do," George said.

"What work?"

"The night life! I've been waiting for you so we could enjoy it together. There's a lot a man can do in Madrid."

My father looked dazed and depressed. He gave George a rundown of his domestic situation. He had been drinking steadily on the train from Paris and looked it. George's answer was, naturally, let's go out and get drunk.

"Put it out of your mind," George told him. "By the time you get back home, Ellie will have forgotten about it."

The director's tireless high spirits did manage to lessen my father's dark mood, at least enough to get a good, relaxed performance out of him in the fluffy romantic comedy they were making with Glenn and Debbie as two sweethearts, both in states of distress about their respective marriages.

Debbie was in the midst of a humiliating scandal. She had been married to singer Eddie Fisher, and the two had been labeled by the fan magazines as America's sweethearts. Eddie was a good friend to showman and moviemaker Mike Todd, who was married to Elizabeth Taylor. When Todd died in a plane crash, Eddie ended up consoling Elizabeth and abandoning Debbie. It was a major Hollywood scandal at the time, topped only a couple of years later when Elizabeth dumped Eddie to consort with Richard Burton on the set of *Cleopatra*.

Debbie would become one of my father's lifelong friends, though not right away. I asked her to recall for me their bumpy start on location in Spain.

I had met Glenn before, but not as a friend. He was one of those who hung out with the guys, like Spencer Tracy, Clark Gable. You didn't meet them anywhere because those guys all hung out with other guys. I knew Eleanor, and I had been to their house, to a charity event—a fashion show on behalf of the Jewish Home for the Aged, girls modeling dresses out by the pool. It was a pretty day. I remember I liked the house very much. Eleanor was just the sweetest person. It seemed like a very happy house. Little did I know . . .

On our first day of shooting in Madrid, we were at the bullring, all made up and ready, sitting in our trailers, and it started to rain. They say they'll tell me when they can start working. And Eva Gabor, who was in the picture, came to the trailer and said, "Dahling, I'm so lonesome, can I sit with you?" And so Eva came in and started telling me stories. It got later, and the sky got darker. Finally, we realized they had forgotten about us. Everybody had left.

We were by ourselves in the dark in a trailer somewhere in Madrid. We had no phone, no pesos, or pesetas, whatever it was. And we were in our little robes. Eventually, we found a car, and Eva offered the driver a piece of her jewelry to take us back to the hotel. And we got there, tired and angry and a little scared. And there was George Marshall and Glenn and the guys in the crew in the lobby bar, drinking and smoking and laughing. They'd been there for hours.

And Eva and I stood there and bawled them all out, and George, who was loaded, said we had no sense of humor, and then we ran to our rooms in tears. That was the first day of shooting! But from then on we were very well taken care of, and it was Glenn who made sure of that. Always running around checking, "Did you get the girls? Make sure you get the girls!" And he became the big daddy, making sure nothing like that ever happened to us again.

We would sit around after work, Glenn, Eva, and I. Glenn finally began to talk about his situation—that he and Eleanor might be separating. I was really sad at that time to hear it because I didn't know the problems and I didn't know what her story was. And he would try to explain himself, of course. And we were taking the girl's side, of course—because Eddie Fisher had just left me, and no man was going to get a good ear from me. He'd want to talk about Eleanor and his marriage, and I really didn't want to hear his side.

I was a little hard on him. And then Glenn started making eyes at Eva. He didn't make eyes at me because I wasn't in the mood. I just had my husband leave me and my two little children. And had he made eyes at me, I probably would have punched him. And Eva had a boyfriend who was arriving any minute, so she wasn't really that interested in Glenn anyway. He had this fabulous wife and son, and he was upset, but he couldn't resist looking and patting. He was hot to trot. He loved women, loved to look at them, to pat them, touch them. I think Glenn flirted with every woman he ever worked with. He liked to play, and he always wanted to have his cake and eat it, too.

I'd say to him, "Why would your wife want to leave you? You're handsome, a little shy. You're wonderful, so why would she leave you? Obviously, you did something awful!"

My father liked Debbie very much as a talent and as a person. She was feminine, strong, funny, down to earth, a straight shooter. And Debbie decided that whatever he had done wrong in his marriage or in his life, she liked Glenn very much too. Despite their differences, they became great friends.

After three weeks on location in Spain, cast and crew returned to Hollywood for several weeks of interiors on the Metro lot. In the intervening time, I think because my mother told my father she wanted a divorce, coupled with Debbie's advice on location, Dad had contemplated his role as husband and father more seriously. Mother did file for separation, but while Dad was finishing *It Started with a Kiss* back home at the studio he was never a better father. From Spain he brought an armload of stamps for my stamp collection. We spent a lot of time together in the workshop. We went to a number of Dodgers baseball games. He even promised me he'd find a role for me in his next film. It was great.

Unfortunately, it was too late. On May 1, 1959 (my father's forty-third birthday, as it happened), my mother filed for divorce in Santa Monica Superior Court. Despite her hope to avoid publicity, it was a headline story, and for weeks the Hollywood gossip columnists speculated about the cause of the breakup.

Dad had wrapped up *It Started with a Kiss* at the studio on April 23, 1959, and enjoyed a party at Debbie Reynolds's home the following day. As he said his good-byes, Dad told Debbie how excited he was that MGM had decided to pair them up in another film to start in just three months. In the week that followed Debbie's "wrap" party, my father attended to projects around the house, worked in his garden, and continued, I think for the first time, to try to be my sincere friend.

I don't think Dad knew what awaited him. I think he might have felt that he had reclaimed Mom's heart and she would take him back, but only a week later he was served the divorce papers. In hindsight, it was odd that Dad was not more proactive in doing anything to make amends to my mother: no flowers or baubles were forthcoming. Perhaps he thought reconciliation would just happen, just like a happy dissolve in a movie. Indeed, it had happened before.

I remember that first week in May as a very unpleasant week. Even though he knew that proceedings had begun, he told my mother he had no intention of moving out of the house—it was his house, too, and he dug in. All the recent happiness I had shared with him vanished in an instant.

The three of us lived together in the house for the next five months. If there had been tensions in the house before, now it was like an armed camp. My father lived at one end and my mother at the other end, with me, back in my familiar place, in the middle. Dad was home every day after his return from Spain, and in June I was home on summer vacation from Buckley School. I was just fourteen and at an age when I really needed a father in my life. But instead Mom and I—and I suppose Dad too—were in a siege mentality.

For nearly five months, seldom was a word spoken between my parents, and when they wanted to say something to each other, I became the interlocutor—the situation was beyond grim.

In the new MGM film reteaming him and Debbie Reynolds, *The Gazebo*, Glenn was playing the part acted on Broadway by Walter Slezak. En route to Spain in the summer of 1959, he took the train to New York, as was his custom, staying over for a few days and attending *The Gazebo* at the Lyceum to study the play and Slezak's performance. "I saw 'Gazebo' tonight," he commented in his diary. "Not too well done. Not sure it would make a good movie."

By July he was back at the studio working with Reynolds on the film version. Both stars needed therapy now. Though Debbie and Eddie Fisher had been divorced on February 12 (before the making of *It Started with a Kiss*), Eddie had married Elizabeth Taylor a few weeks after *Kiss* was completed.

Once again, George Marshall rode to the rescue with his relentlessly upbeat attitude. Making a simple film shot on a soundstage was just what my father needed at this time. It's amazing how successful this MGM dark comedy turned out to be when one considers the depressed mindset of the key participants. It was a testament to their professionalism, to the excellent supporting cast of Carl Reiner, Martin Landau, and John McGiver, and to Marshall's underrated directing.

This little film was one of my father's favorites. The plot had murder mystery TV writer Elliott Nash (Glenn Ford) planning to bury the blackmailer of his wife, Nell (Debbie Reynolds), in the concrete of a new gazebo in his suburban backyard. (Nell had appeared in some risqué photos and lacked the $10,000 demanded by the blackmailer; Nash must eliminate him and dispose of the body—all this unbeknownst to his wife.) Plans for the perfect murder and cover-up go hilariously awry until finally Nash's fate is unexpectedly saved by a pigeon, which deposits the incriminating evidence on the top of a policeman's hat. And did Nash really commit the crime? That remains unclear. This wasn't Hitchcock, but it was fast-paced fun.

The film received mixed reviews when it was released before Christmas but grossed $1.8 million for the studio, turning a tidy profit. And indeed, despite all the turmoil at home, I was given a small speaking part as a page boy—no billing—and got my Screen Actors Guild card. Dad had kept his promise.

The Gazebo finished production in late August. My father decided that to stay in the Cove Way house was futile, and he decided to move in with his mother until he sorted out his life. He started packing his things and by the end of September had moved out completely. I would surreptitiously watch him from behind the curtains of my bedroom window as he went back and forth, moving many of his belongings in suitcases loaded in our old wheelbarrow across the property to my grandmother's garage apartment. It was a sad time.

There were sixteen court postponements as the lawyers dickered. The final settlement hearing was on Mother's forty-seventh birthday, November 21, 1959. The divorce was granted on grounds of "extreme mental cruelty." I guess the gloves were off by now, because when Mother was queried by the press about the term "extreme mental cruelty," she said, "That's exactly what I mean."

Mom received half the community property of $700,000, the house on Cove Way, $40,000 a year for the next six years, then $30,000 a year for the rest of her life, plus $250 a month additional support and custody of me. California law stipulated a one-year interlocutory period before the final decree, but neither of my parents attempted reconciliation. Asked by a reporter about her plans for the future and whether she would return to performing, my mother said, "I don't know what I'll do. I was forty-seven years old last week, but I feel like eighty-nine."

On November 26 my mother decided we needed to get away from Cove Way. She telephoned "Uncle Jim" Juris at her mother's house, and he packed Grandma Powell, my friend Scotty McComas, my mom, and me into his 1959 black Cadillac sedan, and we set off for a one-week vacation in Las Vegas. My mother said she was celebrating the divorce, but I think she and I were both just deflated.

We checked into the Desert Inn Hotel and spent the next week seeing the shows around Vegas and relaxing in the sun. Uncle Jim had always been an anchor for me, an older male to whom I could look for advice. I remember quite clearly that he bought me my first dress suit for this trip and patiently spent time teaching me how to tie my tie. It was seldom that I had a male grown-up to talk to and teach me the lessons that a youngster needs to know about growing up.

My father lived next door with my grandmother Hannah for a time before moving into his own house nearby in Beverly Hills. But he might as well have moved to another planet. He had decided to make a clean break from my mother and me. For the next several years, with few exceptions, unless I made an attempt to contact him, the only time I saw my father was in the movies—like the rest of the world.

As the 1960s began, my father faced a fresh start in his life. His marriage of sixteen years had ended. The family unit that had thrived for better or worse under one roof for so many years was now scattered among three separate households. My mother contemplated going back to work, and she sent me to Chadwick, a boarding school in Palos Verdes, California, to finish my last two years of high school. My dad's mother, Grandmother Hannah, continued to live next door to our home in what had been Charlie Chaplin's converted garage.

My father's alliance with MGM happily continued. In fact, he was pretty close to being the studio's most important star. Two of his final films for MGM, under his original contract, were both superproductions, two of the biggest budgeted films of his career. Both were widescreen remakes of old classics. First was *Cimarron*, which in 1931 had been a best picture Oscar winner for RKO, followed by *The Four Horsemen of the Apocalypse*, which in 1921, as a silent picture, had launched Rudolph Valentino as a star.

Cimarron was based on Edna Ferber's sprawling novel about adventurer and crusading newspaper editor Yancey Cravat and assorted other settlers in the Oklahoma Territory in the 1880s. Anthony Mann was hired to direct. The cast included Anne Baxter, Dad's costar in *Follow the Sun*, Arthur O'Connell, Russ Tamblyn, Vic Morrow, Charles McGraw, Mercedes McCambridge, and, as Yancey Cravat's put-upon wife, the acclaimed Austrian actress Maria Schell (sister of Maximilian). She had been in European films since the 1940s and, more recently, in Hollywood, in *The Brothers Karamazov* for Richard Brooks and opposite Gary Cooper in the western *The Hanging Tree* for Delmer Daves.

Producer Ed Grainger asked my father to drop by his office at MGM so my dad could meet Miss Schell. As my father remembered it, Maria's presence in the room was like a bright beacon, and he was struck by her from the first. "She just captured your full attention the moment you saw her," he recalled.

The *Cimarron* company headed off for a long stay in Arizona, which would replicate the Oklahoma locales. The film's most memorable sequence and the most difficult to shoot was a full-scale re-creation of the Oklahoma land rush, with hundreds of settlers in a furious race to claim parcels of government land. Anthony Mann had a reputation for gritty realism in his action scenes, and he planned for the land rush to involve not only dozens of stuntmen and stuntwomen but also, keeping his camera close, key actors, including Glenn Ford.

My father, as I've mentioned, was an excellent horseman and in addition always felt an obligation to do as many of his stunts as possible. He may have underestimated how tough some shots would be—or perhaps, at forty-three, he was starting to get a little too old for this activity. During a scene in which he was driving a wagon and team of horses on rugged terrain at top speed, he tore the ligaments in his back and shattered two spinal discs. "I ended up," he recalled, "doing most of the picture taped up or in a back brace and shot full of Novocain."

Maria Schell explained that when she arrived in Oklahoma she felt more than a little out of her element with all the cowboys and stuntmen in the company. Behind the scenes it was just as Wild West as in front of the camera. "I didn't know anything about that cowboy world, and they used to have fun with me," Maria recalled. "The first day we were all sitting around the bar of the hotel where we were staying. It was a very 'western movie' atmosphere, and the cowboys kept offering me to eat these Oklahoma Oysters. And they were all having great fun with it, and Glenn Ford was laughing with them because I didn't know what they were—the testicles of a bull! And so all of us at the bar had some Bullshots and some Oklahoma Oysters, and that was my first real experience with my darling Glenn."

Darling, indeed. What might have become just another on-location affair between two costars became instead—according to both participants—something more intense. Maria Schell was a very passionate person (she once told a reporter, "Without love, I cannot glow!"), and my father, whose own emotions were in a raw state three months after his divorce, seems to have surrendered himself wholeheartedly to a romance with his costar. Glenn and Maria became inseparable in Oklahoma and then later back in Hollywood.

"We were soul mates," my father would say. "I wish it had gone on."
Many years later Maria recalled:

> I fell deeply in love with Glenn. It was a beautiful relationship, but at the
> same time very painful. Glenn could not give himself fully to me, because
> he was too hurt because of his divorce. He was unable to start a new life
> and a new love. It was too early, too quick after his ending of a very long
> marriage. I flew to Glenn with such an open heart that he couldn't resist!
> Poor Glenn had absolutely no chance. We had a wonderful, true, and
> deep affair. If he could have committed himself totally, I would have
> stayed with Glenn, I would have married him, but he couldn't do it at
> that moment. I suffered very much through Glenn; I was so completely,
> deeply in love with him.

Maria was in fact married at the time to German director Horst
Hachler. When she went to New York to rehearse for a Broadway production of *Ninotchka*, Glenn stayed in California. Hachler arrived in New York,
and when the play ended its short run, the two of them returned to their
home in Europe.

Looking back, my father would speak of the way it ended with regret.
"I loved her very much, but I wasn't capable of falling in love to the point
where I'd get married then. It was not a good choice on my part. My life
would have completely changed for the better. And then I lost her . . . a big
mistake in my life."

Cimarron turned out to be a well-made film with a number of memorable scenes, including that thrilling land rush sequence, but the long-
winded script often played out more like soap opera than horse opera. The
main attraction for movie fans nowadays may be the torrid love story
going on behind the scenes.

By the summer of 1960 my father was living in a sprawling contemporary
bachelor pad he had leased on Beverly Estates Drive in the hills off Benedict Canyon in north Beverly Hills. I hadn't seen much of my father since
his divorce from my mother the year before, but I heard later that many
all-night bacchanals and other more spiritual investigations were held at
his place. With the constraints of married life lifted from him, Dad was
seeking and embracing a whole new group of friends.

I think it was through famed costumer Walter Plunkett (a friend since
Walter and Dad worked together on *Go West, Young Lady* in 1941) that my
father became entwined with the "artistic intelligentsia" of Hollywood.

Writer Christopher Isherwood and his partner, artist Don Bachardy, Aldous Huxley, actor Roddy McDowall, Somerset Maugham, and other notables from the arts were among those who gathered at Dad's house. Truman Capote and Tennessee Williams were in the mix when they were in town. Many of these illustrious figures, along with mystic explorers of the Vedanta Society, led by Hindu Swami Prabhavananda, were espousing transcendentalism and other experimental forms of consciousness-raising.

It was during this time, I am told, that Dad and Cary Grant got to be fast friends, as they lived mere blocks from each other. I wasn't privy to a lot of what Dad was up to in those days, as my relationship with my father had not yet healed, but when I was home from boarding school on weekends and summer breaks I'd go over to Dad's house to visit, and very often Mr. Grant would drive by in his Rolls Royce and stop, roll down the window, and talk with me and Dad.

My first car was a black 1932 Ford Roadster with a rumble seat. I installed a small-block 283-cubic-inch Chevrolet motor in it, which got me around town in a hurry and in glorious "teenage" style; the car was hot. When Cary saw me on the road he'd say, "Pete, when are you going to trade me that hotrod for my Rolls?" He'd wave and be on his way, and it became kind of a ritual between us.

One night in the fall of 1961 Dad had one of his soirées and invited me over. I was still young and unaware of how famous these people were at the time, but I remember Aldous Huxley and Christopher Isherwood and composers and artists mingling at my father's home. I was always intellectually curious and eclectic in my interests, but I was clearly out of my league at this party, so I just hung back by the bar, had drinks, and watched everyone with great interest.

At some point in the evening, Cary Grant had what he thought was a great idea. Why don't a few people take a ride in Peter's Roadster? Cary had been obviously medicating himself with something other than alcohol that night, and he was determined that he and some of the others should go for a ride. The next thing I knew, Cary herded Mr. Huxley, Igor Stravinsky, and an artist (I believe it was Joan Miró) into my Roadster for a whirl in the hills above Beverly. It was uneventful, and thank God I hadn't had too much to drink, but I often think back to that madcap evening and wonder, What if something dreadful had happened, and I had taken the cream of the world's illuminati over a cliff to their deaths?

With *Cimarron* completed and his next big studio project not scheduled until September, Dad accepted another small film. He had to fulfill an obligation to Columbia, and while he wasn't overjoyed about the script, he always liked to keep busy and make money, and, since the filming was in Los Angeles, he could enjoy his bachelor life on an easy schedule. It helped, too, that Glenn would be reteamed for the sixth time with director George Marshall.

The film was *Cry for Happy*, which William Goetz was producing for Columbia. Goetz had produced *Sayonara* for Warner Bros. in 1957, a Marlon Brando vehicle that had earned Japanese actress Miyoshi Umeki, making her American debut, an Academy Award as best supporting actress. Now Goetz tapped Umeki for *Cry for Happy* and brought Donald O'Connor back to the screen after a three-year absence. He joined my father in this "service comedy" about four Navy photographers after the Korean War who find billets in what they think is an abandoned geisha house only to find it inhabited.

Not a masterpiece, but it was escapist fare shot on a low budget in less than two months' time. One of the better "reviews" came from former president Harry S. Truman; after viewing *Cry for Happy* in a Columbia screening room in New York, the ex-president wrote to the studio that he didn't know when he'd had "so many good laughs and [came] so near to shedding tears." And the film grossed $1.45 million for Columbia, so my father still looked strong at the box office.

Dad attended the Westwood preview of *Cry for Happy* with the French actress Capucine as his date. Whatever deep unhappiness was engendered by his divorce, whatever regrets my father might have had at the time of his breakup with Maria Schell, he always found ways to regenerate his love life.

By the fall of 1960 he had a newfound crush on Hope Lange, the winsome blonde star of *Peyton Place* and *The Best of Everything*. At first he was just smitten, but over time it would develop into something more serious.

Dad was called away to work in Europe. Yet in his letters and diaries from this period it is obvious Hope already had stolen his heart. All he talked about on his next film, with anyone who was foolish enough to ask, was Hope Lange.

In September 1960 Glenn traveled by train and ship to Paris to film *The Four Horsemen of the Apocalypse* with Vincente Minnelli directing. Minnelli wanted to capture a very loose, updated (set during World War II) remake of the Vicente Blasco Ibáñez novel (and Rudolph Valentino silent picture), a story of conflicts among members of a wealthy South American family living in Paris and how they are drawn into the maelstrom of war.

In the Valentino role my father was somewhat miscast (he was a bit old to play the Argentine playboy character), but he would deliver what many consider a very powerful and sensitive performance. The film also gave him an opportunity to work with Ingrid Thulin, the Swedish actress who would perform most famously in a series of films for Ingmar Bergman. (Thulin spoke fluent English, but her overseers in Hollywood eventually decided her accent was too thick, and her voice in the film was overdubbed by Angela Lansbury.)

Work in Paris began on October 17 and turned out to be fraught with hazards. The weather plagued the shooting schedule, with rain pouring down day after day. Even when the sun shone, the production faced difficulties. Director Minnelli had previously filmed all over town with great success while making *Gigi*, but that Oscar-winning glorification of the city seemed to gain him few favors with the local bureaucracy. New regulations required that every single resident in any building being used for filming sign a letter of consent, and naturally there were some hold-outs and curmudgeons at every address.

Much of the film had to be shot on Sundays so the streets would be relatively clear, but between the weather and the delays imposed by French customs, it was very slow going. Much controversy ensued in August, when Minnelli prepared to shoot several sequences involving soldiers of the German Wehrmacht marching around various Parisian landmarks as they had during the Occupation. The sight of Nazi troops so inflamed the citizens in this reoccupation of Paris that French gendarmes had to be called in to calm the populace.

Bowing to public protest, the French government finally canceled the permits for those scenes. "There was a lot of wasted time and effort," my father remembered. "But there are few more pleasant places to waste your time than in Paris. The studio got fed up with all the delays, and in early December everyone came back to Los Angeles to finish the film. I came back a week ahead of the company to attend the gala worldwide premiere of *Cimarron*."

In order to make the premiere on time, Dad had agreed, despite his earlier vow, to fly to New York rather than travel by sea, then the rest of the way by train to Oklahoma City, where the event was scheduled. Perhaps one reason he consented to fly again was that MGM was flying Maria Schell to the premiere from Europe as well as hundreds of critics from all over the world. (Even Anne Baxter made the long flight across the Pacific from her home in Australia for the occasion.) Dad was nervous about seeing Maria again after so many months. He felt beguiled by Hope Lange, but seeing Maria rekindled the old ardor. Passionate as ever, Maria described the bittersweet reunion when I asked her about it: "I came back to America for the opening of the film, and it was like for me breaking into heaven to see him again. And again, he closed his door to me."

After the premiere, *The Four Horsemen* resumed production in Los Angeles in early December and would continue for a few more months. The budget was approaching $8 million, and Sol Siegel, then MGM's man in charge, was hysterical about the runaway costs and delays. Minnelli, in my dad's opinion, was an incurably fussy director who spent more time worrying about the wardrobe on the extras and the foliage on the trees in the background than about moving the production along in an efficient way. It was with great relief to everyone at MGM that the purported twelve-million-dollar production finally was completed on the last day of March 1961.

Working back home in Los Angeles, Dad and Hope began to see more of each other. Then it happened—he fell madly and irreconcilably in love. During the fall of 1961 Dad felt he had finally found his dream girl. Hope had been married to actor Don Murray, but the marriage was ending, and they were legally separated.

Aside from being a lovely woman, funny, intelligent, and a sparkling companion, Hope's appeal to my father—at first—may also have had something to do with her attitude toward love and marriage. After the breakup of her marriage to Murray, Hope wanted nothing more to do with weddings. She was not someone to fall in love easily nor immediately settle down with another man. In addition to her career, she had young children at home to raise. She wanted to—as we'd say now—compartmentalize her romance, not let it interfere with the rest of her life. Hope's only goal seemed to be to live for the moment. My father liked to tell Hope—and tell himself—that all he wanted was the same thing: a fun-filled, guilt-free romance. But for my father, that was easier said than done, and this time he fell hard, with his dream girl remaining as elusive as ever.

11

"Cat's in the Cradle"

Two for the Seesaw was supposed to be next up on Glenn's schedule, costarring the one and only Elizabeth Taylor, but she had become bogged down making *Cleopatra* in Rome for longer than planned. When Elizabeth found herself involved with a married boyfriend, Richard Burton, *Seesaw* was put on permanent hold. In 1962 the film would be made starring Robert Mitchum and Shirley MacLaine.

But then Dad got a welcome offer from superagent Abe Lastfogel, who wanted to put Glenn Ford together with legendary moviemaker Frank Capra for another remake—*Pocketful of Miracles*. Way back in 1933 this Damon Runyon story had been a crowd-pleaser for Capra under the title *Lady for a Day*. The warmhearted plot concerned Dave the Dude, a glamorous bootlegger in Prohibition-era New York who decides to help panhandler Apple Annie pretend to be a grand lady of society for her visiting daughter.

My dad bristled when it was pointed out by some critics that three of his last four films had been remakes. He tended to dismiss critics anyway, but this got under his skin. "Every time Hamlet is played it's a remake, but who cares?" he was quoted. "Everyone is creating something of his own. We're not copying the original movie."

Capra was a living legend in Hollywood, but his heyday had been the 1930s and 1940s. It was my father's name attached to the project that got the film financed, and Glenn's agent negotiated a deal that would make him a coproducer of *Pocketful of Miracles* under this onetime company banner: Franton Productions (a combination of Frank, Capra's first name, and Newton, Glenn's middle name).

My father was paid (or paid himself as producer) $350,000 for his work plus 35 percent of the gross profits. Old Frank arrived with memories of his *Mr. Smith Goes to Washington* days, when he had boasted near complete control of his projects, but he soon found that those days were long ago. In his later autobiography Capra would write with some bitterness about how Glenn threw his weight around during the production of *Pocketful*. The resentment began right away during casting, when Capra chose to hire Shirley Jones for the role of Dave the Dude's girlfriend. According to my father, he didn't realize this when he suggested that his real-life girlfriend, Hope Lange, be cast. Capra countered that my father did know about Jones but insisted on Lange playing the role. Capra fumed and protested, but the part went to Lange in the end. It wasn't a slap at Shirley, as Dad admired her and would work with her on another film.

Dad was pleased to endorse Capra's suggested casting of Bette Davis to play Apple Annie. Dad had enormous respect for Bette as well as eternal gratitude to her for choosing him to be in *A Stolen Life*, and he was happy to be working with her again. (This was before her big "comeback" in *What Ever Happened to Baby Jane?* since Bette's career, like Capra's, had been quietly winding down.)

Beneath the surface there was plenty of tension on this production. Frank Capra suffered from on-the-job stress as well as festering resentment of my father's influence over the decision making. During filming Capra developed terrible migraine "cluster" headaches and was taking regular injections of sodium phosphate for relief. Although my father did not recall having a particularly difficult relationship with Capra, later the director would write of the experience in *Frank Capra: The Name Above the Title* and complain about the compromises he had made for the sake of his star; he wrote that he had "sold out the artistic integrity that had been my trademark for forty years." After the book came out in 1971, my father sent Frank a telegram: "What a shame you did not have the guts to say this to my face—what you said in the book."

Although *Pocketful of Miracles* has many fans today, it was not an overwhelming success when it came out for Christmas 1961. Whatever their differences, my father had enabled Capra to make one last film—there would be no more. Capra tried to put some other projects together in the next few years but failed, and then went into retirement until his death years later. I have my own fond spot for the film because, thanks to Dad, it boasts my second speaking part; I play an elevator operator in a scene with the principals in which my conveyance saves their lives by deflecting some mobster's bullets.

After *Pocketful of Miracles* was completed my father resolved to make a "fresh start," personally and professionally. He decided to build a custom home. He had revived his friendship with Rita Hayworth, who in 1958 had married producer James Hill (who teamed with Harold Hecht and Burt Lancaster in a production company). In 1960 Rita and her husband bought some large pieces of property on Hartford Drive in Beverly Hills, about two blocks away from our house on Cove Way and just a block behind the Beverly Hills Hotel. Rita thought it would be a fine idea to have Glenn living next door, so during his hunt for some land on which to build his dream house, she made a portion of her property available to him. He purchased two-thirds of an acre at 911 Oxford Way, a hilltop promontory between Oxford and Hartford Way.

Dad began collaborating with his architects on a nine-thousand-square-foot contemporary home that would be designed to his own specifications. Made of iron, flagstone, and wood, it featured an atrium with a staircase that descended to a downstairs living room, projection room, recreation/pool room, and guest suite. Thirty-foot-tall rhapis palms reached from the ground floor to the huge skylight at the entry. Upstairs was an expansive step-down living room and a huge, connecting, wood-paneled bar that looked out on the swimming pool and garden filled with fruit trees.

Dad designed a large master bedroom suite composed of a sleeping area fronting a massive stone-faced wood-burning fireplace, a connecting retreat with a full kitchenette that also served as his office, and a two-hundred-square-foot dressing room closet with dozens of drawers and six closets for clothes. The closet area led to a large bath with a walk-in steam shower and deep Japanese tub. This bedroom suite was his sanctuary—here he could shut himself off from the world.

It was a "bachelor pad" on a grand scale, designed expressly for Dad and his lifestyle. As it turned out, three months after Rita and her husband sold my father the lot, she filed for divorce—what a coincidence! Within a short time, beyond the pool and partially hidden by surrounding rose bushes, Dad installed—with his neighbor's permission—a "secret" gateway to the adjacent property of his neighbor so the two friends could visit, talk, and burrow into each other's lives again without fuss and with complete discretion.

Rita's divorce from James Hill terminated her fifth (and last) attempt at marriage. She was truly in a miserable state of mind and shared her grief with my father. Curiously, even as Dad repeatedly sympathized with and comforted Rita, he had made his own life unhappy in ways that mirrored the behavior of Rita's husbands. Both Rita and my mother had idealistic notions about what to expect from a spouse. Whether Dad was unable or unwilling to meet those expectations, he was unfaithful to my mother and continually forsook his marriage vows. Yet my mother never cheated on her husband; nor, as far as I know, did Rita.

I have always wondered if my father's incapacity for lasting intimacy in personal relationships was due to the fact that he gave so generously of himself to his performances on-screen. By the time Dad had exhausted his energies and emotions convincing an audience in a darkened theater of his sincerity and genuineness, might there have been too little left of those qualities, away from the moviehouses, to give to people in his personal life?

In August Dad returned to Columbia one more time to make *Experiment in Terror*, a film by the superb director Blake Edwards. This crime story would complete his Columbia contract, ending a relationship that had lasted continuously for twenty-two years.

The book by Mildred and Gordon Gordon had been purchased in 1960 for the steep price of $112,500. The Gordons adapted their own dark thriller about a psychotic criminal who resorts to murder and kidnapping in his plot to rob a bank. With Glenn playing the FBI agent assigned to the case, the cast included Lee Remick as the bank teller–pawn in the plot, Stefanie Powers as her young sister and kidnap victim, and Ross Martin as the mysterious, ultracreepy villain.

Edwards wanted to film in San Francisco for the color and mystique of the city. All the night scenes were actually filmed at night (not day-for-night, which was the normal custom), sometimes in foggy and congested conditions—especially the movie's exciting climactic chase at Candlestick Park, filmed at night during an actual ballgame between the San Francisco Giants and the Los Angeles Dodgers.

Terror was a project that Edwards and Remick owned jointly, and Dad was merely satisfying his contractual obligation to Columbia. Blake was a strong-willed, consummate filmmaker who knew exactly the effects he wanted to get out of every shot and every page in the script. The hero cop and the damsel in distress didn't have a conventional romantic subplot, nor did they walk off into the sunset together at the end. From start to finish,

Experiment in Terror is a terrific movie, directed with dazzling style, one of those films of the early 1960s that took the suspense-crime film into a new era: grittier, more provocative, and adult. Film buffs now see it as one of the key films to influence the later revolution in the thriller genre in Italy, the so-called *giallos* made by people like Dario Argento and Mario Bava.

In his diary my father comments that the last half of 1961 was like "hell" for him because of all the problems he was having with Hope Lange. The "problems" were not of Hope's making, other than the fact that she was not succumbing to Dad's amorous pursuit. She was not looking for a total commitment to one man. He wrote: "I know my health has suffered and I'm unable to do anything about it. It is absolutely impossible to go on this way much longer without a complete breakdown—impossible to work or think straight."

Glenn had been approached by producer Martin Poll about starring in *The Grand Duke and Mrs. Pimm* in the winter of 1961–62 after completing *Experiment in Terror*. Hope was discussed as his costar, but—whether to punish her or try to get her to change her mind—he himself made the decision that it would be best if they didn't work together. "I love Hope so much," he explained in his diary, "but how could I have worked with her when she ignores me?" When he learned the title of the planned film had been changed to *Love Is a Ball*, he thought the new title an ironic affirmation of his decision. "How can I do justice to the film called *Love Is a Ball* when it isn't—I'm so hung up on Hope? Why not get Audrey Hepburn!"

My father always needed to be "in love" with someone—he was lost without love. He relished having a beautiful young woman on his arm. Raven-haired, blonde, redhead, or brunette, it didn't matter who or what type—he loved all beautiful women. For the most part, they enjoyed his celebrity, charm, wit, and boyish smile. I came to understand that, in many ways, women defined his very existence.

Now, with Hope Lange acting noncommittal, he began seeing a beautiful actress twenty-two years his junior—Connie Stevens. Connie was currently starring as Cricket Blake on the television series *Hawaiian Eye*. They would share New Year's Eve together in 1961, and soon Dad wanted her to share everything in his life.

On January 11, 1962, a chauffeured car from Warner Bros. (Connie's home studio) picked up Connie and Dad, and the two of them left that night for a "date" in Paris. They were winging their way to Europe for the world premiere of *The Four Horsemen of the Apocalypse* with stops on both legs of the journey in New York City. It was a whirlwind, exciting trip, and Connie was left reeling from a ten-day blitz of press coverage, celebrity treatment, gourmet food, and fine wine.

They would reprise that trip in February when she and my father went to Washington, D.C., for the U.S. opening of *Horsemen* at the Capitol Theatre. At the reception held at the National Press Club, they shared cocktails with Barry Goldwater Jr., Mike Wallace, Edward R. Murrow, and Jimmy Roosevelt (then the U.S. ambassador to Spain) and afterward attended a gala given by society hostess Perle Mesta. In the wee hours Glenn and Connie walked back to their hotel arm in arm, stopping for a piece of pound cake and tea at an all-night café.

My father found Connie to be sweet and charming, and he was captivated. But Connie was much younger than my father, and she moved in a young, fresh-faced circle in Hollywood that was being shaped by the medium of television. Their romance did not last long.

But the affairs and flings were countless, it seemed, when you were a big movie star. My father first met Marilyn Monroe in March 1960, when he presented her with a Golden Globe Award for her performance in *Some Like It Hot*, and early in 1962 they met again at a party for Abraham Ribicoff, who was then President Kennedy's Secretary of Health, Education, and Welfare and would soon run for U.S. senator in Connecticut.

My father found Marilyn to be a delightful person, interesting and amusing, he said, but full of insecurities. Late in the evening someone said something to upset her, possibly her psychiatrist, who was there and in strangely close attendance, as Dad remembered. She came up to my father, very distraught. He recalled:

She said, "Glenn, would you give me a ride home?" I said, "Of course, Marilyn." I could see she was upset. She wanted to go right away, without looking back. I followed her outside and took her to my car, and we drove off. I said, "What's your address, Marilyn? I don't know where you live." She said, "No, Glenn, let's go to your home."

We went to my place. She was interested in the paintings that were hanging in my home, and I told her about each of them. There was one in particular she liked very much, and I said, "If you like it so much, I want you to have it." And she was very pleased about that. And then she wanted to drink Champagne. I got out some Champagne, and Marilyn drank the entire bottle in about two seconds. Then she wanted another.

We were in the bar, on the plaid sofa. She said, "Just hold me." And I did. And then she wanted to do more, and we did. . . . She stayed until the morning. And then she forgot to take the painting. I still have it. I never saw her again. A lovable but troubled person. I wish I had gotten a chance to know her better and maybe to help her if there was a way. A few months later she was dead.

After she died, my father, wistful about their brief time together, went and took down the painting he had intended to give to her. On the wood frame on the back he wrote some lines about the night they had spent together so he would never forget, he told me. He drew a red heart in ink and wrote, "When we made love she whispered, 'I wish I could die right now while I'm happy.' . . . Now she is gone."

Dad continued to pine after Hope Lange. He and Hope continued to see each other, but she was insistent about maintaining separate lives. Hope was busy raising her children while my father went off to Paris and elsewhere on acting business, plus Rita was back in his life again, now and then. Yet the thought of marrying Hope Lange absolutely possessed him. She left him breathless. The allure of Hope was so great that Dad decided that he must make *Love Is a Ball* after all with his dream girl as costar.

Martin Poll, the producer, was already in Nice, France, making arrangements for the production. With the start date looming, he was happy for my father to have made any decision as to his leading lady. Even then, Dad had second thoughts, because he couldn't control twenty-eight-year-old Hope—he found out she was seeing other men.

One was a certain twenty-one-year-old semiregular star of the television series *77 Sunset Strip*. Also, as my father learned from a costumer he knew at Fox, when Hope was making *Wild in the Country* with Elvis Presley in November and December 1960, she was rumored to have had a "fling" with the "King." When Dad learned the name of the Elvis film— and worse, that the character Elvis played in the film was also named "Glenn"—it was more than he could bear.

Dad hatched a plan. He reasoned that by stealing Hope away from the temptations of Hollywood, from home, family, and prospective beaus, by casting her in *Love Is a Ball*, he could isolate her overseas and win her heart. However, his plan was compromised when Hope agreed to do the film but only if she could bring her children and her mother with her to France. My father just couldn't seem to separate his women from their pesky children.

Off they went to France. Dad was half defeated already.

Love Is a Ball was going to be directed by David Swift, a multitalent who had left a long alliance with the Walt Disney organization to make his own light romantic comedies. My father had a nice salary and a profit participation deal. Hope, Charles Boyer, Ricardo Montalban, and Telly Savalas were the other names in the cast.

The plot was about a dashing American adventurer (Glenn) working as a chauffeur for Boyer, who's a professional matchmaker trying to arrange a marriage between Montalban and Lange. The marriage is almost consummated when Lange falls in love with Glenn, and a variety of misadventures ensue. The film was intended as a throwback to glamorous romantic comedies of the 1930s like *Midnight* and *Trouble in Paradise* but this time filmed in Technicolor and on beautiful authentic locations in the south of France.

Before the first day of shooting, however, Hope announced that she didn't like her character as outlined in the script, and she wanted to go home. My father wasn't enamored with the script either, but he was committed and needed to complete the film no matter what. Hope was probably bluffing to keep my father off balance, but his diaries are full of concern that Hope would leave France precipitously.

While in Nice, Hope and her family rented a magnificent villa, surrounded on three sides by the sparkling Mediterranean and with a boat landing and a small private beach. Dad took a large suite at the Hotel Negresco across from the promenade in town, but he would spend much of his off-camera time with Hope at the villa. Far from resenting the intrusion of Hope's relatives, he seemed to enjoy being part of a family unit again. And although Hope loved her family, she found time for Dad too. He and Hope threw many dinner parties at her villa, and they spent hours together in the kitchen preparing meals. He began to think of Hope's children, Christopher and Patricia, as his own. He also doted on her mother. Hope's family was his family now. Hope's sister Joy told me, "He was very generous to our mother. He was lovely; he probably gave her some of the most memorable moments of her life. He was just very gracious."

The filming became an incidental experience compared to their idyllic time together. They dined al fresco on Hope's patio, swam in the blue Mediterranean, and made love. In a white 300 SL Mercedes roadster given to my father as part of his contract, he and Hope explored the beautiful French coastline and quaint hill towns beyond. He would remember it as one of the happiest times in his life.

In June 1962 I graduated from Chadwick High School. I had asked my father to please come to my graduation. I had not seen very much of him, other than at some screening appearances and attending some parties at his rented home. He promised me he would attend and would make sure that all his scenes in *Love Is a Ball* would be completed by then. It wasn't long before I got word that *Love Is a Ball* was running over schedule, and Dad just couldn't get home. By this point in our relationship I had developed a very large chip on my shoulder and was angry that he let me down again, even though this time he really was working.

As big a disappointment as it was to me at the time, I had a life-saving epiphany. I reasoned (whether he was working or not) that if he preferred staying on the French Riviera, drinking Champagne with the love of his life in his arms, why should he tear himself away for me? He owed me nothing. It was an Ayn Rand moment for me, one like Gary Cooper had in the film version of *The Fountainhead*. My father would always do what would please him without regard for convention or what was expected of him. In reality, staying in Nice was consistent with his character.

I made a conscious decision that I would no longer wish for a traditional father, one who would interact with me as I always dreamed. Although I was his only child, I was an adult, and it was too late for a traditional father–son relationship. I resolved to accept Glenn Ford not as a "dad" but as the fine movie actor he was, an extremely talented man who never gave a bad performance in any of his films. His talent was shining, and for that alone he should be celebrated, I reasoned. If he brought happiness to so many through his films, why should I try to selfishly claim any part of him for myself? I had no choice anyway. I elected to become a fan.

Believe me, it was a tough decision but a wise one. I had to protect myself. Being the offspring of a movie star is one of the most dangerous jobs in the world, a truth to which dozens of my deceased peers, had they a voice, could attest.

My father was deeply in love with Hope, and he began to see her as someone with whom he could share his life. But Hope did not feel the same way. He did everything he could to convince her that he was a viable beau—he even went so far as to take her dancing, which he loathed. I asked Joy to describe the relationship to me:

> I think in the beginning they had a lot of fun together. It was a lot of fun and laughter. I don't think there's any doubt that he loved her very much.

But I don't know that Hope was ever in love with Glenn. She took it more casually. First of all, Glenn was a lot older than Hope. And he was from another era in a way, very old-fashioned. Glenn did not have a sense of humor about himself, and I have to say we did have some fun at his expense from time to time.

I remember they were in New York for some publicity thing, they were staying at the Sherry-Netherland, getting ready to go out, and I was visiting. And Glenn walked in, wearing this dressing gown with these great big shoulder pads—it must have been something he'd worn in one of his 1930s movies. And he took himself so seriously. Hope and I just burst out laughing, and we laughed more because of the way he didn't think it was funny. But he liked that Barrymore era, and he wanted to remain there.

As my father pushed for a deeper involvement with Hope, she began to pull away from him. It was a blow to his ego to know that he could not have someone he wanted so much. He didn't handle rejection well. They broke up and came back together several times.

Weaning himself from the elusive Hope Lange, he became involved with a number of other women during this period, including Tyrone Power's beautiful widow, Linda Christian. The brief relationship with Linda ended in rancor when the newspaper columns reported that Glenn and Linda had become engaged to be married, and Glenn denied it in such a way that Linda took great offense. The columnists had a field day with this short-lived feud.

There was also a tempestuous affair with the brilliant and troubled Judy Garland. Judy had been through a lot in her spectacular career, a roller-coaster ride of artistic highs and emotional extremes. She had found a period of stability—relatively speaking—during her marriage to Sid Luft, but the marriage had fallen apart, and in the summer and autumn of 1963 Judy was alone and in the midst of a nerve-racking attempt to conquer television with her own variety show.

In my father's diary he noted that he had actually met Judy Garland in Santa Monica when they both were young and she performed as one of the Gumm Sisters. But as friends and neighbors they had known each other for years. They went out to dinner one night, and Judy poured out her heart about her personal life and the problems and pressures of her TV show. Glenn offered a sympathetic ear, a strong shoulder to lean on. Judy was a compelling personality in private as well as on-camera or on the stage. My father recalled:

Judy could make you rock with laughter one moment and make you want to cry with her the next. We began seeing each other. We went out for drinks, had fun. She could trust me, and that meant a lot to her because she felt disappointed by a lot of the people she had known in her life. . . . She insisted I come to the rehearsals and tapings when she had her own TV show, to sit up front, . . . and she would sing to me. . . . What an honor, since there was never a better singer than Judy Garland.

Actor Andrew Prine, who was in a picture with my father, *Advance to the Rear*, during this time, described their relationship:

They had known each other for a long time, but now they were having this love affair. Glenn liked me right away, and I liked him. I was the young guy on the set in those days, and Glenn took me under his wing. And through Glenn I met Judy. Judy loved me; she thought I was funny. And she was such a flirt. She saw us in that silly movie we did—she went to it with us.

Glenn used to throw these wonderful parties, and I'd get to meet these wonderful people, Rex Harrison—scowling at me, looking as if he'd knock me flat if I said a word, which he would—and Oscar Levant, a crazy mother, and Edgar Buchanan. And I got to stay after everybody left, and Judy would keep the piano-player late, and she'd sing to Glenn and me. Moments I treasure.

And we got together at other times. We went to Ciro's and the Crescendo and whatever else was still around of the old nightclubs. We would all dress up and go out, in those days when people still dressed up to go out. And I was with Glenn and Judy to watch her daughter Liza's first television special. And it was wonderful. They were a real couple. But it was brief. Judy had her problems. She was adorable. She was brighter than anybody. Lots of laughs. But she had her problems.

Other books have reported on Judy's problems, her exhausting behavior during this period, recurring bouts of depression and hysteria, the predawn phone calls for help, the overdoses. My father had this to say when I pressed him as to the seriousness of their romance: "She might have wanted to be more deeply involved. I cared too much for her to marry her. I just knew it would have been wrong. I didn't feel it would work for either of us. I could only see problems ahead, and I was having enough problems of my own. I didn't want to compound them with Judy's."

In November 1963 President John F. Kennedy was assassinated. Judy had been a good friend of the young president, and she was inconsolable. She would show up unannounced at Glenn's house. They would sit together in the den, and he would hold her until her tears stopped. Some nights she would cry herself to sleep in his arms. In the morning she would pull herself together and go back to the set for rehearsals.

The romance, if that's what it could be called, had cooled by Christmas of that year. Mel Tormé, in *The Other Side of the Rainbow*, provides a version of the end of the relationship. In Judy's words: "All is bloody over. . . . Finished. . . . I don't know what happened. . . . One minute everything was fine and the next we just weren't seeing each other anymore. Just like that."

My father angrily disagreed with this account. "That's a lie. It was a beautiful ending, not like what's in his book. I cared for Judy very much. I worried about her, and I was very concerned. There's nothing I wouldn't have done for her. We parted dear friends—we were friends until the end of her life."

In early January Judy came by the house just as she was leaving for New York. She left a large wrapped package for my father. He took it inside and opened it up, finding a large black-and-white photograph of Judy in a dramatic pose. She had inscribed a note: "Glenn, dear one, now I can look forward and see the beauty of the sun and the moon and the love you give to me. You have my heart and I adore you. Judy."

If Hope Lange slipped through his grasp, in most other ways my father stayed lucky. He was still young at age forty-seven, wealthy, good-looking, and very eligible. The world was his oyster. He was still getting good roles, as evidenced by *The Courtship of Eddie's Father*.

This was one of my father's most beloved later films, a tenderly made story of a recently widowed father and his young son trying to put their life back together. Made at MGM, it was directed by Vincente Minnelli, with little Ronnie Howard (today a major Hollywood producer-director) as Eddie, Shirley Jones as an interested neighbor, Dina Merrill as a love interest, Stella Stevens as an adorable ditz, and Jerry Van Dyke as a crazed disc jockey. If Dad was becoming something of an old-fashioned star, *Courtship* was an old-fashioned sort of production, a studio-shot family comedy that Hollywood was rapidly losing the ability to make. There was no spectacle, no great sets or production value or controversial content, just a compelling, down-to-earth story and a group of attractive performers making some believable, likable characters come alive on-screen. The bond and tenderness between Eddie and his film father (my real father) was special to behold, and the irony of it did not escape me.

Shirley Jones came to the set eager to work with Glenn, an actor she had long admired, and she described the filming for me:

Oh, gosh, I was a real fan. I just thought he was one of the best actors and especially one of the best western stars. . . . And he was so nice, he came on the set and said, "I'm really so thrilled to be working with you." He was not what I expected. He was much more laid back, relatively shy, almost antisocial. But he was such a pro, and in fact if I had any direction at all on that film, it came from Glenn. I had been so spoiled, working with Fred Zinnemann on my first picture [*Oklahoma!*], because afterwards when I worked with directors like John Ford and then Vincente Minnelli I never got that kind of direction about character. Not that they weren't geniuses in their own right. But Vincente liked to draw pretty pictures with the camera, and it was always for me to move to a certain point, put my hand here when I say this line, but never any direction about character, and I missed that.

And so Glenn would work with me on that, and we would discuss the scenes and rehearse them on our own. I don't think Vincente even knew about it, he was too busy set decorating.

Working with Glenn as an actor was wonderful. But you never really got to know who Glenn was inside, you just never did. I saw the outside man. He didn't share any of his private, private thoughts with you. He always had stories to tell, but rarely anything he wanted to reveal about himself. You never got to know the inside of the human being. It was all something that had happened in a movie or to Bill Holden or somebody else. And a lot about the ladies he knew. He loved to brag about the ladies and thought of himself as a ladies' man, always.

In his own way, when we did *Courtship*, he came on to me very strong that way. Not overtly. It was just in his dialogue and his charm and touching now and then. I just knew if I blinked an eye, it wouldn't take much more.

We became social friends for a while, because I knew Hope Lange before Glenn met her, and she was a girlfriend of mine. And so my husband and I would go to dinner with Glenn and Hope and to parties and so forth. And it's kind of a funny story how that ended. It wasn't funny at the time, but it's kind of funny now. . . .

I was married to Jack Cassidy then, and he was an admirer of Glenn's as well. Anyway, Glenn was having a New Year's party at his home, and Jack and I were invited. It was already very late by the time we got there; we had already done the New Year thing at twelve o'clock. And it was a very lovely party going on. And Jack said to me, "I want to go pop in to another party just around the corner." He said, "You probably won't enjoy it, so if you want to stay here. . . ." Jack was a drinker, and he had some guy friends. So he said, "I'll come back and pick you up in about an hour." And I said, "Fine." There were still plenty of people at Glenn's party, and I was enjoying it.

Well, time went on and on, and I was drinking wine. New Year's was long over, and I was getting so tired. I was a little tipsy. So I thought, I'll just find a little guest room, and I'll lie down and rest until Jack comes to get me. Well, I did that, and I went into a bedroom and I lay down on the bed, fully clothed—I was in a big, long gown. I thought, I'll just lie here until he gets back. He'll find me. And the next thing I knew there was morning light, and I turned over and there's Glenn. He was beside me in the bed, in just his pajama bottoms, with his hands on his chest. And he was so angry. Mad as hell.

I said, "What's happening?" And he said, "Well, this does happen to be my bed." And I said, "Oh, Glenn!" He said, "Don't worry. I didn't touch you. I didn't even look at you." And I said, "Where's Jack?" And he said, "I don't know." Naturally, I was appalled. So I got up and went out, and just as I got downstairs Jack arrived. And of course he tried to apologize. And Glenn was so angry. How dare I do this to him! And I had a bad husband, and I shouldn't have married him! And Glenn literally threw us both out. Well, Jack couldn't let that go. He started telling people. And Jack wanted to be a comic, and he had that real satirical side to him. So at parties he would tell this story . . . how I slept with Glenn Ford. And he built it up. That Glenn liked to sleep with the dead—he was a necrophiliac and all kinds of stuff. Glenn got word of this, Jack making fun of him, and he was furious, and that was the end of our relationship.

Our paths crossed again one night at a party. And Glenn called Jack some terrible name and turned on his heel and walked out. Well, I did see Glenn again at a screening somewhere, and he was fine by then. He came up to me, and we talked, "Nice to see you again," like that, not much, but we spoke. And then much later on we worked together again, and by then it was all forgotten.

There is a bizarre footnote to Shirley's story, which goes to show that Hollywood loves—and is as ready to believe as the outside world—lurid gossip about its stars. Jack Cassidy's jokes about Dad resulted in many people taking them seriously. Even close friends of my father's like Terry Moore began to hear and wonder about Glenn Ford's interest in necrophilia, with the stories getting more elaborate to the point where people whispered about the funeral home he used to visit by secret arrangement so that he could commune with the dead bodies.

Somehow, amidst this abundance of romance and drama in his private life, my father continued to work, making two and sometimes three films a year at a time when many stars of his generation were slowing down.

It was in the summer of 1963 that my father and I began to draw closer. I had turned eighteen and wanted to join the military, and Dad and I had more than a few discussions about which branch of the service I should enter. I wanted to join the Army; he was pushing for the Navy. It seemed that now, without my mom around whenever we were talking, whatever tensions had existed between Dad and me had vanished—at least for the time being. My father even began asking me to spend a few days a week with him. I slept in the downstairs guest suite at the Oxford house on these occasions (he was lonely between girlfriends), but things between us definitely improved.

Following *The Courtship of Eddie's Father*, he made the black-and-white western comedy *Advance to the Rear* (known as *Company of Cowards* in Britain). MGM had bought the film rights in 1956 from a *Saturday Evening Post* story by William Chamberlain, and it had bounced around the studio for seven years with a variety of writers before William Bowers wrote a script everybody liked. Finally, the project ended up on my father's plate.

Advance to the Rear was directed by Dad's good pal George Marshall, the last feature they would make together (though they did get to work again years later when my father made *Cade's County* for television). The cast featured Stella Stevens, veteran Melvyn Douglas, Jim Backus, Joan Blondell, Andrew Prine, and Alan Hale Jr. The story was set in the waning days of the Civil War, with some war-weary soldiers on both sides trying their best not to kill each other, in fact, trying to completely avoid any dangerous activity at all, with farcical results. I had a bit in this film as an aide-de-camp to Backus.

The cast and crew worked quite a bit on the old steamboat that MGM had on its lake on Lot 3, the same boat that was used in the film *Show Boat* and many others. I visited the set almost daily that summer, to see and touch the great paddle-wheeler and visit with all the great folks working on that film. My dad was very welcoming these days, and it was a wonderful opportunity for a kid who grew up immersed in old movies just to walk, unattended, through all the backlot and amongst the sets and behind the facades of a dying era.

I had the opportunity to talk shop with Melvyn Douglas and Joan Blondell. To visit with Alan Hale Jr. and hear Hollywood stories about his dad and him growing up in screenland was a real treat. Andy Prine and I spent a lot of time in Jim Backus's dressing room listening to his war stories about old Hollywood, especially about working with James Dean, playing his father in *Rebel without a Cause*. At the end of the production, sensing my interest, Jim gave me an autographed photo of Dean. It's still a prized item these many years later.

The antics of the "cowardly company" seems to have unofficially inspired the television series *F Troop* and anticipated the later wave of cynical war comedies like *M*A*S*H* and *Kelly's Heroes*. *Advance to the Rear* is an often hysterically funny film, woefully neglected when it came out but still enjoyable nowadays. My father as the befuddled captain and Stella Stevens as a Confederate spy made a wonderful comic team.

Dad and Stella Stevens also made a wonderful team in other regards. The filming was completed in only five weeks, and my father commented in his diary how swiftly the time passed. He enjoyed getting to know the voluptuous actress, of whom he saw a great deal after hours. Hope was still the focus of his dreams, but Stella did a womanly job of helping him forget Hope temporarily. Dad's diary was sprinkled with comments about Stevens's invaluable "help" and explaining why he had a bad back throughout the filming.

Despite the abundance of beautiful and interesting women in his life, my father remained obsessed with Hope Lange, convinced she was the only girl in the world who could make him happy, that is, until Hope found a new man and married him—movie producer Alan Pakula of *To Kill a Mockingbird* fame (and later a very successful director as well). In October 1963 Hope and Alan tied the knot.

Dad did not take it well. "I was hoping I'd be the one," he was publicly quoted, "if she decided to get married again. I'll always love her."

Hope's sister Joy remembered his disappointment:

> I'd been to the wedding. Glenn called me. I forget what movie it was he was making, but they had to close down for the day [of the wedding], he told me. He said he just couldn't go on. He needed to see me, he said.
>
> I went over, and all the shades were drawn. And he was there in the dark, with dark glasses on. He was in total mourning. It was a sight to behold. He was being very dramatic about it. But I think some of it had to do with Glenn getting his way a lot, and he was not used to not getting his way.

"At that time my life suddenly became empty," he would recall when I asked him about it. "Because all my thoughts for a long time, all my desires, were about her. It was like a part of me was cut off. How does an arm feel when it's severed from a body?"

Dad remained inconsolable for months. He went back to work on another film at the end of 1963, *Dear Heart*, costarring the gracious and talented Geraldine Page, and it was a wonderful experience; but he still had Hope Lange on his mind—constantly.

MGM was probably mindful of Glenn's doldrums when the studio asked if he wanted to go to New York in December to promote *Advance to the Rear*. They would send him and a guest on this public relations trip, first class, of course, with a stay at a top-flight hotel and a car and driver at his disposal for two weeks. He could also make an appearance at a benefit for the Actors Fund while he was in New York.

Usually, Dad would find a lady to accompany him on these kinds of trips. This time, he surprised me by asking me to come along and join him in what would be my first trip to the Big Apple.

12

"Auld Lang Syne"

Dear Heart, the third film Dad made in 1963, was a gentle love story about ordinary middle-aged people. It had originally been titled *The Out of Towners*, but the name was changed by studio head Jack L. Warner after preview audiences responded enthusiastically to the film's theme song by Henry Mancini and Johnny Mercer (a follow-up to their huge hit, "Moon River," written for *Breakfast at Tiffany's*).

The story, about a cynical greeting card salesman and ladies' man who meets a charming but lonely spinster while attending a post office convention in the big city, was conceived by writer Tad Mosel, a veteran of "live" television. The producer was Martin Manulis, who also had a long television résumé (*Studio One*, *Suspense*, and *Playhouse 90*), and the director was Delbert Mann, another TV alumnus best known for having guided *Marty* to success on both the small and the big screens, winning a best director Oscar for the latter in 1956.

Dad's contract gave him $250,000 plus a deferred amount of $100,000 out of the first profits, in addition to 25 percent of the gross. His love interest was the exceptional actress Geraldine Page, with a smaller role for a dazzling Angela Lansbury as the ultimate shrew who's burdened with a deadbeat son, Michael Anderson Jr.

First there was a bit of location work in New York, filming the initial sequences at the famous (now razed) Penn Station in October (with the trade papers reporting that Glenn and the poised and beautiful Dina Merrill, who had appeared in *The Courtship of Eddie's Father*, were dating after hours). The rest was filmed at Warner Bros.

Mann spoke with me about the film in 2007, not long before he passed away. He said:

> It was a fun picture to do, for the most part. We shot it all out here [California], all those New York scenes, except for a few shots of the city. Glenn was very good. A shy man, I thought. I found him very shy. Didn't socialize much, but someone who knew how to get the job done and give you exactly what you needed. He had great respect for Geraldine Page. He may have been even a little intimidated by her because she was such a great figure from the New York stage. She was a terrific actress, of course.

As I mentioned, in late December 1963 Dad went to New York City to promote *Advance to the Rear* for MGM, and this was my first trip outside of California with him as an adult. We stayed at the Essex House on Central Park South in two separate and very large rooms on the twenty-second floor; each had an incredible view of Central Park. It had been exactly twenty-five years since Dad first tasted New York City during the brief run of the play *Soliloquy*, and he wanted to introduce his son to the great city he had grown to love.

Traveling with someone in my father's privileged position was like nothing I had ever known. Everything was first class, from the flight to the service and the meals. We were pampered with a limousine and private driver waiting curbside all day, every day, to ferry us anywhere we chose to go. It was an experience that could spoil anyone.

A few weeks before we left I had a role in a TV show, *Mr. Novak*. I played a member of Frankie Avalon's car club. The director was Richard Donner, to whom I introduced Dad when my father came to visit me on the set. Fourteen years later he would direct my father as Jonathan Kent in *Superman*.

I was beginning to think of myself as following in Dad's footsteps, and I was full of myself that Christmas in New York. I was eighteen, I had a recording contract, I had been onstage in a professional play, and I had done some television work as well as a number of bits in Dad's films—life and the future looked good.

Dad and I had made peace. He took me to Coney Island for a Nathan's hot dog (by limo, of course), we had hamburgers at P. J. Clarke's, we ate at the counter of the Oyster Bar in Grand Central Station, and we visited Danny's Hideaway for medium-rare New York steaks. The owner, Danny Stradella, comped our meals, and my father reacquainted himself with a bunch of "wise guys" who hung out there.

One evening we went to the Copacabana to see the show, and afterward we went backstage to meet some chorus girls (I think I saw one of them leaving Dad's hotel room later in the trip). On another occasion we had a drink (I was underage, but no one asked) at Jack Dempsey's restaurant and met the great man himself. Most every night we dismissed the car and driver and walked around aimlessly. My father's philosophy was, when you visit a grand city for the first time, you must walk everywhere to experience it. He introduced me to New York City in this way.

On New Year's Eve Dad and I had drinks at Lüchow's on 14th Street with Hope Lange's mother and sister beneath the giant decorated and lighted Christmas tree and listened to Lüchow's famed German oompah band play. Afterward we were joined by actor Andy Prine, who was in New York on a PR junket for *Teen Screen* magazine and who was also doing publicity chores for *Advance to the Rear*. Dad was going back to Hope's mother's apartment for dinner, and he went by cab so that Andy and I could borrow the limousine.

We bid adieu to everyone, and Andy and I left for a night on the town—and what a night it was. After a stop at the Improv Room, where *Teen Screen* was hosting a Bagel Bash for young performers, we crashed a party at Albert Finney's apartment, and as we walked in, the eccentric artist Salvador Dalí was walking out. An arched brow and penetrating stare were the only answer to Andy's greeting of "Hello, Salvador!" Inside a bacchanal was in progress, awash with beautiful people partying with uninhibited zeal. Andy moved in like a pro and brought me along with him— his protégé. Andy's sobriquet for me was then and is to this day Black Pete.

I can remember bits and pieces of the evening, which didn't end until daybreak. Was that Elizabeth Ashley French-kissing me as I sat in Finney's living room? Who were those naked women in Finney's bedroom (with Finney passed out on the bed) singing Christmas carols to him? And wasn't Andy leaning against the bedroom door for support, crying with the joy of Christmas spirit? And where did I lose my belt?

At some point we were in an outer borough, perhaps Queens, at actress Jill Haworth's party, where we ran into many of the people we had partied with earlier at the Improv Room, Troy Donahue, Sharon Tate, and Lynn Loring among them. So many parties, so many eager revelers that night; all

I can say is that where Dad's stuntmen had failed, Andy Prine succeeded, for which I thank him.

The limo driver dropped Andy at the Edison Hotel and then took me back to the Essex House at daybreak. I finally awoke with a nasty hangover and realized it wasn't just my belt that was missing but my socks, hat, and top coat as well. Yes, life was good.

Lennie Hirschan, my father's newly appointed agent at William Morris, found his next project at Twentieth Century Fox, *Fate Is the Hunter*. *Fate* was based on a novel by Ernest Gann, a specialist in aviation stories, and my father would join Nancy Kwan, Rod Taylor, and Suzanne Pleshette for this story concerning an airline executive (Ford) investigating the circumstances behind a deadly airplane crash that may have been caused by his former World War II war buddy's (Taylor) drinking. The buddy has a fiancée (Kwan), who believes in his innocence, but the investigation hinges on the surviving stewardess (Pleshette).

I worked on this film too, but it was a small part, uncredited. A blurb from the studio touted my involvement: "Glenn Ford and his 18-year-old son Peter are appearing in their fifth movie together. . . . Peter portrays a guide who introduces Ford to co-star Nancy Kwan."

The airplane crash was staged on the Fox back lot, and it was not only realistic on the ground, at camera level, but believable from the sky as well. Burning parts of the plane, five fire engines with red lights flashing, three ambulances, TV and newsreel trucks, as well as several hundred extras milling under the bright studio klieg lights were so convincing that incoming planes landing at Los Angeles International Airport reported to traffic controllers that a major air disaster had taken place that evening beneath their flight path. Actual police and firemen were dispatched to the scene, and director Ralph Nelson and studio executives had quite a time soothing their nerves and annoyed feelings.

Twenty-five years earlier Dad had earned $25 a day on the Twentieth Century Fox film *Heaven with a Barbed Wire Fence*, shot on the same stage—Stage 5, which had a skyline background. Now Darryl F. Zanuck, still running the studio, was paying Dad nearly $10,000 a day on a fifty-five-day schedule. His salary—$500,000—was the highest fee he had yet received for a single film appearance.

Westerns were still popular—with Dad and audiences.

Burt Kennedy was a talented writer-director who had come into the movie business as a protégé of John Wayne and written some of the fine, early Randolph Scott westerns directed by Budd Boetticher. Burt had adapted a Max Evans novel, *The Rounders*, into a terrific comedy script set in the modern West and centered on two hapless old cowboys who barely eke out a living busting broncos.

Dad agreed to play one of the old cowboys, Ben Jones, while the role of his somewhat dimmer pal, "Howdy" Lewis, went to Henry Fonda. My father had top billing, but Glenn and Hank, two wily veterans, played beautifully off each other in the film, with a hilarious rapport. It was like Laurel and Hardy in spurs. The small-scale, closely observed character study of two likeable losers, a picaresque, meandering narrative with no real plot or climax, was more like a European art film than a big Hollywood production.

My father and Fonda had been friends for many years but had never worked together. Kennedy knew them both and had a copy of the script delivered to both actors. The writer-director was prepared for long negotiations and practicing a persuasive speech when Dad and Hank called him back on the same afternoon.

"I like it, Burt," Dad said. "What does Hank think?"

"Man, it's terrific. . . . What does Glenn think?"

From the first day the teaming was harmonious, with most scenes between Glenn and Hank accomplished in single takes. The supporting cast was made up of western veterans who added authenticity and luster: Edgar Buchanan, Chill Wills, Denver Pyle, and Warren Oates. Of course, the stars' sons were also in the film: Peter Fonda and me. We formed part of the street scene when our respective fathers steered the two leading ladies, Hope Holiday and Sue Anne Langdon, across the street, covering their bare behinds with their hats.

In those pre–*Easy Rider* days Peter and I were friends. Together we made a trip to visit our fathers on location. Peter picked me up at the Cove Way house one afternoon, towing his motorcycle behind his Buick Riviera, and we headed east to Arizona for about a week. *The Rounders* was shot almost exclusively on location in the Coconino National Forest and in areas around Sedona.

While filming in Sedona, my father met a man who became one of his most trusted associates, Bob Crutchfield. A young newcomer to the movie publicity business, Crutchfield arrived at *The Rounders* location for his first assignment on an important production with major stars. Bob recalled:

> Glenn was slumped in his director's chair when I came up and introduced myself as the unit publicist. Glenn pushed back his cowboy hat and

looked at me. I was all of twenty-five and looked about ten years old. I could read what he was thinking: Is this what it's come to? But what he said was, "Hiya Bob, welcome. If you ever want anything from me, just let me know." I thought, Great, this is going to be a snap. Then I went over to Henry Fonda, where he was slumped in his chair. And I introduced myself and told him the same thing I just told Glenn. And Fonda looked at me very briefly and said, "You want to know anything about me, ask my agent." Case closed. He didn't want anything to do with some punk kid.

I never spoke to Fonda after that. I was scared of him, but I was enough of a snotty kid to think, Fine, who needs you. So off I went to work with Glenn. And Glenn did whatever we wanted. I had the still man [the photographer who takes publicity photos during filming] working his ass off. It was Glenn, Glenn, Glenn. And finally one day we're shooting Glenn on a bale of hay with the horse, and suddenly I'm aware that someone has come up behind me.

It was Henry Fonda. I said very formally, "Good morning, Mr. Fonda." And in that wonderfully droll voice of his he said, "Hi, guys . . . Watcha doin'?" I said, "Well, we're doing some more publicity photos of Glenn here." Fonda looked at Glenn posing and then looked at the photographer and then looked back at Glenn. And he said, "Ah . . . Well, if you need me for anything, I'll be right over here." A complete turnaround. And from then on he was terrific too.

A couple of weeks later I was getting ready to be replaced by the senior publicist, who had been delayed on another assignment. Glenn heard about this, and he said, "Bullshit. Get your boss on the phone." And Glenn spoke to the head of publicity at MGM, Howard Strickling. I handed him the phone, and he said, "Howard? Glenn Ford. This kid here has done a better job in two weeks than you guys have done in six years. I don't want one of your old farts coming here to replace him. You got that?" And that was that, and we went back to work. And that was the start of my career, really, because somebody that big had given my boss a call and vouched for me in a big way.

In a couple of years Bob Crutchfield would open his own public relations firm, and Glenn Ford would become one of his first clients.

The Rounders always held a special place in my father's estimation. MGM offered this unusual western as part of a double feature, at the bottom of a double bill, for some inexplicable reason, with the mindless *Get Yourself a College Girl*. The few people who saw it loved it, but *The Rounders* was too "small" to get much serious attention. Too bad—it was and is a beautiful picture, hilarious, sweet, and touching without being the least bit sentimental. It is certainly on the list of the top five or six of my father's best movies.

The producer, Richard E. Lyons, wanted to find another project for Dad and Hank Fonda, but Lyons did not fare well with MGM. He had produced two excellent westerns in *Ride the High Country* and *The Rounders*, but MGM had myopic vision, and Lyons ended up doing more westerns for television and the big screen over at Universal.

However, writer-director Burt Kennedy had so enjoyed the ease and camaraderie of making *The Rounders* that he found another project for my dad so they could work together again. It was a very different sort of movie, a dark crime thriller called *The Money Trap*.

The film, adapted from the novel by Lionel White (*The Killing*, *The Big Caper*), was a worthy final attempt to recapture the noir oeuvre. Film historian and writer Alan K. Rode told me: "Despite a cast that comprised a highlight reel from the classic noir period, the prototypical plot was no longer credible. *The Money Trap* is a film noir nostalgia jam that ultimately strikes a depressive chord."

Glenn's wife was played by a sexy young German import, Elke Sommer, with support from Joseph Cotten and Ricardo Montalban. Third-billed, playing the cop's washed-up former girlfriend, was a woman my father had known and worked with for over a quarter of a century, his longtime friend and sometime lover, Rita Hayworth.

It had been nearly twenty years since Rita and Glenn had burned up the screen in *Gilda*. Now, in 1965, Glenn was still playing male leads, but Rita—and her career—had declined. It was one of the inequities of the Hollywood system that the male stars seemed to go on and on with their careers while the leading ladies had to struggle for good parts once they reached forty. Rita was now forty-six and not in the greatest physical or emotional shape. As Rode observed, "Who wanted to believe that Johnny Farrell and Gilda would reunite in middle age as a corrupt cop and a used-up waitress?"

Publicist Bob Crutchfield, who worked on *The Money Trap*, recalled:

> I was at his house a lot in those years, and Rita of course lived next door. She was always calling Glenn or would just appear through the gate in the backyard. Sometimes Champagne bottles would precede her arrival. . . . She'd throw the bottles toward the skylight that covered the atrium. Glenn finally put up chicken wire or something to stop the bottles coming through.

He was always tender and sweet with her, no matter how she acted. . . . I made a terrible mistake one day. Glenn was doing an interview. They were taping, and the phone rang. I answered it right away so it wouldn't interfere with the interview. I told the caller that I was sorry, Glenn was doing a radio interview at the moment. She said, "I don't care! I must speak to Glenn!" I said, "Who is this?" "It's Rita!" I said, "Rita who?" It didn't dawn on me, because I was really still listening to Glenn talking to the interviewer. She screamed, "Rita who?!" And she followed with a stream of screaming and four-letter words.

I quickly mumbled her name to Glenn, and he immediately stopped the interview. The tape recorder was turned off, and he excused himself to grab the phone. "Now, love. . . . What's wrong, dear? What's wrong? Yes . . . yes . . . I'll come over . . . right away!"

He was very caring and sweet with her always.

My father was never more protective of Rita than during the filming of *The Money Trap*, and the haunted actress gave a poignant performance, but in more ways than one her glory days were over.

Bob Crutchfield recalled:

Rita had come up to the stills department, and there on the table were all of these 11 by 14 blowups of her. . . . They were not flattering, and you could see all of the crow's feet, the age lines in her face. Rita went crazy when she saw them. She scooped up a big handful of them and stormed over to the Thalberg Building and barged into the office of Max Youngstein, who was the producer. She threw the pictures down in front of him and screamed, "What the hell is this?" Youngstein was startled. "What? What do you think? They're the stills from the picture." Rita cried, "What do you mean? They aren't retouched. . . . They're just lying out where people could get their hands on them!" And Youngstein said, "Well, that's the way it is." And he just acted like she was no longer there. Rita seemed stunned. She said, "You aren't serious. . . . They look terrible. . . . I look like an old whore." And without missing a beat Youngstein said, "Why do you think we hired you?"

I never told Glenn what happened. He probably would have knocked Youngstein's teeth down his throat.

This was how Hollywood treated the former Love Goddess. After *The Money Trap*, Rita would work in only a few more movies, mostly obscure films into the early 1970s. By the last of these she was clearly suffering from the early stages of the disease of the mind that would consume her.

By contrast, Glenn Ford was still a busy and well-paid movie star in 1965, and his place in the Hollywood hierarchy seemed secure. With hindsight, though, it is clear that he too was nearing the end of something. New stars and styles were about to take over the picture business. The films my father had been making were the sort few regarded anymore, small-scale, black-and-white pictures such as *Advance to the Rear* and *The Money Trap*, pictures intended for the top of a double bill and sometimes even the bottom.

It didn't matter how good *The Money Trap* might have been; pictures like that were—or were perceived to be—irrelevant and old-fashioned. Burt Kennedy's dark thriller received scathing reviews from all quarters. The *Daily News* called it unconvincing. *Time* magazine said the film was overburdened with social significance and a sloppy script. Kevin Thomas, a friend of my father's, called it "dumb" and "implausible" in the *Los Angeles Times*.

Even if he didn't know it yet, my father was heading for a crisis in his career and in his life.

It was after I graduated from high school—Chadwick School in Palos Verdes—that my interest in show business became more serious. With two major stars for parents, it was not surprising that I felt the urge. I had grown up in a world of creative people, and now I felt ready to go out into the world and see what I could do for myself.

After high school I attended Lake Forest University north of Chicago for one semester, but the weather was cold, I was homesick, and, frankly, I had been medicating myself liberally with pills to get through the Illinois winter. My in-dorm pharmacy dispensation center, which I shared with some of the other students, was not well received by the administration, so it was resolved that I should leave the environs of higher education and go back to Los Angeles.

Happy to do so, I enrolled at Santa Monica City College and began taking classes in the fall, but in my spare time I was trying to find acting jobs, and I also pursued my love of singing. Mom was often on the road, dancing around the country, and I shared the twenty-room house on Cove Way with a number of different housekeepers who came and went in their employment. Although my mother continued to be a wonderful and doting parent whenever she was around, nowadays she was away from home for many months each year. In looking back at my upbringing, before and after the divorce, I think it could be said that in many ways I was raised by employees of my parents.

Perhaps my new acting aspirations excited Dad's interest. Or perhaps because I was older now he became more comfortable dealing with me as a near-adult rather than as a needy young child. I saw the first change when we were in New York at Christmas and New Year's. Then, in the spring of 1964 (after I had just turned nineteen), he came to a performance of a play I was appearing in at the Pasadena Playhouse. I had landed a part in a revival of *A Member of the Wedding* with Ethel Waters in the role she played in the film.

Ethel had worked with Mom on Broadway in 1935 in *At Home Abroad*, and when my mother came to the opening night of my play, she and Ethel had a warm reunion. Ethel always called me "Son," and I called her "Mom." My father had attended the dress rehearsal and graciously spent some time with Ethel and the cast. He gave me some encouragement and seemed pleased with what he saw.

Whatever his motives, my father began to allow me back into his life on a more regular basis. He always needed someone to ease his loneliness, so I began to get included at dinner and holiday parties. Then, in the summer of 1964, after Dad completed *The Rounders*, I was surprised to get a call from him with an offer to accompany him on a publicity trip to northern Europe in July. MGM was opening *Advance to the Rear* in Scandinavia, Belgium, the Netherlands, and France; additionally, Twentieth Century Fox was planning a fall release for *Fate Is the Hunter*. The two studios had got together to arrange for Dad's trip across the Atlantic to promote both films.

I was thrilled, and on July 20, 1964, we flew together on SAS first class to Copenhagen, Denmark. It was a ten-hour flight with a stop in Strømfjord, Greenland. At the airport Dad bumped into a friend traveling home to the States, and he asked him to join us for lunch—author James Michener. That was the VIP beginning of a VIP tour.

We were greeted at each stop by press conferences and full media attention. Limousines transported us to and from every event, and the days in each city to which we traveled were fully scheduled for my father. All the city's papers had multipage articles, with photographs, covering our every move. Wherever we went people recognized my father. We were mobbed by autograph seekers.

Copenhagen, Helsinki, Stockholm, Amsterdam, Brussels, Antwerp, and finally Paris—the tour lasted three weeks. Everywhere we went there were publicity duties, but there was also time for me to sightsee. I had seen falling snow for the first time in my life the previous Christmas in New York City (which was pretty exciting for a native Californian), but to visit Anne Frank's house in Amsterdam, ride in a parade with the king of Belgium, be photographed with my dad, both of us buck naked while enjoying a hot sauna, covered only by a sprig of strategically placed birch leaves, in Helsinki, walk down the Champs-Élysées and visit the Louvre and then spend a night on the town, see the performers at the Crazy Horse Saloon in Paris—it was a dream trip.

One incident sticks out in my mind after all these years, and perhaps you'll understand why. In Stockholm when my father and I held a press conference at the Grand Hotel, I met a young man, Peter Krueger, who befriended me. Throughout our stay he and I and his young Swedish friends (gorgeous females) hit the nightclubs and kept each other company. The day before we left for the next stop on the publicity tour he introduced me to a six-foot-three, incredibly beautiful exotic dancer he knew named Monica.

Well, the next day we were taking a flight to Amsterdam. Before noon, much to my surprise, who should show up at my hotel door but Monica. She had stopped in to say good-bye—and then she proceeded to do so in the most engaging way. Monica was so enthusiastic in her adieus that I suggested she pass on her bounty to Dad also, which she did. What a good son I was, thinking about my father's welfare, but suffice it to say, we almost missed the plane.

That same afternoon, as we rushed to catch our flight, the airport was crowded with young people. I was warming to the idea of all the hoopla attendant on traveling abroad with Glenn Ford and figured, of course, they were here to wish him and his son farewell; what else could it be? It was actually the mop-haired Beatles, who were arriving in Stockholm's Arlanda Airport and about to be mobbed by their fans.

The airport personnel asked my father to pose for some photos with the Fab Four when they arrived for their press conference, probably looking for the publicity angle of "Young British Rock-and-Rollers meet Aging American Movie Star." They offered to hold our plane with everyone else onboard. Dad deferred to me and asked if we should wait for the Beatles to deplane or just get on with our travels. I told him not to bother; it wouldn't be fair to our fellow passengers, and besides, the Beatles were not my cup of tea. Bad decision.

In many ways that trip changed the map of our relationship—Dad and I had become more like brothers than father and son. In later years Dad asked me to accompany him on a number of junkets: to England, France, Hawaii, Brazil, Australia, Japan, Korea, and Tahiti. These were colorful adventures for me, and not all of them were entirely G-rated. I was of an age that Dad felt he could relax and enjoy himself with me, though this period was to be short-lived.

It took a few years before my father got over Hope Lange marrying producer-director Alan Pakula, and then, only after many months of playing the field with a lot of casual female friendships, Dad became seriously involved with another woman.

She was an actress, professionally known as Kathryn Hays, a beautiful, elegant brunette in her early thirties. An Illinois native, Kathy had started her career in Chicago as a fashion model in television commercials. Then she moved to New York to study acting and theater. She got her first big break when she landed a role on the Manhattan-based police drama *The Naked City*, which led to more television work in Los Angeles. She had been married once before and then divorced, and she had a little daughter named Sherri.

In Hollywood Kathy had signed on with the William Morris agent Lenny Hirschan, who also represented my father. No doubt Lenny had talked up the charm and beauty of his new client and introduced them in December 1964 while Dad was making *The Money Trap*. Kathy described their meeting:

> I had started working a lot in California. I used to fly out and guest star in television shows. When I met Glenn I was there doing one at Universal. Lenny Hirschan told me about Glenn and that he would like to meet me. Well, that seemed very nice, but I was working on whatever show it was, and I said I usually didn't go out during the week. I then called Betty [Mrs. Don] Murray, who had been a friend of mine for years, because I knew she and Don knew Glenn. . . . I called to find out about him, you know . . . what was he like, and was he seeing anyone. The following week we met.
>
> It was a charity dinner dance. I found him to be a fascinating, wonderfully complex man. He asked me to go to dinner with him the next night, but I was working. He said, "Well, you have to eat." He promised that if I had dinner with him, he would have me home early. So I agreed, and the next day I called to tell him when I'd be finished. He said, "I'll come and pick you up." He brought me back to the house, and indeed we had a lovely dinner. And I remember something that touched me very much. I

was still wearing the heavy makeup from the studio, and he helped me take it off with some makeup remover and Kleenex. I thought that was sweet and considerate. True to his word, he took me home after dinner.

Then I saw him again over the weekend. We had many quiet times together. We sat by the pool, we swam.

Dad pretty quickly decided he had found someone very special. Early on he took Kathy to meet his mother, who was now living in the little guest house on the Oxford property. If he was looking for some reassurance from Grandma Hannah, he got it, as she liked Glenn's new girlfriend very much. Kathy was renting an apartment in Brentwood but spending much of her time at my father's house. They became "exclusive," and my father seemed very happy about it. Kathy was very pleased that he liked little Sherri a lot and treated her very kindly.

After many happy weeks in each other's company their careers began to drive them apart. After appearing in a western called *Ride Beyond Vengeance*, in August 1965 Kathy went to New York to begin working on a Broadway-bound production scheduled for an October opening called *Hot September*, a musical version of *Picnic*. That same month Glenn signed a five-day contract to play Gen. Omar Bradley in the film *Is Paris Burning?* And within days he was headed for France to join an all-star cast that included Kirk Douglas, Charles Boyer, Yves Montand, Tony Perkins, Leslie Caron, and Orson Welles. The separation had the effect of deepening Dad's and Kathy's feelings for each other, however. Dad had made contractual arrangements with Paramount Pictures to stay in Paris for three weeks after his five days of work, but this time he felt disconnected and alone in a city that had always stimulated and soothed him. All he could think of was Kathy. He wanted to go home.

When he returned from Paris in mid-September, Glenn stopped in New York to see Kathy, and their reunion persuaded both of them that their romance had become serious. Kathy's show folded after a few days, she returned to California, and she and her daughter moved into my father's big house in Beverly Hills.

For the better part of 1965 my father did not do any film work. It was a rare time for him to relax and enjoy his home. He had made a dozen films in five years, and at nearly fifty years of age he was admittedly weary. He took a few junkets for different studios and traveled to Reno, Nevada, to accept the first annual Golden Spur Award for his many outstanding portrayals in motion picture westerns.

My father relished the opportunity to tend his garden. He had always enjoyed plunging his hands in the soil, so to speak, and his time had passed pleasantly at Cove Way, raising chickens and growing all manner of plants and vegetables. He invited me to the Oxford Way house on weekends, and together we built raised beds and cultivated the land. I was older now, and it was a pleasure to labor and help construct his horticultural refuge as an unconscripted volunteer.

In March director Burt Kennedy asked my father to join him and his wife and producer Richard E. Lyons and his wife on a publicity trip to the Far East to promote *The Rounders*. There was a tie-in with Inflight Motion Pictures, and *The Rounders* helped launch the concept of watching movies on planes on the PAL (Philippines Airlines) flight between San Francisco and Manila. It was a fifteen-hour journey with a stop in Honolulu. Dad asked Kathy Hays to come along.

The group ventured from city to city in the Philippines and had an exciting few days in Hong Kong. On the return leg they had a long stay at the newly built Kahala Hilton Hotel (now the Mandarin Oriental) near Diamond Head in Hawaii. Dad and Kathy had never spent so much time together; they had every opportunity to share their feelings, and they returned committed to each other more than ever.

On November 19, 1965, they threw a cocktail and buffet party for sixty or so invited guests, including Debbie Reynolds, George Marshall, and Rod Taylor. It was supposed to be a going-away party before Glenn left for Mexico to make his next picture, *Rage*, but Dad surprised the gathering with the announcement of his engagement to Kathy, presenting her with a five-and-a-half-carat diamond ring.

Kathy accompanied Dad on location to Mexico City and Durango, Mexico, in December. *Rage* was a gritty drama about a struggling backwater doctor who contracts rabies and then must fight against time to save his own life. The sexy Stella Stevens was back as Dad's costar, playing the hooker-with-a-heart-of-gold type. But Dad was on his best behavior under Kathy's watchful eye. The rest of the cast consisted of Mexican performers—notably, David Reynoso, the country's biggest star.

Mexico had long sought to become a major player in the international film market, and this project was the vehicle that many Mexicans felt would fulfill that ambition. The driving force behind the film was the producer, director, and writer Gilberto Gazcón. *Rage* was a coproduction between Dad's old home studio, Columbia, and Mexico's Cinematográfica Jalisco, along with the Mexican National Film Bank. The executive producer was Richard Goldstone, who was in Mexico to safeguard the American studio's interests, but the film had a small budget of $640,000, an amount less than my dad's salary in better days.

My father had not worked in a year and itched to get before the cameras again. Considering the modest budget and the bare-bones production values, it was a commendable film, and my father gave an extraordinary performance as the down-at-the-heels doctor in trouble. Mexico's top color cinematographer, Rosalio Solano, contributed to the film's artistic success—though of course *Rage* never scored big at the box office and didn't stand a chance really, when competing against so many other higher-cost studio investments.

Turning twenty in 1965, I decided to concentrate my aspirations on singing rather than acting. I had been a music devotee all my life and been led to think I had a chance to succeed. I had a talent agent at General Artists Corporation (GAC) and a personal manager. All I needed, I mused, was a lucky break. I was very fortunate to come under the wing of a man who was a pioneer in rock and roll, songwriter and record producer Robert "Bumps" Blackwell. Bumps discovered Little Richard and Sam Cooke and in the 1940s had Ray Charles in his band. Bumps encouraged my singing, but I had signed a contract with Capitol Records, and my producer, Jim Economides, insisted that my first song selections be in a tamer "white" vein than I would have liked. Still, I loved music, and it was a wonderful time.

I cut some tracks and made small club appearances with my band, the Creations (Dave Thomas, Curt Chandler, and Bill Karp). I later signed with Phillips Records and, under the tutelage of Mike Curb, recorded some singles, most notably a song called "Blue Ribbons" written by Jackie DeShannon and Sharon Sheeley. That record, which scraped the lower reaches of the top 100, received enough airplay on the West Coast that I began appearing on all the local music television shows of the time: *American Bandstand*, *The Regis Philbin Show*, *Hullabaloo*, and *Ninth Street West*. Because of my singing career I appeared on *The Dating Game*. I also became a semiregular on an early ABC TV teen-oriented soap opera called *Never Too Young*, portraying a bass player in Alfie's (David Watson) band. Features in teen magazines, a spread in *TV Guide*, and a lot of other publicity seemed to support my career momentum.

My band and I continued to appear at nightclubs and discotheques in the Los Angeles area as well as the Whisky A-Go-Go in San Francisco and the El Cortez Club in Las Vegas. Like so many other wannabes during those pre-Woodstock days, we were trying to find our niche in the burgeoning rock-pop culture. We thought we had all the makings of a great band. It never happened, but we tried.

However, my little bit of success affected me in a devastating way. I had spent a lot of my youth bottled up with anger and repression. From the time when Dad left the house after the divorce through my teenage years at boarding school, then home alone when Mom was away working, and now on the road myself with opportunities for mischief, I had been living a life of excess.

In San Francisco we worked very near to the Playboy Club, with many of the "bunnies" often in the audience. The boys and I shared a houseboat in Sausalito as our home away from home while working at the Whisky. While in Vegas . . . well, in Vegas there was temptation everywhere, and I was my father's son after all. I pursued the sex, drugs, and rock-and-roll lifestyle with a vengeance. But I finally reached a point where I literally all but self-destructed.

In the summer of 1966 I was scheduled to appear with my group in San Diego on a bill with the English pop duo Peter and Gordon, an important gig for us. But the unimaginable happened. Prior to the booking I was struck with a crippling pain throughout my body; my bones and joints were in agony, and I could barely walk. Within weeks I became totally bedridden. I was in excruciating agony at all times. The doctors described it as a rare form of severe, crippling arthritis. There was no known cure for the disease, and I was told I'd most likely be in a wheelchair for the rest of my life.

I saw numerous physicians and specialists in the months ahead, and after intense medication with steroids and the ingestion of various drugs—Indocin, Prednisone, and Butazoladine, among many others, and finally gold injections—doctors wrote me off as a hopeless case and repeatedly stated that I would likely never walk again.

In looking back now, I believe God had sent me a message to slow down and probably saved me from myself. But at the time all I knew was that I watched all the good fortune and promise of my musical career fade to black. Just when success had come within my reach, it was snatched away. I refused to accept this fate, however.

After a period of months of despair and resignation came renewed determination. I began working on my own health regimen to mend my broken body. I gave up red meat, liquor, and everything else I'd ever heard was "bad for you." Torturously at first, I forced myself to resist the pain, to exercise, and to make my body function again. Eventually, I was able to stand for a time, then crawl from my bed to the bathroom, then walk with the help of crutches and a cane. Pain remained a constant; I was forced to rely on drugs, now not for perceived pleasure but in order to function in anything like a normal life. My mother and I prayed for my health to return. I slowly recovered, but with a new perspective on the meaning of life.

13

"Hard to Say"

On March 27, 1966, Glenn Ford and Kathryn Hays were married at the Westwood Community Methodist Church. I was the best man. The matron of honor was Kathy's friend Betty Murray, Don Murray's wife. Kathy's six-year-old daughter, Sherri, was the flower girl. Robert Goulet sang the Lord's Prayer. Among the guests were Edward G. Robinson, Don Murray, Rod Taylor, the Van Heflins, Elke Sommer, Oscar Levant, and Andy Williams. As *Photoplay* in June 1966 reported, "Kathy was beautifully dressed in an empire A-line gown in a daffodil color, the bodice of reembroidered lace encrusted in diamondette paillettes and caviar beads, with a matching double-tiered capelette."

The reception immediately followed at the Oxford Way residence. Andy Williams serenaded the newlyweds back at the house and dedicated the Hawaiian wedding song ("Ke Kali Nei Au") to the happy couple. Photographers and reporters from several news media and movie magazines were among the invited guests.

The newlyweds went on a grand tour of Europe, culminating at the Cannes Film Festival in the south of France. My father intended to dazzle Kathy with his international star status, and he did a pretty good job of it, I'm told. Everywhere they went photographers were in abundance. In London they went to see the new Noël Coward play, and Dad took Kathy backstage to meet Mr. Coward himself. And at a reception hosted by Dad's old friend Joan Crawford they were introduced to Lord Mountbatten, the famous admiral and member of the royal family. To everyone's delight, Lord Mountbatten professed his great admiration for one of my father's old westerns, *The Sheepman*. "He was," Dad recalled for me, "fascinated by a fast-draw trick I had done in the film and had to know how it was done." The trick—flipping a poker chip in the air from a glass, shooting it, and having it land back on his hand—was a very elaborate combination of skill and movie trickery involving a wire and a small amount of buckshot to make hitting the chip a certainty.

On the Riviera the honeymooners attended Princess Grace's Red Cross Ball, and in Nice they had dinner with Dad's old friends and fellow actors Alec Guinness and Jack Hawkins. Everywhere they went they were trailed by press writers and photographers.

Although Kathy was suitably impressed, she was a down-to-earth person with a great sense of fun and refused to take the pomp and circumstance too seriously. "That's one of the reasons Glenn liked me," she would recall. "When things seemed silly to me I'd laugh . . . or I'd do something silly myself and make Glenn laugh."

Of course, the problem with honeymoons is that they don't last forever. When Glenn and Kathy returned to California they were almost immediately separated for long periods by their professional obligations. Kathy learned that a pilot she had shot with Barry Sullivan and Glenn Corbett was being picked up by NBC for the fall season, and the producers needed her at once. A starring role on *The Road West*, a weekly television series, meant exhausting work and long, long hours. My father had been attracted by her charisma and talent—it's no surprise that performers find an easy rapport with other performers—but he had not given much thought to her career. My father didn't have any intention of altering his own ambitions, for Dad's generation believed that the man was the breadwinner and the wife, whatever her talents, was there to take care of him.

In June, while Kathy was busy in Los Angeles, Glenn headed out to Kanab, Utah, to shoot a Civil War era western, *A Time for Killing*, which reunited him with producer Harry Joe Brown. He and Dad had made another western, *The Desperadoes*, in that same rugged location in the early 1940s. Inger Stevens, Paul Petersen, George Hamilton, and Max Baer Jr. were also in the cast.

But young maverick director Roger Corman tangled with the producer from the start. Corman was trying for an epic feel and the look of a John Ford film, shooting lots of vistas and grand compositions in Zion National

Park. Producer Brown wanted to economize, stick to the story line, and make a basic chase picture. Corman left the production after a couple of weeks and was replaced by Phil Karlson, a journeyman director who did whatever the situation dictated.

Kathy was able to take some time off, and she, Bob Crutchfield, and I drove to Kanab, Utah, to spend a week visiting. I had been cast in a small role for one scene with beautiful Inger Stevens, so for me it was a paid vacation. I remember an extremely hot location and meeting a young fellow in the film with the same last name as mine—Ford.

Harrison Ford was playing his first role as a billed character—Lieutenant Shaffer—albeit seventh-billed. Harrison and I often ate lunch together, and I remember him as a nice guy just getting started in the business. Great things awaited him. Harry Dean Stanton and Timothy Carey, two real-life characters, to say the least, were also in this film, and two more likeable guys you could never meet. Paul Petersen, the former Walt Disney Mousketeer and star of *The Donna Reed Show*, and I became good friends on *A Time for Killing*, and he, Dad, and I would share many good times ahead in life.

George Hamilton was dating President Lyndon Baines Johnson's daughter Luci, and one day she and her entourage flew from Washington, D.C., to visit George on the set. I can recall the afternoon when LBJ's daughter arrived. We were filming in a canyon when a helicopter delivered her in the midst of our day's setup. Earlier in the day, Bob Crutchfield and I had been relaxing in our directors' chairs, and I pointed out the men I saw standing on the tops of the surrounding mountains. We couldn't figure out what they were doing up there, but it looked like they had binoculars and were holding rifles. As soon as Luci Baines Johnson plunked herself down among us, Bob and I realized that those were Secret Service agents positioned on the hilltops to protect her. I also recognized that I was dressed for my role in the film wearing a Civil War outfit with a holstered side arm. There were no bullets in the gun, but I had this queasy feeling that I'd better not make any sudden moves in her direction.

The completed movie had some strong scenes, but there was a choppy, unfinished feeling to it, perhaps a result of the directorial transference. *A Time for Killing* went virtually unnoticed on release. Incidentally, George Hamilton dated his preoccupation with his now trademark "Coppertone persona" to this film, when he noticed my father, in an effort to avoid using makeup, sunning himself daily.

236

The new trend in westerns was crude language and graphic violence, as exemplified by *The Wild Bunch*, starring Dad's friend William Holden. But the ones my father continued to make were far more conventional and modest in budget, conception, and impact.

The Last Challenge, shot in late 1966, was the final film directed by Richard Thorpe and the only one he ever produced. A veteran MGM workhorse, Thorpe had made some of the *Tarzan* pictures in the 1930s and over one hundred motion pictures in all, including many westerns. Despite *Challenge*'s pedestrian story about an older fast-gun and his young challenger, Thorpe's direction gave it a swift pace.

A solid cast supported my father, including the sultry Angie Dickinson (they had dated briefly in his bachelor years), a young Chad Everett as the young gunslinger, Bette Davis's ex-husband Gary Merrill, and our old western friend Jack Elam. The one month of filming took place mostly around Old Tucson and Palmdale, Arizona, on a large-scale western set that was originally built in the 1930s for the film *Arizona* before final interior shots were completed at MGM and on locations in Alpine Butte, sixty miles north of Los Angeles.

The weekend after *The Last Challenge* was finished, Dad traveled with Bob Hope and other celebrities to Mexico. Bob was going to tape his annual *Bob Hope Special* from a festival at which Dad's film *Rage* was to be featured. Among the others gathered together for Bob's special were Michael Caine, Cantinflas, Elke Sommer, Dolores del Rio, Merle Oberon, Jayne Mansfield, and Gina Lollobrigida.

Jack Valenti, the president of the MPAA (Motion Picture Association of America), was there to be honored by Hope for his twenty-five years of service to the film industry, but he must have flinched at the conduct of the U.S. contingent. Jayne Mansfield did a striptease at a local club—Tequila A-Go-Go—that was so risqué Hope couldn't use the footage on American TV. Even the young revelers in attendance were shocked. Then at the airport as they were leaving Mexico, Elke Sommers was detained over the nonpayment of a thirty-two-thousand-dollar hotel charge. She had thrown a big Champagne party for everyone and had interpreted the "all expenses paid" invitation to mean just that. Mexico's film bureau sighed, dug deep, and paid the bill.

Despite such frivolity, the Bob Hope trip signaled a solemn turn in my father's life as he began to give generously of himself to various charitable and patriotic causes. The war in Vietnam, an increasingly controversial

237

and bloody quagmire, was raging in the late 1960s, and Hope's trips to Southeast Asia to entertain the troops, often broadcast on TV, were well known—in some quarters, they were as controversial as the war itself. My father also believed that, whatever one thought of the intentions and strategies hatched in Washington, one should always support the troops, the young people serving their country and risking their lives. Many celebrities were making USO-sponsored visits to Vietnam to lend cheer and support, and Dad was eager to do the same.

My father had always felt some regret that his time in the Marines had not been more distinguished and ended before he could see action overseas. On occasion, when he had drunk too much, he unfortunately exaggerated his war record. Some of these "exaggerations" had found their way into print articles and interviews. But he lent a hand to the military in many other ways he didn't tout.

Having many friends and acquaintances in the military hierarchy, Dad sought a commission in the Naval Reserve, and in November 1957 he was accepted as a public information officer, charged with promoting the Navy's interests and helping to produce or narrate promotional films on their behalf, duties he would take seriously in the years ahead. He was given the rank of lieutenant commander (with special duty in public information), and after many years of hard and dedicated work on behalf of the military, on August 1, 1963, he was appointed a full commander in the United States Naval Reserves.

In January 1967 Dad finally got his wish to serve in a combat zone when the Navy requested him for active service for one month; he would be charged with narrating a documentary called *Global Marines*. On January 5, 1967, two days after he was "activated," Dad took off for Saigon. At Tan Son Nhut Airport, in his naval commander's uniform, he was met by his liaison, Colonel Jim Williams, a tough, good-humored Texan who was a highly decorated pilot and veteran of both World War II and the Korean War. Williams was determined not to treat his famous visitor "like a movie star." As he told me, "As a matter of fact, I damn near got him killed, several times. Not that I did it intentionally. Hell, I didn't want to get killed either!"

My father's forays on the front lines were many, rugged, and often dangerous, as Colonel Williams confirmed. Dad took part in Operation Deckhouse Five, working south of Saigon in the Mekong Delta region in a gunboat. He also traveled in a jeep on a road north of Da Nang, he and Williams on that occasion being the only Americans in an ARVN convoy (the South Vietnamese army). One of the trucks ahead of them hit a land mine. The truck exploded, and soldiers riding inside were scattered all over, some of them blown to pieces. Williams and my father got out of their jeep and ran to help. There was pandemonium, but the colonel would recall that my father kept his cool and went about helping to get the wounded into another ARVN truck and on the road to medical help in Da Nang.

On another occasion a helicopter pilot new to the region got lost and took his whirlybird—with Dad and Colonel Williams his passengers— across the border into enemy territory in North Vietnam. "You're gonna get us shot the hell out of the air!" Williams screamed at the young pilot when he realized the mistake. "That pilot spun us around and shot the chopper across the DMZ [demilitarized zone] like a bullet," my father recalled. "I never saw a helicopter move that fast."

On another day their helicopter was dropping them off at a Marine battalion encampment when they came under fire. They were filming at Marble Mountain, just north of Da Nang. The First Corps was fighting nearby. The helicopter took off right away after depositing them, and Colonel Williams and my father found themselves in a rice paddy, knee-deep in water, and exposed to enemy snipers. A Marine sergeant in the foxholes nearby screamed at them, "Come on, you dumb bastards, get out of there!" My father said he ran like hell to the levee. The Marines set up mortars and traded fire with the snipers for the rest of the morning.

Colonel Williams inscribed a photograph of the two of them in uniform for my father. He wrote: "Glenn, when we were being shot at in the Delta, mingling with the crowds in Saigon market, or on a lonely Laotian border, you were always a brave and truly great American of which our country and its people can be proud."

Back in California, Kathy's television series, *The Road West*, was canceled; however, she got another good break as the leading lady opposite Charlton Heston in a Universal film called *Counterpoint*. Unfortunately, the film was not a great success, and her career stalled.

Kathy spent much time shuttling between New York and L.A. looking for acting jobs, and the occasions when Dad and Kathy traveled together lessened. In June 1967 Dad was called to host some fund-raising events in the Midwest, with stops at Cincinnati, Columbus, and Indianapolis; this was in his capacity as the national cochairman of the Seeing Eye Dog Foundation. Bob Crutchfield, his publicist, accompanied him, but Kathy chose to stay home. While in Indianapolis he participated in the Indianapolis 500 parade festivities to commemorate the rain-plagued forty-first running of the famous race.

A month later, however, Dad and Kathy were winging their way to Canada and British Columbia's Campbell River to fish for salmon — Dad enjoyed mentoring the women in his life, and he wanted to teach Kathy how to fish. It was a busy summer, and they had some good times together, but by the following year, after a two-year marriage, the relationship was beginning to break down. In April 1968 they were officially separated.

In mid-May the couple went to court. Much of the strife in the marriage seemed to center on Glenn's objections to Kathy Hays's professional ambitions. Kathy told Superior Court Judge Roscoe Farley that her husband had repeatedly given her the "silent treatment" when she tried to discuss her acting aspirations. "Before we were married," she stated, "my husband advised me to sign a film contract, but after we were married Mr. Ford indicated he did not want me to continue with my acting. . . . If I tried to discuss a matter, his frequent defense was not to talk to me at all." Her mother, Mrs. Daisy Gottlieb, backed her up and said Glenn was given to "long periods of silence."

Kathy was granted an interlocutory decree and given a substantial cash settlement. My father was despondent, and to a reporter who asked about his failed marriage he said curtly, "I don't imagine I'll ever marry again. I couldn't go through another divorce."

Kathy continued to pursue her career. In the early 1970s she took a part on the daytime soap opera *As the World Turns*, and in the role of Kim Hughes she would become one of the show's beloved players and an icon of daytime television. Extraordinarily, Kathy portrayed this character until the cancellation of the show in the fall of 2010.

Oddly, the picture Dad made next after *The Last Challenge*, called *Day of the Evil Gun*, was directed by Jerry Thorpe, Richard's son. This must be the only case in film history where the same star made back-to-back movies directed first by a father and then by his son.

Evil Gun had a plot similar to *The Searchers*, with two men journeying through the wilderness to rescue their kinfolk kidnapped by the Indians, but the comparisons with John Ford's masterpiece ended there. Both Glenn and costar Arthur Kennedy gave gritty, credible performances, but there was a sense that both men were getting a little old for this sort of thing. Most of the filming was done on rough locations near Durango and

Torreón, Mexico, and it was exhausting, all that rolling around and fighting and waiting in the desert sun.

"We're doomed, Peter. We're doomed!" Arthur used to say to me at every opportunity during the shooting. He and Dad had become good friends while making *Trial*, and the three of us spent quality time together in those desolate Mexican locations. I had signed to play a nice role in the film and spent over a month on location. Hal Clifton and Bob Crutchfield were along for the ride, too.

Earlier in 1967, before the cast and crew even arrived on location, rains had washed away the town that had been constructed for the film—a town that cost $40,000 to build. Virna Lisi was supposed to be the female star, but the filming had to be postponed while the crew rebuilt the town, and Barbara Babcock stepped in. It rained every day we were there, and the planned thirty-four-day film took two months to complete.

The rain wasn't as bad as the sickness; everyone got sick—really sick—during the first weeks. I thought my reaction to the food or water was the dreaded Mexican *tourista*, so I took to my bed for a few days, but it didn't help. Finally, a doctor was found, and he gave me a shot of something. At least I *think* he was a doctor, but they called him "The General," so I'm not really sure. What I was sure of was that I was gravely ill, ravaged by a 103-degree fever, and I didn't care what they had to do to cure me. "The General" really might have been a traveling veterinarian, because not only did he arrive by horseback, but the needle he stuck in me looked like a harpoon and felt worse.

I was diagnosed with typhus, not *tourista*, and all I could think of as I lay on a straw-filled mattress on a cot in a dingy room of a shabby motel was that I might actually die in Durango, Mexico. As soon as I recovered, Dean Jagger, one of the costars, became ill. He was so sick that they had to take him back to the States for treatment before he could return and resume filming. One after the other everyone fell ill—it was like something right out of Agatha Christie's *And Then There Were None*.

Lon Chaney Jr. flew in to play a small role. When he arrived he was very inebriated and obviously not ready to work. The director asked me to run Lon's dialogue with him and help get him in shape to go before the cameras. I spent many hours with him in his room, but it was a lost cause. Jerry sorely wanted to give this once-fine actor a special moment on-screen, but Lon was unable to pull himself out of his delirium. The once fearsome "Wolf Man" broke down crying in my arms when he was sent home without having done a single scene.

Another MGM film crew was working in Durango at the time, making *Guns for San Sebastian*, starring Anthony Quinn, Charles Bronson, and Anjanette Comer. The other production was also affected by the bad weather, and there was a lot of misery shared by the casts and crews in the bars around town. There was not much to do in Durango in those days, but everyone looked forward to Sundays, when you could visit the jail and buy trinkets fashioned by the prisoners.

For the past few years things had been good between my father and me, but the Mexico location revived the old problems. For weeks Dad had been giving me a hard time (I don't know what else to call it), continually teasing me in a hostile and mean manner. I wasn't the only one who felt his wrath or ill mood. I would often end the day at the Tropicana Bar with actor Royal Dano, Bill Hart (Dad's stunt double), and Red Morgan (stunt-man), and between copious amounts of tequila and beer we talked the situation over, and they tried to comfort me.

I kept a diary during these years. "I'm getting a little disgusted with him—I among others," I wrote in my diary. "He's rude, arrogant, moody and at times very strange. I guess I'll never know my father. He seems to drift farther and farther from me. I'm no gem, but it is difficult for me to realize sometimes that we're cast from the same mold."

Many things contributed to my father's unhappiness: the long delays in filming; the fact that, for the first time in his career, one of his films was going to be marketed first to TV and not to the big screen; and once again he was having "wife" problems with Kathy Hays. Dad was stranded in this hellhole of a location with his marriage falling apart, and someone had to answer for it—guess who that was?

Here was Glenn Ford, on-screen the defender of all persons powerless and voiceless, treating his own son like a pariah. If I had been the child of someone else, he would have challenged that person to stop this nonsense. It was a troubling time between us. When my father was dating someone, there seldom was a problem between us; but when he was married or deeply committed, a transformation was likely, worthy of Dr. Jekyll and Mr. Hyde.

I had to return to Los Angeles because I was starting my senior year at USC, pursuing a BA in English; as a consequence, I couldn't fulfill my role in the film. But I did escape Mexico ahead of the others, and away from my father I tried to put my life back together.

The single most positive factor in my recovery was the introduction in my senior year to a fellow student at USC, a sharp-minded, tender-hearted, beautiful young woman named Lynda Gundersen. We had our first date in December 1967. It was three years before we would marry, but I knew from the moment we met that this was the woman with whom I wanted to spend the rest of my life.

After we had been seeing each other for a while I naturally wanted to introduce her to my parents. My mother had invited us over a few times with no formalities, but the first time Lynda met my father was when he invited us to Christmas dinner at his home in 1967. It was an intimate family occasion with just Dad and Kathy, my grandmother, Bob Crutchfield and his date, Dixie, and Lynda and me. I'll let Lynda recall her introductions to my family:

> The first time I met Peter's mother, I was of course apprehensive, because this was the mother of the guy I was nuts about, and I wondered if she'd like me. She was a famous woman—would I measure up to her standards? And we got to her home, and she was on the stairs of her two-story house, on her hands and knees with all these cleaning supplies, cleaning the railing. She greeted me warmly, and she was just wonderful. I remember saying to her after we were introduced, "I don't know what to call you . . . Mrs. Ford? Miss Powell?" And she said, "Call me Mom."
>
> The first time I met Peter's father was at Christmas dinner. . . . It was a rather formal evening, and I had never been to a house for dinner where I was catered to by servants. And then I met Glenn Ford. He was rather reserved, playing the host, showing me around the house. I was very impressed with the size of the house and noted that he took great pride in all the unique features of the home he had built. After cocktails we were called to dinner and sat in the baronial dining room at a table prepared for a dozen people. When food was to be served, he pressed a little buzzer under the table that rang in the kitchen to summon the servants. I had never seen anything like it. We had a lovely dinner.
>
> But then, at the end of the meal, I had left a small morsel of something that I didn't particularly care for on my plate. Everyone was finished and was preparing to return to the living room for dessert and Champagne, and I expected that Mr. Ford would push his buzzer again for the plates to be cleared. However, with a deadly tone, Peter's father looked over at me and said, "No one is going to leave the table until Lynda finishes her plate." I was embarrassed by his rudeness. I didn't think that was a very hospitable thing to say; after all, I wasn't his child—I was his son's date.

He was clearly out of place, and I wasn't nice [about it] either. I replied, "Well, you better get a good book, because it's going to be a long wait." I remember Bob, the publicist, later told me he wanted to slide under the table. But Glenn just paused a moment and said, "Okay, dinner's over." And that was that.

Dad had met his match. He always enjoyed testing people in some fashion, and one never knew if he were serious or not in his sometimes cruel probing techniques. I was pleased and impressed by Lynda's unflappable resolve and glad to have her on my team.

Day of the Evil Gun was followed, in my father's career, by another western, *Heaven with a Gun*—even the titles began to sound the same. Dad prevailed on me to accompany him to the Tucson, Arizona, location in mid-1968. Dad's marriage was all but over by then, and in his needy state of mind he wanted a companion on location. I went in the official capacity of dialogue director, but, as always, I was also trying to improve our father–son relationship.

The film's producers were the King brothers, three siblings who had been in the business for more than twenty-five years but whose staple was low-budget, quickly made fare. (This would be their last production.) Glenn had tried mightily to get his old friend George Marshall to direct the film; however, George was committed to Jerry Lewis's *Hook, Line and Sinker*, and he wasn't available. The King brothers selected director Lee Katzin, a veteran of TV series, to make his debut in features.

Carolyn Jones, Barbara Hershey, David Carradine, Noah Beery Jr., and a host of veteran western regulars filled out the cast. My father played a gun-toting minister who was determined to save the innocent local sheep men terrorized by a ruthless cattle baron and his gang. My father had dipped into that formula a decade earlier with *The Sheepman*, but this time the script was humorless. The film showed some of the new permissiveness of the era, with more brutal violence and some frank sexuality, but it was basically a traditional western with a modest budget and a very old-school look to it.

We spent six weeks filming in Patagonia, Arizona, and in Old Tucson before returning to Los Angeles. Although, as ever, Dad gave a solid performance, he seemed burdened by introspective woes. He was in his fifties now, and life was hurrying along. He seemed grateful for my companionship, and we got along better—better than that difficult time in Mexico, that's for sure.

Within a month of finishing *Heaven with a Gun* Dad accepted a role in *Smith!* for the Disney Studios. A contemporary western in which he played a tolerant rancher helping an Indian accused of murdering a white man, *Smith!* was Disney's first attempt at what might be called a "message picture." It was the first and last big-screen feature of TV director Michael O'Herlihy, an Irish native and brother of actor Dan O'Herlihy.

Nancy Olson, Dean Jagger, and Keenan Wynn were in the notable supporting cast, but actor Chief Dan George stole the show. I was the dialogue director on this film and worked closely with seventy-year-old Chief George on his big courtroom speech, in which his beautifully characterized old Indian, Ol' Antoine, gave a long eulogy defending his people, leaving the audience spellbound. Making this film introduced my father and me to the struggles of the American Indian competing in a white man's world at a severe disadvantage. Actor Jay Silverheels worked on this film as well, and through Jay both my father and I became active in Jay's Indian Actors Workshop, a training facility to empower Native Americans in film. My father continued to advocate Native American causes throughout his life.

The film itself received lukewarm reviews from most critics. There were a number of theatrical features ahead and a few more good roles, but essentially, with the release of *Heaven with a Gun* and *Smith!* my father's thirty-year career as a leading man came to an end. It was a tumultuous time in Hollywood. The big studios were in disarray, changing production chiefs every week and unsure of an equally fluid market. The older audience, the generation that had flocked to see *Gilda, Blackboard Jungle,* and *3:10 to Yuma,* was not going out to the movies as much anymore, and moviemakers aimed more of their product at America's newly empowered youth.

Lynda and I both graduated from USC in 1968, and I was accepted at the USC law school, with halfhearted intentions to become an attorney, while Lynda chose to pursue a master's degree in education.

The relationship between my father and me was back on an even keel, harmonious again. He wasn't focused on a romance with anybody (Kathy was pursuing divorce), so he would encourage Lynda and me to stop by for a spontaneous barbeque or an afternoon spent just sitting by his pool. Lynda had her own apartment, I was living with my mom, and I spent time shuffling between both my parents' homes.

Dad had a New Year's party at the end of 1968. The tension that had been between us in Mexico was now all but vanished. He told me he was lonely and asked me to move in with him. The following Saturday I packed my things and took up residence on Oxford Way. Mom was fine with the move; I had been spending more and more time with my father working and traveling. I had decided to just try and be friends with my father (forget love), but Mom was still emotionally scarred and sought nothing more than to have a quiet life in retirement while reserving her best thoughts for the happiness of her son and future daughter-in-law. My mother's home on Cove Way was only a few blocks from my father's, and Lynda and I easily shuffled between her apartment and both residences.

Dad suddenly had plenty of time on his hands, and he filled it with interesting activities. Somehow he got entrée to sessions of the Sirhan Sirhan trial in Judge Herbert V. Walker's courtroom on the eighth floor of the Hall of Justice for the Los Angeles Superior Court. Sirhan Bishara Sirhan had assassinated Senator Robert F. Kennedy on June 5, 1968, at the Ambassador Hotel in Los Angeles. He was being tried for murder. Dad wangled two press passes through his connections and dragged me along. I remember Sirhan's mother's testimony on behalf of her son as a moving plea by a desperate mother. Dad would offer me many opportunities and experiences like this over the next few years, and whenever he said, "Saddle up," I tightened the cinch and rode off with him.

Though I pursued work as an actor and singer, my father's intense feelings of loneliness made it difficult for me not to tag along when I was asked. Lynda was remarkably understanding, and her trips to the airport to say her good-byes to me became something of a family joke. I must say I never tired of traveling first class with overnights in the world's finest hotels while dining on epicurean cuisine. But Lynda continued her graduate studies at USC while I bounded off hither and yon to see the world, playing the role of Dad's sidekick.

In March 1969 my father and I attended the international film festival in Rio de Janeiro. Dad took Barbara Babcock, his costar from *Day of the Evil Gun*, as his guest. It had been sixteen years since I had gone to Brazil, I had forgotten all but a few words of Portuguese, and the country had changed drastically. As always, we were treated royally by the press, our hosts, and the movie fans. We each had an incredible suite overlooking Copacabana Beach. This trip was strictly for pleasure, and Dad was back in his bachelor mode.

Just before we left for Brazil I appeared for the second time on *The Dating Game* TV show. A female contestant asked questions of three prospective "dates," who were screened from her view, and then she would select her preferred date — sight unseen — based on the answers. In 1965, when I first appeared on the show and was chosen by a young lady, we went on a date to the Los Angeles opening of *The Spy Who Came in from the Cold*. By December 1968 *The Dating Game* had become a wildly popular prime-time show, and the destinations of the date were appropriately more grandiose.

The show paid union scale of about $375, plus a new tuxedo, win or lose. I was happy for the money and new tux, but I was also interested in the national TV exposure to promote a record of mine that had just been released—my eyes were no bigger than that. Of course, explaining the fact that I was contemplating going on *The Dating Game* to my fiancée was a bit awkward, but we could use the money, so Lynda unenthusiastically gave me her OK.

One day in February, therefore, I drove to ABC television studios in Hollywood, where I appeared alongside teen idol Bobby Sherman and RCA recording artist Rod Lauren. Peggy Clinger of the singing Clinger Sisters was the prospective date asking the questions. At one point she asked each of the three of us to serenade her, a cappella, with a love song. So I crooned a few lines of "Try a Little Tenderness," the audience sighed, and after a few more questions and answers she finally picked contestant number two—me.

I wasn't overly concerned when they announced that in April Peggy and I would be winging our way to Lahti, Finland, on our date. I called Lynda and broke the news that I had won, but I assured her I'd never go to Europe with a strange girl; after all, Lynda and I were engaged to be married. Then the unimaginable happened. Within the week Dad called and said that in April he had a trip lined up to New York, London, and Paris to do promotional work for Disney and *Smith!* He wanted me to join up with him and the Disney publicist, Tom Clark, in London.

His trip and my *Dating Game* journey coincided. To compound matters, the trips were scheduled during Lynda's Easter vacation, which we had planned to spend together—it was a perfect storm.

I promised her I'd behave, but Lynda was appropriately incredulous first that I'd fly off to Brazil without her and then that I was willing to go to Finland on a date with Peggy Clinger and a chaperone provided by the television show. To her credit, she rolled her eyes and forgave me. I promised that this would be the last escapade of her future mate, but it was not to be.

Peggy and I spent three days sightseeing in Helsinki and Lahti, riding in horse-drawn sleighs through the Finnish snow and immersing ourselves in saunas—all shown on American television for Lynda and the world to see—before we flew back through London.

As planned, I had an open-ended return ticket, so I left Peggy and our chaperone during the layover and joined Dad and Tom Clark at the Savoy Hotel. My father was in the company of a newly crowned Miss BBC—a nineteen-year-old beauty from Leeds—who was acting as our local guide. From London we went north to Manchester in central England to appear on the first of BBC North's new *Personal Cinema* shows. It was in Manchester that for the first time I met my English relatives (my grandmother Ford's brothers and sister), who visited us from our family's city of origin, Horwich, in Lancashire.

The three of us then took the train to Dover, crossed the English Channel to Calais, and journeyed on to Paris. To be in Paris on an unlimited expense account is intoxicating. We stayed at the fabled George V hotel, and the first night Dad, Tom, and I shared escargots, filet mignon, and a dessert of *fraises des bois* with whipped cream along with vintage Dom Pérignon Champagne. Believe me, we toasted Walt Disney and his famous mouse.

I missed Lynda terribly and felt really guilty, but it was Dad and Tom—not I—who got into some mischief with some girls from the Lido whom they brought back to the hotel. I spent my time visiting museums and enjoying the street life of Paris. My hanky-panky days were over, but not Dad's (or Tom's).

On our last night Tom had the concierge find him a date. Keep in mind, Tom was a fellow who had had a torrid relationship with Rock Hudson at a time when the public didn't know Rock was bisexual. Tom heard that Rock was in Paris staying at another luxurious Paris hotel, the Plaza Athénée. What a great idea, he thought, if he, Rock, and I were to party together with some live performers. Personally, I'm a red-blooded heterosexual, so this was not my scene; and Rock couldn't be found, so Tom resorted to having just a young damsel as his overnight guest. When we all checked out the next morning, this French beauty was with Tom in the lobby. Thankfully, I never had the experience of paying for a hooker, but out of curiosity I asked Tom what something like that costs. He said he didn't know; the hotel just added it to his room charge. Walt Disney, the purveyor of family entertainment, would have rolled over in his grave.

We were home only a month before we were back on the road again, this time to Cody, Wyoming, where Dad was to make an appearance at a dedication in the Buffalo Bill Museum (Dad was then being paid as a goodwill ambassador for the Winchester company). "It'll be a fun trip, Pete," he told me. "We'll have a good time there."

My father, Bob Crutchfield, and I flew to Denver, Colorado, where we boarded a private plane that would take us to Cody. Thanks to the attentions of the stewardesses in first class, our glasses were refilled with Champagne many times, and we were generously gifted with extra half-bottles from the galley for the second leg of the trip.

We were all pretty loaded as we changed planes, squeezing into a tiny Piper aircraft—the owner-pilot and three passengers with luggage. No sooner did we take off than our pilot opened a big bottle of Jack Daniel's and offered it to us. We began combining the whiskey with the Champagne the stewardesses had given us. No one seemed to think this was a bad idea, including the pilot, who joined us for a snort.

The next thing I knew I was in the pilot's seat. "Look, Dad, I'm flying!" How I managed to navigate the plane I don't know, but no one was complaining. We were all in pretty bad shape when we landed and had to exit the plane by some small aluminum steps. Bob went out first and promptly tumbled to the ground at the feet of the gathered museum representatives and members of the press. His briefcase popped open, and the dozens of small bottles of alcohol that he had collected on our journey and was carrying in it spilled all over the tarmac. And that was just our arrival.

Things went downhill from there. On the day of the Buffalo Bill Museum's dedication, everyone sat in bleachers outside the entrance to hear the speeches, concluded by a high-ranking official from the governor's office of the state of Wyoming. The ceremony was to have a climactic ending with the arrival of a live buffalo dangling in a harness beneath a helicopter and lowered to the ground.

I'm sure it had looked spectacular in the planning stage, but the helicopter pilot brought the buffalo directly over the assembled dignitaries. The buffalo, harnessed above us, now fully terrified to be flying instead of grazing, began peeing and defecating. The helicopter rotors blew the feces and urine right onto the gaping audience. I think my father, Bob, and I were the only ones who found it funny. Someone yelled into a loudspeaker, "Everyone inside!" But the fast thinkers were already running for cover, laughing like crazy.

During the summer of 1969 my own career heated up. I got a call from actor George Montgomery, who asked if I would be interested in going to South America to appear in a big role in an American western being shot there with Chuck Connors, Cesar Romero, José Greco, and Aron Kincaid among the cast. (Montgomery was the coproducer but didn't play an on-screen role.)

It was a tough decision, because if I agreed to go, it would mean the end of law school and a career as an attorney. I talked it over with my parents, and both said I shouldn't leave, but the thought of three months riding horses in the wilds of the mountains of Bogotá, Colombia, acting a good role, was a temptation I couldn't resist.

I left Lynda, my mom and dad, and any thoughts of attending law school and set out for the pampas of Colombia to play "Billy" in *The Proud and the Damned*, directed by Ferde Grofé Jr. The experience was worth it: rugged filming conditions, wonderful cast, memorable incidents galore. Ironically, it was my biggest film role ever, and few people ever saw it. *The Proud and the Damned* took a few years to get released in America and then quickly sank from notice.

Even though I hadn't followed Dad's advice, my decision must have resonated with my father as the kind of thing he would do—taking an audacious stab at life.

By August 1969 there was a serious film offer for my father to consider. Tony Ward of Screen Ventures International wanted Dad to star in a film about the April 14, 1969, downing of an EC-121 Constellation, an unarmed American reconnaissance plane shot down by North Korea. All thirty-one U.S. servicemen aboard were killed. This was in the aftermath of the incident in which North Korea captured the USS *Pueblo* and held eighty-two surviving crew members captive for eleven months.

Once again, Dad invited me to accompany him on this trip, along with—for some reason I still can't quite fathom—Choo Choo Collins, a Hollywood starlet and girl around town. We went to Seoul, Korea, and Tokyo, Japan, supposedly on a fact-finding trip. I think Tony's main goal was to introduce Dad to some investors in the Orient who might bankroll his project. The film might never happen (it didn't), but my father was never one to opt out of a free first-class trip somewhere.

Like father, like son, I suppose. I remember the penthouse suites at the Hotel Okura in Tokyo as the most incredible I had ever seen. I had a huge suite all to myself that overlooked Emperor Hirohito's garden behind the Imperial Palace. Every morning the hotel staff changed my satin sheets and bedding with different pastel shades: light pink, violet, soft blue, and then peach. The whole experience was beyond luxurious. Strangely, though, Dad didn't have much contact with Choo Choo; I spent more time with her than he did, actually. Maybe he felt that having a young voluptuous miniskirted babe in his retinue would impress the Asian dignitaries we met.

It was edifying to experience the colorful Ginza shopping and entertainment district in Japan, as contrasted with the stark and rather depressing military complex that was Seoul at the time. I found myself wishing Lynda was with me, and I'm sure she was wondering if these happy-go-lucky trips with my father would ever end.

14

"Devil or Angel"

My father inevitably drifted into television. It was a drop in prestige for most movie stars, but others had preceded him: Barbara Stanwyck, James Stewart, and Oscar winner Donna Reed come to mind. But working on a major network series paid well enough, attracted a huge audience, and, just as important to my father, allowed him to remain a star and leading man; a switch to character parts at this time in his life was something his pride and machismo would not have allowed.

As I've mentioned, my father had appeared on television as early as 1949, when he and my mother were guests on a local CBS show in New York City called *We the People*. Over the next two decades he appeared on at least half a dozen other shows, including my mother's TV show, *The Faith of Our Children*, two episodes of *This Is Your Life* celebrating fellow actors (Tom Moore and Walter Brennan), and an occasional syndicated TV game show like *The Movie Game*.

In March 1970 he first dipped his toes in the water as the host-narrator of a one-hour prime-time national special called *America*. Dad and I spent two weeks taping the segments at historical sites across America. Guests who sang tributes to our great nation included Connie Stevens, Lou Rawls, Bill Medley, Gary Plunkett, and Mac Davis. Stops included Washington, D.C., Arlington National Cemetery, and Independence Hall and the Liberty Bell in Philadelphia. The whole show was a culturally enriching trip for us, and we drew closer. I'm sure the experience was financially remunerative for Dad, and I also earned a few dollars as the show's dialogue director.

He took the next step in 1970 with the opening of the sixth season of CBS's *Thursday Night Movie* and a leading role in *The Brotherhood of the Bell*. This was a suspense tale about a professor in conflict with a powerful secret society within his university, what was referred to as a "WASP mafia," based on Yale's notorious Skull and Bones organization. Nowadays the film is considered by some to be a cult classic, and my father found the job to be very satisfying, working with a terrific director, Paul Wendkos, and a well-written script by David Karp. Both Wendkos and Karp were nominated for Emmy Awards for my father's first made-for-TV film. When talk of him doing a full-time network series came up, he was now ready to listen.

The banner headline on page 1 of the April 17, 1970, *Daily Variety* read: "Glenn Ford Gets 500G CBS-TV Half-Hour Series Deal." At first, the network suggested a half-hour sitcom about a policeman running a half-way house for juvenile delinquents, no doubt with memories of *Blackboard Jungle* in someone's mind, but this, thankfully, did not pan out. By the fall of 1970 the plan had evolved into a one-hour series with the lead (Dad's role) a sheriff riding a jeep in place of a horse in the modern West. Dad and a creative team got busy developing the show that eventually would be named *Cade's County* after his character, the tough but low-key Sam Cade.

Dad was restless where work and women were concerned. I was luckier: Lynda was a keeper who tolerated my youthful wanderings and persevered with me. We were married on Sunday, December 6, 1970, in the living room of my father's home, bathed in the glow of a lighted Christmas tree festooned with ornaments. The Reverend Wales Smith, Ken Wales's (actor, producer, and electronics wizard) father, performed the ceremony. In attendance were my mother, my grandmother Hannah, her caregiver, and assorted friends, including two of Lynda's sorority sisters, Pam Baker and Mimi Stermer.

After the ceremony my mother hosted a dinner at Don the Beachcomber's restaurant in Hollywood. Our reception was held the following Saturday with guests who included next-door neighbor Rita Hayworth, Jim Nabors, Cesar Romero, Edgar and Millie Buchanan, Jack Oakie, George Montgomery, and, of course, my mother, joining our family and friends at Dad's home. We cut the chocolate wedding cake with my grandfather Newton's cavalry sword.

Cade's County was custom-designed from the start. Dad would play an archetypal "Glenn Ford role" as Sam Cade. He was directly involved in creating the character, screening a number of his old films for story editor Cliff Gould, and determining in advance certain details about Sheriff Cade's outlook, style of living, and beliefs. My father said, "If the show catches on, it could go for years and years, like *Gunsmoke*, so I want to make sure this guy is a comfortable fit."

Although it was set in the mythical Southwest, in truth Maricopa, Arizona, was the model county for the series. The filming, however, never left the Los Angeles area. The town was actually the old "Peyton Place" on the Fox lot, and the wilderness was mostly the Fox ranch in Malibu Canyon. One of the reasons Dad agreed to the show was that he could work from home for a change. "I had them put it in my contract," my father recalled. "I had to be back in Beverly Hills every evening by six."

Dad handpicked the regular cast and crew. He chose one of his oldest and closest friends, Edgar Buchanan, to play his deputy, and I signed on as the series dialogue director; then, to my surprise, I was added to the cast as a county forensic deputy working on-camera. Keeping it in the family, Lynda also became a part of the production, playing a county resident in many episodes. She had joined the guild when she started teaching elementary school and had been getting quite a few calls on various shows. Attractive, hardworking, and responsible, she earned more as a background player in films than she did as a teacher, and soon she turned to acting full time.

Many actors as well as directors, stuntmen, and behind-the-camera personnel counted themselves in Dad's circle; my father had worked with some of them going back to the beginning of his career.

The series debuted on Sunday, September 19, 1971, in the 9:30–10:30 p.m. slot (PST) under the direction of award-winning veteran TV director Marvin J. Chomsky (a cousin of Noam Chomsky). The twentieth episode, titled "Ragged Edge," was a special event for my father. The director was eighty-year-old George Marshall, and this episode marked their final collaboration after having made eight films together since 1941. Watching his octogenarian friend moving around the *Cade's County* set, my father would reflect warmly, "You know that man directed his first picture—*Across the Rio Grande*—in 1916. D. W. Griffith had just made *The Birth of a Nation*. There were no stars to speak of, no big studios. I wonder how many people seeing old George working here today realize they're looking at one of the people who invented the movies and this place called Hollywood."

Richard Donner directed three episodes, and he recalled Glenn's affection for his old buddy Edgar "Buck" Buchanan and, even more vividly, the day his star was nearly killed on-camera. "Bucky played the old deputy," remembered Dick Donner. "A wonderful guy and as good as they come. And Glenn loved this guy and protected him at all costs. If he blew a line, Glenn protected him. He would come in with a pickup line or he would jump in and say, 'I didn't get that, let's go again.' I thought it was just beautiful." One day Donner shot an action sequence involving a buzzing helicopter and my father driving his jeep. "The chopper came sweeping down too low—it came down so close that a rotor clipped the top of the jeep's antenna. Glenn's head was about five inches away!"

My father, fully middle-aged now, still enjoyed doing some of his own stunts on-camera. One scene in the show involved Sheriff Cade jumping from the moving jeep. The scene was shot first with his stuntman, Bill Hart, doing the leap; then it was going to be re-created with Dad behind the wheel for the cut-ins. But instead of simply miming the start of the jump and staying behind the wheel, my father did the jump for real, landing hard on the dusty ground. After the shot everyone rushed up to help him, wondering if he was all right. He was. "Well, it just felt right," Dad said. "I saw the spot and I went for it."

Cade's County was a good show, with good scripts and likeable characters and a realistic approach to the new West, including episodes addressing minority discrimination and the plight of modern Indian tribes. But quality on television was usually trumped by ratings, and the show was a hard sell in the Sunday night slot. It ran for only twenty-four episodes before CBS pulled the plug.

The cancellation was a tough blow to my father. He enjoyed working on a show with so many friends as guest stars, and I think he generally felt that the ratings were good enough for a second year.

Within a few months Dad signed for *Santee*, his first feature since *Heaven with a Gun* in 1969. This "oater" originally started filming on videotape to save time and money, but after a few weeks the company had reverted to film stock. But it was really a television western in most ways, and it didn't help that *Santee* was director Gary Nelson's first feature after two decades in television—it showed.

This unexceptional western was filmed mainly around Santa Fe and Albuquerque, New Mexico. Dana Wynter was Dad's lovely leading lady and, besides his sizeable paycheck, the best thing about this project for

Dad. It would be three years before he would make another film and then in a much smaller, featured role in an all-star cast, portraying Rear Adm. Raymond Spruance in *Midway*.

Dad returned home from *Santee* to consider his future as an actor and, with his usual zeal, attend to his languishing love life. For my father to be without a woman in his arms was not an option.

Eva Gabor was his constant companion in those days, but in December 1972, while making an appearance on *The Dean Martin Show*, he was smitten by one of the program's young attractive Golddiggers, Suzie Lund. They began an amorous relationship that I believe was more fantasy on Dad's part and patience on Suzie's.

Lynda and I had opened an art gallery in Century City, California, to subsidize our income while we both pursued work in the entertainment industry. We featured some of Dad's abstract art. He had taken up oil painting in his spare time and over the span of twenty years had created about two dozen very interesting pieces. *This Is Your Life: Glenn Ford*, hosted by Ralph Edwards in late 1972, reunited Dad with former coworkers and old friends from his little theater days in Santa Monica. Ralph's initial "surprise" of Glenn Ford was shot at our gallery and helped showcase Dad's talent as an artist.

It wasn't long before Dad had a shot at another TV series, *Jarrett*. The feature-length pilot was shot in January 1973 in anticipation of a weekly berth on NBC. David Gerber, the producer of *Cade's County*, badly wanted to work with Dad again, and he convinced the network to take on this series.

Jarrett was about a globe-trotting investigator whose specialty was art crimes. It was intended to be a sophisticated comedy-mystery series, with a touch of James Bond, aided by the input of writer Richard Maibaum, who had scripted early Bond movies. Contrasting with Sheriff Sam Cade, the character of Jarrett was far from a "custom fit," and my father knew it. The publicity department had him posing for photographs staring intently at various works of art or pretending to be reading a thick volume of art history. It was true he could paint, but the poses looked more appropriate for an actor like James Mason, and my father was concerned he wouldn't be accepted by a public more accustomed to seeing him in a cowboy hat or a soldier's uniform.

He never was a complainer, however, and the producer was so enthusiastic. Dad was pleased, regardless, to be back on the old Columbia lot where he had made so many films. It was called Screen Gems now, and, unlike the old Harry Cohn days, the lot was almost deserted. "It's been twenty years since I've been here. And it's kind of eerie. A lot of ghosts around," he was quoted in an interview.

I was with him when he visited his old dressing room, empty now. He had it unlocked and asked me to meet him back on the stage where we were working—he wanted to be left alone in the room for a while. He sat in a chair, thinking, I'm sure, about Rita, Bill Holden, and the "terrible" Harry Cohn, imagining the hustle and bustle of the old days.

I was the dialogue director on *Jarrett*. "Jeez, they're giving me a work-out on this thing," he complained to me at the time. "I'm crashing through windows, banged on the head. . . . I was watching one of these other detective shows on the TV last night, the one with Buddy Ebsen [*Barnaby Jones*], and they didn't make him do any of that stuff."

Dad shared his doubts about *Jarrett* with his good friend Debbie Reynolds. "Why are you doing it?" she admonished him. "Do you need the money that much? You're too old. You're a movie star; you don't need to do this." But Debbie was wrong. He did need to do it. And he didn't want to be told he was "too old" for an acting job. Psychologically, he was not ready for older parts and letting some younger actor get the girl. In any case, he needn't have worried. *Jarrett* did not make it past the pilot stage after the one episode aired in March 1973.

There were television junkets, too, and within a few weeks after *Jarrett* wrapped, CBS sent Dad and me to Australia on a two-week trip to promote *Cade's County* (which, ironically, was a huge hit Down Under). I got to go—dear Lynda was left behind again—because I had a substantial part in the series. Michael Cole from *Mod Squad* and Gail Fisher from *Mannix* also came along to promote their respective TV shows. On the way we stopped at Tahiti, Moorea in French Polynesia, and Fiji. The islands were incredibly beautiful and isolated, and Dad, like his sometime friend Marlon Brando, announced that he intended to buy property there one day and build a home for himself and our family.

In Australia Dad was going to receive the prestigious Australian Logie Award for lifetime film excellence. But our trip was not without controversy. For the first few days in Sydney everything went exceptionally well and according to a busy planned schedule; when we flew to Melbourne, however, to attend the Logie Award banquet at the Southern Cross Hotel, all hell broke loose.

It started when my father refused to shake hands with Australia's minister of the media, Senator Douglas McClelland. McClelland was supposed to sit at our table. My father became upset about some things he had seen in the media about anti-American sentiments, generally negative comments about the United States, his friend President Richard Nixon in particular, and the conduct of the Vietnam War; antiwar sentiments had been expressed by the new labor government led by Prime Minister Gough Whitlam. I guess Dad's sense of decorum was compromised by too many cocktails that evening, but of one thing you could be certain—he was always one to speak his mind. He was always an American patriot.

Dad's awkward moment with McLelland was just the start. Michael Cole let slip a swear word on a live broadcast of the occasion on national TV, and my father was accused of being a racist for not wanting to sit next to Gail Fisher, a talented black actress. Dad insisted on sitting next to me. Words flew between attendees and press alike, and I remember my father screaming for all to hear that if he was such a racist, then how was it possible that Pearl Bailey was his son's godmother (which she was). Before the end of the trip Prime Minister Whitlam was quoted as saying: "Someone should have put a bucket over Glenn Ford's head." My father challenged Whitlam to do it himself—if he dared. Quite a brouhaha, and later the U.S. ambassador, Walter Rice, felt obliged to offer a formal apology to the nation of Australia. My father and I, buddies in this escapade, returned home to find many letters of support from Australians who shared Dad's views about the Labor government.

During the years after the breakup of his second marriage, after a brief period of depression and self-recrimination, my father returned to his old bachelor habits. Yes, he was getting older, but his interest in the female of the species was still strong. He went out socially with a number of prominent and beautiful ladies in this period, including dear friends Rhonda Fleming, Loretta Young (with whom he had an affair of some substance), and Terry Moore and new ladies in his life, including Jill St. John, Diane Baker, and starlet Kathy Kersh.

Some relationships were more "industrial" than heart to heart. Gangster Mickey Cohen's moll, Liz Reney, memorialized my father in her encyclopedic autobiography, *My First 2,000 Men*, as ranking number 5 among her best lovers. That's taking your credits where you find them. I must say that I liked Liz; she was as honest a person as you would ever want to meet. There was no pretense about being something she was not, which is rare in

Hollywood, and from princesses to prostitutes my father was an equal opportunity lover.

The delightful Debbie Reynolds has always been adamant that their relationship was never a "romance," but she and my father (whom she called "Pa") saw each other frequently in those years, and on several occasions Dad declared that he and Debbie should get married. Ever since they had known each other in Spain in the late 1950s Debbie had been a close and loving friend of my father's, but after her own experiences in marriage and knowing all of Dad's foibles, she didn't consider him promising husband material.

In love or work, Dad just didn't like to be idle. If he wasn't acting in a film or on television, then he wanted to be on the go, keeping busy, traveling for publicity purposes with Bob Crutchfield and/or me. Publicity junkets rescued him from boredom, you might say. People and organizations showered him with endless travel opportunities, and to my knowledge he never personally paid for any of those many trips to exciting places around the world.

I fondly recall a trip to Arizona for Dad to do a segment on the top-rated syndicated television show *Virgil Ward's Championship Fishing* and the two days of fishing at Hoover Dam with Ward, a world-class fisherman, cameras grinding. Unfortunately, despite cold beer, Jack Daniel's, and sunburn, the fish weren't biting, and the two large bass caught by the camera being pulled from the water and netted by Dad and Virgil came from the local market—probably the first and last time Virgil Ward caught dead fish.

On the way home we made an overnight stop in Las Vegas at the Sands Hotel, where Sammy Davis Jr. was the headliner. Dad, Bob, and I attended his exceptional dinner show, and Sammy introduced my dad, a friend of his, to the appreciative audience.

But it was the woman whose act preceded Sammy's that night who got Dad's attention (and mine). I don't remember exactly what Mamie Van Doren did that night (sing, I think), but it really didn't matter; she emerged clad only in an emerald green skintight matte jersey dress that revealed every pulsing inch of her. We went backstage afterward to say hi to Sammy, and then Dad said he'd see us later and disappeared. Dad joined us at the bar later. I never asked what exactly, if anything, happened backstage between Dad and Mamie, but we all returned home with stories about that trip—and when I told them to Lynda, including the Mamie Van Doren part, I was forbidden ever to leave the house again on a father–son bonding trip without her. "The fruit doesn't fall far from the tree," she reminded me.

In all seriousness, what I didn't know was that Lynda was prescient; this would be the last trip my father and I would ever take together. And worse than that, by the end of the year, a pall would descend on our family and nearly destroy it forever.

My father and I had always been passionate advocates for better treatment by our government of Native Americans. In the spring of 1973 a situation in Wounded Knee, South Dakota, grabbed my father's attention. My father and Jay Silverheels (who had worked on *Santee* with him) were quite concerned when in February what was called "The Siege at Wounded Knee" occurred.

In February a group of Oglala Sioux from the Lakota Nation reclaimed Wounded Knee in protest over the treatment of their people by the U.S. government. The standoff lasted seventy-one days. Two tribal members were killed, and a U.S. marshal was shot and paralyzed. My father was friends with President Nixon, and he had many talks with the president and then–attorney general Richard Kleindienst, who hoped Dad and Jay might serve in the situation as mediators. It never happened, but Dad's desires were sincere.

By this time Lynda and I had worked long and hard and saved enough money to leave our apartment in West Hollywood and buy our first home. It was a big decision for us. My mom was barely hanging on in her rented duplex in South Beverly Hills and was now surviving by virtue of Dad's monthly alimony payments. Taking great trips with my dad was pleasant and diverting, but I knew I was on my own when it came to making my living as a married man.

My father had come from a humble background, and he made sure that I realized the value of a dollar and hard work. I might have been a movie star's son, but when it came to daily expenses and tangibles, it didn't help a single iota that my father was famous and wealthy.

Certainly, Dad helped open many doors to film jobs, for which I am eternally grateful. I helped out on another TV show he did in the early 1970s called *The Glenn Ford Summer Show*, with Dad as on-camera host and me juggling cue cards and coordinating the script for guest celebrities—a two-week job and a lot of fun.

The occasional job came through that did not arrive on Dad's coattails: dialogue director on *Mephisto Waltz* for director Paul Wendkos, for example, working primarily with Alan Alda and Jacqueline Bisset. Or dialogue director over at Fox for *The New Perry Mason* show, working mainly with Monte Markham, who had Raymond Burr's old role as Perry Mason. I also played a recurring role as costar Dane Clark's (Lt. Arthur Tragg) assistant. The series only lasted for fifteen episodes on CBS, but the actors were a joy to work with.

Lynda worked constantly in films nowadays too, but I was no "Glenn Ford" and constantly worried about my future in show business.

Dad was inactive for most of the end of the year that I was working on *Perry Mason*. Lynda and I were busy decorating our new home, which didn't leave as much time to be with my father as in the recent past. He invited me on a few trips, but they always conflicted with my schedule—and especially in light of the Vegas sortie, my vigilant wife wasn't eager to let me out of her sight.

I felt bad for Dad because I know he wanted a friend on call. A guy friend was fine for Dad; a girlfriend was better. For all of his escapades, my father still felt periods of intense loneliness and a desire to have one woman to love and to love him. However, it had to be the perfect woman, who would mother him, take care of him, and submit herself completely to her role as a stay-at-home companion.

Dad had gone out on an arranged date with a woman named Sandra McCabe. They got along fine, but there were no sparks. Sandra mentioned that she had a twin sister living in New York. The sister, Cynthia Hayward, was a divorced, attractive twenty-something, an aspiring hand and leg model, originally from San Diego, trying to make ends meet in the Big Apple. Sandra reasoned that her sister would be a perfect fit for Glenn, and she convinced my father that he should send a plane ticket to Cynthia to come to Los Angeles so they could meet. He did send a ticket, and on December 6, 1973, Cynthia flew out to Los Angeles first class on a TWA flight.

Dad invited her to the house for a drink. They chatted for a couple of hours and decided to go out to dinner. They went to Nicky Blair's restaurant that night, and when the owner, Nicky, came by to greet Glenn and meet his date, according to Cynthia, my father said, "This is the person I'm going to marry." It was meant as a joke, I guess, but Dad was certainly smitten by the woman, though she was thirty years his junior.

They spent the next three weeks in close company, including Christmas and New Year's parties in Dad's home. Glenn pulled out every stop to flaunt his new girlfriend at the holiday parties. At home and on dates at other celebrations, she was introduced to the crème de la crème of Hollywood royalty. In a rush, Dad was certain that this time he had found his life's mate, and, for her part, Cynthia was swept off her feet by the whirl of glitz and glamour and the very real possibility that she might be the next Mrs. Glenn Ford.

The two-week whirlwind courtship completed, Cynthia went back to New York to disentangle herself from her past and prepare for a new life in the arms of Glenn Ford. Lest her new beau have second thoughts, she mailed Dad a large manila envelope, stamped "Confidential," with a revealing series of seminude photos of herself in the embrace of a hunky barechested male model. Apparently, hands and legs weren't the only body parts that Cynthia modeled, and, knowing my father, these photos must have clinched the bargain.

They pursued each other via long distance telephone for a short while. My father enlisted Debbie Reynolds, who was in New York appearing on Broadway in *Irene* at the time, to meet the girl backstage and, Dad hoped, bestow her "approval." Debbie reported back that she found Cynthia lovely and very youthful, but she later wondered if this "audition" had been such a good idea. Within months, Cynthia moved out to Los Angeles, determined to marry Dad.

She moved into the mansion on Oxford Way in Beverly Hills, and at first Dad truly was madly in love. He was nearly sixty years old, not working steadily anymore. His standing as an actor had fallen another notch in post-Nixon Hollywood, but Cynthia's genuine adoration of him and her youthful enthusiasm invigorated him and reflected well on his machismo. The press covered their every move. My father squired Cynthia everywhere with tremendous pride.

The next step was to encourage Cynthia to give acting a try, and Dad arranged for her to act a small part in his next project, another TV pilot he made in February 1974, the charming *Punch and Jody*. This prospective NBC series followed a drifter who leaves his wife to join the circus and many years later finds his life complicated when he meets a pretty teenage girl who turns out to be the daughter he never knew existed. Cynthia (billed as Cynthia Hayward) played the part of Aurora, a trapeze artist (the "catcher," I presume), and I was the bus driver and dialogue director. The ninety-minute telefilm was broadcast in November 1974, but the network declined to pick it up for series development. Dad was disappointed but undaunted, and Cynthia would take other stabs at acting.

In the early months of their relationship Cynthia sought Lynda's and my counsel on how to ingratiate herself with my father. She seemed like an uncomplicated and pleasant person, and initially we judged her as having Dad and our family's best interests at heart. My father needed someone in his life, and Cynthia seemed good for him.

She visited our home to discuss all of his preferences, from food to fashion, what pleased him and displeased him, how to cope with his moods—anything and everything Cynthia needed to do to make sure the relationship revolved around their mutual love. This devotion was the kind of thing we knew Dad craved, and at the time it seemed like the right recipe, finally, for my father's happiness.

Soon, however, she became "actress" Cynthia Hayward and no longer liked to be referred to as Dad's "girlfriend." She acquired a prestigious agent for commercial representation at Herb Tannen & Associates, and over time she broadened her horizons via numerous lessons in French, stained-glass making, photography, Asian cooking, and more. Together they threw and attended parties, traveled to celebrity gatherings and luxury resorts, greeted and mingled with fans. My father was enjoying the perks of stardom again through fresh eyes and youthful spirits, and he seemed overjoyed. Her role in his life grew exponentially, no longer girlfriend, now interior decorator, social director, personal manager, and de facto gatekeeper.

It wasn't long before my father's Oxford Way home became a redoubt, and the passage to Xanadu became impenetrable to all but a few chosen callers. We were too busy to notice the gradual changes during the summer and fall of 1974, and Glenn and Cynthia were busy too. They took a cruise to the Mexican Riviera, followed with another voyage on the *Stella Solaris* through the Greek Isles. By August Cynthia was sporting a fourteen-carat pear-shaped diamond ring.

Dad made another attempt at a prime-time series in 1974 when he filmed another pilot for NBC called *The Greatest Gift*, costarring Julie Harris and Lance Kerwin. Cynthia flew with him to Statesboro, Georgia, where the pilot was filmed, and Glenn did an admirable job in capturing the spirit of the Reverend Holvak, a poverty-stricken small-town preacher who is struggling to keep his family and rapidly dwindling congregation together in the face of adversity in the contemporary South. *The Greatest Gift* was broadcast in November 1974 as one of NBC's two-hour *Monday Night at the Movies*, and shortly thereafter, finally, Glenn received a network telegram: "We are delighted that you are again a member of the NBC family and that you will be seen on the NBC television network. . . . Best Wishes, Herbert S. Schlosser, President." NBC had bought the idea of a series but reset the locale during the Great Depression. Like *The Greatest Gift* but now called *The Family Holvak*, the series would follow the story of a rural southern preacher and his family struggling to survive during the Great Depression.

Any similarities to CBS's *The Waltons* and NBC's *Little House on the Prairie*, two hit shows about homespun rural families, were probably not coincidental. But the part of the Reverend Tom Holvak was a comfortable fit for Glenn's style and personality, and he got to work with Julie Harris, an exceptional talent who reprised her role from the pilot, playing his wife, Elizabeth. However, *The Family Holvak* proved another setback to Glenn's TV hopes, lasting for just ten episodes. But he had Cynthia to occupy his time. While most men his age were slowing down, Dad was revitalized by Cynthia's tireless energy. He had always taken good care of himself, and now the years fell away as he kept pace with Cynthia. He looked a decade younger than his age. He was blessed with his looks, he well understood, and they were part of his longevity in the business—they and many other things, including his relentless drive.

My mother chose a different path and retired gracefully as a champion, unlike so many who hold on too long, hoping to hear that last glorious applause. Dad would soldier on not for the money and the fame—he had plenty of both—but in part because he was driven by the fear of losing all the other benefits, not the least of which was Cynthia.

Television movies and foreign syndicated series became the source of most of Dad's lucrative employment for the rest of the decade. My father starred in *The Disappearance of Flight 412*, an unusual and well-made story about the Air Force and UFOs, shown as an NBC World Premiere Movie in 1974. He was in the *Once an Eagle* miniseries (1976), a top-quality depiction of war, and had good starring parts in *The 3,000 Mile Chase* (1977), *No Margin for Error* and *Evening in Byzantium* (both 1978), and *The Gift* and two miniseries, *Beggarman, Thief* and *The Sacketts* (all 1979)—respectable work.

Friends of Man, a Canadian Broadcasting Network series of forty-five episodes in which he acted as host-narrator, explored the relationship of humans and animals across the globe and was a popular show.

The telefilm about UFOs reflected Dad's lifelong fascination with otherworldly and supernatural phenomena. On his own he delved into mysticism and the extrasensory, studied astrology and numerology and

264

psychic powers, and through the years consulted with practitioners in the various forms of these disciplines.

My first memory of these interests harks back to when I was very young. Dad paid a handsome sum to a Mr. Ed Hall to have elaborate numerological charts prepared for him, my mother, and me. Later, he would consult this numerological information when important decisions had to be made regarding travel, execution of contracts or agreements, and other milestone occasions.

In the early 1960s, when Dad was still diligently pursuing Hope Lange, he became a friend and mentor to the Dutch psychic Peter Hurkos. Dad had many parties at his house where Peter gave readings to my father's celebrity friends. He seriously tried to produce a movie about Hurkos's life, and my father's diaries are full of references to Hurkos predicting that certain things would happen in his life. My father took Hurkos's pronouncements to heart, and this was not just an idle fancy. For many years he was under Hurkos's spell until finally, after many failed interpretations, he and the psychic parted ways. To be honest, many people in Hollywood have dabbled in the occult; this is not necessarily a repudiation of a godly world but rather an interest in the possibility of the magic of transcendence.

My father believed that the human mind held secrets and depths of knowledge beyond everyday consciousness. For that reason, in the early 1960s, at the suggestion of his friend and neighbor Cary Grant, he even participated in a scientific study of LSD use sponsored by nearby UCLA researchers. Dad found the hallucinogenic to be a powerful sensory experience but in no way "enlightening." He tried it once, under supervision, and never again.

In an experiment sponsored by the University of Southern California, Dad submitted himself to hypnotherapy treatments. During these sessions he was observed to "regress" into other personalities and "past lives." Intrigued by the results, in the mid-1970s, ostensibly to research a film project about Dr. John Kappas, the first president of the American Hypnosis Association, he returned to controlled hypnosis sessions with the goal of recalling more about his previous life experiences. These sessions were taped, and the recordings are eerie.

With my father sunk into a deep trance, the hypnotist led him backward in time. In a vague, groggy-sounding voice, my father would begin to speak of incidents from his past, his known past to begin with, including traumatic experiences like the humiliation he had undergone from director Ricardo Cortez when making his first feature film, recalling certain incidents and precise dialogue in detail. The hypnotist then sent him back farther in time, to childhood, then to a memory of his birth, and finally, slowly, to a time before he was born.

In response to the hypnotist's steady questioning, my father began speaking in an altered voice and persona, revealed to be that of a cowboy, a trail boss named Charlie Bill, born in Cheyenne, Wyoming, in 1855. He spoke freely and in detail of his life and daily activities. Eventually, the hypnotist moved him to an even more distant time, my father breathing and mumbling as if half asleep. New voices and identities rushed forward: a British merchant sailor of the seventeenth century, fleeing the Great Plague in London; a Christian from third-century Rome. Altogether, five of these so-called previous lives were revealed during my dad's unsettling hypnosis sessions.

More than once Dad himself listened to the taped playbacks. He couldn't have known, consciously, about some of the things he described, including the degree of detail with which he discussed remote places and times and professional activities. His "other" identities were inexplicable by conventional reasoning. He was too wary of his public image to say he was completely convinced, but he did not take the experiments lightly, and their revelations lingered in his mind.

As I have mentioned, it was not unusual for my father to confabulate on occasion. He would tell stories about owning homes in various locations, like France and Tahiti; he would boast of breeding racehorses, meeting Winston Churchill, and being in Europe in May 1945 to celebrate VE Day (actually, he was at Warner Bros. making *A Stolen Life* with Bette Davis at the time). No one ever checked the veracity of these anecdotes, and in time they became a part of his (and our family's) life story, part myth and part publicity.

He did live an incredibly rich life, but it was as though reality was never enough. In some ways my father never came to terms with who "Glenn Ford" really was. In many ways he conducted his life in a way inconsistent with his grounded, spiritual upbringing, and I think, through other-worldly exploration, he hoped his inner self, the essence of his soul, would be revealed.

Ladies were part of this reinvention of self. If his career was stalled, if he was bitterly disappointed in his failed marriages, why not erase the past and create a new history that wouldn't haunt him?

Just before Christmas of 1974, there was a family schism. Dad and Cynthia were not yet married, but the new woman in his life helped to manufacture a deep rift in our family that lasted for decades.

It's hard for me as his only child to explain how and why he could have repudiated Lynda and me so egregiously, but it happened. Could his resentment of me as a child contributing to the breakup of his "dream marriage" to my mother been festering all this time? This I know—my father was the puppeteer, and Cynthia was merely his instrument. He would make little suggestions, and then Cynthia would take action. As though fascinated by his godlike powers, Dad would observe the consequences and perhaps engage in a little hand-wringing at the carnage, but someone had to be sacrificed in this Greek tragedy, and it was us.

We were invited to my father's home in mid-December to help decorate his Christmas tree, and all was well on that occasion, but by Christmas Lynda had received a nasty phone call and letter from Cynthia telling her she was "no longer welcomed at Glenn's home."

Lynda is a private person who tends not to interfere in other people's affairs, but Cynthia, most likely at the behest of my father, insisted that she and Lynda become the interlocutors to heal any breaches, past or present, between my father and me. Lynda did not feel comfortable meddling with Glenn and her husband's relationship. "Let's leave the boys to themselves," she told Cynthia repeatedly.

More than once Cynthia became furious, and this time in frustration she told Lynda, "Go fuck yourself." Lynda was incredulous and hung up on her. Shortly thereafter, Cynthia's letter of "excommunication" arrived in the mail.

Before all this happened we had given Dad and Cynthia a thoughtful Christmas gift. Just before Christmas our gift was unceremoniously returned, unopened, on our doorstep. Lynda heard a noise one evening, looked out our front window, and saw Cynthia and her sister running to their car after making the front-porch deposit.

In an interview before they wed, my father said the new lady in his life had saved him from the despair of a failed marriage. He and Cynthia were pictured in his home, both smiling for the cameras, obviously in love. "She brought me back to life again," Dad said. "In many ways she saved me from God knows what. I was dying. There was a terrible void inside of me. . . . Unlike other women I've known she doesn't come to me with her hand out. She's a giver not a taker."

She was a "giver" all right—and we were the recipients of a lot of pain. Gradually, my father began to distance himself from some other long-term friendships. It seemed to many that his older relationships were plowed to fallow in order for the new one to thrive.

Debbie Reynolds, after nearly twenty years of closeness with my father, found that her calls to him went unreturned. She eventually stopped calling. Bob Crutchfield, Dad's publicist, friend, and confidant since the mid-1960s who had been in weekly contact with my father for over a decade, was cut off from Dad without a word. Edgar and Millie Buchanan's calls were likewise ignored. Actor Dean Jones, a friend for two decades, was banished. I heard many similar stories from longtime friends. When people asked Dad about these drastic changes in his life, they met with indifference or denial. If they pushed, he would give them some "good reason" why he no longer saw this person or that person. The new people in my father and Cynthia's circle were the Gregory Pecks, the George Kennedys, and Frank and Barbara Sinatra.

Cynthia was the center of his universe, and any complaints about her drew an angry rebuke, even if, I was told, they came from his beloved mother, Hannah, now living on Oxford Way in the attached guest house and confined to a wheelchair.

During Cynthia's redecorating phase of the Oxford Way house Hannah had pleaded to have her own familiar surroundings left alone, but my father allowed drastic changes to be made. So it came to pass that my grandmother, whose home was stylishly decorated in a palate of lavender and ivory, found herself living in a blaze of Cynthia's favorite colors: canary yellow and chartreuse.

Even if we were not made welcome in my father's life in those years, we still kept in close contact with my grandmother Ford. She was mystified by the strained relationship between her son and grandson, and we discussed it often, but she could only wring her hands. We visited her as often as possible for dinner and card games.

My father's house was huge (it had five levels), and we could walk in and out of Grandmother's house, using her side gate, unnoticed if necessary. However, to avoid a potential confrontation, we were kept apprised of my dad and Cynthia's comings and goings and made it a point to try and stop by when the coast was clear.

My grandmother had a companion-caregiver who attended to her needs, and the four of us would enjoy dinner and an evening of conversation over a game of canasta. However, one time my father caught us visiting and provoked an ugly incident. He happened to be home, and of course he didn't know that Lynda and I were coming over to have dinner with his mother. Glenn appeared in her guest house and asked for Grandmother's magnifying glass for Cynthia to use. Dad was cordial to Lynda and me, but after about a minute, when I thought he was well out of earshot, I said to Grandmother (referring to her magnifying glass), "Well, that's the last time you'll ever see *that* again." In a flash my father appeared from where he had been lurking just around the corner and dared me to repeat what I had just said—which I did as I stood up from the table.

He came toward me with clenched fists. I advanced and beckoned him forward with the challenge, "Come on, Dad, let's get it on." I think I might have said a few other negative things about Cynthia, because my adrenaline was pumping and I was ready for a fight. It never went any further—thank God. He backed down and left. I was thirty-two years old, and at 6 feet 2 inches tall and 220 pounds I was facing a man of sixty-one; it's chilling to think of what might have happened.

But we continued to visit my grandmother, especially when we could see her interact with her great-grandson, Aubrey Newton, our first child, who was born in January 1977. We introduced him to his great-grandmother as soon as we were able. She adored little Aubrey, and we are proud to have photos of the two together.

Fortunately, Dad and Cynthia were often out of town, working on television shows or appearing at publicity events, accepting honors at film festivals, traveling for weeks or months at a time. Dad delighted in introducing his less well traveled wife to the foreign cities and countries and world capitals he loved. These luxury trips (everything first class and an honorarium besides) were always sponsored by sincere, well-funded fans who basked in Dad's presence. He was a pioneer, for example, on the "movie star cruises," or "film festivals at sea," as they were sometimes called, sailing four times on different cruises with other stars, including June Allyson, Olivia de Havilland, director King Vidor, Gloria DeHaven, Helen Hayes, Cornel Wilde and his wife, Jean Wallace, Ann Blyth, and Rita Hayworth. Daily screenings were followed by question-and-answer sessions with the stars. I know my father relished the chance to reminisce about his old pictures and discuss his creative process, and he would hold court in the lounge each night long after his official obligations were over.

On one notorious trip Rita Hayworth was less cooperative, offering perfunctory replies in the talk-back sessions, clearly uncomfortable with the public scrutiny. She had a pair of attorneys with her who helped keep people at arm's length. Only once did she come out of her shell, and that was on a night when a live band played, and, transported by the music, she danced up a storm with her old flair and joy.

Rita's friendship had survived all of my dad's relationships with women, and it survived Cynthia's (although, I heard, Rita refused to have her picture taken with Cynthia onboard the cruise ship). For years their relationship had been so close and casual that Dad would often come home to find Rita at the bar fixing herself a drink or sunbathing by his pool. Sometimes she wanted to talk and unburden herself about something, other times she wanted to be left alone. His home was an escape for her, and my father respected her whims. They would go out to dinner on occasion or accompany each other to events and premieres. During the "Cynthia years" Dad saw much less of Rita but still stayed in touch. When he called to check on her now and then she seemed either in a perpetual state of unreal enthusiasm or on the verge of tears. Suspicious of most people, she seldom admitted visitors or came to the phone. Sadly, she was an alcoholic, and much of her depressed and erratic behavior was due to her drinking.

In 1979 Rita sold the house next door and took an apartment in Beverly Hills, and most people agree that she was never the same. She had fallen in with some people who took control of her life, and they did not serve her well. Much later we learned that Rita was suffering from a debilitating disease few people had ever heard of at that time: Alzheimer's. It slowly eroded her mind, with tragic results. It wasn't long before Rita's loving daughter, Princess Yasmin, decided to bring her mother back to New York to live with her in a large condo on Central Park West. My father stayed in touch with Yasmin, but he declined to visit Rita in New York. He found the prospect too heartbreaking. "I wanted to remember her as she was," he said.

Rita's house was sold and torn down. A fence went up to block the old passageway between Rita's former property and my father's. But he kept the little gate that had served as the portal for so many visits between them. Many times he would sit outside by the pool, smoking his cigars, looking off into the distance, musing about his beautiful friend. But long before her death in 1987, she was gone.

My father was one of the pallbearers at Rita's funeral.

My father and I went to MGM studios to see Mom dance in *Duchess of Idaho*, November 1949. It was an exciting day for me to see my mother dancing. I had lunch with my parents and the film's stars, Esther Williams and Van Johnson, in the MGM commissary.

Glenn Ford and Gloria Grahame rehearsing a scene for director Fritz Lang during the making of *The Big Heat*, March 1953.

Left: A "loving" photo of Dad and Geraldine Brooks in a funicular after work in *The Green Glove*, June 1951. After their affair went on the rocks he was driven in despair to try and join the French Foreign Legion.

Glenn Ford and director Richard Brooks appropriately pose before a blackboard during the making of *Blackboard Jungle* at MGM studios, December 1954. This was a breakthrough film for my father. Dad began a long-term contract at this storied Dream Factory after making this film.

Top right: Glenn Ford and Marlon Brando playing yet another game of chess in my father's dressing room, June 1956. The competitiveness of these two acting pros would lead to a rivalry during the making of *Teahouse of the August Moon*.

Bottom right: Glenn Ford and Van Heflin appear in the 1957 western film classic *3:10 to Yuma*, December 1957. John Barrymore told my father early in Dad's career never to turn down the part of the villain. In this film he took Barrymore's advice with great success.

Dad and a love of his life, Maria Schell, have a playful moment during the making of the film *Cimarron*, January 1960. Dad fell in love with Maria. They never married and both regretted it their entire lives.

Dad and Hope Lange hit the dance floor for an uncharacteristic (for my father) bit of dancing, in this case the Twist, August 1962. He was desperate to prove to Hope that he was the "young man" of her dreams.

Dad and I on the set of *Brotherhood of the Bell*, on this day filming at the Huntington Library in San Marino, February 1970. It was my father's first appearance in a television production. I worked as the dialogue director on this cult classic and we would rehearse Dad's lines between shots.

Top left: My father dropped by Gold Star Recording Studios in Hollywood to see me record "Blue Ribbons" for Phillips records, July 1965. My A&R man, Mike Curb, and engineer, Jack Tracy, are working the mixing board.

Bottom left: Dad and actress Kathy Hays, his second wife, enjoy their honeymoon on a gala trip through Europe, May 1966. They attended the Cannes Film Festival on this occasion and were followed relentlessly by the paparazzi.

Dad and his young soon-to-be third wife, Cynthia Hayward, April 1975. Lynda and I accepted her into our family in hopes that she would bring Dad happiness. She did for a while but at great cost to us and eventually to him as well. She eventually abandoned him when he became ill.

The four-hour TV-movie *The Sacketts* was presented on NBC, May 1979. Dad, Tom Selleck, Sam Elliott, and Glenn's old friend Ben Johnson acted in this Louis L'Amour story in what was to be one of the last appearances that my father made in a quality western. Dad loved making westerns.

A family dinner at the Oxford Way home with Dad and his family: son Peter, daughter-in-law Lynda, grandchildren Aubrey, Ryan, and Eleanor Powell Ford with their grandpa in the living room, Thanksgiving 2004. Dad was eighty-eight years old.

15

"Lyin' Eyes"

Dad spent 1977 traveling, and of course it was financially fortuitous that he was able to take Cynthia on an around-the-world honeymoon *before* the wedding by virtue of his employment as the host-narrator for *When Havoc Struck*. The couple went to London, Paris, Wales, Monte Carlo, Italy, and on a virtual tour of the United States, as well as islands in the Caribbean Sea, in the quest of documenting the different locales where spectacular disasters had occurred throughout history. The BBC through Lord Lew Grade's ITC Corporation produced this series of twelve episodes. My father and Cynthia got to be on the road together, while Lynda and I had a chance to come by Dad's house and visit my grandmother without any uncomfortable confrontations.

On September 10, 1977, at precisely 11:00 a.m., after a two-and-a-half-year courtship, Glenn Ford and Cynthia Hayward were married at his home at 911 Oxford Way. The date and exact time of the ceremony were chosen by famed Hollywood astrologer Carroll Righter. The officiating minister was the Reverend Robert Schuller of Crystal Cathedral fame. Dad's best man was William Holden accompanied by Stefanie Powers. Among the guests were John Wayne with his date, Pat Stacy, the Jimmy Stewarts, the Frank Sinatras, George Kennedy and Vera Miles, the Henry Hathaways, the Robert Goulets, and members of both families among the one hundred guests. This was a happy day for my father and Cynthia.

Lynda and I sat inside the house with my grandmother at the table reserved for family and staff. The celebrities were seated outside by the pool, which was afloat with miniature "barges" laden with small palm trees, birds of paradise, red torch ginger, and all manner of tropical fruit. A three-piece Hawaiian band played my father's favorite music on the lawn by the swimming pool. Cynthia wore a white silk suit and pink blouse. The maid of honor was her sister, who had initiated the relationship, Sandra McCabe.

My father's glow of happiness wasn't only in the personal realm. He and Cynthia had just returned from Canada, where he appeared in a brief but important role in a big-budget film about a comic book hero, 1978's *Superman*. Dad was given the chance to appear in one last major film by his old pal director Dick Donner, whose suggestion it was that he play Superman's earthly father, Jonathan Kent. Dick promised my father that this was not going to be some drive-in comic book movie but grand-scale entertainment.

The scenes with the Kents—Glenn Ford, Phyllis Thaxter playing his wife, and young actor Jeff East as Clark/Superman—were shot outside Calgary. When Dad arrived for wardrobe fittings on location, to his dismay the production people outfitted him with a bulky white wig to make him look older. Dick Donner recalled:

> The producers hadn't instructed the wardrobe people. They just took it upon themselves. Glenn didn't want it, but he's a trouper. Glenn was such a gentleman. Late one afternoon I'm coming through the lobby of the hotel and head for the desk to get my messages. Glenn came up behind me and asked to talk. I said, "Sure thing, you've got it." And Glenn said, "Richard, I just want to know if you really think I should wear this?" And I put down my messages and turned around to look at him and saw him with this big white hairpiece on. It was ridiculous, like a Harpo Marx wig. It was a fright wig! I fell on the floor laughing.
>
> Well, I was laughing so hard, and he started to laugh, and we both wound up hugging each other and laughing in the middle of the lobby, looking insane. Glenn said, "You don't want me to wear it?" And I said, "Of course not!" He took the wig off, and there was a bellhop walking by us, and Glenn tossed it to him and said, "Boy, would you burn this?" And it turned out to be a very wise decision. Glenn looked touchingly real in the role he portrayed, and with his own hair.

Of the actual filming, Donner recalled:

Glenn has this great scene with the kid . . . and then gets a heart attack. I'll never forget when we shot the scene. He already had it planned out in his mind. When he did it, he grabbed his arm and looked up and said, "Oh no . . ." And I'll tell you something, we're on-camera, and the crew, everybody, looked at each other like, Oh God! We thought we were watching an actor have a heart attack. And Glenn fell to the ground, and there was this moment when you think, Do we let it run because it's a great scene, or do we say, "Oh my God!" and run over and see if he needs help.

The film, starring Christopher Reeve and Gene Hackman, was a box-office sensation and, as my father suspected it would be, a great piece of entertainment enjoyed by people of all ages and around the world. Additionally, *Superman* introduced my father to a whole range of younger movie-goers who heretofore would have not been aware of him. He received some of the highest praise from many critics for his work in a small role in this major motion picture. Richard Donner directed it wonderfully. And although Dad continued to work in films for another thirteen years, I like to think of *Superman* as a fitting finale to my father's career. Even the fact that he had made his contribution in Canada, where his own life began over sixty years earlier, gave it the feeling of closing a circle.

The Sacketts was another matter altogether. My father looked forward to making this 1979 television western, but the stresses he faced due to aging, constant travel, and fewer quality opportunities to pursue his profession had begun to take their toll. It was on *The Sacketts* that for the first time my father started to drink during filming. He had always enjoyed a nip or more but always after work or in social situations; now I had heard from Bill Hart, Dad's double and stuntman, that my father was not confining his imbibing to after hours.

Even though my little family of three was not seeing much of my father, I was concerned. The reviews of this two-part, four-hour NBC TV-movie were mixed, and I could see things in his performance that troubled me. Irrespective of all the game-playing that had hurt our relationship, I was an admirer of Dad's acting and hated to see it slide.

Dad still got interesting parts in the occasional feature. *The Visitor*, aka *Stridulum*, an occult–science fiction Italian-American coproduction, had a stellar cast of similarly aging personalities: Mel Ferrer, Shelley Winters, and director-actors John Huston and Sam Peckinpah. It was not the finest hour of any of these people.

285

Dad threw himself into more film work at the end of 1979, making the TV miniseries *Beggarman, Thief* and an epic fifteen-million-dollar Japanese film called *Virus*. He played President "Richardson" of the United States in this big-budget doomsday film about lethal germs ending life on Earth. He had a small role that he shot in only a few days' work at Toronto's Kleinberg Studios. But he was not in the best physical shape and from things I heard at home from his household staff and my grandmother, he was often moody and short-tempered.

In December 1979 Dad gave a masterful performance, working with Julie Harris again in a two-hour TV-movie adaptation of Pete Hamill's novel *The Gift*. He played a grizzled, one-legged, alcoholic Irishman struggling to come to terms with his son. This was a laudable must-see job of acting, and in my opinion one of his finest works. I wish he could have stepped away from the cameras after this film, but he could not bring himself to do so.

My father employed some of the best publicists in the business to spin stories that cast him in a favorable light. Yet I was greatly amused, after he filmed *The Gift*, to spot Dad and me on the front of the *Midnight Globe* (April 9, 1979) in a large, cheerful photo taken back when I visited my father on the set of *Experiment in Terror* in 1963. The caption read: "WHY GLENN FORD IS A SO SAD DAD." The tabloid wrote that making *The Gift* was incredibly painful for my father because of his own rift and lack of communication with his real-life son, Peter. "But Glenn wants to change all that 'before it's too late,'" the article said. "His decision to reach his son has come because of his latest role in *The Gift*, the story of a man and his son—a story very much like Ford's. Ford, 62, was close to tears as he spoke of the gap that he has been unable to bridge between himself and Peter."

If the strained relationship between us motivated his performance, then at least something good came out of it, but I doubted there was any truth to the story. It was just an opportune time for some good PR—like the good old days back on Cove Way.

We maintained contact with my father as best we could in the years that followed, but the distance between us seemed to stretch and grow. I concentrated on my own life and family. I continued to find work in the film industry for a while, but the work was unsteady. I occasionally had a role in TV series like *Cannon* and *Police Story*, but on an episode of Buddy Ebsen's *Barnaby Jones* I had a life-altering experience. I was working with actor James Woods, and he and I were almost killed in an airplane accident. I was portraying a drug-runner, and I had landed my airplane, exited, and was approaching Jim to engage in some dialogue when my plane broke lose from its moorings and began taxiing toward my turned back.

The camera crew was shooting over Jim toward me, and the next thing I knew Jim had pulled us both to the ground as the plane swept over us and slammed into the fleeing crew and camera equipment. Some of the members of the crew were hurt, and a lot of damage occurred, but after the paramedics arrived and new equipment was organized, filming continued. I took this as an omen, however, and decided there really was little future for me in acting as the family breadwinner. I began to devote my time to another passion of mine, carpentry, and soon found steady work in woodworking and as a carpenter for hire.

Ironically, it was the non–show business child, Lynda, who continued to make a good living appearing in virtually every TV series in production at the time (she played Harrison Ford's wife in the miniseries *Dynasty*, we always like to brag) and some blockbuster features such as *The Towering Inferno, Chinatown,* and *The Poseidon Adventure.* Together we continued to buy, remodel, and sell homes. Lynda and I did almost all the work on the building projects ourselves. She sewed the drapes, did the exterior landscaping, and decorated. I did most of the construction, and we both did all the painting.

Whenever we finished the improvements on a house, we took a breath and sold it, gathered our profits, and like nomads moved on to the next. Personally, I was very happy to return to doing something I had always loved, building and working with my hands, and at last, with my own abilities, I felt some control over my family's future.

Naturally, once I had established a home construction company, many of my clients were show business contacts. My first major building project for hire was for Walter Coblenz, who produced, among other films, *The Onion Field* and *All the President's Men.* I went on to build and remodel homes for many well-known clients, including producer Steve Tisch (*Risky Business* and *Forrest Gump*), superagent Jeff Berg, Don Simpson (the producer of *Top Gun* and *Beverly Hills Cop*), once-marrieds Charles Shyer and Nancy Meyers (*Private Benjamin* and *The Holiday*), actress Jo Beth Williams, health guru Richard Simmons, actress Sally Kellerman (*M*A*S*H*), Blake Edwards and Julie Andrews, as well as three projects for world-renowned architect and 1989 Pritzker Prize winner Frank Gehry.

The 1980s brought winds of change for us and my father. The first year of the decade Lynda announced we were going to have another child. We told Grandmother Ford the good news, but we were not in contact with my father and assumed she would tell him. I'm not sure if she did, as we never heard from him. But after seventeen weeks of pregnancy, we lost the baby. Lynda was in the hospital for three days and returned home devastated.

My father worked sporadically over the next eleven years. He made six features with diminishing returns. On television he made a few guest appearances as himself and in 1981 hosted and narrated a documentary about sharks, *The Great White Death*. Turning seventy, he played a role in *My Town* (May 1986), a one-hour Disney TV Sunday Movie, and had third billing in *Final Verdict* (September 1991), a made-for-cable (TNT) courtroom drama from the book by Adele Rogers St. John about her real-life father, famed criminal attorney Earl Rogers, reputedly the model for Perry Mason.

For the Disney Channel Dad hosted a four-part special titled *World War II: A Personal Journey,* which aired in late 1991. This would be his last appearance as a professional performer after a fifty-two-year career of work that began with a studio paycheck in 1939. Sometimes, still, the paychecks were big; in 1979 he received $100,000 for two days of work on a turkey called *Day of the Assassin*. Cynthia often accompanied him, as part of the deal, on locations.

In Canada in 1980, while Dad was shooting a pretty good horror film called *Happy Birthday to Me*, he and Cynthia had made an overnight stop in Quebec City, spending a few days at the luxurious Château Frontenac hotel so Dad could show his wife the city where he was born and raised. They went down the St. Lawrence River toward Trois-Rivières to visit the Ford family compound in Portneuf so that Cynthia could meet some of the clan still living there. Dad showed her the places he remembered as a child. He had not been back there since he visited in 1941 for the opening of *So Ends Our Night*.

They visited Woodend Cemetery, where Dad's father, Newton Ford, had been reinterred in a double plot that in the future would be the final resting place for Dad's mother. He planned to be buried there himself one day next to his parents, he told Cynthia. My father always was a careful planner. He wanted Cynthia to know what his wishes were. Little did Cynthia know that in less than three months she would be back in Portneuf again—this time with her sister and not my father—but at this very location.

Always restless, in September 1980 they were back in Europe again, invited to attend the Deauville Film Festival, where six of Dad's films were being screened, propitiously on the third anniversary of their marriage. From Deauville they went to the Ritz Hotel in Paris for a long stay. They visited Olivia de Havilland, who was living there, and hosted her and some French friends in their fifteen-hundred-dollar-a-day suite. The Paris side trip was part of the arrangement with Deauville.

They had been back in Beverly Hills for only a short while when they got a call that Grandmother Ford was ailing. I had not seen my grandmother for many months due to the family tensions. She had been sent to a nursing home but was brought back to the Oxford Way house when it was determined that she was seriously ill and going to die.

On December 2, 1980, Dad's mother, my grandmother, passed away at age eighty-six. Her severe rheumatoid arthritis had grown rapidly worse, and her passing was an almost insurmountable loss for my father. Her love had been unconditional, and her support and belief in him, he felt, had made everything in his life possible. The sense of loss seemed not to fade with time but to deepen, as it does with many people. No diversion would calm his grief. Cynthia and her sister, Sandra (without my father, who could not bear to go), took my grandmother back to Canada, laying her to rest next to her husband at Woodend Cemetery.

The deaths of friends also haunted my dad. I sometimes think 1979 is the year my father's world really started to crumble. His friend the durable John Wayne succumbed to lung and stomach cancer. This happened only a week after a television tribute to him, *When the West Was Fun*, was broadcast. My father and about every living western actor had gathered at the ABC Studios to pay homage to the Old West and John Wayne. Everyone knew Duke was seriously ill, but the finality of this American icon's death was a blow to his friends in the industry and fans around the world.

Less than a year after my grandmother's passing another tragedy occurred. Bill Holden and my father had been good pals for most of their lives, although there were times when years went by without them seeing each other. Holden had spent much of the 1960s and 1970s in Switzerland and in Kenya when he wasn't making films all over the rest of the world. They would keep in touch by phone and letter, however, and when Holden returned to Hollywood to work or visit, the friendship would resume as close as ever.

In 1981 Bill was living back in the States again, splitting his time between a house in Palm Springs and an apartment at the beach in Santa Monica. On Dad's birthday Bill showed up at the Oxford Way house with a present. It was one of the capes the actor had worn in his first starring role in 1939's *Golden Boy*. "This is something very special to me," Bill told him, "and I would like you to have it. We have been through a lot together. You are my very best friend."

Later in the fall, Bill Holden dropped by the house one day, full of excitement. He had secured the rights to a script called *Dime Novel* about two over-the-hill cowboys, one a lawman and the other a sheriff. It was going to be a project for the two old friends, he declared. They were going to shoot it in Mexico, and they were going to get Blake Edwards or maybe Burt Kennedy to direct. They went outside with their cocktails, and my father barbecued steaks while Bill told him the story and how the film was going to use footage of the two of them as young men in their 1941 picture *Texas* for certain flashback sequences. Dad loved the idea of a reunion picture with Bill after all those decades. Over the next weeks they met for dinner and drinks to discuss the project. Bill said he had one more movie to make first, *That Championship Season*, and then the two of them would head off together for Mexico.

Holden was a heavy drinker, and in middle age it had begun to take its toll on his health and his appearance. Still, what happened next came as a brutal shock to everyone who knew him. On November 11 Bill was alone in his apartment in the Shorecliff Towers in Santa Monica, drinking too much, it's assumed, and he fell and hit his head on his end table. He lay on the floor for days, unable to reach a telephone to call for help, and he died where he had fallen.

Dad was shattered. It was like losing a family member, a brother. Glenn and Bill had come up in the business together, known each other for forty years, seen each other at their best and worst, understood each other as few people could outside their rare world.

My father's own alcohol dependency had been increasing since his mother's death. With the news of Bill's untimely passing, he went on a bender that landed him in St. John's Hospital in Santa Monica. He came home for a week and then collapsed again and was admitted to Cedars-Sinai Medical Center in Los Angeles. Unfortunately, it wouldn't be the last time he would need treatment for alcohol or depression.

Following Bill Holden's funeral, my father made another escape from home. This had become his usual method of dealing with his melancholy. Cynthia and my father winged their way to the comfort of my father's old friend Maria Schell in Munich, Germany.

I don't know if Cynthia was privy to Dad's intense feelings for Maria at one time in his life, but she and Dad checked into the Hotel Vier Jahreszeiten and used it as their base of operations for the frequent trips to see Maria at her home in Wasserburg and to visit the Bavarian countryside. The woman with whom he had once had a tempestuous love affair was a gracious host to Glenn and his young companion.

Before the visitors left Germany, Maria surprised my father with a present: a six-week-old long-haired dachshund. Maria told him the dog's pedigree rivaled that of the German aristocracy, and with that in mind my father named him Bismarck. He had the puppy shipped home to him in Beverly Hills. Bismarck would become his pride and joy and in some ways, in the mind of my father, the "child" that he and Cynthia wanted but could not conceive.

The calamities continued. My dear mother, Eleanor Powell, was diagnosed with cancer in the early 1980s. She had been living a contented life in retirement for some years. Although she had toured steadily with her successful stage act until 1964, paying the salary and travel expenses of her troupe of dancers and musicians meant that the money she brought home for herself was meager.

In the years since her divorce from Dad she had lived very modestly. She had taken a loan out against the Cove Way house to pay for her dancing comeback, and she never climbed out of debt until she sold the house in December 1969. I moved back in with her for a time after I graduated from college, and I did what I could to help run the house, but eventually it became clear that she would need to sell it and move somewhere less grand and more affordable.

I really think Mother did her best acting when it was time to sell the house. On the day of a showing to a prospective buyer, Mother and I would spend many hours cleaning. She would purposely make the real estate broker's appointments in the afternoon in order to give us enough time to make the place look immaculate. When the client eventually showed up with his or her agent, Mom would always make sure she was outside, lounging in the sun by the pool. She played the part of the retired movie star perfectly. She was entirely believable—reading a glamour magazine, wearing her dark glasses, and doing her best imitation of Joan Crawford. Who would have believed that just minutes before she had been furiously scrubbing the toilets, with me following behind with the vacuum and dustcloth?

In her sixties, still a warm and vibrant personality, she devoted herself to her charity work, her faith, and her first grandchild, Aubrey Newton Ford. She was a spiritual woman whose comment one day on her religious TV show, *The Faith of Our Children*, became something of a famous saying: "What we are is God's gift to us. What we become is our gift to God." This is the credo that she followed all her life.

After she retired, my mother got used to the idea that people had forgotten about her, until MGM released the first of the *That's Entertainment* movies, the hugely successful documentary compilations of Metro's musical heyday. Now a whole new generation of fans got to see Eleanor Powell's spectacular dancing highlighted on the big screen. In *That's Entertainment*, when Frank Sinatra introduced the film clip of Mom and Fred Astaire dancing to "Begin the Beguine" in *Broadway Melody of 1940* with the words "You know, you can wait around and hope, but I tell ya, you'll never see the likes of this again," it made me proud. She was delighted by the upsurge in attention and the waves of fan mail that followed the movie's success. All I can say is that my mom was an even better mother than a dancer—and as a dancer she was unparalleled.

She insisted that no one be told about how sick she was. It was just her nature to maintain her modesty and dignity to the end. She especially insisted that we not tell my father about her decline. At last there reached a point where I felt I could not obey her wish.

That December, when my father was in the hospital after Holden's death, I called him there and told him how ill Mom had become and that she too was hospitalized and being treated for advanced stages of cancer. "If you have anything you want to say to her," I told Dad, "you better do it soon; otherwise, it will be too late."

He phoned her. They had a long good-bye, and as usual Mom was more concerned about my father's condition than she was about her own. When Lynda and I took my mother home from the hospital, she spoke little of their conversation. All I knew was that it had been a wistful talk. "Glenn," my mother had said to him, "where did all the time go?"

She was strong and positive to the end, ready to put herself in God's hands. Eleanor Powell, the greatest dancing star who ever lived, died at home on February 11, 1982. Sadly, she would never meet the other two children Lynda and I brought into the world: Ryan Welsie in 1984 and Eleanor Powell Ford, Mom's namesake, in 1988.

My father's life with Cynthia continued in the same vein for the next couple of years, or so it appeared from the outside. With my grandmother's passing there was no reason for us to visit Oxford Way, and besides, we were not invited. They hosted dinner parties, attended professional and charitable events, and went on trips and cruises. But Dad's behavior became erratic; he was depressed much of the time. His drinking was becoming a serious problem, eventually to be compounded by an addiction to pills. In Hollywood there are always "doctors to the stars" who will prescribe whatever feels good to their celebrity clientele, regardless of the consequences.

Henry Fonda's passing, six months after my mother's, set Dad off again. So many deaths had come in quick succession—Bill Holden, his mother, Hannah, and my mom, old pals John Wayne and Henry Fonda. My father took each loss very hard, I was told.

By the early 1980s Father was experiencing episodes of agoraphobia (fear of wide open spaces and crowds), and he did not often want to leave the house. The once gregarious world traveler and party host became withdrawn and sullen. Cynthia and my father had exchanged their marriage vows before the Reverend Robert Schuller, promising mutual fidelity for better or worse, richer or poorer, "till death do us part." Yet for the past six years she only had experienced the better and richer parts; now she faced the other, tarnished side of the marital coin. In my father's journal there is a poignant handwritten note: "Any kind of illness offends Cynthia—she simply won't accept it—certainly not from her husband." Except for a cruise to Barbados and a trip to Montreal for the film festival, my father stayed home for most of 1983. His garden had always been there to distract and uplift him from day-to-day problems, but now, it seemed, only cuddling his little dog, Bismarck, brought him any happiness. His behavior in public became problematic.

After a few embarrassing moments here and there, the invitations to celebrity events or other stars' homes began to dry up. Cynthia complained they weren't being invited anywhere anymore. Dad became increasingly dependent on Cynthia even as she was becoming increasingly dissatisfied with her husband's degenerating condition. She began making frequent trips to New York and told my father that she was pursuing personal interests— and indeed she was.

Debbie Reynolds was on a flight from Los Angeles to New York City. Coincidentally, she was seated in first class next to a gentleman whom she didn't know but who would play a part in our family's future. After a few hours in the air the pleasantries between the two seatmates turned to "where are you from?" and "where are you going?" The well-dressed gentleman confided that he was returning home after visiting his girlfriend, who, by the way, was trapped in a loveless marriage with a has-been movie star who was drinking himself to death.

I don't know if he didn't recognize Debbie Reynolds or didn't know about her connection to my father, but Debbie later related to Lynda and me that she sat in astonished silence as the man poured his heart out over several hundred miles about the plight of his beloved Cynthia, married to the has-been actor Glenn Ford.

Evidently, the man had had a fond relationship with Cynthia that predated her marriage to my father, but recently he had begun to see her in a new light. She now spoke French, was well traveled, and was accomplished at managing a large household and staff; she moved in the circles of the rich and powerful. This made her all the more attractive to the young entrepreneur, a bachelor from Connecticut.

On April 27, 1984, Cynthia called to ask if I would help her take my father to Pasadena's Las Encinas Hospital, a dependency care facility. He had grown very ill, but in an effort to save his marriage he had consented to go to an addiction cure center and stay there for a month for treatment for depression and chemical dependence.

Since the first of that year, 1984, for reasons we couldn't fathom but welcomed, Lynda and I had been encouraged by all parties to reenter my father's life. A sense of stability had returned to our family relations, and for my birthday my father took his grandson, Aubrey, and me to dinner at Scandia, a well-known Scandinavian restaurant on the famed Sunset Strip. It was a nice all-generation evening. I didn't know it at the time, but the reason became clear when later Cynthia told me that, while she was concerned about her husband's health, she needed to move on with her life. They had been together for eleven years—six and a half years as a married couple—but now that my father was in this weakened condition, Cynthia had decided to hand the reins of his care over to Lynda and me. She told Dad she was leaving him—hence, his hospital stay.

Against his doctor's wishes, however, he checked himself out early, hoping that by coming home he could salvage his marriage. On that day, May 28, he wrote in his diary, "Cynthia has come several times, the last time she has told me she is separating from me and I am broken-hearted." Four days later Cynthia filed for legal separation.

In the months ahead my father continued to seek a reconciliation, but Cynthia would not nibble. Dad went into a tailspin, returning to the booze and pills. In September I took him to St. John's Hospital and checked him in. Not really remembering how he got there, Glenn awoke in the CDC (Chemical Dependency Care) unit. He spent three weeks in the alcohol detoxification program. He was X-rayed, CAT scanned, and examined by various psychiatrists and neurologists. According to his doctors, the CAT scan showed evidence of serious brain damage, likely from the alcohol abuse.

We decided to stage an intervention, with all his old friends who earlier had been banished from his life. Elizabeth Taylor came and spoke gently to Dad to give him courage and urge him to transfer to the Betty Ford Clinic in Palm Springs. He listened to everyone's concern but was focused on coming home and seeing his dog, Bismarck. "The rest of the problems," he said, "I will deal with later."

However, before he left St. John's Hospital he befriended one of the nurses at the clinic. Her name was Pekay, a good-looking young blonde he would later hire to look after him while he recuperated. The treatments he received had done some good. We got him home, and he swore off liquor and promised the family that he would behave.

For decades, Dad had gotten into the habit of speaking his thoughts into a tiny tape recorder, and he resumed this habit as he settled back into the house alone. "It was so good to see Bismarck," he spoke into the whirring tape recorder. "He peed all over the floor when I came in. He won't leave me for a moment; he's next to me all the time. I think he's afraid I'm going to run away again."

My dad needed to be strong if he was to succeed in this fight for his life, and I challenged him when I found a note he had stashed in the drawer of his end table: "Vodka puts a safe distance between me and my insecurity and fears. But you must live with the facts of life."

"What are the facts, Dad?" I asked him. "We can't fight this for you. You have to want to get well, too."

Dad was pleased to find a script waiting for his consideration—a company in Germany was offering him a part in a new film. "It's nice to know someone still wants me to act again," he said. But for once he wasn't eager about the job. He worried about taking Bismarck on a long flight or leaving him behind for so long.

"I miss Cynthia so much," Dad spoke poignantly into the tape recorder. "All the dreams I had for the both of us are just shot. I think of her constantly, constantly. I love her so deeply and I pray, please, Cynthia, come home. Maybe God will answer my prayer. I won't say maybe. No. God will answer my prayer. In the name of Jesus I ask, please bring Cynthia home to me."

But it didn't happen. Cynthia pursued the divorce. My father was miserable. As the weeks went by he continued to record his thoughts on tape, a sad record of his sorrow and depression:

> I've cried an awful lot. This whole thing is tearing me to pieces. Maybe it's for a reason. I don't know. Maybe I'll come out stronger. But at my age now I can't pick up the pieces. It's too late. If I was younger I would bounce back up and everything would be fine. I depended on her for so many things. I don't know how to keep the bills or how to do anything. I'm just completely at a loss.
>
> I'm too old to find somebody else. . . . It gets worse and worse as the days go by. I hope I don't lose my mind and do something that stupid. I'm very capable of it. I haven't heard from Cynthia in so long. . . . I sit and watch television. I can't even concentrate on a book for one reason or another. . . .
>
> Thank God for little Bismarck, who stays with me all night. He understands and puts his head on my lap when I cry as though he understands. . . . I'm frightened. Is this the way my life is going to end up, in deep sadness? I don't know if I'm even capable of working. I'm very insecure. I think I've lost it. I don't know if I can handle memorizing lines. My mind is so shook up. I don't know. . . .
>
> "I've thought about taking my own life. It's a drastic thing to do—a horrible thing to do. But I don't think I can go on living like I am now. . . . I'm lost. I'm just completely washed up. I'm finished.

My father had two wonderful employees working at the house, John and Ida Nooner, who cooked, cleaned, and maintained his immense home for him. Lynda and I would come by often to check on him, but we could do little to stop him if he wanted to destroy himself.

My father had placed all the legal authority for his life into the hands of his business manager and attorneys, so our role was to monitor, not to manage, even though we continually advised him that he needed more help and supervision. One day in November 1984 he was heading out to the kitchen when he slipped and fell. The pain was excruciating. He had fractured his hip. Dad was rushed by ambulance to St. John's Hospital, where doctors operated. A steel ball was inserted in his hip, and his recovery was slow and painful.

After three weeks he returned home, barely able to stand up with a cane, still suffering tremendous pain. Pekay, the nurse Dad had befriended in the St. John's Hospital CDC, agreed to serve as his private nurse for a few months until he was fully mobile. She started working at the house for twelve-hour shifts each day. His condition improved little by little until my father could walk without the cane, but the pain diminished very slowly.

Things briefly seemed to return to normal. We spent New Year's Eve at my father's home with the nurse, and we introduced my dad to his newest grandson, Ryan Welsie. We were finally reunited as a family and looked forward to sharing my father's happy retirement.

On Tuesday, April 29, 1985, my father's divorce from Cynthia became final. The financial settlement was still up in the air and had been the subject of prolonged discussions between attorneys on both sides.

Then in October a letter arrived at the house from Cynthia. It read:

> I would have hoped that after eleven years we could have sat down together and resolved the financial settlement together. . . . The $300,000 you're offering me now & the $300,000 in your will is not enough, divided like that. . . . I can't earn enough interest on the $300,000 yearly to live. . . . Had you offered me the entire sum now I would have taken it. Had you offered me $450,000 now and $300,000 in your will I would have accepted that. In the beginning I thought—well if Glenn would offer me $400,000 now, and maybe half of the house in his will, that would be my nest egg—my future stability—what difference does it make to you when you're gone Glenn? I'm sure your son and family will now inherit everything and rightly so—but think back on those eleven years—I don't remember them being there for you or your mother. I guess the lesson in all of this for me is "nice guys get dumped on"—it's better to be a selfish, greedy and uncaring person—those are the ones that win in the end—
>
> Love, Cynthia.

Keep in mind that it was Cynthia who dumped my father when the going got rough. Her true nest egg was her lover, who would become her next husband, living on a huge Connecticut estate.

Whoever was at fault, the "Cynthia Era," as we called it, was over. Our family had drifted away from Dad, but now there was hope of mingling our lives anew. I was prepared to move ahead without rancor or recriminations. Then lightning struck again.

It wasn't long before, to my horror, the same pattern of events began to repeat itself. The ambitious girlfriend-wife was replaced by a scheming nurse. Unbelievably, this time the situation was worse.

Pekay, the nurse from St. John's Hospital, orchestrated a concerted effort to keep my family away from my father. The locks were changed on the house gates and doors, and my father was allowed to drink again.

I begged his business manager to allow me to intervene and take away his alcohol, but I was told that Dad was competent and all decisions were his to make. His business manager once wittily told me, "Peter, your father is a cottage industry," and by that he meant that a team of accountants, lawyers, and business managers depended upon his bank account for billable hours. This team of "advisors" could not afford to have him ruled incompetent. As long as he had air to breathe and a fat bank account, he could be billed for something—and he was.

His "advisors" stonewalled us. No one would help us, and we finally had to walk away. We didn't see Dad except on rare occasions for almost six months. We kept in contact with things at the house through John and Ida, who shared all the news, good and bad, with us clandestinely.

Dad reverted to his old habits and again became distant and unapproachable. Pekay took up permanent residency at the house and became his primary care coordinator, aided by a group of assistants, whom she guided.

Within five months of his divorce from Cynthia, Dad and Pekay were in London, attending film festivals together and appearing on *Lifestyles of the Rich and Famous*. He was in love again, but, unlike his last wife, this woman cleverly kept him at arm's length. She had her own beau and correctly reasoned that a well-paid caregiver-girlfriend was a better role to play than a stay-at-home wife.

My father and Pekay went on exotic trips, dined in the finest restaurants in Beverly Hills, and revived Dad's social life with Hollywood celebrities. She used his credit card, drove his Mercedes Benz, decorated her condo at his expense, and did her best to plant seeds of venom about Lynda, me, and our children. We heard it all: that I was an atheist, that my father should not admit to being a grandfather because it was not in keeping with being a movie star, and more.

At first, he willingly put himself under her spell, infatuated by this shapely Svengali, but eventually his health became such that he could not keep up. She convinced him that he couldn't live without her medical supervision, but we later learned that while Dad stayed home under the care of Pekay's "helpers," she traveled to Europe without him—on his dime. She went with her boyfriend, using my father's luggage, staying at the hotels at which she and my father had stayed, dining in the same elegant restaurants, and partying with the same people to whom my father had introduced her. All this was done without my father's knowledge on his expense account. Her boyfriend even wore my father's fur-lined topcoat.

Despite all this, in the late 1980s my father continued to seek work. With all the trauma he had experienced, however, his acting abilities had been affected. The jobs were few and far between. My father still managed a few romances, and he took a few junkets, but Pekay was always waiting for him in his house when he returned.

Nearly eight years after my father had starred in *Happy Birthday to Me* he accepted a role in his eighty-sixth motion picture. In April 1989 he flew to Morocco via Paris to appear in *Casablanca Express*, written, directed, and produced by Sergio Martino, a prolific Italian filmmaker making his first and only English-language feature film. For this low-budget yarn about a kidnapping attempt on Winston Churchill by the Nazis, Dad earned $50,000—for just three days of work—and he had one of his favorite perks, a first-class trip to Europe besides.

In September my father was back in Old Tucson, Arizona, for a week portraying a sheriff in writer-director Chris McIntyre's *Border Shootout*, an uninspired adaptation of Elmore Leonard's novel *The Law at Randado*. My father was top billed in an attempt to lure audiences into theaters, but it was really a small supporting role for which he was clearly too old. Bill Hart, Dad's stunt double, worked with my father for the last time, performing all the action scenes when the sheriff thwarts the bad guys in a fight. This was Dad's last western—after this he holstered his gun and hung up his spurs—but he was paid $75,000 and took pride at still earning good money in his profession.

In August 1990, at the age of seventy-four, Dad made his last on-camera appearance in a movie. Filmed in Mobile, Alabama, *Raw Nerve* was a crime drama, with Glenn and Jan-Michael Vincent as two police detectives who try and solve a whodunit involving a serial killer and a psychic race car driver (Ted Prior) whose sister (Traci Lords) is the next target. Not a significant film in my father's career, except for being his last, but it was pleasant entertainment.

In March 1991 it was announced that he would play a role in Oliver Stone's *JFK*, but illness stopped him. Dad's health began to deteriorate rapidly, beginning with prostate surgery in May. A brief weekend trip in

August to the Telluride Film Festival would be his last public appearance. For the next nine months my father was admitted ten different times to either St. John's or Cedars-Sinai for various medical emergencies.

On May 14, 1992, Dad was admitted to St. John's Hospital with chest pain and breathing difficulties. Tests showed blood clots in his lungs. In the hospital, apparently, he developed pneumonia. Days later, I received a call from actress and family friend Roberta Collins, who had been filling the role as one of the substitute caregivers when Pekay was off duty. "Peter," Roberta solemnly said, "I think you better come to the hospital right away and say good-bye to your father. He's going to die this weekend."

16

"Yesterday"

I rushed to the hospital. Dad was alone in his room and looked haggard and pale. His hair was matted; his fingernails were extremely long. Purring monitors charting his vital signs were at his bedside, and intravenous tubes were stuck in both arms. It took me a moment to process what I was seeing—was this my father, or was it Howard Hughes in his last days? As I stood by his bedside and touched his arm, he opened his eyes and looked at me with a hopeful look.

"Where have you been, Pete? I needed you."

"But Dad, you're the one who kept me away."

"I'm dying. . . . They're trying to kill me," he answered. "Please help me."

What did he mean, "They're trying to kill me"? I panicked, found the nurse on duty, and identified myself. She showed me his chart, which had a "No code—DNR" instruction written on it, and informed me that Nurse Pekay had been appointed by my father's handlers with durable power of attorney for his health care. I asked her what DNR meant. She told me that Pekay, now the ultimate authority in my father's health decisions, had left instructions that if he were faced with a life-threatening problem, the hospital staff would not take any heroic measures to save him. DNR meant "do not resuscitate." I was in shock, disbelief.

My father slipped into a semi-coma at the hospital and developed pneumonia. For days he lay on the verge of death. Lynda and I, fearing for my father's welfare, began sorting out what had happened over the past six months. We hired an attorney and petitioned the court to be granted a temporary conservatorship of my father's "person."

A probate investigator was sent to visit him in the hospital and determined that, indeed, Dad was not capable of handling his own health decisions. The investigator reported this fact to the court. However, my father specifically instructed this investigator that he wanted me, his son, to be his conservator.

My dad's stated preference for me as his conservator threw all his current "keepers" into a panic. Subsequently, my family and I were barred from seeing my father; in fact, when the probate investigator arrived to assess Dad, Nurse Pekay called his attorney and was told to try and prevent the investigator from talking to my father. She tried in vain to have him removed from my father's hospital room.

In California there are two types of conservatorships: a conservatorship of the person, whereby the conservator (a responsible person) is legally empowered to make day-to-day decisions for the benefit of the protected person; and a conservatorship of the estate, which protects the finances of someone who can't competently handle his or her own debts and income or who can't resist unfair financial pressure from others. Lynda and I did not petition the court to conserve Dad's estate, because we felt this would alarm his business manager and attorneys; it was my father's life that we cared about, not his money. We were granted the conservatorship of his person, and within the week we went to his house, met a locksmith, and changed all the locks.

It was essentially a palace coup to save my father's life, or at least that was our intention. We posted a guard outside his front door with instructions that no one other than Lynda and I, his business manager, or his attorneys should enter. I dismissed Nurse Pekay and all the other nurses when Lynda and I discovered that his bathroom countertop resembled a well-stocked pharmacy with dozens of bottles of medications—Zoloft, Valium, Zantac, Coumadin, Darvocet, Librium, Haldol, and Percocet, to name a few. We hired a new nurse to care for Dad, the liquor was put away, all his medications were tailored to what he actually required for his health, and we set about getting my father under the care of his former trusted doctor, who had earlier been replaced.

Our enemies were incensed. They decided that my father should be brought home prematurely from the hospital to fight my conservatorship. Dad should have remained in St. John's Hospital for continued care, as he was gravely ill, but they checked him out anyway. He needed to be in his own bedroom, pretending that nothing was wrong; he had one more acting job to do. Within a few days, Dad's handlers had prepared a script for Dad to memorize. Pekay was his dialogue coach for this performance, and Dad was scared into believing that he mustn't allow me to become his conservator (or play any other important role in his life). Armed with his bank account and coerced cooperation, they petitioned the court to defeat my bid as conservator.

I opposed them at great personal expense (read: attorney) but was defeated again. Then the tabloids unleashed their fury, yielding weeks of front-page headlines: "Glenn Ford Partied Hard Until He Dropped," "Glenn Ford in Bitter Battle with His Son over $20 Million Fortune," "Tears Flow as Glenn Ford & Son Reunite at Hospital Bedside." In the end, I was portrayed as trying to steal my father's fortune while he was incapacitated because he had cut me and my family out of his will—which, at the behest of his minions, he actually did.

Glenn Ford, world-famous movie star, was now under house arrest.

Unfortunately, as I say, he should not have left the hospital when he did, because a short time later my father had to be rushed back to the hospital (this time Cedars-Sinai) in critical condition, with blood clots blocking the circulation in his legs. Surgery was performed, and Dad remained in critical condition for days before finally being discharged. My father never walked unassisted again.

It was during this hospital stay that another nurse laid eyes on my father and made plans to secure *her* future. Oh yes—this is the never-ending saga.

Finally, legal matters sorted themselves out. I became conservator. It took a while to mend fences with my father again, but I did. In his clouded state of mind he was easily made suspicious and angry, and the general decline in his health was clear. We ushered good friends like Debbie Reynolds and Angie Dickinson back into his life. Others would come by, and he would sit up to chat with them while they sat at his bedside. But when Dad was invited to leave the house to venture into public, despite his loneliness, he almost always refused.

However, when the young blonde Jeanne Baus, the nurse from his last hospital stay, began working at the house to take care of him, it invigorated his libido—at age seventy-six! It wasn't long before he proposed marriage to her a number of times, and eventually she said yes. She was a divorcée with a young daughter. Lynda and I didn't know what to think, but we knew Dad was very lonely, and we felt it was better to encourage the relationship and hope for the best.

My father and Jeanne were married at the Oxford Way house on March 6, 1993. Dad's fourth marriage lasted precisely forty-nine days. Suffice it to say that my father and Jeanne had different expectations. Apparently, we found out later during the divorce, Jeanne had consulted a psychic, who had predicted that my father didn't have very long to live and in a short time she would be a rich widow. On his part, my always pragmatic father thought he was acquiring a full-time nurse, a wife, and a mother, all as a marriage bonus, while saving on Jeanne's salary. This was an expensive miscalculation for which, I must admit, Lynda and I must bear some responsibility. The divorce action mandated Dad to pay Jeanne $8,500 a month for three months until she had completed a nursing course. She was allowed to keep her $25,000 engagement ring.

Jeanne disappeared from our lives, and a new nursing staff was employed. Dad continued to have health crises and was in and out of hospitals. He fell more than once and began to spend more of each day confined to his bed. Lynda and I went to the house as often as possible, visiting and bringing his favorite dishes. We began staying overnight in the guest house (my grandmother's former home).

Shortly after his brief marriage to Jeanne mercifully ended and the divorce became final, I retired from my home-building business. We sold our house, and my family moved into the Oxford Way house permanently. Our daughter, Eleanor, learned to ride her bike in Dad's bedroom (yes, it was that big), my father helped my son Aubrey on his quest to become an Eagle Scout, and Ryan spent many days sitting with his grandpa watching films and talking about the golden days of Hollywood. We were happily underfoot, and Dad seemed to like it.

I slowly began to try and sort out the chaos of my father's personal and business affairs of the previous ten or more years. His business manager had been paying his bills, but there was no oversight. If a bill materialized, it was paid without scrutiny. Supporting my father and running his home was an incredible money pit, peopled with "yes men," redundant employees, and hangers-on.

Dad's swimming pool, which he had not used in years, was heated year-round at great expense. Meals for caregivers were ordered at and delivered by restaurants instead of cooked on the premises. Unoccupied rooms were heated or air-conditioned. For years his business office rented rotary phones from Pac-Bell at $60 a month, phones that could have been replaced with Radio Shack ten-dollar push-button versions. Business accounts in private banks charged $5 for every check written in his name. Many of his personal possessions—valuables, collectibles, gifts, his pipes, and his Rolex watches—were missing. Dad's gold coin collection, works of art, and bearer bonds were all gone—sold off for cash or stolen.

Learning from a former nurse and Pekay's ex-boyfriend that Pekay had two storage garages full of my father's belongings stashed away near her condo in Marina Del Rey, I went to the police and filed complaints. I consulted with lawyers. But charges were hard to prove, and the statute of limitations restricted my options. To this day I still find an occasional item of Dad's showing up at auction or on eBay.

Before his marriage to Cynthia, Dad's estate had been estimated at about $14 million. Most of that had vanished. The home he loved, that he had designed and built on Oxford Way, was literally all that remained of his once valuable estate, and it was his wish to stay in his home and not to go to an elder-care facility. Although his various union, military, and government pensions brought him a retirement income of about $125,000 per year, this amount barely covered half of the expenses of running the house and grounds while taking care of his living expenses and employing two rotating full-time caregivers. We never told my father that we had to supplement his income to take care of him, but we made up the difference.

My father's continued maintenance and care would eventually consume all of Lynda's and my savings as well. We were finally able to end the relationship with his business manager and my father's attorneys, but it took a lot of time to pry them loose—his money was gone, and there was no reason for any of them to remain in his life. I obtained power of attorney but never told him. He had always been the captain of the ship, so why not let him believe he still commanded the helm? However, frail and dependent as he was, Dad was still a difficult and demanding captain right up to the end.

One minute he might seem unaware of anything happening around him, but then, if an orange went missing from his beloved temple orange tree by the swimming pool, which he could see from his bedroom, woe betide the person who plucked it, even if that person was Lynda making orange juice for *him*. He'd sometimes wake up in the middle of the night and want a Grand Marnier soufflé or something similar, as though he were aboard a cruise ship or at the Ritz in Paris pampered by twenty-four-hour room service. He had been spoiled his entire life, he was still spoiled, but that was fine; we had people on hand to make him happy and comfortable, and we tried our best.

Dad's doctor forbade him to drink alcohol, but he was totally un-cooperative. He demanded that his bottle of vodka and glass always be on the table by his bed. Gradually, without his ever noticing it, we added more and more water to the bottle until there was only water—he'd pour himself a drink, never realizing it was only water. He could not tell the difference.

Lynda and I would arrange a few dinner parties every year for Dad, complete with Scotty Bowers, his favorite bartender—drinks for the guests but tea-colored water ("Scotch") for Dad. His old circle was back, friends like Debbie Reynolds, Anne Francis, Angie Dickinson, Stella Stevens, Dean Jones, Bill Hart, Ken Wales, Tony Martin, Cyd Charisse, and more. He was now bedridden, so at these social get-togethers the guests would take turns visiting his room off the pool, sitting next to his bed and chatting with him.

Like many people with age-related illnesses, my father's memory came and went, but while he might often forget things that happened a week before, he could be clear and sharp about events of forty and sixty years ago. He expressed a desire to write his memoirs; he had always kept a diary and had already made hundreds of tape recordings about his early life, career, and professional experiences. So we decided to try and work on his biography together.

These were informal sessions, conversational, with Dad recalling people and events at his own pace. When one of his old movies would come on the television or when I would get ahold of them on tape or DVD, we would watch them; Dad made comments and recalled incidents from the time they were made. The movies and the memories might make him laugh with delight or bring tears to his eyes. Sometimes he would just sit in silence, lost in the flickering reflections from his past. One time, when one of his movies ended, after a long silence staring at the screen, he leaned his head forward in his hands and sighed, seemingly moved by what he had just seen.

I asked, "What are you thinking, Dad?"

He answered, "I'm thinking that was the worst piece of crap ever made."

He didn't have much patience for the contemporary movies that he saw. Either the subject matter didn't interest him or the plots weren't well constructed, and he had no taste for the extremes of sexuality and violence in newer films. Many times he would look at the screen and shake his head and simply say: "These people can't act."

Twenty years before his passing my father and I had gone to Gates, Kingsley & Gates, a mortuary in Santa Monica, and Dad had picked out his casket—solid bronze, lined with white satin. For years he had said that he wanted to be laid to rest at "home" in Woodend, the cemetery in Portneuf, next to his mother and father. Then, toward the end of his life, he changed his mind and decided he wanted to be interred in the mausoleum at Woodlawn Cemetery near Santa Monica High School in Santa Monica, California.

Dad was the director of his own funeral. He said that he did not want to be buried in the ground; he specified in which chapel he wanted his memorial and exactly where in Woodlawn he wanted to be interred. He set down elaborate instructions about the conduct and the content of the service: Masonic rites and a sole bagpiper playing "Amazing Grace" at the entrance to the mausoleum, with a color guard at the ready and a bugler playing taps. The list of pallbearers continually changed as close friends predeceased him: Frank Sinatra, John Wayne, William Holden, David Niven, Henry Fonda, Cary Grant—he outlived them all. After his beloved dachshund, Bismarck, died, we had him cremated, because Dad wanted his dog's ashes buried with him.

As the years went by and his world shrank to his home and garden, I think he grew weary of living. More than once he said to me, "Pete, I just want to die." I told him that God would call him when it was time. We encouraged him to stay vital, and I personally pushed for the Academy of Motion Picture Arts and Sciences to honor him with a Lifetime Achievement Oscar. It still upsets me that after a career spanning seven decades of fine film work he was never honored in this way.

I tried the American Film Institute, approaching officials about granting him a Lifetime Achievement honor, but I was told that he had never supported that organization. I produced a certificate signed by director Robert Wise: "The Members of the Board of Trustees of the American Film Institute Are Pleased to Honor Glenn Ford as a Founding Member of the Professional Guild"—it didn't help. The Screen Actors Guild was equally unresponsive. I even appealed to the Toronto Hall of Fame in Toronto, Canada, which honors Canadian native sons and daughters, but had no luck there either. The people in charge said they had never heard of him. He had outlived his celebrity.

Lynda and I planned a big celebration for his ninetieth birthday. On May 1, 2006, the American Cinematheque helped us arrange a special celebratory event in Hollywood. There were many VIP guests, including Debbie Reynolds, Shirley Jones, Martin Landau, and Jamie Farr, who spoke to the standing-room-only crowd at the Egyptian Theatre. My father had wanted to attend to greet everyone, and in fact Lynda and I made a rehearsal run in traffic to time everything out, but his frail health made it impossible. Instead, we arranged for him to tape a special greeting to be played on the large theater screen at the event. He didn't look too robust, but you could see the spark of joy in his eyes—that twinkle that made women swoon throughout the years—as he faced a camera and an audience one last time.

The summer of 2006 came. On the next to last day of August, I looked in on my father. We spoke. I grasped his hand in mine, told him that I loved him. In the afternoon I was downstairs working on my computer writing this book when I heard Dad's on-duty caretaker urgently call my name. I ran upstairs, and Lynda followed.

Dad was not visibly breathing, and his color was pale. Lynda called 911. Two teams of paramedics arrived very quickly. Six paramedics surrounded Dad in the bedroom, working to revive him. After what felt like forever one of them ushered me out of Dad's bedroom to the hall and said there was nothing more they could do.

The police came and went, we telephoned the mortuary, and after everyone left I went into the room one last time and sat beside my dead father in his bed.

My mind was blank. I was numb—so much had happened between us, and now that part of my life was over. Dad's eyes were open, and I reached over and closed them. I went to his desk, and I took his scissors and cut some locks of my father's hair, as I had done when my mother had passed nearly twenty-five years earlier.

I sat alone on the steps at the front of the house waiting for the men to arrive from the mortuary. They took Dad away from his precious home for the last time.

Per Dad's request, we had an open-casket chapel service. We dressed him in his Mason's apron over his favorite gray suit, and I tucked a picture of his mother, Hannah, with the inscription "Mother—always beautiful," along with the small tin of Bismarck's ashes, inside his coffin. Before we left for the cemetery, Dean Jones placed a crucifix that Dad had purchased from Notre Dame Cathedral when we were all in Paris together in 1964 on his breast. My father had always kept that crucifix on the table next to his bed.

A. C. Lyles, a friend of the family since the early 1940s and still working as a producer at Paramount Pictures, gave the eulogy. Mickey Rooney stood up and said some words of remembrance. Grace Godino, Dad's friend (and Rita Hayworth's stand-in) from his earliest days in Santa Monica "little theater," led the six pallbearers (my sons, Aubrey and Ryan Ford, Bob Crutchfield, Bill Hart, Ken Wales, and Sammy Yates) to the hearse, with good, faithful Debbie Reynolds walking behind and leading the solemn procession.

When we arrived at Woodlawn Cemetery in Santa Monica, everything was as Dad had "directed": a kilted bagpiper playing "Amazing Grace"; a full military color guard and military salute; a trumpeter playing taps. At the end of the service the American flag that draped Dad's coffin was presented to our family.

A few days after Dad was buried I determined to go back and finish my father's biography, the story of his life that we had worked on together in his last good days.

A movie star never really dies, not as long as his or her work remains. At the time of my father's passing I received letters, cards, and e-mails from all over the world, from people of all ages—strangers compelled to write to me with their prayers for my father, speaking of their memories of his films, and the pleasure and meaning he had lent to their lives. There were teachers who had been inspired by his role in *Blackboard Jungle*, a widow who remembered seeing *Gilda* sixty years earlier on a first date with the man she would marry (naming their daughter Gilda), a young man in Paris whose favorite movie was *3:10 to Yuma*, and hundreds more. I continue to receive such letters and messages to this day.

The life and career that began so long ago in school plays and amateur productions and touring companies, leading to Broadway, B movies, major motion pictures, awards, and recognition as the number one box-office star in the world . . . that life has ended. Something else begins: Glenn Ford's legacy.

I once asked my father where *he* thought he stood as an actor among his peers and his public. He paused and reflected simply, "A tree is best measured when it's felled."

Acknowledgments

My father documented his life in diaries, on cassette tapes, in letters, and in notes. At every opportunity he recorded his thoughts, fears, and observations. The abundance of material I had at my disposal to construct this biography was as vast as it was daunting.

Also, I had the privilege of sharing personal experiences with many luminaries of the Golden Age of Hollywood and I've incorporated some of these memories as well, but to a specific few I owe a great debt of gratitude.

To actress Anne Francis, who years ago prodded me to begin this biography—bless you. I was aided immeasurably in my first attempt to write this book by the perseverance of Christopher Nickens. Thanks also to others who pushed the project on to another stage. And to Patrick McGilligan, who encouraged me through it all; I doubt I would have succeeded without your counsel—I am deeply indebted to you.

I am grateful to the kindness of my friends upon whose knowledge I could rely to guide me: teacher and author Rob Davis, author and historian Alan Rode, and actor Aron Kincaid, first and foremost. To actor Andrew Prine, director Joel Freeman, and film historian Joel Blumberg, thank you for your generous support and encouragement. Appreciation also goes to friends Jim Dawson and Allen Brandstater for their technical assistance and to Glen Marcotte in Quebec, Canada, for help with early Ford family history.

For access to library collections and archival material, I'd like to thank Pat Hanson at the American Film Institute and the Margaret Herrick Library of the Academy of Motion Picture Arts and Sciences—in particular my guide Sandra Archer.

I am indebted for many reasons to Harlan James Juris. Regarding accurate family history, he provided much of what had been lost to time—blessings to you, Jim. And to another significant person in my life, Robert Crutchfield: I couldn't share all we experienced together, Bob—decorum dictates some discretion, at least for the present.

And lastly, thanks to my indefatigable researcher and friend in Belgium, Leo Verswijver—your kindness and help has provided me with an abundance of material for which I shall forever be indebted.

Filmography

Night in Manhattan
Filmed: March 28–29, 1937
Released: July 29, 1937

Heaven with a Barbed Wire Fence
Filmed: June 8–31, 1939
Released: November 3, 1939

My Son Is Guilty
Filmed: October 19–November 2, 1939
Released: December 28, 1939

Convicted Woman
Filmed: November 27–December 12, 1939
Released: January 31, 1940

Men without Souls
Filmed: January 14–February 1, 1940
Released: March 14, 1940

Babies for Sale
Filmed: March 29–April 13, 1940
Released: May 16, 1940

The Lady in Question
Filmed: May 16–June 22, 1940
Released: August 7, 1940

Blondie Plays Cupid
Filmed: July 16–August 17, 1940
Released: October 31, 1940

So Ends Our Night
Filmed: August 10–week ending October 18, 1940
Released: January 21, 1941

Texas
Filmed: May 9–June 26, 1941
Released: October 9, 1941

Go West, Young Lady
Filmed: July 16–August 14, 1941
Released: November 27, 1941

The Adventures of Martin Eden
Filmed: November 4–December 5, 1941
Released: February 29, 1942

Flight Lieutenant
Filmed: March 16–April 18, 1942
Released: July 9, 1942

The Desperadoes
Filmed: June 22–August 26, 1942
Released: March 25, 1943

Destroyer
Filmed: November 16, 1942–January 25, 1943
Released: September 2, 1943

A Stolen Life
Filmed: February 14–June 23, 1945
Released: July 6, 1946

Gilda
Filmed: September 4–December 10, 1945
Released: April 25, 1946

Gallant Journey
Filmed: March 4–June 1, 1946
Released: September 24, 1946

Framed
Filmed: September 6–October 30, 1946
Released: February 27, 1947

The Man from Colorado
Filmed: February 24–May 26, 1947
Released: November 11, 1948

The Mating of Millie
Filmed: June 23–August 14, 1947
Released: April 29, 1948

The Return of October
Filmed: September 18–October 31, 1947
Released: January 20, 1949

The Loves of Carmen
Filmed: November 15, 1947–February 24, 1948
Released: October 7, 1948

Undercover Man
Filmed: May 4–July 16, 1948
Released: April 20, 1949

Mr. Soft Touch
Filmed: August 9–September 23, 1948
Released: July 28, 1949

Lust for Gold
Filmed: October 25–December 13, 1948
Released: May 29, 1949

The Doctor and the Girl
Filmed: May 16–week ending July 2, 1949
Released: September 28, 1949

The White Tower
Filmed: August 6–October 24, 1949
Released: June 24, 1950

Convicted
Filmed: December 12, 1949–January 19, 1950
Released: August 31, 1950

The Redhead and the Cowboy
Filmed: April 25–May 22, 1950
Released: March 14, 1951

The Flying Missile
Filmed: July 11–August 14, 1950
Released: December 25, 1950

Follow the Sun
Filmed: September 29–week ending November 18, 1950
Released: April 25, 1951

The Secret of Convict Lake
Filmed: January 29–March 15, 1951
Released: August 2, 1951

The Green Glove
Filmed: April 19–July 7, 1951
Released: February 28, 1952

Young Man with Ideas
Filmed: September 4–week ending October 26, 1951
Released: May 2, 1952

Affair in Trinidad
Filmed: January 25–March 25, 1952
Released: July 29, 1952

Terror on a Train
Filmed: April 4–May 28, 1952
Released: September 18, 1953

The Man from the Alamo
Filmed: August 25–November 3, 1952
Released: August 7, 1953

Plunder of the Sun
Filmed: November 3, 1952–January 5, 1953
Released: August 19, 1953

The Big Heat
Filmed: March 17–April 18, 1953
Released: October 14, 1953

Appointment in Honduras
Filmed: May 18–week ending June 13, 1953
Released: October 16, 1953

The Americano
Filmed: late July–September 8, 1953; June 14–late August 1954
Released: February 2, 1955

Human Desire
Filmed: December 14, 1953–January 25, 1954
Released: July 5, 1954

The Violent Men
Filmed: April 12–May 15, 1954
Released: January 5, 1955

Interrupted Melody
Filmed: September 15–November 13, 1954
Released: July 1, 1955

Blackboard Jungle
Filmed: November 15–December 20, 1954
Released: March 20, 1955

Trial
Filmed: April 2–May 16, 1955
Released: October 7, 1955

Jubal
Filmed: July 29–September 13, 1955
Released: April 6, 1956

Ransom!
Filmed: September 26–November 8, 1955
Released: January 20, 1956

The Fastest Gun Alive
Filmed: January 5–week ending February 2, 1956
Released: July 6, 1956

Teahouse of the August Moon
Filmed: April 16–week ending August 2, 1956
Released: December 25, 1956

3:10 to Yuma
Filmed: November 28, 1956—January 17, 1957
Released: August 7, 1957

Don't Go Near the Water
Filmed: March 4–April 26, 1957
Released: November 14, 1957

Cowboy
Filmed: June 14–July 26, 1957
Released: Oklahoma premiere, January 7, 1958; New York opening, February 19, 1958

The Sheepman
Filmed: September 30–November 13, 1957
Released: May 7, 1958

Imitation General
Filmed: January 20–May 3, 1958
Released: July 18, 1958

Torpedo Run
Filmed: April 7–May 22, 1958
Released: Washington, D.C., premiere, October 23, 1958; nationwide release, October 24, 1958

It Started with a Kiss
Filmed: March 7–April 23, 1959
Released: August 19, 1959

The Gazebo
Filmed: July 20–week ending August 28, 1959
Released: January 15, 1960

Cimarron
Filmed: November 30, 1959–March 3, 1960
Released: December 1, 1960

Cry for Happy
Filmed: June 20–week ending August 26, 1960
Released: March 7, 1961

Pocketful of Miracles
Filmed: April 20–week ending June 30, 1961
Released: New York opening, December 20, 1961

The Four Horsemen of the Apocalypse
Filmed: October 17, 1960–week ending March 31, 1961
Released: Washington, D.C., February 7, 1962

Experiment in Terror
Filmed: August 7–week ending November 17, 1961
Released: New York opening, April 13, 1962

Love Is a Ball
Filmed: March 20–June 25, 1962
Released: Los Angeles, March 6, 1963

The Courtship of Eddie's Father
Filmed: August 2–September 19, 1962
Released: New York opening, March 3, 1963; Los Angeles opening, March 20, 1963

Advance to the Rear
Filmed: July 15–August 28, 1963
Released: San Francisco opening, April 15, 1964

Fate Is the Hunter
Filmed: January 20–March 20, 1964
Released: Boston opening, September 30, 1964

Dear Heart
Filmed: October 3–November 22, 1963
Released: three-day Oscar-qualifying run in Los Angeles, December 3–5, 1964; nationwide opening and premiere, Radio City Music Hall, New York, March 6, 1965

The Rounders
Filmed: May 4–week ending June 19, 1964
Released: Denver opening, March 3, 1965

The Money Trap
Filmed: November 30, 1964–January 20, 1965
Released: Baltimore opening, February 2, 1966

Is Paris Burning?
Filmed: July 19–December 8, 1965 (Glenn filming in early September)
Released: Paris premiere, October 24, 1966; Los Angeles premiere, November 9,
    1966; Los Angeles and New York openings, November 10, 1966

Rage
Filmed: December 1, 1965–February 4, 1966
Released: Boston opening, November 30, 1966

A Time for Killing
Filmed: June 7–August 15, 1966
Released: November 10, 1967

The Last Challenge
Filmed: October 17–November 16, 1966
Released: Atlanta, Georgia, opening, September 29, 1967

Day of the Evil Gun
Filmed: August 7–October 4, 1967
Released: March 1, 1968

Heaven with a Gun
Filmed: May 20–week ending July 5, 1968
Released: New York opening, June 11, 1969

Smith!
Filmed: July 15–week ending September 6, 1968
Released: March 21, 1969

Santee
Filmed: May 30–July 21, 1972
Released: Houston premiere, August 1, 1973; Los Angeles release, July 24, 1973;
    nationwide release, September 24, 1973

Midway
Filmed: May 15–July 20, 1975
Released: June 18, 1976

Superman
Filmed: March 24, 1977–October 1978 (Glenn filming in September 1977)
Released: Washington, D.C., premiere, October 12, 1978; nationwide release
    December 15, 1978

The Visitor
Filmed: April 24–May 26, 1978
Released: Los Angeles, March 14, 1980

Day of the Assassin
Filmed: July 7–October 8, 1980
Released: date unknown

Virus
Filmed: August 4, 1979–March 26, 1980
Released: shown at Cannes, France, May 22, 1980; Tokyo premiere, June 28, 1980

Happy Birthday to Me
Filmed: July 7–September 12, 1980
Released: May 15, 1981

Casablanca Express
Filmed: April 10–August 24, 1989
Released: Italy, December 22, 1989

Border Shootout
Filmed: September 26, 1989; end of production unknown
Released: date unknown

Raw Nerve
Filmed: August 27, 1990; end of production unknown
Released: May 24, 1991

Bibliography

Archive

The Glenn Ford Library and Archives, Beverly Hills

Encyclopedias and Film Annuals

The American Film Institute Catalog of Motion Pictures Produced in the United States: Feature Films, 1931–1940. Berkeley: University of California Press, 1993.
The American Film Institute Catalog of Motion Pictures Produced in the United States: Feature Films, 1941–1950. Berkeley: University of California Press, 1999.
The American Film Institute Catalog of Motion Pictures Produced in the United States: Feature Films, 1961–1970. New York: R. R. Bowker, 1976.
Blum, Daniel. *Screen World.* New York: Biblo & Tannen, 1949–51.
———. *Screen World.* New York: Greenberg, 1952–65.
Variety Film Reviews. Vol. 6, 1938–1942; vol. 7, 1943–1948; vol. 8, 1949–1953; vol. 9, 1954–1958; vol. 10, 1959–1963; vol. 11, 1964–1967; vol. 12, 1968–1970; vol. 13, 1971–1974; vol. 14, 1975–1977; vol. 15, 1978–1980; vol. 17, 1907–1980 index. New York: Garland, 1983–85.
Variety Film Reviews. Vol. 18, 1981–1982; vol. 19, 1983–1984. New York: R. R. Bowker, 1984–86.
Willis, John. *Screen World.* New York: Crown, 1966–92.

Newspaper Articles

Adler, Dick. "'Bob & Carol' & Then What?" *New York Times*, July 26, 1970.
Anderson, Susan Heller. "It's a Bird! It's a Plane! It's a Movie!" *New York Times*, June 26, 1977.
Bart, Peter. "TV Studios Turn to Feature Films: Reply to Movie Competition with Bid for New Market." *New York Times*, July 24, 1964.

Barthel, Joan. "Biggest Money-Making Movie of All Time—How Come?" *New York Times*, November 20, 1966.

Brady, Thomas. "Hollywood 'Alert': So Far Japanese War Has Little Effect on Studios, but Boxoffice Reacts." *New York Times*, December 14, 1941.

———. "Hollywood's Uneasy Labor Truce: Studio Strike Deadlock Is Broken— Sentiment Turns Against Washington Investigation—Assorted Production Activities." *New York Times*, November 2, 1947.

———. "Thinning Out the Ranks." *New York Times*, September 15, 1940.

Colton, Helen. "Coaching the Stars to Enunciate Properly: Dialogue Director Polices Speech Habits and Helps Interpret Meaning of Lines." *New York Times*, August 6, 1950.

Falk, Ray. "Bivouac at an Okinawan 'Teahouse' in Japan: M-G-M Troupe Acquires Customs, Cast in Making Movie of Broadway Play." *New York Times*, June 10, 1956.

Herbers, John. "Brezhnev Leaves the West on a Note of Informality." *New York Times*, June 25, 1973.

McDonald, Thomas. "Focus on the Non-stop Glenn Ford: 'I Like to Work,' Says Actor Now Involved in Four Features." *New York Times*, September 18, 1960.

Pryor, Thomas M. "U.S. Asks Studios for Their Support: Urges More Participation at Foreign Film Festivals to Reflect Life Here." *New York Times*, March 19, 1954.

Raines, Halsey. "Talent Hunt: Comparative Unknowns Cast in New Movie." *New York Times*, March 6, 1955.

Rothwell, John H. "'Tucson': Movie Mecca: Noted Arizona Screen 'Set' Attracts 'Badlanders' Troupe and Tourists." *New York Times*, March 9, 1958.

Schumach, Murray. "Business Managers of Hollywood Stars Gaining Importance." *New York Times*, August 17, 1963.

———. "Hollywood Maverick: Unusual Points of View Held by Frank Capra." *New York Times*, May 28, 1961.

———. "M.C.A. Tries to 'Save' Hollywood: Hopes Its Efficiency Will Help Revive Movie Capital—Many Film Leaders Dubious on Move by Big Concern." *New York Times*, May 10, 1962.

Severo, Richard. "Glenn Ford, Leading Man in Films and TV, Dies at 90." *New York Times*, August 31, 2006.

Stanley, Fred. "Hollywood's Veterans." *New York Times*, September 16, 1945.

———. "Hollywood Takes the Saddle." *New York Times*, February 18, 1945.

Strauss, Theodore. "No Assembly-Line Ford." *New York Times*, March 22, 1942.

Thompson, Howard. "'Best Man' On the Job: Henry Fonda Scans a Notable Career while Analyzing His Profession." *New York Times*, April 26, 1964.

Wilson, John M. "The Global Film: Will It Play in Uruguay?" *New York Times*, November 26, 1978.

Books

Aherne, Brian. *A Proper Job: The Autobiography of an Actor's Actor*. Boston: Houghton Mifflin, 1969.

Baltake, Joe. *The Films of Jack Lemmon*. Secaucus: Citadel Press, 1977.

Barrymore, Ethel. *Memories: An Autobiography*. New York: Harper & Brothers, 1955.

Basinger, Jeanine. *Anthony Mann*. Middletown, CT: Wesleyan University Press, 2007.

———. *The Star Machine*. New York: Alfred A. Knopf, 2007.

Baxter, Anne. *Intermission: A True Tale*. New York: G. P. Putnam's Sons, 1976.

Black, Gregory D. *Hollywood Censored: Morality Codes, Catholics, and the Movies*. Cambridge: Cambridge University Press, 1994.

Boetticher, Budd. *When in Disgrace*. Santa Barbara, CA: Neville, 1989.

Bogdanovich, Peter. *Who the Devil Made It*. New York: Alfred A. Knopf, 1997.

———. *Who the Hell's in It*. New York: Alfred A. Knopf, 2004.

Borgnine, Ernest. *Ernie: The Autobiography*. New York: Citadel Press, 2008.

Brando, Marlon, with Robert Lindsay. *Brando: Songs My Mother Taught Me*. New York: Random House, 1994.

Brown, Peter Harry, with comments by Kim Novak. *Kim Novak: Reluctant Goddess*. New York: St. Martin's Press, 1986.

Bucknell, Katherine, ed. *Christopher Isherwood: Volume One, Diaries 1939–1960*. New York: HarperCollins, 1996.

Buhle, Paul, and Dave Wagner. *Radical Hollywood: The Untold Story Behind America's Favorite Movies*. New York: New Press, 2002.

Cameron, Ian. *A Pictorial History of Crime Films*. London: Hamlyn Publishing Group, 1975.

Canham, Kingsley, with Clive Denton. *The Hollywood Professionals*. Vol. 5, *King Vidor, John Cromwell, Mervyn LeRoy*. New York: A. S. Barnes, 1976.

Capra, Frank. *The Name Above the Title: An Autobiography*. New York: Macmillan, 1971.

Clarke, Gerald. *Get Happy: The Life of Judy Garland*. New York: Random House, 2000.

Dalio [Marcel]. *Mes années folles: Récit receuilli par Jean-Pierre de Lucovich*. France: Éditions J.-C. Lattès, 1976.

Davis, Genevieve. *Beverly Hills: An Illustrated History Featuring Interviews with Celebrity Residents*. Northridge, CA: Windsor Publications, 1988.

Davis, Ronald L. *The Glamour Factory: Inside Hollywood's Big Studio System*. Dallas, TX: Southern Methodist University Press, 1993.

———. *Just Making Movies: Company Directors on the Studio System*. Jackson: University Press of Mississippi, 2005.

Dick, Bernard F., ed. *Columbia Pictures: Portrait of a Studio*. Lexington: University Press of Kentucky, 1992.

———. *The Merchant Prince of Poverty Row: Harry Cohn of Columbia Pictures*. Lexington: University Press of Kentucky, 1993.

Dmytryk, Edward. *It's a Hell of a Life, but Not a Bad Living: A Hollywood Memoir*. New York: Times Books, 1978.

Donati, William. *Ida Lupino: A Biography*. Lexington: University Press of Kentucky, 1996.

Durgnat, Raymond, and Scott Simmon. *King Vidor, American*. Berkeley: University of California Press, 1988.

Eames, John Douglas. *The Paramount Story: The Complete History of the Studio and Its 2,805 Films*. New York: Crown, 1985.

Edelman, Rob, and Audrey F. Kupferberg. *Angela Lansbury: A Life on Stage and Screen*. New York: Birch Lane Press, 1996.

Eerens, Patricia. *The Films of Shirley MacLaine*. New York: A. S. Barnes, 1978.

Epstein, Edward Z., and Joseph Morella. *Rita: The Life of Rita Hayworth*. London: W. H. Allen, 1983.

Fernett, Gene. *American Film Studios: An Historical Encyclopedia*. Jefferson, NC: McFarland, 1988.

Finch, Christopher. *Rainbow: The Stormy Life of Judy Garland*. New York: Grosset & Dunlap, 1975.

Finch, Christopher, and Linda Rosenkrantz. *Gone Hollywood: The Movie Colony in the Golden Age*. Garden City, NY: Doubleday, 1979.

Finler, Joel W. *All-Time Movie Favorites: Comedies, Thrillers, Epics, Musicals, Love Stories, Westerns, War Films and Others*. London: Sundial Books Limited, 1975.

———. *The Hollywood Story: Everything You Always Wanted to Know About the American Movie Business but Didn't Know Where to Look*. New York: Crown, 1988.

Fisher, Eddie, with David Fisher. *Been There, Done That: An Autobiography*. New York: St. Martin's Press, 1999.

Fowler, Karin J. *Anne Baxter: A Bio-Bibliography*. Westport, CT: Greenwood Press, 1991.

Fujiwara, Chris. *Jacques Tourneur: The Cinema of Nightfall*. Jefferson, NC: McFarland, 1998.

Fultz, Jay. *In Search of Donna Reed*. Iowa City: University of Iowa Press, 1998.

Garcia, Roger, and Bernard Eisenschitz, eds. *Frank Tashlin*. Locarno: Éditions du Festival International du Film de Locarno in collaboration with the British Film Institute, 1994.

Garrett, Betty, with Ron Rapoport. *Betty Garrett and Other Songs: A Life on Stage and Screen*. New York: Madison Books, 1998.

Goodman, Ezra. *The Fifty-Year Decline and Fall of Hollywood*. New York: Simon & Schuster, 1961.

Grant, Barry Keith, ed. *Fritz Lang Interviews*. Jackson: University Press of Mississippi, 2003.

Hadleigh, Boze. *Bette Davis Speaks*. New York: Barricade Books, 1996.

Hammond, Lawrence. *Thriller Movies: The Movie Treasury — Classic Films of Suspense and Mystery*. London: Octopus Books, 1974.

Hannsberry, Karen Burroughs. *Femme Noir: Bad Girls of Film*. Jefferson, NC: McFarland, 1998.

Harvey, James. *Movie Love in the Fifties*. New York: Da Capo Press, 2001.

Heisner, Beverly. *Hollywood Art: Art Direction in the Days of the Great Studios*. London: St. James Press, 1990.

Henreid, Paul, with Julius Fast. *Ladies Man: An Autobiography*. New York: St. Martin's Press, 1984.

Herman, Jan. *A Talent for Trouble: The Life of Hollywood's Most Acclaimed Director, William Wyler*. New York: G. P. Putnam's Sons, 1995.

Higham, Charles. *The Art of American Film, 1900–1971*. Garden City, NY: Doubleday, 1973.

———. *Merchant of Dreams: Louis B. Mayer, M.G.M. and the Secret Hollywood*. New York: Donald I. Fine, 1993.

Holden, Anthony. *The Oscars: The Secret History of Hollywood's Academy Awards*. London: Little, Brown, 1993.

Jeavons, Clyde. *A Pictorial History of War Films*. London: Hamlyn Publishing Group, 1974.

Kass, Judith M., and Stuart Rosenthal. *The Hollywood Professionals*. Vol. 4, *Tod Browning, Don Siegel*. New York: A. S. Barnes, 1975.

Kennedy, Burt. *Hollywood Trial Boss: Behind the Scenes of the Wild, Wild Western*. New York: Boulevard Books, 1997.

Keyes, Evelyn. *Scarlett O'Hara's Younger Sister: My Life In and Out of Hollywood*. Secaucus: Lyle Stuart, 1977.

Kiersch, Mary. *Curtis Bernhardt: A Directors Guild of America Oral History*. Metuchen, NJ: Scarecrow Press, 1986.

Kobal, John. *Rita Hayworth: The Time, the Place and the Woman*. New York: W. W. Norton, 1977.

Kramer, Stanley, with Thomas M. Coffey. *It's a Mad, Mad, Mad, Mad World: A Life in Hollywood*. New York: Harcourt Brace, 1997.

Lasky, Jesse L., Jr. *Whatever Happened to Hollywood?* New York: Funk & Wagnalls, 1975.

Leaming, Barbara. *If This Was Happiness: A Biography of Rita Hayworth*. New York: Viking Penguin, 1989.

———. *Orson Welles*. London: Phoenix, 1985.

Leigh, Janet. *There Really Was a Hollywood: An Autobiography*. Garden City, NY: Doubleday, 1984.

Levy, Emmanuel. *Oscar Fever: The History and Politics of the Academy Awards*. New York: Continuum International Publishing Group, 2001.

Madsen, Alex. *Stanwyck*. New York: HarperCollins, 1994.

Mann, Delbert. *Looking Back . . . at Live Television and Other Matters*. Los Angeles: Directors Guild of America Publication, 1998.

Martin, Linda, and Kerry Segrave. *The Continental Actress: European Film Stars of the Postwar Era—Biographies, Criticism, Filmographies, Bibliographies*. Jefferson, NC: McFarland, 1990.

McBride, Joseph. *Frank Capra: The Catastrophe of Success*. New York: Simon & Schuster, 1992.

———. *Searching for John Ford: A Life*. New York: St. Martin's Press, 2001.

McCarthy, Todd. *Howard Hawks: The Grey Fox of Hollywood*. New York: Grove Press, 1997.

McClelland, Doug. *Forties Film Talk: Oral Histories of Hollywood, with 120 Lobby Posters*. Jefferson, NC: McFarland, 1992.

McGilligan, Pat, ed. *Backstory: Interviews with Screenwriters of Hollywood's Golden Age*. Berkeley: University of California Press, 1986.

———, ed. *Backstory 2: Interviews with Screenwriters of the 1940s and 1950s*. Berkeley: University of California Press, 1991.

———, ed. *Backstory 3: Interviews with Screenwriters of the 60s*. Berkeley: University of California Press, 1997.

———. *Fritz Lang: The Nature of the Beast*. London: Faber and Faber, 1997.

Medina Cotten, Patricia. *Laid Back in Hollywood: Remembering*. Los Angeles: Belle, 1998.

Minnelli, Vincente, with Hector Arne. *I Remember It Well*. London: Angus & Robertson, 1975.

Mirisch, Walter. *I Thought We Were Making Movies, Not History*. Madison: University of Wisconsin Press, 2008.

Montand, Yves, with Hervé Manon and Patrick Rotman. *You See, I Haven't Forgotten*. Translated by Jeremy Leggatt. New York: Alfred A. Knopf, 1992.

Moseley, Roy. *Bette Davis: An Intimate Memoir*. New York: Donald I. Fine, 1990.

Munn, Michael. *Hollywood Rogues: The Off-Screen Antics of Tinsel Town's Hellraisers*. London: Robson Books, 1991.

Norman, Barry. *Talking Pictures: The Story of Hollywood*. London: Hodder and Stoughton, 1987.

Nowlan, Gwendolyn Wright, and Robert A. Nowlan. *Cinema Sequels and Remakes, 1903–1987*. London: St. James Press, 1989.

O'Brien, Pat. *With the Wind at My Back: The Life and Times of Pat O'Brien*. Garden City, NY: Doubleday, 1964.

O'Hara, Maureen, with John Nicoletti. *'Tis Herself: A Memoir*. New York: Simon and Schuster, 2004.

Parish, James Robert, and Ronald L. Bowers. *The MGM Stock Company: The Golden Era*. Shepperton: Ian Allan, 1973.

Parish, James Robert, and Alvin H. Marill. *The Cinema of Edward G. Robinson*. New York: A. S. Barnes, 1972.

Parker, John. *Five for Hollywood: Their Friendships, Their Fame, Their Tragedies.* New York: Lyle Stuart, 1991.

Pickard, Roy. *The Hollywood Studios.* London: Frederick Mueller, 1978.

———. *Who Played Who in the Movies.* New York: Schocken Books, 1981.

Poague, Leland, ed. *Frank Capra Interviews.* Jackson: University Press of Mississippi, 2004.

Quirck, Lawrence J. *The Films of Fredric March.* New York: Citadel Press, 1971.

———. *The Films of William Holden.* Secaucus: Citadel Press, 1973.

Reed, Rex. *Big Screen, Little Screen.* New York: Macmillan, 1968.

Reynolds, Debbie, and David Patrick Columbia. *Debbie: My Life.* New York: William Morrow, 1988.

Ringgold, Gene. *The Films of Rita Hayworth: The Legend and Career of a Love Goddess.* Secaucus: Citadel Press, 1974.

Robertson, Patrick. *The Guinness Book of Movie Facts and Feats.* London: Guinness, 1988.

Robinson, Edward G., with Leonard Spigelglass. *All My Yesterdays: An Autobiography.* New York: Hawthorn Books, 1973.

Rogers, Ginger. *Ginger: My Story.* New York: HarperCollins, 1991.

Roscow, Eugene. *Born to Lose: The Gangster Film in America.* New York: Oxford University Press, 1978.

Royce, Brenda Scott. *Donna Reed: A Bio-Bibliography.* Westport, CT: Greenwood Press, 1990.

Scherle, Victor, and William Turner Levy. *The Complete Films of Frank Capra.* Secaucus: Citadel Press, 1977.

Schickel, Richard. *Brando: A Life in Our Times.* London: Pavilion Books, 1991.

Schultz, Margie. *Eleanor Powell: A Bio-Bibliography.* Westport, CT: Greenwood Press, 1994.

Selby, Spencer. *Dark City: The Film Noir.* London: St. James Press, 1984.

Sherman, Vincent. *Studio Affairs: My Life as a Film Director.* Lexington: University Press of Kentucky, 1996.

Shipman, David. *The Story of Cinema: An Illustrated History—Volume Two—From "Citizen Kane" to the Present Day.* London: Hodder and Stoughton, 1984.

Signoret, Simone. *Nostalgia Isn't What It Used to Be.* New York: Harper & Row, 1978.

Silver, Alain, and James Ursini. *What Ever Happened to Robert Aldrich? His Life and His Films.* New York: Limelight Editions, 1995.

Silvester, Christopher, ed. *The Grove Book of Hollywood.* New York: Grove Press, 1998.

Springer, John. *The Fondas: The Films and Careers of Henry, Jane, and Peter Fonda.* Secaucus: Citadel Press, 1970.

Stine, Whitney. *"I'd Love to Kiss You . . .": Conversations with Bette Davis.* New York: Softcover Books, 1990.

Stuart, Gloria, with Sylvia Thompson. *I Just Kept Hoping.* New York: Little, Brown, 1999.

Sweeney, Kevin. *Henry Fonda: A Bio-Bibliography*. Westport, CT: Greenwood Press, 1992.

Swindell, Larry. *Charles Boyer: The Reluctant Lover*. Garden City, NY: Doubleday, 1983.

Terrace, Vincent. *Complete Encyclopedia of Television Programs 1947–1979*. New York: A. S. Barnes, 1980.

Thomas, Bob. *Joan Crawford: A Biography*. New York: Simon & Schuster, 1978.

———. *King Cohn: The Life and Times of Harry Cohn*. New York: G. P. Putnam's Sons, 1967.

Thomson, David. *Marlon Brando*. New York: DK, 2003.

———. *Showman: The Life of David O. Selznick*. London: André Deutsch, 1993.

Toeplitz, Jerzy. *Hollywood and After: The Changing Face of Movies in America*. Translated by Boleslaw Sulik. Chicago: Henry Regnery, 1974.

Verswijver, Leo. *"Movies Were Always Magical": Interviews with 19 Actors, Directors and Producers from the Hollywood of the 1930s through the 1950s*. Jefferson, NC: McFarland, 2003.

Walker, Joseph B., with Juanita Walker. *The Light on Her Face*. Hollywood: ASC Press, 1984.

Wellman, William. *A Short Time for Insanity: An Autobiography*. New York: Hawthorn Books, 1974.

Widener, Don. *Lemmon*. New York: Macmillan, 1975.

Wiley, Mason, with Damien Bona. *Inside Oscar: The Unofficial History of the Academy Awards*. Bromley, UK: Columbus Books, 1986.

Winecoff, Charles. *Split Image: The Life of Anthony Perkins*. New York: Dutton, 1996.

Wolper, David L., with David Fisher. *Producer*. New York: Scribner, 2003.

Youngkin, Stephen D. *The Lost One: A Life of Peter Lorre*. Lexington: University Press of Kentucky, 2005.

Index

Page numbers in italics indicate illustrations.

Australia, 257–58
Australian Logie Award, 257–58
aviation, 14; films about, 42, 69–70, 106, 220; "no fly" clause in contracts, 124, 174–75; Peter's impromptu piloting experience, 249

Babcock, Barbara, 241, 246
Babies for Sale, 31
Bachardy, Don, 196
bachelor pads, 129–30, 195, 202
Backus, Jim, 214
Bacon, James, 174
Baer, Max, Jr., 235
Bailey, Pearl, 258
Baker, Diane, 258
Baker, Pam, 253
Ball, Lucille, 35
Banks, Lionel, 40
Barrymore, Ethel, 114
Barrymore, John, 34
Baus, Jeanne, marriage to, 304
Baxter, Anne, 112, 193, 198
Beal, John, 20
The Beatles, 227
Beery, Noah, Jr., 244
Beggarman, Thief (television series), 264, 286
Bennett, Charles, 114
Benny, Jack, 21, 125
Berg, Jeff, 287
Berman, Pandro, 103, 150, 156, 177
Bernhardt, Curtis, 57–58, 103–4, 148–49
Beverly Hills, residences in, 3, 57, 66–69
The Big Heat, 134–36, 143, *273*
Bill Haley and the Comets, 153–56
Billingsley, Sherman, 36
Bill (pet German shepherd), *91*, 106, 125–26
biopics, 69, 111–13, 148–49
Bismarck (pet dachshund), 291, 293, 295–96, 307, 308–9
bison, flying, 249
Bisset, Jacqueline, 261
bit parts, 15–20
Blackboard Jungle, 149–56, *274*, 309

blacklist, 25, 113, 158, 161
Blair, Janet, 70
Blondell, Joan, 46, 214–15
"Blue Ribbons," recording of, *178*, 231
Blyth, Ann, 269
B movies, 31
The Bobby Soxers of America, 66
Boehm, Sydney, 135
Boetticher, Budd, 131–33, 139
Bogeaus, Benedict, 137
Bond, Ward, 25
Border Shootout, 299
Borgnine, Ernest, 164–65, 184
Born to Dance, 17, 45
Born Yesterday, 101, 108
Bowers, Scotty, 306
Bowers, William "Bill," 182, 214
Boyer, Charles, 46, 229
Boy Scouts, 10
Brand, Neville, 131
Brando, Marlon, 151, 165–66, 171–74, 257, *275*
Brazil, 139–41, 246–47
Brenan, Frederick Hazlitt, 111
Bridges, Lloyd, 104, 106
Briskin, Sam, 185
Broadway Melody of 1936, 45
Broadway Melody of 1938, 45
Broadway Melody of 1940, 45, 292
Broadway productions, 20–21
Brooks, Geraldine, 114–18, *272*
Brooks, Richard, 150–53, 155, 156, 161, *274*
The Brotherhood of the Bell (television program), 253, *279*
Brown, Harry Joe, 235–36
Brown, Robert, 137
Brown, Stanley, 18
Buchanan, Edgar "Buck," 30, 39–40, 71, 182, 253–55, 268
Buffalo Bill Museum (Cody, Wyoming), 248–49
Burton, Richard, 188, 200

Cabot, Bruce, 30
Cade's County (television series), 253–55
Cagney, James, 46

Woods, James, 286–87

World War II: Coast Guard Auxiliary enlistment of Glenn prior to, 38; films set during, 177, 184, 197–98; Marines, Glenn's enlistment in, and service during, 49, 54; *World War II: A Personal Journey* (television special), 288

World War II: A Personal Journey (television special), 288

Wrangler, Jack (Jack Stillman), 131

Wurtzel, Sol, 22, 24

Wynn, Keenan, 177, 245

Yates, Sammy, 309

Young, Gig, 99

Young, Loretta, 258

Young Man with Ideas, 120, 147

Zanuck, Darryl F., 14, 111–12

Ziegfeld, Flo, 44

Made in the USA
Columbia, SC
27 May 2020